American technology and the British vehicle industry

American technology and the British vehicle industry

WAYNE LEWCHUK

Department of Economics and
Labour Studies Programme
McMaster University
Hamilton, Ontario Canada

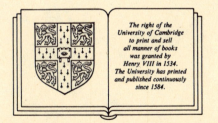

The right of the
University of Cambridge
to print and sell
all manner of books
was granted by
Henry VIII in 1534.
The University has printed
and published continuously
since 1584.

CAMBRIDGE UNIVERSITY PRESS

Cambridge

London   New York   New Rochelle

Melbourne   Sydney

Published by the Press Syndicate of the University of Cambridge
The Pitt Building, Trumpington Street, Cambridge CB2 1RP
32 East 57th Street, New York, NY 10022, USA
10 Stamford Road, Oakleigh, Melbourne 3166, Australia

First published 1987

Printed in Great Britain at the University Press, Cambridge

British Library cataloguing in publication data

Lewchuk, Wayne
American technology and the British vehicle industry:
a century of vehicle production in Britain.
1. Automobile industry and trade—Great
Britain—History
I. Title
338.4'76292'0941   HD9710.G72

Library of Congress cataloging in publication data

Lewchuk, Wayne

American technology and the British vehicle industry.
Bibliography.
Includes index.
    1. Automobile industry and trade—Great Britain—
History.   2. Automobile—Great Britain—Technological
innovations—History.   3. Mass production—Great Britain
—History.   4. Automobile industry and trade—United
States—History.   5. Automobiles—United States—
Technological innovations—History.   I. Title.
HD9710.G72L48   1987   338.4'56292'0941   86-30994

ISBN   0521 30269 2

TM

Contents

Preface

The recent rise of Japan as a major producer of manufactured goods has given debates over technical change and labour productivity a new sense of urgency.[†] It has caused European and North American managers to re-examine the formulas which were successful in generating profits in the 1950s and the 1960s. Between 1890 and 1920, a similar debate was carried on within British circles as British manufacturers responded to the challenge created by the rise of the United States as a manufacturing force. The focus of this book is this earlier period and its impact on the methods of production adopted in the British motor vehicle industry.

The book departs from the conventional economic methodology which tries to explain shifts in technology in terms of simple market forces and the relative prices of inputs. The central problem with this approach is that the relative price of labour is meaningless without information on the amount of effort labour supplies. For much of this century, economists ignored the relationship between earnings and effort, preferring to study the relationship between earnings and leisure time. It was implicitly assumed that markets worked efficiently in converting labour time into effort. In the last few years, this assumption has been challenged by a number of economists who have shown a renewed interest in the role of non-market institutions. Studies of authority, power and ideology are creeping back into the discipline. In what follows, it is argued that this new interest in non-market economic institutions requires a dramatic revision of existing economic models of technical change.

In writing this book I have benefited from the cooperation, encouragement and criticism of a large number of people. I would like to express particular appreciation to Leslie Hannah who provided invaluable guidance and advice throughout the period when the manuscript was being prepared. Jon Cohen was

---

[†] See, W. Abernathy, *The Productivity Dilemma* (Baltimore 1978); W. Abernathy, K.B. Clark and A.M. Kantrow, *Industrial Renaissance, Producing a Competitive Future for America* (New York, 1983); R.B. Reich, *The Next American Frontier* (New York, 1983); B. Bluestone and B. Harrison, *The Deindustrialization of America* (New York, 1982); M.J. Piore and C.F. Sabel, *The Second Industrial Divide, Possibilities for Prosperity* (New York, 1984).

largely responsible for stimulating my interest in economic history and without his early encouragement, this book never would have been attempted. I would like to thank William Lazonick who provided comments on earlier drafts and whose work is providing a focus for a new generation of Institutional Economists. I would also like to thank the following who commented on my work at various stages of the project: Roy Church, Alfred D. Chandler, Peter Clark, Melvyn Dubovsky, Bernie Elbaum, Patrick Fridenson, Knick Harley, Nelson Lichtenstein, Gavin MacKenzie, Nigel Mason, Donald McCloskey, Stephen Meyer III, Roger Moore, Richard Price, Richard Whipp, and Paul Willman.

A number of individuals and organisations provided access to records in their possession. I would like to thank the Engineering Employers Federation and H.K. Mitchell; Coventry & District Engineering Employers Association and J. Viggars; Amalgamated Union of Engineering Workers and John Boyd; Coventry East Section of the Amalgamated Union of Engineering Workers and H. Clarke; British Motor Industry Heritage Trust, B.L. plc. and Mr A.D. Clausager; Leyland Historic Vehicles Ltd and R.A. Westcott; the Veteran Car Club and D.C. Field; Edison Institute and D. Bakken and D.R. Crippen; BBC and Peter Pagnamenta; Ford (UK) and D. Burgess-Wise; Transport and General Workers, Union for Access to the National Union of Vehicle Builders papers; and A.G. Cave.

D. Rimmer guided me through the papers held at the Coventry Record Office. I would like to thank Richard Storey and Alistair Tough for providing invaluable advice regarding the holdings of the Modern Records Centre and for making the Centre an outstanding source of post 1850 archival material. The papers from the Ford Archives used in the book represent the original deposit of the Henry Ford Museum/Greenfield Village complex.

The Social Sciences and Humanities Research Council of Canada funded this project over a period of years.

A special thanks to my colleagues, Marguerite Boux, Martin Dooley, Peter George and Robert Storey whose unflagging support made the whole project that much easier.

I would like to thank my mates on the Ford Windsor 351 and 400 engine lines who helped me to appreciate the relationship between technology and the effort bargain first hand.

Finally I would like to thank Dale Brown for her support and for her many contributions which made this a better book than I alone was capable of writing.

Wayne Lewchuk
Hamilton
July 1986

1

Introduction

Economic historians and historians of technology have been aware for many years that the methods of production employed by British and American manufacturers began to differ around the middle of the nineteenth century.[1] Although recent work by Hounshell has qualified our picture of mid-nineteenth century American production methods, it is still widely accepted that the Americans showed a preference for labour saving and skill displacing methods of production, sometimes referred to as the American system.[2] The British on the other hand, continued to employ the labour intensive methods characteristic of the early nineteenth century European factory system.

Economists studying the differences in British and American production methods have concentrated on explaining the differences in the proportion of factor inputs such as capital and labour employed in the two economies. They have used the competitive market as the framework of analysis and the relative prices of factor inputs as the main explanatory variables.[3] In studying the history of production methods in the British motor vehicle industry, we have come to the conclusion that the existing economic models fail to address a number of important questions and fail to incorporate important explanatory variables. The existing models are deficient in that they focus mainly on what we have called production techniques, the physical aspects of the production process, which can be quantified and subjected to standard neoclassical analysis. They have failed to examine the institutional context of the production process, including authority patterns, managerial structures, labour organisations, mechanisms for monitoring and enforcing the effort bargain, political ideology, all of which play an important role in determining the productivity of production techniques.

Since the 1920s, when the division of labour between economics and sociology was finalized, economists have been reluctant to examine the formation and evolution of institutions.[4] A recent attempt by an economist to break with this tradition was prefaced with the claim that: 'Our insistence that important advances in the understanding of the processes of institutional innovation and diffusion can be achieved by treating institutional change as endogenous to the economic system represents a clear departure from the tradition of modern analytical economics.'[5] Economists have been so busy trying to prove scientifically that perfectly competitive markets are wonderful, or at least could be if the government stopped intervening, that their models have become increasingly divorced from the real world whose institutional context bears little resemblance to the economist's institutional fantasy.[6] It has become necessary in the opinion of Schotter, 'to liberate economics from its fixation on competitive markets as an all-encompassing institutional framework'.[7]

Recently, as economists have tried to deal with the problems associated with imperfect information, the cost of monitoring exchanges and unenforceable contracts, there has been a recognition of the limits of competitive markets and a renewed interest in economic institutions.[8] North and Davis, who defined an institution as an arrangement which guides competition and conflict between economic agents, were amongst the first modern economists to examine the role of institutions.[9] Further study has suggested that institutions have an important role to play in providing information on the expected behaviour of economic agents which complements the information provided by markets on the scarcity of factors of production.[10]

One area in which institutions are particularly critical is the production process. A new literature has emerged which focuses on the labour contract or the effort bargain, and the complex process through which labour time is converted into labour effort and ultimately goods and services.[11] This literature has shown that difficulties associated with enforcing and monitoring labour contracts limit the power of the market to discipline economic agents and create the need for non-market authority structures. The realisation that non-market authority structures are important provides the starting point for our interpretation of the history of technical change in Britain.

The most serious weakness of existing economic models of technical change and the existing attempts to explain differences in British and American production methods is the treatment of labour. Labour has been modelled as an inanimate and passive input. It has been assumed that labour productivity and the level of labour effort can be treated as given or, in more complex models, can be derived from observed human capital characteristics. This has allowed economists to avoid the troubling question of how labour time is converted into labour effort. Within this context, new technology is seen largely as helping labour to do what it is physically unable to do. Technology's potential to control labour, to enforce effort bargains, to make labour do what it is unwilling to do, has been largely ignored. This is seen to be critical, as our research has suggested that the conversion of labour time into labour effort was an important question facing early nineteenth-century employers and was a major factor influencing their choice of technology. We will argue that it was the difference in the ability of British and American employers to convert labour time into labour effort that explains differences in the history of technology, not differences in relative factor prices.

Before moving on to a detailed examination of economic models of technical change and an alternative framework for examining the differences in British and American production methods, we will provide a brief outline of the model which we have employed. This is intended for those readers who are not well versed in the terminology used by economists and who might wish to skip Chapter 2 and proceed directly to the historical analysis.

Our model is built around the interaction between the effort bargain and shifts in the capital–labour ratio. Unlike most economic models which limit their analysis to the buying and selling of labour time, we will extend the analysis one stage further to the process by which labour time is converted into labour effort.[12] Because of measurement costs, imperfect information, and the impossibility of writing contracts to cover all possible contingencies, the effort bargain is only partially market enforced. This opens up possibilities for both the buyers of labour time and the sellers of labour time to invest in institutions which shift the effort bargain in their favour. For the buyers of labour time, this may involve investment in shop floor monitoring, the implementation of payment systems which try to link effort and earnings, or investment in good relations with labour to try to convince labour that it is in its interest to work harder. For the sellers of labour time, this might involve investment in shop floor labour organisations, attempts to link up informally with other workers, political activism, or the promotion of payment systems which they feel they can control. The buyers of labour time may also change production techniques to ease the task of monitoring labour and enforcing the effort bargain. One of the differences between our model and earlier economic studies by Williamson and Leibenstein of the effort bargain is that both buyers and sellers of labour time will be allowed to invest in institutions which shift the effort bargain.

It might be thought that the objectives of the buyers and the sellers of labour are relatively straightforward. Surely, the buyers of labour time want to maximise effort per unit of labour time purchased and the sellers of labour time want to minimise the amount of effort per unit of time sold. The realities are much more complex. It may not always be in the interest of the buyers of labour time to maximise the amount of effort extracted per unit of time, nor is it necessarily in the interest of sellers to minimise effort.

The buyers of labour time have two concerns. The first is the amount of effort extracted per unit of time, and the second is the cost of effort. Other things being equal, the buyers of labour time will want to maximise effort per unit of time in order to maximise the productivity of the capital equipment employed by the workers. In a large number of cases, the speed at which capital equipment operates, and hence its productivity, is a direct function of effort norms. But the buyers of labour time must also be concerned with the net cost of each unit of effort. Herein lies the buyer's dilemma. Over a wide range of cases, the buyer can always increase the level of effort per unit of labour time purchased by offering to raise wages in return for more effort or by investing in monitoring and controlling institutions. The additional cost of an extra unit of effort per unit of labour time is not likely to be constant. In fact one can safely predict that it will rise as the pace of work increases. Hence the buyer of labour time is faced with the complex problem of balancing increases in effort per unit of time which will increase profits, and increases in the cost of a unit of effort which will decrease profits. It will generally be true that the buyer's interest in controlling effort per unit of time will increase as the capital–labour ratio increases and that the buyer's interest in controlling the ratio of wages to effort will decrease as the capital labour ratio increases.

For the sellers of labour time, the minimisation of labour effort per unit of time is an optimal strategy only in the very short-run. Rational sellers of labour time will also take into consideration the link between current effort and expected future income streams, a link which the historical record suggests labour recognised. In a capitalist system, the seller's future job prospects depend on the continuing profitability of the firms they work for. Burawoy, who has done some excellent work in this area, suggests: 'Proletarian existence rests not merely on today's wage but also on tomorrow's and the next day's . . . Capitalist labourers depend on the production of profit. Their future interests, as organized under the capitalist mode of production, lie in the production of surplus value.'[13] Hence for the sellers of labour time, the decision to supply effort is a function of the rate at which effort is rewarded in the short-run and their expectation of how their future income streams will be influenced by the current profitability of their employer.[14]

The links between the struggle over the effort bargain, the capital–labour ratio and technical change are complex and subtle, and can only be fully appreciated as the reader works through the historical chapters. Keeping in mind that technology, as we have defined it, can be divided into production techniques and production institutions, two main sets of forces are at work shaping technical change.

New technology will emerge as new knowledge is added to the existing pool of knowledge. Most economists have rejected models where new knowledge is discovered in a random and unplanned fashion. We believe the model developed by P. David provides the most plausible basis for a solution to this problem.[15] David argued that what is discovered is very much a function of what is searched for, and that the search for new knowledge is directed by attempts to resolve the problems thrown up while using the existing technology. Learning by doing can produce technology which enhances the productivity of existing inputs without necessarily shifting the effort bargain, or it can generate new technology whose main effect is to shift effort norms or the effort bargain.

The process of learning by doing will generate both new production techniques and new production institutions. This brings us to a second type of technical change which is stimulated by disequilibriums between production techniques and institutions. Production techniques and production institutions are in disequilibrium when the existing effort bargain does not allow the profitable use of new or existing production techniques. Schotter, in his work on institutions recognised the potential for an economy to develop the wrong set of institutions. He wrote:

Those societies that create the proper set of social institutions survive and flourish; those that do not, falter and die. The distressing fact is that what is functional to meet today's problem may be totally inadequate in meeting the tests our society faces tomorrow. Social institutions are our adaptive tools; we cannot survive without them.[16]

We will argue that institutional crises can be found within the production process and that they tend to stimulate dramatic changes in technology. Either or both production techniques and institutions must change to restore equilibrium or else the firm will fail. We will argue that the British motor vehicle industry was in such a disequilibrium on two occasions during the time period we are studying. At the end of the nineteenth century, British firms began introducing the production techniques pioneered in America. However, they were unable to alter production institutions which continued to be based on the institutions employed during most of the nineteenth century when the production process revolved around the skilled artisan. The industry's response to this disequilibrium was to alter both the American production techniques and the European institutions creating what we have called the British system of mass production. The industry found itself in disequilibrium a second time in the late 1960s and early 1970s. Again, British firms were trying to adopt American production techniques while employing the production institutions which had evolved in Britain under the British system of mass production. The resolution of this second crisis led to the nationalisation of the industry and, it will be argued, led to the belated transition to American style production institutions.

The remainder of this book will be organised as follows. In Chapter 2, we will examine various theories of technical change and develop an alternative model which will be used to organise our historical analysis. In Chapter 3, we will use this model to explain the evolution of Fordism in Ford's American factories. Chapters 4 and 5, focus on how the initial shift to mechanised factory production techniques in Britain in the latter half of the nineteenth century created new pressures on the existing effort bargain and led to what was known to contemporaries as the 'Labour Crisis'. In Chapter 6, we will examine the evolution of production techniques in the pre-1914 British motor vehicle industry. Chapter 7 will examine the evolution of pre-1914 production institutions. Chapter 8 will focus on the interwar response of British vehicle makers to the Fordist challenge and the rise of the British system of mass production. Chapter 9 will examine the collapse of this system and the emergence of an alternative system of production under M. Edwardes. Chapter 10 will summarise the analysis and show how the model developed in Chapter 2 can be used to explain the sequence of events in the industry.

2

Economic models of technical change

The modern economic analysis of technical change dates from the 1960s when empirical work indicated that only a small portion of the growth of total output over the last 100 years could be explained by the accumulation of factors of production.[1] This set in motion a search for new models capable of explaining changes in the productivity of factors of production. Most early models relied on relative factor input prices as the main explanatory variables and built on the earlier work of J. R. Hicks. Hicks made a distinction between technical change which was the result of substitution between known techniques, and technical change which was the result of the discovery of new techniques. He argued that both of these processes would be influenced by relative factor prices. As an input became relatively more expensive, entrepreneurs would search for existing known techniques which used relatively less of the now more expensive input. The change in factor prices would also induce entrepreneurs to search for yet to be discovered techniques which used less of the more expensive input. He wrote:

The real reason for the predominance of labour-saving inventions is surely that which was hinted at in our discussion of substitution. A change in the relative price of the factors of production is itself a spur to invention, and to invention of a particular kind-directed to economising the use of the factor which has become relatively expensive.[2]

Salter argued that Hicks' analysis was logically flawed. If one accepted that a change in factor prices led to substitution between known techniques, a process which would equate the marginal revenue and the marginal cost of each factor of production employed, then it must be argued that after such substitution all factors are equally scarce. In short-run equilibrium, economic agents would be indifferent to the factor saving bias of new techniques. Their only concern would be the magnitude of the reduction in costs.[3]

Salter suggested that the key to understanding the observed long-run trend toward mechanisation was not factor prices but, rather, improvements in labour productivity within the capital goods producing sector of the economy. He wrote; 'The essence of technical progress is that it enables commodities to be produced with less labour and capital, and so reduces the price of commodities in terms of labour.'[4] Salter did not provide an explanation for this increase in productivity. He rejected increases in the personal efficiency of labour due to increases in effort, skill or intelligence. He could then argue that:

Technical progress in the manufacture of capital goods produces a continuous pressure throughout industry for the substitution of capital equipment for labour. .... The supply of capital goods per worker rises parallel with the increasing productivity of that part of the labour force devoted to the manufacture of capital goods. This increasing supply of capital goods is reflected in a declining price relative to wages which, in the long-run at least, induces their absorption through the substitution of capital equipment for labour.[5]

If changes in personal labour productivity were allowed, either through more effort or the accumulation of human capital, then the Salter result would be less straightforward.

Induced innovation and technical change

In response to Salter's criticism of Hicks' inducement mechanism, Kennedy proposed shifting the analysis from changes in relative input prices to changes in an input's share of total cost. Kennedy argued that an entrepreneur would focus the search for new techniques on inputs which represented a large share of total cost.[6] It was suggested that an increase in the relative price of an input would increase this input's share of total cost, assuming the elasticity of substitution was less than one, and hence bias the search for new techniques which saved the relatively more expensive input. Kennedy suggested the following model[7]:

$$r = Yp + Xq, \tag{2.1}$$

$$q = f(p) \quad q_p < 0, \tag{2.2}$$

where Y = share of capital costs in total costs; X = share of labour costs in total costs; p = proportion of capital saved by new technology; g = proportion of labour saved by new technology; and r = proportional reduction in total costs due to new technology

The key to Kennedy's model is Equation (2.2). For any fixed research budget, an increase in the search for techniques which save capital must be accompanied by a reduction in the search for new techniques which save labour. This tradeoff can be seen in the Innovation Possibility Frontier shown in Fig. 2.1

The optimal allocation of resources, in the search for factor saving techniques, is found by maximising Equation (2.1) subject to the constraint Equation (2.2). For any given set of factor prices and factor shares, Equation (2.1) will be at its maximum when $\partial p * Y = -\partial q * X$, or point A in Fig. 2.1.[8] It can easily be seen that an increase in an input's relative price, which will change the ratio of factor shares, will bias the search for new technology toward saving that input. Ahmad pointed out that if Equation (2.2) was respecified so that a given investment in

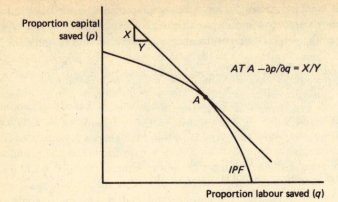

Fig. 2.1. Innovation possibility frontier.

the search for new techniques reduced factors usage by an absolute rather than a proportional amount, the conclusion that factor saving is biased toward the input which accounts for the largest share of total cost would be invalid.[9]

Kennedy's Induced Innovation Model has other serious weaknesses. As pointed out by Ahmad, the model provides few clues as to the factors which shape the IPF or Equation (2.2). Quoting Ahmad: 'The innovation possibility curve thus conceived is not the result of any economic choice, it is a purely technological or laboratory question.'[10] David argued that what Kennedy had done was to substitute one intractable problem for another. He wrote:

Since the shape and position of the IPF are not really accounted for by the theory of induced innovation, its application here has succeeded only in taking an old, familiar, historical problem and restating it in new, more precise and considerably more esoteric terms.[11]

Nordhaus argued that Kennedy's model not only failed to define the IPF, but it also failed to explain how the IPF might shift over time as new inventions were discovered. Nordhaus emphasised the point by suggesting that unless it was assumed that realised inventions deplete potential inventions at the same rate as they expand them, then invention must cause the IPF to shift.[12] David's proposed solution to these problems produced a major advance in attempts to explain the process of technical change.

Learning by doing and technical change

The Learning by Doing approach to technical change was the second general response to Salter's criticism of Hicks' inducement mechanism. Building on Arrow's earlier work, David constructed a model of technical change where factor prices were given a secondary role in explaining bias in long-run factor saving. The role of relative factor prices was replaced by a model of learning, where new knowledge was generated through experience.[13]

The learning process would begin when entrepreneurs chose a technique from the stock of known techniques on the basis of relative factor prices and short-run profit maximising behaviour. Through the use of a technique, its weaknesses would become known. These weaknesses would become the focus of the search for ways of improving productivity. A new body of knowledge would be generated allowing new methods of production to be developed. The critical assumption of the Learning by Doing model was that this new knowledge was local in nature and only production techniques similar to the one in use could benefit from any discoveries. Hence the new techniques invented would tend to resemble the techniques being used. Beyond making the initial choice from the stock of known techniques, the entrepreneur had no control over what was learned or what was invented. David wrote:

Technological learning depends upon the accumulation of actual production experience, short-sighted choices about what to produce, and especially about how to produce it using presently known methods, also in effect govern what subsequently comes to be learned.... The element of guidance present in the long-run process is attached in large measure to the circumstances surrounding those choices, and involves no forward-looking, induced innovational responses to current market signals or future portents.[14]

Fig. 2.2 shows a possible learning path, or improvement ray, of an economy using technique *B*. The initial choice of technique *B* is a result of entrepreneurs making short-run profit maximising decisions given factor prices and known techniques. Experience gathered using technique *B* will lead to the discovery of

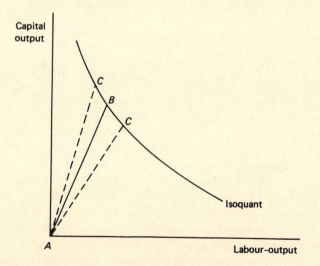

Fig. 2.2. Learning by doing and technical change.

new techniques which resemble *B*. The direction of technical change will be random within the boundaries *AC*. These boundaries reflect possible supply and technical bottlenecks should input ratios diverge radically from the existing input ratio. The improvement ray *AB* represents the expected path of technical change after random elements have been balanced out.[15]

International comparisons of technical change

Economic historians have used the preceding models to explain long-run biases in technical change and international differences in this bias. The willingness of American entrepreneurs to shift to more capital intensive production techniques has been contrasted with the British preference for labour intensive methods. By 1907, American firms had invested twice as much capital per worker as had British firms.[16] Habakkuk argued that the availability of land in the United States raised the minimum wage needed to attract labour into factories. This in turn induced technical change with a labour saving bias in the United States, accounting for the different experiences of British and American firms.[17]

Temin was critical of the Habakkuk thesis arguing that it could not explain the higher American interest rates during the nineteenth century. If we assume that Britain and America both faced identical production functions, then it could not follow that America could have higher interest rates, higher real wage rates and a higher capital–labour ratio. The higher capital–labour ratio should push down the marginal product of capital which should lead to lower interest rates. This led Temin to the conclusion that the differences in British and American practices must have been the result of differences in their production functions. These differences were not the result of a Habakkuk-type inducement mechanism. They were argued to be the result of asymmetries of information flows between Britain and America. Temin wrote:

As the Americans seem to have been more interested in British discoveries than the British were in American developments, an asymmetry in the flow of information may be postulated. This asymmetry gradually led to a divergence of the two technologies, with that of America in the van.[18]

The ensuing debate, generated by Temin's work, resulted in a number of attempts to explain Anglo–American differences using various multi-input models. Williamson and Brito constructed a model with three inputs, capital, skilled labour and unskilled labour. They argued that it was unskilled labour rates which were particularly high in America. The relative differential for skilled workers was lower because skilled labour was more mobile between countries and hence could respond to wage differentials. They also argued that the relatively lower American price for skilled labour encouraged American entrepreneurs to search for and adopt capital intensive methods of production because they required relatively large amounts of skilled labour. The Brito and

Williamson thesis may apply to certain classes of technical change, such as construction, where armies of unskilled navvies were replaced by new mechanical devices. However, their analysis is not consistent with the evolution of production techniques within manufacturing industries where the dominant effect of the American system was to reduce the demand for skilled artisans who were replaced by unskilled machine minders.[19]

Harley's analysis of Edwardian Britain reflects the weakness of the Brito–Williamson analysis. Harley argued that skilled labour was abundant in Britain and hence relatively cheap, the exact opposite of Brito and Williamson. It was then argued that British managers resisted the shift to the capital intensive methods of production, being pioneered in the United States because they replaced skilled workers with the unskilled. Such a change in input proportions was less attractive in Britain where skilled labour was cheap. It is very difficult to reconcile the Brito–Williamson and Harley stories. In the first, the low relative wages for skilled workers encourages the adoption of and search for capital-using technology, while in the latter, the relatively low wages of skilled workers retards the adoption of and search for capital-using techniques.[20] Clearly, this is more than just a problem of getting the facts straight, there are fundamental differences of interpretation regarding the nature of new technology.

Attempts to measure the degree of induced technical change in the British and American economies have lent, at best, weak support to the thesis. Patterson and Cain, studying technical change in America between 1850 and 1914, conclusively proved the existence of biased technical change. Of 19 manufacturing industries, 12 exhibited labour saving bias, two capital saving bias and seven material using bias.[21] Patterson and Cain did not test if this bias was caused by changes in relative factor prices, though they did note that the discovered biases were consistent with known changes in factor prices and the induced technical change model. Phillips tested directly for the existence of induced technical change in the British economy during the late Victorian period. His results do not support the existence of a link between changes in factor prices and biases in technical change. He concluded that: 'The impression given is that induced innovation was a rare phenomenon for British entrepreneurs. ... It is possible to claim that induced innovation is of little consequence to economic development and rarely occurs except in extreme cases such as the cotton famine.'[22] The inducement model is also unable to explain why Germany, with labour costs even lower than those found in Britain, adopted a capital intensive technical strategy.[23]

David's explanation of the differences in British and American technical change rejected any direct link between changes in factor prices and an induced bias. Instead, he suggested that the critical feature of the new machine systems being introduced around 1850 was their tendency to use larger amounts of raw material inputs relative to existing labour intensive techniques. David concluded that American entrepreneurs originally employed the new machine systems because they had access to relatively cheap raw material inputs. For British entrepreneurs, it was uneconomical to employ the new machines because they were forced to pay much higher prices for raw materials. It was suggested that this initial choice, based on short-run profit maximising criteria, influenced what was learned in the United States and introduced a bias toward capital-using technical change as the Americans accumulated better knowledge of how machine systems operated.

The critical weakness of the above models is their focus on production techniques while virtually ignoring production institutions. This is particularly critical for the period after 1850 when significant changes took place in the organisation of the firm, labour relations, labour organisations, managerial structures and strategies.[24] Collectively, these changes amounted to a Second Industrial Revolution. During this revolution, there was a fundamental change in authority patterns on the shop floor. In the process, the knowledge which the skilled worker had employed to maintain some control over the machines introduced during the First Industrial Revolution was expropriated by an emerging class of factory bureaucrats or managers. The notable feature of the First Industrial Revolution was the virtual absence of either a managerial class, or a perceived body of managerial theory.[25] Supervision, planning, accounting, costing and rate fixing departments were, for the most part, products of the Second Industrial Revolution.

Accompanying the rise of management was a fundamental change in the nature of labour markets. It has been argued that the growth in the spatial area of goods markets, and the accompanying growth in the size of firms, dramatically altered the relationship between employee and employer. The impersonal nature of the employment relationship in large firms and new forms of competition between firms strained capital–labour relations. As labour came to see its interests conflicting with those of the owners of capital, new forms of capital–labour conflict emerged. This polarisation of economic agents into two conflicting classes complicated the problems facing the new managerial class, especially their attempts to control labour effort norms. They found it necessary both to coordinate the more complex production systems and to control an increasingly resistive workforce. Late nineteenth-century labour violence in the United States, and the rise of formal systems of collective bargaining, ca'canny and socialist movements in Britain, symbolised the changing problems facing the owners of capital.[26]

The Second Industrial Revolution, and the different experiences of Britain and the United States during that revolution, requires a change in both theories of technical change, and explanations of Anglo–American differences. It is generally accepted that the rise of management and the shift of control over production from labour to management was slower and less complete in Britain than in the United States.[27] In Britain, the set of production institutions that emerged to perform the tasks of coordination and control were not the bastions of a new managerial class, as was the case in the United States. This different experience during the Second Industrial Revolution continues to be reflected in the modern British factory where the quality of management and the degree of labour control over factory operations is pointed to as a leading cause of the low levels of British productivity. By focusing on factor prices and capital–labour ratios, economic models of technical change have ignored a range of institutional changes which had a significant effect on productivity and may help explain the unexplained 'residual' which stimulated economists' interest in technical change in the first place.

The Neo-Ricardian model and technical change

The role of capital–labour conflict in economic development has been the hall-mark of Marxian analysis.[28] In recent years, the Marxian analysis has been reformulated, on a more rigorous mathematical foundation, by Sraffa and his followers.[29] One might expect that the Sraffian model, given its links with the Marxian model, might provide a basis for an alternative theory of technical change which explicitly takes into account institutions. However, the Sraffian model suffers from many of the same weaknesses as the neoclassical model because it all but ignores the institutional context of production.[30] Sraffian models use input and output matrices such as those in System 2.1.

$$\mathbf{A} = \begin{vmatrix} a_{1,1} & a_{1,2} & \cdot & \cdot & \cdot & a_{1,n-1} \\ & & & & & \\ & & & & & \\ & & & & & \\ & & & & & \\ a_{m-1,1} & a_{m-1,2} & \cdot & \cdot & \cdot & a_{m-1,n-1} \end{vmatrix} = \text{Non-labour inputs}$$

$$\mathbf{AN'} = |a_1 \quad a_2 \quad \cdot \quad \cdot \quad \cdot \quad a_{n-1}| = \text{Labour inputs}$$

$$\mathbf{P} = |p_1 \quad p_2 \quad \cdot \quad \cdot \quad \cdot \quad p_{n-1}| = \text{Prices}$$

$w = \text{wage rate (scalar)}$
$\pi = \text{rate of profit (scalar)}$
$m = n$

System 2.1

The rows in the matrix $\mathbf{A}$ indicate the industries in which the mth commodity is used as an input. The columns indicate the inputs needed to produce one unit of the nth commodity. Matrix $\mathbf{AN}$ represents the labour inputs needed to produce each commodity. The matrix $\mathbf{P}$ is the price vector. Only basic commodities, defined as those commodities which enter either directly or indirectly into the production of all other commodities, are considered. Joint production has been ruled out. Making the further assumption that profits are earned on non-labour inputs, and that production is completed in one period, gives us Equation (2.3) which, by simple manipulation, gives Equation (2.4). In Equation (2.4) wages are an inverse function of profits. The inverse relationship between wages and profits, known as the wage–profit curve, is supposed to reflect the fundamental conflict between labour and capital in a capitalist economy. However, Hahn has shown that the neoclassical model, given the same information, would also generate an inverse relationship between wages and profits.[31]

$$\mathbf{PA}(1 + \pi) + w\mathbf{AN}' = \mathbf{P} \tag{2.3}$$

$$w\mathbf{AN}' = \mathbf{P}[\mathbf{I} - \mathbf{A}(1 + \pi)] \tag{2.4}$$

Any attempt to use Equation (2.4) to explain the choice of technique or the direction of technical change is seriously hampered by the failure of either Sraffa or his followers to explain how the input coefficients in the matrices of System 2.1 are generated.[32] The Sraffian's do not have a theory of technical change, they only have a theory of choice of technology given the matrices **A** and **AN**'. Nonetheless, a careful examination of the latter can help point us toward the type of model which might explain technical change.

In order to make sense out of the Sraffian analysis, it is necessary to be aware of the precise meaning of technology versus technique. The entire matrices **A** and **AN**' together represent the technology of the economy. Each column of **A** and the corresponding labour input from **AN**' represents the technique used by a single industry. The analysis that follows makes a distinction between models capable of describing the choice of technology, of which there are a number, and models capable of describing the choice of technique.

Wage/profit curves and the choice of technology

Models found in Hicks' *Capital and Growth* and *Capital and Time*, Pasinetti's *Lectures in the Theory of Production*, and Harris' *Capital Accumulation and Income Distribution*, use a form of Equation (2.4) to analyse the choice of technology in the absence of technical change. These authors do not attempt to extend the analysis to the choice of technology or technique where the input coefficients are allowed to change.

Following Harris' analysis, which is representative of this approach, the problem is framed as follows.[33] The entire specification of a technology can be found on each page of a book of blue prints. Each technology generates a unique wage–profit curve. With only two pages in the book of blue prints, the problem facing entrepreneurs is shown in Fig. 2.3. The envelope of outer points, *ABC*, represents the technological frontier for this economy. If we assume profit maximising entrepreneurs, and take the wage rate as given, the problem becomes one of choosing the technology which is on the frontier. In our example, with a

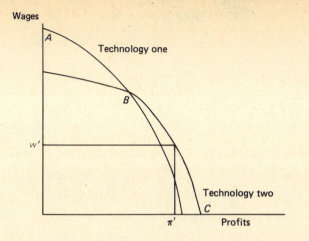

Fig. 2.3. Wage–profit frontiers and the choice of technology.

wage rate of W', the economy should adopt technology two and earn profits π'. The limitations of this approach are obvious. First, it only allows us to describe the choice of technology from a given book of blue prints. It tells us nothing about how new technologies are discovered. Second, by assuming that the wage is given, it implies that the wage rate is unaffected by changes in technology. Third, the above system does not explain why each individual entrepreneur picks the technique specified by the technology. Fourth, the above system does not allow producers in the same industry to use different techniques. If they did, either capitals would earn different rates of profit, or two prices would have to exist for the same good.

Wage–profit curves and the choice of technique

We can extend the model to the case of an individual entrepreneur choosing a new technique by assuming that any cost reductions made possible by the new techniques raises either wages or profits in the innovating firm. This implies that the vector of commodity prices is unaffected by an innovating firm choosing a new technique. Studies suggest that at least in the short-run, changes in process technology do not change prices.[34]

System 2.2 represents our modified input output data.[35] The first $n - 1$ columns are identical to System 2.1. The nth column represents a new technique for producing one unit of the $n - 1$th commodity.

Using the first $n - 1$ columns of the above matrices we could generate a set of price vectors $\mathbf{P}$ for the different wage and profit pairings. Using the assumption that prices are initially unaffected by a firm's decision to change techniques, the innovating firm can use these prices as given. The decision to choose a new

$$A' = \begin{vmatrix} a_{1,1} & a_{1,2} & \cdot & \cdot & a_{1,n-1} & a_{1,n} \\ \cdot & & \cdot & \cdot & & \cdot \\ \cdot & \cdot & \cdot & \cdot & \cdot & \cdot \\ \cdot & \cdot & \cdot & \cdot & & \cdot \\ a_{m-1,1} & a_{m-1,2} & \cdot & \cdot & a_{m-1,n-1} & a_{m-1,n} \end{vmatrix}$$

Old technology   New technique

= Non-labour inputs

$$AN' = |a_1 \quad a_2 \quad \cdot \quad \cdot \quad a_{n-1} \quad a_n| = \text{Labour inputs}$$

System 2.2

technique will be based on the wage–profit tradeoffs generated by Equation (2.5) which is simply the nth column of the above matrix.

$$P_n = PA'_n(1 + \pi + \pi') + (w + w')AN'_n \qquad (2.5)$$

In Equation (2.5), w and π are the wage and profit rate in the entire economy, while w' and r' represent labour's and capital's share of any surplus generated by the new technique. The decision to adopt a new technique depends on the value of π'. However, before we can solve Equation (2.5) for π' we need to make some assumptions about the institutional context and the distribution of any surplus between labour and capital.

One possible assumption, the one implicit in most Sraffian analysis, is that capital claims the entire surplus. Setting $w' = 0$, capital would face a single curve mapping wage rates in the old economy with different levels of surplus profit π'. If π' was positive, then the firm should adopt the new technique. Alternatively, we could assume that labour and capital share any surplus. In this case there would be one linear $w' - \pi'$ curve for each combination of w and π. Choice of technique would depend on both the wage rate ruling in the rest of the economy and the expected distribution of any surplus in the innovating firm.

The preceding analysis allows the extension of the Sraffian model to the choice of technique by individual firms. However, it raises some serious questions regarding the original formulation of the Sraffian model which used an envelope of wage–profit curves, each representing a specific technology. At the limit, each point on the wage profit frontier would correspond to a different technology.[36] Technologies will appear on the frontier if they yield *pareto optimal* distributions of income, in the sense that the technology provides at least one factor with a higher payment without reducing the payment to any other factor. As Hahn has shown, the neoclassical production function would produce exactly the same result.[37] Both the neoclassical model and the Sraffian model assume that if a new technology can raise the payoff to either capital or labour, the technology will be adopted. The neoclassical model assumes that competitive forces will generate this result, while the Sraffian model assumes the owners of capital control the choice of technology and will choose technologies which raise their profits, given wages. The Sraffian assumptions about labour institutions reflect a longstanding Marxian position that labour has little power to alter its working environment.[38]

The Sraffian model and the neoclassical model make extreme assumptions. The one assumes capitalist control and the other perfectly competitive markets. Without these assumptions, the problems of choice of technology and technical change become more difficult. Technical change reduces costs and creates a potential surplus which can be used to increase the welfare of labour, capital or consumers. The neoclassical model assumes that the benefits all go to consumers, while the Sraffians assume they all go to capitalists. It is only under highly restrictive assumptions that the gains from technical change will be distributed in such a fashion. The problem is compounded if, as the historical record suggests, markets are imperfect and the relative bargaining power of capital and labour is in some way a function of technology. If we assume that both labour and capital try to maximise their individual welfare, and if their ability to do so depends at least partially on their bargaining power, then there is no reason to argue, as do both the neoclassical economists and the Sraffians, that *pareto optimal* distributions have any special relevance. It is entirely plausible to argue that the introduction of a new technology, which has a zone of pareto superior distributions, may in fact leave one party worse off after taking into consideration changes in relative bargaining power.[39]

The Sraffian model, which at first glance appeared to deal with competition between classes, in fact simply restricts the analysis to a rather crude institutional framework which gives capital the power to expropriate the entire gain from technical change. The Sraffian model may be correct in assuming that labour has little control over wages paid per unit of time. However, a growing body of literature suggests that labour's bargaining leverage is likely to emerge as a shift in labour effort per unit of time, a question which the Sraffian model fails to consider.

Labour, management and the effort bargain

We have argued that attempts to use the neoclassical and the Sraffian models to examine technical change are seriously hampered by their failure to examine the role of production institutions. For economists, the unique characteristics of the labour contract and the costs associated with specifying, monitoring and enforcing this contract, has stimulated a new interest in the institutions of production.[40] Baldamus, a forerunner of this approach, argued that the major weakness of the standard economic analysis of production was the focus on the allocation of labour time. Baldamus suggested that the critical variable was the amount of labour effort extracted from a given amount of labour time and that this relationship could only be understood if economists extended their analysis beyond the simple framework of choice based on market signals to the role of non-market institutions designed to control labour. He wrote: 'What we are proposing then, is that the social problems of efficiency are ultimately problems of the control of human effort.'[41] Further research has suggested that the firm, systems of supervision, technology, labour relations, schooling and ideology play a role in controlling labour.

Economists are in general uncomfortable with concepts such as control, preferring instead to model the world as one of choice subject to budget or cost constraints and mediated through the invisible hand of the market. The focus on choice allows economists to assume a degree of natural harmony between economic agents. But, as Williamson has stated, it is this very assumption of natural harmony which needs modification if the effort decision is to be understood.[42] Much of the new work on labour assumes, either explicitly or implicitly, that the buyers and sellers of labour time have conflicting interests over the effort bargain, and that these conflicts are resolved by a combination of choice based on market forces and command through non-market institutions. The conflict between buyer and seller is more than simple malfeasance or the product of human nature. As Bowles has argued, an element of malfeasance may exist in human nature; however the conflict between buyer and seller of labour time will also be influenced by the institutional context. Institutions that breed suspicion, mistrust and exploitation will increase conflict while those that breed cooperation and trust will reduce conflict. According to Bowles, capitalism is dominated by institutions of the former type, and hence is forced to invest significant resources in controlling conflict.[43]

It might be argued that the conflict between the buyer and seller of labour time can be resolved through the market in the same fashion as the conflict between the buyer and the seller of any other input. But as Malcolmson has argued, the labour transaction is unique in that:

Even after the contract terms are agreed, the employer has to deal with economic agents who still have their own interests (and indeed a conflict of interest) at stake, which is not the case with the purchase of other inputs. Ceteris paribus, employees, unlike other inputs to the production process, retain an interest in working less hard.[44]

The effectiveness with which the market enforces the effort bargain is also reduced by the complex role of labour in the production process, which precludes writing complete labour contracts, and the high cost of monitoring effort. Williamson's work, within a transaction costs framework, has pointed to the role of non-market production institutions in monitoring and enforcing effort norms.[45] Williamson argued that the problem is compounded by the inability of buyer and seller to process all available information and their unequal access to information. This creates the potential for strategic or opportunistic behaviour by either buyer or seller and opens up interesting new avenues for analysis. Williamson argued: 'Economic man, assessed with respect to his transactional characteristics, is thus a more subtle and devious creature than the usual self-interest seeking assumptions reveal.'[46]

Leibenstein's X-efficiency model was one of the first of the new attempts to understand the effort bargain. In his opinion, the critical weakness of neoclassical theory was the implicit assumption, 'that inputs have a fixed specification and yield a fixed performance.'[47] Instead, Leibenstein chose to focus on the factors which would minimise the difference between maximum potential output and actual output from given inputs. He termed this difference X-inefficiency. The neoclassical model assumed away the problem of X-inefficiency by assuming that market forces would guarantee that actual output equalled maximum potential output.

X-inefficiency in the use of labour was seen as a distinct possibility. Labour was felt to be particularly susceptible to such a problem because of the special nature of the labour contract. Leibenstein wrote:

Human beings, ... the source of human inputs, cannot be purchased outright. What is usually purchased are units of labour time. But these are not the units critical for production. What is critical is directed effort, at or beyond some level of skill. Directed effort, however, involves choice and response to motivation on the part of those directing their efforts.[48]

In making an effort decision, labour must balance the increasing utility associated with higher wages against the increasing disutility associated with the higher effort needed to earn higher wages.[49] Labour's effort decision is further complicated by the socio-economic context within which labour operates. Labour functions within an 'employment situation', which is modelled as an order-signalling set of institutions. In making its decision, labour is subjected to signals from above, the vertical authority relation which, in general, encourages labour to work harder and to signals from its peers, horizontal authority relations, which, in general, encourages lower effort levels. The worker who ignores these signals may face dismissal, peer opprobrium or other socio-economic penalties.[50]

The need to consider how effort decisions might influence and be influenced by authority relationships has led Leibenstein to the conclusion that the analysis of the effort bargain must be done within a non-parametric framework. The shift to non-parametric analysis has important implications for both microeconomics and the study of technical change. With non-parametric models, agents can no longer predict the return from their strategies without considering the response of other agents. Such a situation can be modelled as a game between economic agents, each trying to pick a strategy based on the expected behaviour of other agents. An example of such a game is chess or checkers, 'in which each person makes alternate moves and no move by any individual can have a unique value since, by the rules of the game, we cannot control the moves of the other individual'.[51] We will argue that the effort bargain can be modelled as a game between the buyer and seller of labour time. Neither buyer nor seller is in full control of his respective payoffs, and changes in technology and institutions reflect attempts by both coalitions to change the rules of the game to increase expected payoffs.

Much of the more recent analysis of the effort bargain has been directed toward finding the optimal employment contract when either principal agent problems exist and monitoring is costly, or when contracts are implicit in the sense that that they cannot be expressed in a fashion which is formally enforceable in the courts.[52] Without going into details, much of this work makes use of a common set of modelling tools. The sellers of labour time face a tradeoff between wages and effort. The monitoring of effort is costly and requires the buyers of labour time to invest in some form of supervision which increases the probability that shirkers will be caught. If an employee is caught shirking, the most common penalty is dismissal, although a number of models make use of denial of promotion or denial of deferred income. The seller's effort decision is a function of his/her tradeoff between wages and effort and his/her expected income if caught shirking. In the termination models, the expected income of a dismissed worker is a function of both the expectation of finding another job and the support income available, for example unemployment insurance, if no job is found. These models have yielded interesting insights into involuntary unemployment, optimal investment in supervision, the existence of job ladders, mandatory retirement clauses and wage discrimination.

In general, these models have made limited progress in examining the link between the labour contract and technology. Nor has there been much of an attempt to examine the collective response of the sellers of labour time to supervision, termination or demotion. Termination and demotion may not be feasible if they create a collective response by labour which increases the cost of monitoring and supervising the effort bargain. This latter weakness reflects the failure to construct models of the effort bargain in a non-parametric framework and to consider the possibility of sellers developing strategies to counteract strategies adopted by buyers.[53]

The link between the effort bargain and technical change has been studied by an alternative, largely non-economic literature. Much of this work has been stimulated by Braverman's path breaking study.[54] Following closely, but independently, the approach of the labour economists, Braverman pointed to the unique features of the labour contract. The employer, and owner of capital, buys labour for a specified time period, but of an unspecified intensity. Buyer and seller come into conflict over the level of labour effort, forcing the buyer to seek mechanisms for controlling labour time.

Braverman suggested that employers responded to early nineteenth-century labour strategies, strategies which gave the sellers of labour time a large degree of control over the effort decision, by embarking on a search for new production techniques which separated the conception of work from its execution. This came to be known as 'deskilling'. It reduced the cost of monitoring and enforcing effort bargains by weakening the skilled artisans' monopoly control of the 'mysteries' of production. Having gained control over the knowledge of the production process, employers were able to simplify the work process and introduce mechanical aids whose express task was not to help labour do what it was physically unable to do, but rather to make labour do what it was unwilling to do. 'Machinery offers to management the opportunity to do by wholly mechanical means that which it had previously attempted to do by organisation and disciplinary means.'[55] This strategy came to be known as Direct Control. According to Braverman, Direct Control was the ultimate capitalist strategy.

Braverman all but ignored the response of labour to these managerial strategies and ignored the possibility that there might be more than one way to shift the effort bargain.[56] Friedman proposed that employers had two alternatives open to them; they could pursue a strategy of Direct Control, as Braverman suggested they had done, or they could pursue a strategy of Responsible Autonomy. Under the latter strategy, the sellers of labour time retained a greater degree of control over production decisions and hence the level of effort. This loosening of managerial control over labour time would be accompanied by complementary managerial techniques designed to elicit self-regulation of effort norms by labour. Fox termed these low-trust and high-trust labour environments. Friedman's work forces us to consider carefully the precise nature of the conflict of interests between buyers and sellers of labour time and the strategies available to mollify that conflict. It cannot be assumed, as was the case in Braverman's analysis, that the buyers and sellers of labour time have diametrically opposed interests regarding effort, or that the buyers are limited to deskilling and machine pacing to control effort.

Other work in the labour process tradition has shed further light on the nature of the relationship between the buyer and seller of labour time, and the role of the effort bargain. Burawoy argued that there were reasons to believe that buyers and sellers did not always view each other in oppositional terms. He wrote: 'History suggests, however, that the outcome of class struggle mollifies the opposition of interests and frequently coordinates the interests of labour and capital.'[57] Through schooling and other social institutions, ideologies evolve which amplify common interests between employee and employer while de-emphasising conflicting interests. He wrote: 'The capitalist mode of production is not just the production of things, but simultaneously the production of social relations, a lived experience or ideology of those relations.'[58]

Littler advanced this line of analysis by suggesting that if control over labour can be attained outside of the work place, it may be overly simplistic to suggest that the primary objective of technical change was to increase the employer's control over labour, as Braverman argued.[59] His work offered both support for Burawoy's analysis and an important corrective regarding the link between technical invention and labour control. He argued that labour control was not the only, and perhaps not the most important, reason for changing production techniques. In some areas, technical needs for precision or strength might stimulate new inventions. Noble, on the other hand, while accepting that changes in technology can be motivated by non-control concerns, continues to argue that employers always have a number of ways to achieve these non-control goals and that, other things equal, they will search for and develop techniques which maintain or improve their control over labour.[60]

Littler's work also provided a more sophisticated model of the relationship between buyer and seller of labour time. For Littler the relationship was one of both mutual opposition but also mutual dependency. He argued:

Capitalists are faced with the problems of continually transforming the forces of production. This, in turn, entails stimulating motivation and harnessing labour's creative and productive powers. Thus capitalists must to some degree seek a cooperative relationship with labour. It cannot just exploit those capacities that can be brought into play by bribery and coercion. Similarly, side-by-side with labour's resistance to subordination lies the fact that workers have an interest in the maintenance of the capital/labour relation and the viability of the units which employ them.[61]

This same point was made by Noble in his analysis of the rise of American management. He wrote:

The engineers. . . . went a step further to ensure that their technical work meshed with the imperatives of corporate social relations; rather than restricting their attention to technical matters, they consciously undertook to structure the labour force and foster the social habits demanded by corporate capitalism. . . . The engineers thus worked to meet the interwoven imperatives of scientific technology and corporate capitalism in two ways; in their technical work proper, as designers of the machinery and processes of production; and in their broader activities, as managers, educators and social reformers.[62]

Research on the labour process has clarified the link between the effort bargain and technical change. It has also shown that the link is not a simple one. On the one hand, the incomplete nature of the labour contract gives buyers of labour time an incentive to increase their control over labour. On the other hand, managerial control can never be total and hence employers must seek a bargain with labour and a degree of voluntary cooperation or self-regulation. The relationship between the buyers and sellers of labour time is neither the natural harmony of the simple neoclassical model nor the polar opposition characteristic of early writing on the labour process. In the words of Burawoy: 'The labour process, therefore, must be understood in terms of the specific combination of force and consent that elicit cooperation in the pursuit of profit.'[63] In the final section of this chapter we will show how incomplete labour contracts, and the mutual antagonism and mutual dependence of buyers and sellers of labour time can generate a model of technical change capable of explaining the different technical histories of Britain and the United States since 1850.

The effort bargain and technical change in the modern factory

In general, economists have not made the link between incomplete labour contracts and the process of technical change. Most of the economic writing continues to focus on specifying labour contracts which reduce the cost of monitoring and enforcing effort bargains. Exceptions include Leibenstein, who briefly referred to the possibility of 'effort stretching' changes in technology and Bowles who suggested that new types of technology might be developed to economise on the collection of the data needed to enforce effort norms.[64] The most comprehensive attempt to link the effort bargain and changes in technology can be found in the work of Lazonick, who has investigated both the need to control labour effort through non-market institutions and the potential of technical change to provide more attractive combinations of effort, wages and profits, which he called the 'terrain of compromise'. He has also suggested that the importance given to controlling effort levels changes as production techniques change. He wrote:

With the introduction of mass production methods based on expensive capital inputs and designed to achieve high levels of throughput, the capitalist became dependent on the reliability, dependability, attentiveness and loyalty of the semi-skilled worker. The efficacy of *capitalist* mass production methods required that the machine operative be disposed to take orders from above and, what is the other side of the same coin, indisposed to sabotage the rapid flow of production from below.[65]

Our objective in the remainder of this chapter is to build on Lazonick's model by, first, making the relationship between changes in production techniques and the changing need to control effort levels more explicit and, second, by casting the problem in a game theoretic framework to capture the mutual interdependence and antagonism between the buyers and sellers of labour time.

We will begin our analysis by presenting a simple choice of technique model along standard neoclassical lines. The only difference from standard production theory is that we will base our model on a labour effort variable, rather than labour time. The market enforces the effort bargain. The level of output (Q) will be a function of inputs of capital equipment (M), labour time (L) and labour effort per unit of labour time (E). An important assumption of our model, one which we feel reflects the reality of most manufacturing technology, is that once a method of production is adopted the ratio of machinery to labour time is fixed. Little, if any, gain in output can be achieved by having two workers drive a truck at the same time, or having two workers operate a machine at the same time. This assumption of fixed factor proportions means that once a production technique is adopted the level of employment is technically determined and the level of productivity is solely a function of effort levels.[66]

How can sellers of labour time influence the level of effort and through this the level of output? They can reduce effort per unit of labour time worked. This would lead to slower machine speeds, lower levels of output and higher unit costs. Alternatively, they might take actions which surface as changes in the amount of downtime per working hour. Downtime will be influenced by the length of sanctioned and unsanctioned rest breaks, absenteeism and industrial disputes. Grunberg found, in his comparison of a French and a British motor vehicle plant, that British workers enjoyed two-and-one-half times as much relief per shift as their French counterparts. Much of the difference was due to the British workers ability to prevent management from substituting downtime created by breakdowns for negotiated relief.[67] Productivity will also be influenced by machine breakdowns, lack of working stock and material wastage, some of which could be prevented if sellers of labour time were inclined to take appropriate action. This last point reflects the complex nature of labour effect, which involves much more than simply physical effort.

An implicit assumption of the model is that as the production process becomes more capital intensive, variations in labour effort will have larger effects on the level of output. Since the level of labour effort controls the productivity of capital equipment, obviously, the more capital equipment employed per unit of labour time, the greater will be the effect of changes in effort levels.

Equation (2.6) represents the production function described above.

$$Q = \alpha f(E) \qquad Q_E > 0 \tag{2.6}$$

where

$$\alpha = f(M/L) \qquad \alpha_{M/L} > 0$$

Sellers of labour time will try to maximise expected utility (U) which is an increasing function of income (Y) and a decreasing function of effort (E), given the rate (W) at which units of effort are rewarded. For the moment, we will ignore how sellers evaluate the tradeoff between income and effort and simply assume the utility function as given.[68] In this simple model labour markets clear and involuntary unemployment is ruled out. As will be discussed below, the assumptions made regarding how labour markets clear has an important bearing on equilibrium levels of wages, effort and profits. We will call Equation (2.8) the income–effort curve (IEC). By changing W, we can use Equations (2.7) and (2.8) to produce a supply of effort curve.

$$U = f(Y,E) \qquad U_Y > 0, \quad U_E < 0 \tag{2.7}$$

$$Y = f(E,W) \qquad Y_E > 0 \tag{2.8}$$

Buyers of labour time will try to maximise profits (π) by choosing the system of production (T) and the rate at which units of effort are rewarded (W). We will initially assume that employers have complete control of (W), an assumption we will later relax.

$$\pi = f(T,W) \tag{2.9}$$

In the short-run, given the system of production, the stock of capital (K), the price of output (p), and the rate of interest (r), employers will choose a rate of rewarding effort which maximises Equation (2.10) which we will call the profit–effort curve (PEC).

$$\pi = p\alpha f(E) - WE - rK \qquad (2.10)$$

Buyers have no direct control over effort levels. Effort levels can be changed only by changing the rate at which effort is rewarded. Herein lies the employer's dilemma. Buyers wish to raise effort levels because this improves the productivity of capital equipment and has a positive effect on profits. However, more effort can be bought only by changing W. If we assume that the substitution effect of changing W on E is stronger than the income effect, than more effort requires a higher W. However, raising W puts downward pressure on profits.

We can simplify the presentation, by assuming that the level of output is directly proportional to the level of effort. Equation (2.10) reduces to (2.11), which generates the profit–effort curves found in Fig. 2.4.

$$\pi = (P\alpha - W)E - rK \qquad (2.11)$$

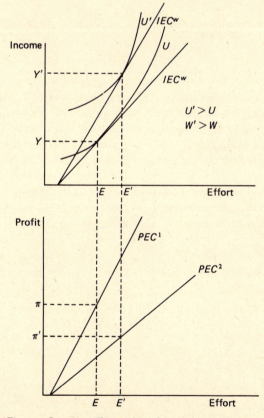

Fig. 2.4. Income–effort and profit–effort curves.

On the income effort plane, sellers choose the level of effort where the ratio of the marginal utility of effort to the marginal utility of income equals the rate at which labour effort is rewarded. On the profit effort plane, increases in the level of effort will cause a shift upwards along the profit–effort curve. Changes in W will cause the profit–effort curve to rotate. As the wage per unit of effort increases from W to W', the profit–effort curve will rotate clockwise from PEC^1 to PEC^2. In Fig. 2.4, sellers offered wage W would supply E effort, and based on PEC^1 yield profit π. An increase in wages to W' would increase effort to E', while profits based on PEC^2 would fall to π'.

In order to close this model and solve for E and W, assumptions must be made about the institutional context. Following the analysis of Lazonick, we can close the model by assuming that sellers can change jobs without incurring any transaction costs.[69] The opportunity cost of an employee with firm A using wage equation A is simply working for firm B using wage equation B. As Lazonick points out, this assumes a relatively strong bargaining position for sellers. Sellers can use their mobility to bid up the wage per unit of effort until employers earn a normal return on capital. Equations (2.12) and (2.13) show the level of income and rate at which effort would be rewarded under these assumptions.[70]

$$Y = P\alpha f(E) - r(K) \tag{2.12}$$

$$(\partial U/\partial E)/(\partial U/\partial Y) = P\alpha f'(E) = W \tag{2.13}$$

Alternatively, we could limit the sellers' bargaining power to choosing the effort level on the supply of effort curve, given the wage rate. Assuming further, a single firm and no possibility of entry, buyers would set W so as to maximise profits. Profits would be maximised when Equation (2.14) is satisfied.

$$\partial E/\partial W * P\alpha f'(E) = \partial W * E \tag{2.14}$$

When (2.14) is satisfied, the change in cost generated by changing the reward per unit of effort equals the change in cost associated with sellers changing effort levels and hence changing the productivity of capital and changing the level of output.

Using this simple framework, and either of the solutions proposed, it is possible to identify the types of production techniques that the buyers of labour time will prefer. A change in technique will appear in this model as a change in the slope and the position of the profit–effort curve. Effort saving changes in production techniques will shift the profit–effort curve to the left. Production techniques which are labour saving will raise the ratio of capital equipment to labour time which will increase α. This will rotate the profit–effort curve in a counterclockwise fashion.

The model makes it clear that simply looking at relative factor prices is likely to be misleading. It is necessary to take into account the relationship between wages and effort levels which will be influenced by a number of factors including

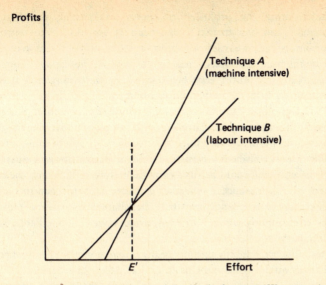

Fig. 2.5. Choice of technique and the level of output (*W* constant).

the institutional context. New production techniques will be introduced if at the expected new *W* and *E*, profits are higher. One possible motive for introducing a new production technique might be to change the relative bargaining power of the buyer and seller of labour time, making possible a more favourable combination of *W* and *E*.

As indicated above, one of the implications of our analysis is that the buyer's expectations regarding the level of effort will influence the choice of production technique. Fig. 2.5 examines two techniques whose profit–effort curves cross at effort level *E'*. Holding labour's utility function and the wage per unit of effort constant, employers will pick the labour intensive method of production *B* if they expect effort levels below *E'* while they will pick technique *A* with a higher ratio of capital to labour if they expect effort levels higher than *E'*.[71]

To this point, our model fails to capture any of the insights of the research on the effort bargain discussed above. The market enforces the labour contract. Competition between sellers of labour time insures that sellers supply the level of effort stipulated by the tangents of the income–effort curves and the seller's utility function. The buyers of labour time control the supply of effort only to the extent that they can change the rate at which effort is rewarded, which is itself partially determined by the institutional context.

The value of this model is that it helps clarify how the introduction of the labour effort variable complicates the analysis of technical change. For any given technique, employers have to be concerned with both the ratio of wages to effort, which will rotate the profit–effort curve, and the level of labour effort which will cause shifts along the profit–effort curve. In general, the higher the capital–labour ratio, the greater is the incentive for buyers to control effort levels. In contrast, at lower capital–labour ratios, control of the ratio of earnings to effort might become more critical. Regardless of the capital–labour ratio, buyers of labour time must always be aware of any shifts in relative bargaining power caused by shifts in production techniques.[72]

The main weakness of the basic model is its misrepresentation of the labour contract and the employment relationship. As discussed above, the existence of transaction costs normally precludes the existence of labour contracts which specify effort levels. Even if a contract could be drawn up, it is questionable whether market forces would be strong enough to force sellers onto their supply of effort curve in the absence of non-market enforcement mechanisms. Much of the new literature on labour suggests that sellers have an incentive to move to the left of the effort supply curve, while employers try to enforce bargains to the right of the curve.

In order to incorporate the insights of the research on the effort bargain, two sets of changes will be made to the basic model. First, it is necessary to consider, in a more explicit fashion, the role of non-market institutions on the effort bargain. This is not to deny that labour contracts and market forces are unimportant. It simply recognises that markets are imperfect and that both sellers and buyers of labour time will try to exploit these imperfections. Leibenstein's concept of an employment relationship as a complex signaling institution, with vertical and horizontal authority relationships, is useful. Management, the vertical authority relationship, can be expected to invest in control systems which shift the effort bargain to the right on the income effort plane. Labour will invest in control mechanisms which shift the effort bargain to the left on the income effort plane.

The employment relationship can be modelled as buyers and sellers of labour time investing in non-market effort controlling institutions. Denoting the seller's investment by CL and the buyer's investment by CM we can modify Equations (2.7) through (2.9) as follows.

$$U = f(Y,E) \tag{2.7}'$$

$$Y = f(E,W,CL,CM) \quad Y_{CL} > 0, \quad Y_{CM} < 0 \tag{2.8}'$$

$$\pi = f(T,W,CL,CM) \quad \pi_{CL} < 0, \quad \pi_{CM} > 0 \tag{2.9}'$$

Examples of effort controlling institutions are not hard to find. For the buyers of labour time examples include new forms of supervision, threats of dismissal, improved cost accounting, labour relations and to a large extent the late nineteenth-century development of a managerial class. The sellers of labour time have available a number of formal and informal devices. Edgeworth, long ago, recognised that unions might increase labour utility not only by raising wages through restricting the supply of labour, but also by enforcing, 'a certain quantity of remuneration in return for a certain quantity of work done'.[73] In the British building trades such restrictions of effort were very real. Bricklayers agreed amongst themselves to restrict production to 800 bricks per day, a standard which remained in effect for nearly 60 years whereupon it was reduced to between 400 and 600 per day.[74]

In this context, it might be more appropriate to consider the supply of effort curve as a psychological constraint, representing the concept of a 'fair day's wage for a fair day's work'. Rather than defining equilibrium income effort tradeoffs, the supply of effort curve influences the response of sellers of labour time to proposed income effort bargains. Sellers of labour time continue to prefer effort bargains to the left of the curve, but their willingness to invest in effort controlling institutions will increase as we move to the right of the curve.

This model differs from earlier attempts to model the effort bargain in that it allows both employers and employees to invest in effort controlling institutions. Much of the earlier work by Williamson and others focused on managerial strategies to control effort levels. There was a simplistic, and unwarranted, assumption that unless forced to, labour would do no work and labour had no capacity for developing its own strategies to challenge managerial control. By allowing both the buyers and the sellers of labour time to invest in effort controlling institutions we enrich the range of potential strategies available.

The problem is also made significantly more complex in that the seller's income now depends on the buyer's investment in control institutions, while the buyer's profits depend on the seller's investment in control institutions. The basic model assumed that buyer and seller acted in isolation within a given parametric world. This is a feature of most neoclassical analysis and, as pointed out by Schotter:

It robs the model of any behavioral or strategic complexity or interest. The neoclassical agents are bores who merely calculate activities at fixed parametric prices. They are limited to one and only one type of behavior – that of acting as automata in response to the auctioneer. No syndicates or coalitions are formed, no cheating or lying is done, no threats are made – merely truthful parametric behavior.[75]

In the revised model our economic agents no longer have sole control over their payoffs. For all economic agents, payoffs are dependent upon the strategies adopted by all other agents. Such a situation can best be modelled within a game theory framework.

The analysis of the effort bargain within a game theoretic context has two advantages.[76] First, it generates a model where neither buyer nor seller has complete control over the effort bargain. Shubik writes: 'A game of strategy is one with two or more players each with partial control over the environment, where, in general, the payoff to each player depends not only upon his actions, but also upon the actions of others.'[77] Second, it forces sellers and buyers of labour time to anticipate the reactions of other players when making their choices, opening the possibility of strategic behaviour, behaviour designed to elicit a particular response from the other players in the game. Commenting on this aspect of game theory, Elster has argued that, with the neoclassical model: 'The agent thinks of himself as a variable and of all other as constants.'[78] Whereas in game theory models: 'The agent acts in an environment of other actors, none of whom can be assumed to be less rational or sophisticated than he is himself. Each actor, then, needs to anticipate the decisions of others before he can make his own, and knows that they do the same with respect to each other and to him.'[79]

It is not our intention to engage in a highly abstract and theoretical analysis of technology within a game theoretic context. It is our desire to use the basic concepts of game theory to organise and interpret the historical record. Our energies will be spent showing how game theory can help us interpret history, not how history can help us understand the remaining controversies within the field of game theory. Such a project does not require the abstract analysis characteristic of most game theory analysis. Rather, what is necessary is an intuitive understanding of the concepts being used.[80]

The effort bargain can be modelled as a non-cooperative game with imperfect information played by two non-over lapping coalitions, which for simplicity will be called labour and capital.[81] The game is non-cooperative in the sense that labour and capital are trying to maximise their individual payoffs, and no mechanism exists for enforcing agreements which would allow them to cooperate and seek the optimum joint payoff. Knowledge is imperfect in the sense that neither labour nor capital has full information regarding the other coalition's payoff vector. Capital lacks information regarding labour's utility function and hence the supply of effort curve, the ability of the market to force labour onto the supply of effort curve and labour's investment in effort controlling institutions. Labour lacks information regarding the production function, market forces and capital's investment in effort controlling institutions. Following Harsanyi, each coalition will make estimates of all missing information based on past experience.[82] There is no reason to assume that labour and capital will end up with identical assessments of the payoff vectors.

Once the payoff vectors have been estimated, we will make use of a solution strategy pioneered by Harsanyi. Each coalition will adopt a strategy which it believes will maximise its payoff while recognising that the other coalition is also playing the game and trying to maximise its own payoff. In making their strategy choices, labour and capital will employ what Harsanyi termed the 'principle of mutually expected rationality'. Harsanyi wrote:

We have defined game situations in which each player's payoff depends not only on his own strategy but also on the other players' strategies. If a player could regard the other players' strategies as given, then the problem of rational behavior for him would be reduced to a straight forward maximization problem. ... But the point is precisely that he cannot regard the other players' strategies as given independently of his own. If the other players act rationally, then their strategies will depend on the strategy that they expect him to follow, in the same way that his own strategy will depend on the strategies that he expects them to follow ... The only way that game theory can break this vicious circle, it seems to me, is by establishing criteria for deciding what rational expectations intelligent players can consistently hold about each other's strategies.[83]

It is obvious that, in our revised model, the buyers and sellers of labour time face a more complex problem with a richer range of choices than was the case in the basic model. As in the basic model, labour faces a tradeoff between effort and income which generates a supply of effort curve. Under perfectly competitive markets, our excursion into game theory is of little use, as labour will be forced onto the supply of effort curve. If market enforcement mechanisms are imperfect, a conclusion which is strongly supported by the research on labour and effort bargains, then labour must also make choices regarding investment in strategies leading to income effort bargains off the supply of effort curve. Here our game theoretic framework is highly useful. Labour can invest in effort controlling institutions such as shop stewards, sabotage, strikes, quitting or trade unionism. Labour's willingness to invest in such institutions will be a function of labour's expectations regarding the strength of market enforcing mechanisms, the return to a particular investment and, perhaps most critically, capital's likely response to a labour strategy.

Capital, on the other hand, can now choose the method of production, the rate at which effort will be rewarded, and institutions for controlling labour effort. Again, if markets enforce effort bargains, capital's investment in effort controlling institutions is likely to be insignificant. However, as argued above, the nature of the effort bargain makes this unlikely. In making its decision to invest in effort controlling institutions, capital must consider the strength of market enforcing mechanisms, the return to increases in effort which will depend critically on the capital intensity of the production process, and finally the expected response of labour to different control strategies.

The advantage of the revised model is that the sellers and buyers of labour time have a richer range of strategy choices. Buyers can continue to use the labour contract and the incentive of higher wages, or they can invest in non-market mechanisms for controlling effort. Buyers must consider the possible interaction between changes in production technique and changes in effort bargain. One dimension of this problem is the relationship between changing capital–labour ratios and the return from increasing labour effort. Buyers will tend to invest more heavily in effort controlling institutions as the capital–labour ratio rises. There is also the question of the impact of new production techniques on the efficiency of existing institutions for monitoring and enforcing effort bargains. Some changes in technique will increase the buyer's control over labour, while others will reduce control.

It is our thesis that changes in production techniques, and the rise of management over the last 100 years represents, in part, strategies for shifting the effort bargain. These changes reflect not only economic forces but also institutional forces and in particular the relationship between labour and capital. This is likely to be particularly true in international comparisons of technical history where the forces moving different countries to common institutions are likely to be weak. The impact of these institutional forces should not be underestimated. Clark, writing on the American managerial revolution suggested:

Profitable and efficient organizations of work differ among capitalist economies because of the mistrust between social groups which must engage together in production... This mistrust played an important role in shaping the new techniques adopted in the course of the managerial revolution. Under other social arrangements many of the old market relationships removed by the [managerial] revolution would have been efficient.[84]

By using the Harsanyi methods for filling in information gaps and choosing strategies, we have a model where both history and expectations of the future count. Labour and capital 'learn by doing'. Unlike the model proposed by David, which limits learning to improvements in production techniques, our model allows economic agents to learn about each other and in the process design production techniques and production institutions.

One of the implications of such a model, and one which was clearly evident in David's analysis is that the evolution of such a system depends to a critical degree on where the process starts and, once the process of learning starts, it is difficult to shift from one learning path to another. Writing on the link between history and the evolution of institutions, Schotter wrote: 'The set of institutions existing at any point in time is really an accident of history and that what exists today could have evolved in a very different manner. All that we know about the institutional history of a society is what happened, not what could have happened.'[85]

We can use our model to shed new light on the question of why Britain and the United States developed not only unique production techniques but also unique production institutions. In the following chapters, we will argue that American buyers of labour time found it relatively easy to control effort norms. This led to further development of capital intensive production techniques which in turn stimulated the development of new effort controlling production institutions such as management. In Britain, buyers of labour time were less successful in controlling effort levels. This led to lower investment in capital intensive production techniques which in turn reduced British interest in new effort controlling production institutions such as Scientific Management and Fordism. American technology was capital intensive and management intensive. British technology was labour intensive and management poor.

3

The American motor vehicle industry, 1889–1930

When one thinks of the history of the motor vehicle industry, one immediately thinks of the American producers and especially of Henry Ford and the Ford Motor Company.[1] The French were the early pace setters, but by 1905 it was the Americans who were setting the standards which manufacturers from other countries strove to emulate.[2] They pioneered the volume production of motor vehicles and experimented with Scientific Management. By 1914 they had moved beyond volume production to mass production and, led by the Ford Motor Company, perfected a production system which is today known as Fordism.[3] Our intention in this chapter is to describe the production techniques and production institutions of this new technology and explain the reasons for its adoption. We will show how attempts by labour and management to shift the effort bargain played a central role in shaping the new Fordist system. This will help us to explain in the following chapters why Fordism was ill-suited to British needs and why British manufacturers developed an alternative method for the mass production of motor vehicles.

The American system of manufacture and the roots of Fordism

Research over the last ten years has dispelled many of the myths associated with nineteenth-century American technology.[4] The employment of unskilled assemblers and machine operators, producing standardised goods with interchangeable components, came to be known as the American system. In contrast, the European system relied on skilled labour to individually fit non-standardised components into finished goods. In 1899, H. Binsse, described the unique characteristics of the American system as follows:

The American method, and it is a vital point in the American system, is to work between fixed, predetermined limits of inaccuracy or error. Other builders make their machine details more or less imperfect and correct the faults as well as may be in the assembling, while Americans seek to have the details right and perfect, reducing to the lowest possible the number and importance of the imperfections.[5]

Careful historical research has shown that the claims made for the American system, by contemporary British and American observers, were often exaggerated. The earliest products of the American system were not fully interchangeable, nor were the new techniques accepted by American workers with open arms.[6] Merrit Roe Smith and Paul Uselding have shown that American workers tried to protect themselves from the impact of deskilling and the loss of craft control on the shop floor associated with the new technology.[7] It was also claimed, particularly in British circles, that many American firms achieved interchangeable production by simply setting very loose standards of fit.[8]

What the research on nineteenth-century American production practices has revealed is that a new system of production was emerging slowly and at great cost in government subsidised armouries. Interchangeable methods of manufacture appealed to buyers of arms, not because they reduced production costs but, rather, because of the great strategic advantage interchangeable components would provide when attempting to repair guns under battlefield conditions. For many years armament firms using the American system were unable to deliver either the volume of arms desired or arms at a cost comparable to American firms using the European system.[9]

The technical innovation perfected by the armouries was a simple one. Components were to be made to standard size through the use of absolute gauges or, in its more advanced stage, through the use of go–no–go gauges. In the current age of spectacular 'high-tech' innovation, it is easy to underestimate the importance of this simple innovation. As Hounshell has pointed out:

This may seem an elementary geometric principle, if B = A and C = A then B = C, but its application is an intellectual leap, for it means deciding to make parts to a standard gauge (in this case the model lock) rather than shaping parts similar to the pattern and then fitting the component parts together to form a complete-and unique-lock.[10]

Adopted with an eye to easing the task of battlefield repair, production based on standard gauges set in motion a process of technical and institutional learning. The era of the skilled worker handcrafting parts into unique products was drawing to an end, while the era of the unskilled worker employing new types of machinery to produce identical goods was dawning. On the institutional side, the era of craft workers control over the effort bargain was also drawing to an end to be replaced by a new set of production institutions which significantly enhanced managerial control of effort norms. Fordism was the ultimate manifestation of the new technical and institutional framework.

The revolution which the new technology would make possible materialised slowly. Hounshell has shown that many of the leading nineteenth-century American firms, including Singer and McCormick, used a technology much closer to the European system than the American system.[11] A major bottleneck in its economical application was the state of machine technology. Even in the mid-1800s, machines were unable to work economically on hardened heat treated metal. Metal had to be machined in its untreated soft state and then hardened, which often distorted it and defeated the attempts at standardis- ation. This problem was resolved in two stages. The first stage involved the adoption of drop forging and later stamping technology which reduced the amount of steel which had to be machined. The second stage involved the perfection of grinding technology by H. Leland and the Brown & Sharpe Co. in the 1880s. Precision grinding made it possible to machine parts after the metal was hardened removing the problem of distortion altogether.[12]

By 1880, most of the technical elements of the American system were in place, but the institutional context had yet to emerge. The American system reduced capital's dependence on skilled workers and paved the way for a transfer of authority over effort norms from labour to a new managerial class. The institutions of craft production were replaced by the institutions of mass production. As the contradictions between the new production techniques and the old institutions became more obvious, both labour and management searched for alternatives. For labour, a new set of institutions would not emerge until the 1930s when industrial unionism swept across North America. For capital, the innovations were much more rapid. Even before F.W. Taylor had popularised Scientific Management in the 1890s, American capitalists had moved to strengthen their control of the shop floor.

The American revolution in managerial methods has been extensively examined elsewhere and there is no need to examine it in detail here. There is a general consensus that this revolution led to the emergence of a new class of professional managers, who became responsible for the tasks of factory coordination and control, tasks which had formerly been the preserve of skilled workers. Litterer, in an analysis of American managerial innovations during the 1880s, called the emerging institutions 'Systematic Management', which he described as follows:

Perhaps the most common of these approaches was that which can be called 'Systematic Management', and which was basically concerned with the managerial functions of directing and controlling, but not with other such functions as planning, organizing, or facilitating. Systematic management was basically concerned with making sure that the work which had to be done would be accomplished on time, and with as little duplication of effort or confusion as possible. This was to be done by supplying administrative machinery to assist in certain parts of the managerial function.[13]

Noble has also shown how the new institutions of management became the tools of the buyers of labour time and were used to control and enforce effort norms. This was not inevitable. That the institutions of management developed in this fashion supports the thesis that institutional innovation is neither accidental nor do institutions fall as manna from heaven. They are created by competing interest groups to serve their interests as part of the process of economic development.[14]

By the time the American motor vehicle industry began production in the 1890s, many of the technical and institutional problems associated with interchangeable production had been resolved. What remained for Ford was to perfect the application of the new technology to motor vehicle production and develop an institutional context which would allow their potential to be realised in the mass production of motor vehicles. As Hounshell has argued, in the process Ford and other American manufacturers would leave behind the American system and truly move into the domain of Mass Production.

The employment relationship in Detroit motor vehicle factories

In Chapter 2, we argued that buyers and sellers of labour time invest in institutions which alter effort levels. Shifts in effort norms were predicted to have an impact on the buyer's decision to adopt and develop new production techniques. Limitations of space prevent us from examining the pre-1914 American institutional context in detail, however we will show how American, and in particular Detroit, workers were unable to establish institutions to control effort levels. In Detroit, trade unions virtually ceased to exist after 1907, making the city, in the words of one contemporary observer, the 'Open Shop Capital of America'. The labour market proved to be labour's best defense against unilateral managerial control of effort norms. The period 1900 to 1920 was one of almost continuous labour shortages.

Craft unions had established bases in Detroit during the 1880s and 1890s. At the Olds Motor Works, the skilled workers had joined the Machinists' Union. They called a strike in 1898 for improved working conditions but were defeated when Olds replaced them with strike-breakers.[15] The Machinists struck the motor vehicle plants again in 1901, demanding higher wages and shorter hours, as part of the national campaign being conducted by the International Association of Machinists. This conflict intensified the attack on trade unions led by the National Association of Manufacturers, whose president was D.M. Parry head of the Overland Automobile Company. The Employers' Association of Detroit led the local campaign.[16] The established craft unions were relatively easy prey. The manufacturers found a ready ally in the American courts who were quick to issue injunctions against strikers. Through creative interpretations, the courts also ruled that union tactics could be declared illegal under the provisions of the Sherman Anti-Trust Act, an act originally directed at curbing the monopolistic practices of employers.[17]

Labour was also hampered by the make-up of the industrial workforce. Prior to 1920, American immigration policies had attracted workers from many different ethnic and cultural backgrounds. Such a labour force, while rich in ideas and experiences, found it difficult to build the solidarity needed to offer an alternative to the emerging employer controlled managerial institutions. The ending of immigration in 1920 did little to remedy this weakness. The Department of Labour used this pause in the inflow of labour to deport what it viewed as undesirables. The outflow reached an average of 38 000 workers per annum in the late twenties, and, in the process, the labour movement was stripped of many of its ablest activists.[18]

The employers were also aided by the policies of the unions and the American Federation of Labour which resisted changes such as the shift from craft to industrial unions and the extension of union influence in the political arena. They were unable to jettison the institutional framework of labour restrictionism, a labour strategy which was workable as long as labour retained a monopoly control of the supply of knowledge, but which failed miserably under the conditions of unskilled factory work. The AFL, in an attempt to retain its own control over the labour movement, and in order to enforce its vision of labour's best interests, had weakened city central labour unions. Central labour unions were perhaps the only labour body which could mobilise local workers on a broad enough scale to challenge the emerging institutional order.[19] Gramsci was probably correct when he concluded that the anti-union forces of the era presented themselves as the progressive forces and attracted valuable community support from the groups which unions supposedly served.[20]

Heliker points to 1907 as the last major battle in Detroit between the unions and the employers. In that year, the Machinery Moulders Union struck for the 9-hour day and a $0.30 minimum hourly wage. The union was soundly defeated after which: 'Trade Unionism ceased to exist as a significant factor in policy calculations of the absolute autocrats of the evolving mass production industries.'[21] The Employers' Association of Detroit, became a permanent fixture in local labour relations, defending the rights of employers and adopting a sophisticated strategy to insure that the unions remained in a weakened state. They made active use of the clergy and the press to advance their own view of the ideal industrial system in contrast to the socialist vision promoted by unions such as the International Workers of the World.[22] The Association advised its members not to exploit to an excess their short-run advantage over the unorganised workers, as they feared a general resurgence of interest in trade unions. The president of the Employers' Association argued against wage cuts in 1910, and H. Leland, the head of Cadillac and a leading actor in the open shop movement from 1901 to 1905, argued in 1911 that the movement should stop short of total elimination of unions. Between 1900 and 1910, despite the success of the local open shop movement, Detroit labour did not suffer cuts in real wages relative to other areas of the United States. In fact, they reached a real wage peak in about 1910 before conditions began to deteriorate, a situation which was reversed when Ford revolutionised the return to labour with the Five Dollar Day in 1914.[23]

This pattern of wages reflects the local labour shortage in Detroit prior to World War I. The Employers' Association, aware that the local shortages worked in labours' interest, intervened to bolster the supply of suitable workers. In 1906, its Labor Bureau listed over 40 000 workers, approximately one-third to one-half of the Detroit workforce. This provided both a ready source of blacklegs to break strikes and made it relatively easy to blacklist troublemakers. It actively recruited new labour and in 1907 encouraged immigration authorities to direct eastern and southern Europeans to Detroit.[24] An Association campaign in 1910 attracted about 20 000 labourers, many coming from Poland, Italy, Austria and Hungary. Advertisements in 200 North American cities attracted what were known as 'Buckwheats', the surplus male labour from midwestern and Ontario farms, while World War I brought an influx of southern black labour.[25]

For many years to come, the divisions within the Detroit workforce produced by these waves of labour migration made it difficult to combat the anti-union stance of the employers or to challenge the emerging institutional framework.[26] In the words of one writer:

From this mass of uprooted, unorganized immigrants and migrants divided by experience, custom, faith and language, the Ford Motor Company recruited the workers who manned the Highland Park Plant during its first historic decade.[27]

Between 1906 and 1914 there were a number of minor strikes including one in the Ford core room in 1912. The only major strike was conducted by the IWW at Studebaker in 1913. The Studebaker strike collapsed without any concessions to labour and marked the end of the IWW in Detroit.[28] Participants in the IWW drives later recounted that in 1913, the IWW had neither the vision nor the structure to organise the massive new workforce employed in the Detroit vehicle plants.[29] At Ford, the new immigrant workers were less militant and less able to challenge their employers. In 1914, the Ford Sociology Department indicated that 85 percent of the labour trouble could be attributed to 25 percent of the workers who were native born and spoke English.[30] Immigrant workers had many reasons for accepting managerial control including their experiences in Europe, their expectations of life in North America and their precarious position as unskilled workers. They were well aware that without the protection of skill they were easily replaceable.[31]

Formal trade unionism was kept at bay until well into the 1930s.[32] The inability of Detroit workers to organise formally did not mean that management had unilateral control over labour and the effort bargain. For the steadily shrinking skilled portion of the workforce there remained vestiges of craft control, the product of craft workers' monopoly control of essential production knowledge. For the unskilled majority of the workers, there remained informal organisation, about which we know little other than its potential. Informal links between workers, and between workers and low-level supervisors, provided potent mechanisms for regulating factory life. Montgomery has pointed out that it was the very success of workers, particularly new immigrant workers, in using these informal organisations to control the pace of work that prompted the post 1890s interest in personnel management.[33] Evidence of the success of these informal mechanisms of control in Detroit can be found in the employers' continuing concerns about labour unrest, even in the absence of formal trade unions.

The most potent weapon in the unorganised worker's arsenal was quitting. In the context of the tight Detroit labour market, where the demand was for unskilled labour, workers found it easy to find new employment. Labour turnover rates in the early motor vehicle plants averaged between 200 and 400 percent per annum which, when combined with the estimated $100 cost of breaking in a new worker, imposed significant costs on employers.[34] Competition between employers for workers was so severe in 1912 that the Employers' Association intervened and called a truce between the largest employers. They agreed to stop poaching each others workers or to engage in advertising designed to attract workers from one Detroit plant to another. In the meantime, the Association stepped up its advertising campaign designed to attract new workers to Detroit.[35]

The open shop campaign changed the return to employers and employees investing in effort controlling institutions, but it did not eliminate the need for such investment. The problems associated with incomplete labour contracts and the high costs associated with measuring and enforcing effort norms continued to haunt both buyers and sellers of labour time. For the capitalists, the new techniques presented both new opportunities and new problems in their attempts to regulate the effort bargain. As Lazonick has argued, mass production required a new type of worker willing to accept a new type of discipline:

Mass production technology ... heightened ... the reliance of the capitalist on the willingness of the workers to work hard at jobs over which they exercised no control ... The social relations of craft production disappeared; the social relations of mass production came into being.[36]

Ford's revolution led to one strategy for resolving the capitalist's new problems.

Henry Ford: early failures and formative influences

Henry Ford came from a modest background, spending his early years on his parents' farm just outside of Detroit. He was largely self-educated, his formal training ending with the early grades of primary school. His technical training was obtained through the practical experience of maintaining farm equipment and later in the repairing of watches for a local jeweller. One of Ford's earliest acquaintances was Thomas Edison, the inventor, whom he met in 1895. Edison provided Ford with employment at the Detroit Edison Company, where he built his first car, pirating the basic technical information from trade journals.[37] In

1899, he gave up this position to devote all of his time to the production of automobiles. His first company, the Detroit Automobile Company was set up in 1899, but went into receivership in 1901 after producing about 20 poorly designed cars manufactured with European craft techniques.[38] Ford and a few of his directors purchased the bankrupt company and renamed it the Henry Ford Company. Ford was the dominant technical contributor, spending his time on design problems and the company's racing cars. His inability to settle on a vehicle design and begin production brought him into conflict with the board of directors. He resigned from the company in 1902, receiving a token payment, his racers and an agreement that the company would change its name, becoming the Cadillac Company.

During 1901 and 1902, Ford was exposed to two important innovations in the emerging American system of vehicle production. Ransom E. Olds had established the Olds Motor Works where he produced the Oldsmobile, one of the earliest of the light and inexpensive vehicles which was to make Detroit synonymous with motor vehicle production. Olds formulated a strategy which eased the capital burden of entering the new industry. He contracted out the production of components such as motors and transmissions, which required heavy capital investments, to firms such as the Dodge Brothers, reserving for his own shops, the design and much less capital intensive tasks of assembly.[39]

On the production side, Ford was exposed to interchangeable manufacture and armoury practices in his short and stormy contact with H. Leland, whom we have already referred to regarding the development of grinding equipment. Leland was hired by the Henry Ford Company in 1902 as a result of the directors' concern regarding Ford's inability to begin volume production. Ford and Leland quickly came into conflict over the way cars should be made. Leland was critical of Ford's 'cut-and-try' techniques, the techniques of the trial-and-error mechanic.[40] Leland was one of the earliest of the Detroit vehicle makers to use armoury practices and his success was evident when he took three Cadillacs to London, disassembled them, scrambled the parts, and then reassembled them into three cars, which to the marvel of many observers actually ran.[41] Ford would go on to perfect the innovations of both Olds and Leland.

In 1903, after some difficulty, Ford found new backers and set up the Ford Motor Company. In return for his accumulated knowledge and patents, Ford received just over one-quarter of the initial share issue. The first issue had a nominal value of $100 000, but Ford managed to raise only $28 000 in cash. The rest of the shares went as payment for goods or in return for promises to supply goods. The most important investors were the Dodge Brothers who agreed to produce chassis and engines for the new company.[42]

Given the difficulty that Ford had in raising even small sums of capital, it is clear that he had to conserve this scarce resource. He used labour intensive production techniques and he followed Olds' example by buying most of his parts from outside suppliers, restricting himself to design and assembly. He also

Table 3.1. *Financial statistics, Ford Motor Company, 1903–24*

	Total Assets ($000's) (1)	Net income as a % of (1) (2)	Net earnings as a % of (1) (3)	Accumulated retained earnings as a % of (1) (4)	Dividends as a % of net earnings (5)
1903	146	25	13	4	65
1904	301	82	72	45	41
1905	301	86	60	40	102
1906	490	24	13	40	0
1907	1 401	83	54	67	1
1908	not available				
1909	2 867	107	96	70	130
1910	5 295	79	87	81	50
1911	13 363	55	54	74	24
1912	20 430	66	64	82	47
1913	35 033	77	70	86	46
1914	59 801	41	55	90	28
1915	127 827	18	63	89	25
1916	158 834	36	18	84	29
1917	166 243	16	19	94	27
1918	298 407	14	24	68	35
1919	284 554	25	—	44	—
1920	263 368	20	—	59	—
1921	409 820	19	—	71	—
1922	445 351	—	—	77	—
1923	568 101	—	—	78	—
1924	644 624	—	—	84	—

Percentage of net earnings over total assets 1903–18 = 33
Percentage of net income over total assets 1903–21 = 23

Notes: The difference between columns (2) and (3) is the result of different accounting methods and accounting periods. After 1924, Ford accounts became too complex for such a simple presentation.
Sources: Column (2) A. Nevins, *Ford; The Times, The Man, The Company* (New York, 1954), p. 647; Columns (1), (3), (4), (5), Ford Archive, Acc. 96, Box 8, *Balance Sheets*.

minimised investment in work-in-progress by pursuing a sales policy which insured rapid turnover and prompt payment for finished goods. On his third attempt, Ford had found a rich, untapped seam in the motor vehicle market. The new company did $1 162 836 worth of business in its first year of production. Tables 3.1 and 3.2 indicate that Ford enjoyed a high rate of return on capital, that he was able to use retained profits to finance his rapid expansion and that he still paid out significant dividends. Within a few short years, Ford bought out his initial partners, becoming the sole controller of one of the largest firms in the world. Over the next ten years, Ford's major dilemma would be organising the production process to cope with the high level of demand for his vehicles.

Table 3.2. *Ford Motor Company profit margins, 1903–24*

	Sales ($ooo's) (1)	Net income as a % of sales (2)	Markup on costs of vehicles (%) (3)	Markup on parts (%) (4)
1903	142	26	—	—
1904	1 162	21	—	—
1905	1 901	15	—	—
1906	1 491	7	—	—
1907	5 773	20	—	—
1908	4 701	24	—	—
1909	9 041	34	—	—
1910	16 711	25	—	—
1911	24 656	30	—	—
1912	42 477	32	37	—
1913	89 108	28	33	—
1914	119 489	20	33	36
1915	121 130	19	38	39
1916	206 867	—	36	48
1917	274 575	—	14	31
1918	308 719	—	30	31
1919	305 637	—	27	36
1920	913 763	—	17	62
1921	546 049	—	22	39
1922	—	—	25	44
1923	—	—	15	37
1924	—	—	17	31

Sources: Columns (1), (2), A. Nevins, *Ford; The Times, The Man, The Company* (New York, 1954), pp. 645 and 647; Column (3), Ford Archive. Acc. 96, Box 8, *Balance sheets*; Column (4), Ford Archive, Acc. 11, Box 21.

The Evolution of Fordism: 1903–14

In 1903, Ford's workshop was small, employed skilled workers and used the European system of production. By 1914, he was a mass employer of unskilled workers using the American system developed in the armouries. Ford had gone a stage beyond armoury practice, linking tasks together into uninterrupted, and in some cases mechanically paced, lines of work flow. In this section we will focus on the changes in production techniques, leaving production institutions and the role of the effort bargain to a later section.

The production process in a motor vehicle plant was composed of two types of activity, assembly and manufacture, or, in the terminology of the nineteenth century, the domain of the fitter and the turner. The predominant function of manufacturing departments was to machine metal into components such as cylinder heads, engine blocks, gears and body panels. These components would be passed on to assembly departments where they were assembled into units such as transmissions, axles and engines, which in turn were delivered to final assembly departments where the vehicle was assembled. As a general rule, manufacturing departments were highly mechanised while assembly departments relied on hand labour using simple tools. The evolution of techniques differed somewhat between assembly and manufacturing departments, but in both cases there was a general deskilling of production work, a reorganisation of tasks along flow lines, and an enhancement of managerial control of factory coordination and effort norms.

Pre-assembly line chassis assembly 1903–13

Ford, like most other early American motor vehicle firms, used stationary trestles to assemble vehicles in 1903. Each skilled assembler, working mainly with files and simple hand tools, was responsible for a major section of the vehicle. Workers used their knowledge and skill to individually fit the less than perfectly standard components into a working vehicle. In some cases they might even be called upon to manufacture a component on a lathe or a drill. The efficiency of the final product's performance depended on the skill shown in lining up shafts, scraping bearings and fitting gears accurately. W. W. Pring, who assembled cars for Ford from 1899 to 1902, described assembly techniques at the Cadillac Company (the former Henry Ford Co.) shortly after Ford left: 'It was all done by hand. There were no fixtures, no jigs in those days. It was done with a tape line. We would just measure it out and put them on there. We would do our operations right on the spot.'[43]

Prior to 1906, Ford was predominantly an assembler, fitting together major components such as axles, engines, transmissions and bodies which were purchased preassembled from outside parts suppliers such as Dodge. F. Rockelman, a tester in those early days, recalled that Dodge delivered chassis with engines already mounted on them.[44] J. Wandersee, who began working for Ford in 1902 as a metallurgist, described Ford assembly techniques in that year as follows:

All we did was put the wheels and the body on.... The cars were assembled on the spot. They would bring the chassis and the motor and the body to one place. I would say there would be ten or fifteen spots for the assembly and there would be one or two men for each assembly.[45]

Rockelman's description of Ford's Mack Avenue plant gives a similar picture:

All we had to do was to put the body and the wheels on. ... In those days the cars were assembled in units. ... There was no machine work done there at all. It was just simply an assembly. In the back room we had a little lathe and had a drill press and we had a grinder. ... I don't think there was over 75 or 80 men there.[46]

For the first few years, even though Ford was limited to assembling major components purchased from outside parts suppliers, he still found it necessary to employ skilled fitters:

Table 3.3. *Distribution of labour by wages,*
Ford Motor Company, 1905

Wage per day	Number of workers
1.00	7
1.25	2
1.50	3
1.75	19
2.00	16
2.25	20
2.50	13
2.75	9
3.00	10
3.25	6
3.50	1

Source: Ford Archive, Acc. 235, Box 6, *Time Book*,
September to December 1905.

At Fords and in all other shops in Detroit, the process. . . . still revolved about the versatile mechanic. . . . Ford's assemblers were still (1908) all-around men. . . . To be sure time had added some refinements. In 1908 it was no longer necessary for the assembler to leave his place of work for trips to the tool crib or the parts line. Stock runners had been set aside to perform this function. Nor was the Ford mechanic in 1908 quite the man he had been in 1903. . . . The job of final assembly had been split up ever so little.[47]

Parts were not sufficiently standardised, nor had assembly been divided into sufficiently small tasks, to allow the extensive use of less skilled labour. In 1908, on the eve of the introduction of the Model T, the average assembler's task cycle was 514 minutes.[48]

Fragments of data from late 1905 suggest that less skilled, or at least low paid workers, may have been employed in assembly earlier than most accounts suggest. The data in Table 3.3 has been drawn from a Ford time book, covering 103 workers during the last four months of 1905. Nevins suggested that unskilled workers were earning as much as $2.52 per day and skilled workers $3.78 for nine hours. Both of these numbers seem relatively high given that the moulders tried in 1907 to establish the $3.00 day for skilled labour but failed, and that in 1908 the average Ford production worker earned around $2.00 per day. Even if we assume that workers earning less than $2.00 were unskilled, that still makes one-third of the workforce unskilled.

A critical feature of stationary assembly techniques was the need to deliver each part to every assembly stand. A.L. Litogot, who began working for Ford in 1912, gave this description of parts delivery: 'They had the stock on trucks. These trucks would come along and follow right along they'd throw that and that off for every car at every place. The next operation would come along with

Table 3.4. *Production costs, chassis and body Ford touring car (Home Plant) 1906–26*(*)

	Material ($) (1)	Labour ($) (2)	Overhead ($) (3)	Total ($) (4)	Percentage material in total (5)	Labour hours (6)	Labour hours normalised (7)(**)
DEC. 1906	415.73	20.03	24.85	460.61	90	134	151
MAR. 1913	184.72	17.39	23.13	249.00	84	67	70
JUN. 1914	165.87	24.07	32.10	222.04	74	42	39
JUN. 1915	186.62	18.70	24.93	230.26	80	38	38
JUN. 1916	174.25	26.50	40.21	241.27	72	52	47
JUL. 1917	203.73	37.05	55.61	296.42	68	60	52
JUN. 1918	230.97	42.15	61.67	334.81	69	67	58
MAR. 1919	230.68	40.82	43.97	315.48	73	54	49
MAR. 1920	279.65	48.96	67.47	396.08	70	64	56
MAR. 1921	266.34	38.05	53.08	357.49	74	50	46
MAR. 1922	183.97	38.33	30.90	253.20	72	50	45
MAR. 1923	195.16	34.63	19.11	248.90	78	42	41
MAR. 1924	198.49	30.31	20.40	249.20	79	37	37
Fordor with balloon tires							
OCT. 1925	259.14	93.19	88.68	441.01	59	114	84
MAR. 1926	253.55	79.29	89.15	421.99	60	97	73

Notes: (*) the estimates for wages found in column (1) of Table 3.10 have been used to convert moneys costs into labour hours in column (6). A certain amount of caution must be used with this data as Ford was continuously changing the parts of the car which he actually manufactured. In 1913, the cost of wheels purchased from outside suppliers was included. A set of four wheels cost $24.00. In 1916, Ford began painting bodies in his own shops, and in 1917 began assembling his own bodies from knocked down kits purchased from outside suppliers.

(**) Column (7) was normalised to try to adjust for the changing amount of bought out parts used by Ford. June of 1915 was taken as the base observation. In all other years, production time was adjusted in relation to the change in share of materials bought out. This adjustment is still relatively crude, and while we believe column (7) shows the broad direction of change, it is still subject to a high level of error.

Sources: For 1906 Ford Archive, Acc. 96, Box 8, Manufacturing Statement; 1913–24 Ford Archive, Acc. 125, *Model T Cost Books*; 1925–26 Ford Archive, Acc. 736, *Cost Books*.

Table 3.5. *Growth of output and employment (Home Plant), 1906–13*

	Output	Employment	Output per worker
1906	2 798	700	4.00
1907	6 775	575	11.78
1908	6 015	450	13.36
1909	12 448	1 655	7.52*
1910	19 233	2 773	6.93
1911	41 981	3 976	10.55
1912	88 966	6 867	13.10
1913	183 572	14 366	12.80

*The dramatic change in productivity in 1909 reflects the impact of the new Model T adopted in late 1908.
Sources: A. Nevins, *Ford: The Times, The Man, The Company* (New York, 1954), p. 648; Ford Archive, Acc. 96, Box 9, *Table prepared by Hawkins Gies Company*.

whatever they needed to begin the next one.'[49] As output levels grew, the demands of the parts delivery system became a critical bottleneck in the production process. Indicative of the scale of the problem was the final assembly hall at Ford which in 1913 was 600 feet long, housed over 100 assembly stands and employed 500 assemblers and 100 component carriers.[50]

It was during the last years of the period of stationary assembly that much of the labour deskilling associated with Fordism occurred. During the early stages of stationary assembly, both the assemblers and the vehicle remained stationary. This limited the division of labour. At Cadillac, eight assemblers were responsible for the entire vehicle, two for each axle and four for the body. Between 1907 and 1910, Ford moved to a more sophisticated system where the car remained stationary but the assemblers moved between cars carrying out their appointed tasks. This resulted in a dramatic increase in the division of labour and the shortening of task duration to an average of 2.3 minutes by August of 1913, before the first lines were adopted.[51]

Estimates of productivity during this period are highly unreliable. They are subject to standard measurement errors plus the added complication that firms were constantly changing the share of bought out components. The data available suggests an irregular pattern of productivity improvement, with productivity growth stalling on the eve of the switch to the assembly line. Pring suggested that in 1901–02, it took four or five assemblers a week of 60 hours to complete one vehicle, or about 250 hours. We have no data on the share of bought out components and can only assume that it was very high. By 1906, Ford had reduced assembly time to between 130 and 150 hours. Table. 3.4 suggests that the amount of labour used changed little between 1906 and mid-1913. Seventy hours of labour time was needed in December of 1913, after the first line was installed. If we work backwards from this observation, and accept the majority of accounts which suggest the first lines halved labour requirements, we obtain a pre-assembly line time of 140 hours. This estimate is broadly consistent with Arnold's estimate of preassembly line labour requirements of 12 hours and 28 minutes to assemble the chassis only, which represented about a tenth of total assembly operations.[52]

Further evidence suggesting a stall in productivity growth can be obtained from various Ford production statistics. Meyer used one set of data to suggest that after 1910, labour productivity at the Ford Detroit factory improved, but at a constantly falling rate. Labour productivity increased 41 percent in 1911, 14 percent in 1912 and only five percent in 1913.[53] Ford data presented in Table 3.5, based on Ford output data and Nevins' estimate of home plant employment, tells a similar story.

The introduction of moving assembly lines

By the end of 1913, perhaps stimulated by the decline in the growth rate of labour productivity, Ford managers began extensive experiments with moving assembly lines. The principle behind the new system was simple. Instead of moving labour to the stationary assembly stands, the object to be assembled was moved to the now stationary workers. It is widely recognised that the idea was not terribly novel and that other industries in a number of countries had employed it prior to 1913.[54] In the motor vehicle industry, Olds may actually have used the system as early as 1901 when engines and chassis were assembled on wooden stands fitted with casters which could be pushed by hand past stationary assemblers and their stock bins.[55] According to Pring, the idea of assembling vehicles on moving lines was explored in Detroit in 1908 and had been suggested at Fords where an experimental line may have been tried during the last days of the Model N, by Ford and Sorensen, his chief assistant.[56] M. Wollering, machine shop superintendent at Ford Manufacturing and the Ford Motor Company during 1906 and 1907, gave the following description of chassis assembly during the last days at Piquette:

It was not powered in any way. It was all done by hand. The first unit that came along was the frame, and first thing that happened was we made what you might call a buggy. We attached the front axle and the rear axle and put the wheels on. Now it was ready so it would roll by pushing it. Then we would push it along from station to station.[57]

Despite these experiments, the new assembly hall at Highland Park used stationary assembly techniques. No explanation has survived to explain why moving assembly techniques were dropped in 1910, but we will return to this question later in this chapter.

Ford's continued use of stationary assembly techniques is in contrast to the practices of two local firms who made the shift to moving assembly prior to 1913. It appears that the first real breakthrough into flow production was achieved by the EMF Company in 1910 or 1911. The links between EMF and Ford are numerous. They were located in the same area of Detroit. W. E. Flanders, trained at the Singer Manufacturing Company[58] and a founding partner of EMF, was in charge of all manufacturing operations at Ford's Bellevue and Piquette plants in 1907. Max Wollering, who became a key figure at EMF, played a major role in organising Ford Manufacturing in 1906 where he was production superintendent.

The EMF assembly line had about thirty work stations. It did not move continuously. Instead, a clerk recorded when each task was completed and once all operations were finished the entire line was moved forward one station. The line was designed to produce about 100 chassis per day, a figure consistent with EMF's output of 22 555 in 1911.[59] Wollering described this first line as follows:

We kept pushing them and then we thought we'd try to pull them (chassis). We took two elevator drums, put a couple of motors on them with cables, and had proper hooks attached to the cable that would grasp the front axle of the car to tow it along.[60]

A second automobile firm which used assembly line production before 1913 was the Brush Company, owned by A. Brush and W. Phipps. This firm built a new plant in 1910 or 1911 to build the Brush Runabout. A local firm, Palmer Bee, installed a chain link track along the floor. Pring recalled:

Up at the Brush we had what you call a link that would catch the cars and draw them up. It wouldn't go any more than 25 feet and then she would go back again. Along came another one, and it would just pick it up and go a little further and then come back.[61]

Output from the Brush plant was about ten chassis per day.

It was not until April of 1913 that flow assembly began to appear in some of the Ford sub-assemblies, while serious experiments on the final chassis line did not begin until August or September of that year.[62] In the first instance, a rope attached to a windlass was used to pull the cars along.[63] A contemporary observer provides a clear picture of exactly what was involved in the move to continuous production:

Once the idea of quantity production along the lines instituted by Ford... had kindled in the minds of men who were making the industry, it spread like wildfire. *Doubling the output involved merely the rearrangement of the plant* and provision of an adequate supply of materials properly timed in their arrival at the machine.[64]

It is important to appreciate that the new assembly lines were very simple affairs with relatively small capacities. Contemporary reports indicate that they were efficient with as low a capacity as 50 vehicles per day. Litogot reported that the first assembly lines at Ford held only five or six cars. The first line at Highland Park was only 150 feet long and employed 140 assemblers. In 1915, a number of Ford's branch assembly plants using the line produced between 30 and 50 vehicles per day.[65] Nor did assembly lines represent major investments in new capital equipment. Quite the contrary, they may have saved capital given they reduced demands for floor space and work-in-progress, two of the largest components of capital invested in early motor vehicle plants. Even in the twenties, it was still possible to set up what were called temporary assembly lines, according to W. C. Klann, who began as a machinist in 1905 and soon progressed to foreman of engine assembly. These lines were set up for two or three weeks when production exceeded the demands of the existing Ford plant.[66]

The new system did little more than reorganise work formerly done by gangs moving between vehicles, into work done by the same gangs in front of a moving vehicle. The actual work tasks were altered little. The real extension of the division of labour had taken place in the last years of stationary assembly when task duration fell from 514 minutes to 2.3 minutes. The new lines reduced task cycles to 1.19 minutes.[67] This reduction was made possible by eliminating the labour necessary to push vehicles down the line, by eliminating the need to move from chassis to chassis, and by regularising the rate at which the chassis moved forward thereby regularising the pace of work and reducing opportunities for on the job leisure.

Early in 1914, Ford assembly lines were mechanised by hooking chassis to a continuously moving chain. Investment in assembly departments remained relatively small. C. T. Bush, a contemporary engineer in Detroit, gave the following description of early mechanised lines. 'They (Ford) did what all the old engineering companies did; they had I beam tracks. That was the easiest, simplest and quickest way, a most inexpensive system.'[68] In 1919, the vehicle assembly line department employed only $3490 worth of capital equipment, compared with the $658 341 worth of equipment in the cylinder block department. By 1922, capital investment in the assembly department was $38 832, while investment in the cylinder block department stood at $1 176 155.[69]

The most widely quoted estimates of the moving assembly line's impact on labour productivity can be found in the work of H. L. Arnold and F. L. Faurote, two American engineers, who were doing a series for the Engineering Magazine when the first lines were installed. They estimated that the best time achieved for assembling the chassis only, using stationary assembly techniques, was 748 minutes. On the first assembly line, labour time was reduced to 350 minutes, with further adjustments reducing assembly time to between 158 and 177 minutes.[70] The impact of mechanising the assembly line was nearly as great as the initial shift to line assembly. Arnold estimated that in the month following the introduction of the mechanised assembly line, and after the shift to the Five Dollar Day, the time needed to assemble a chassis fell to 99 minutes.[71] Within six months, labour productivity on the chassis final assembly line had increased nearly eight times. The Ford data found in Table 3.4 above indicates that productivity growth was less spectacular in the plant as a whole. Using the Arnold and Faurote data to generate an estimate for productivity in early 1913, it seems reasonable to conclude that the time needed to assemble and manufacture

Table 3.6. *Value-added Ford Motor Company, 1906–26*

	Value-added per labour hour ($)	Value-added per $ of wages paid ($)
1906	4.36	29.16
1913	5.46	21.04
1914	7.71	13.50
1915	6.67	13.55
1916	3.57	7.01
1917	2.62	4.24
1918	3.28	5.23
1924	3.83	4.73
1926	3.68	4.51

Sources: Table 3.4; Price data A. Nevins, *Ford: The Time, The Man, The Company* (New York, 1954), pp. 646–7.

an entire motor vehicle fell 50 percent to 70 hours with the initial shift to flow assembly and a further 50 percent to 39 hours with the mechanisation of assembly flows. After these initial improvements, productivity levels remained stagnant until after World War I when they resumed their upward trend.[72]

The value-added measures found in Table 3.6 provide alternative measures of labour productivity which avoid the problem of shifts in the share of bought out components. The weakness of this data is that it depends on final product prices which are sensitive to imperfections in product markets. For Ford, who at times had a near monopoly of the light car market, high levels of value-added may reflect either the firm's market power or high levels of productivity. Value-added per work hour remained relatively constant during the preassembly line period. In 1914, the year after assembly was reorganised on the line principle, value-added per labour hour increased 41 percent. Thereafter it declined steadily to around three dollars per hour. Value-added per dollar of wages paid, a figure more in line with our interest in the effort bargain, showed a somewhat different pattern. It declined steadily throughout the period other than the years 1914 and 1915 when the moving assembly line and the Five Dollar Day resulted in a temporary pause in the long-run downward trend.

While the final chassis assembly line was perhaps the most spectacular and successful application of the new flow techniques, it also was adopted with impressive results in other areas of the plant. The parallels between chassis and engine assembly are such that there is no need to go into details. In 1907, engines were assembled on stationary stands. Output was 50 to 70 per day. Prior to November of 1913, when the line was installed, 1100 men assembled engines, each engine taking 594 minutes to assemble. The first lines with 84 work stations and staffed by 104 assemblers reduced assembly time to 272 minutes.[73] Table 3.7, which provides data on the cost of assembling and manufacturing engines,

Table 3.7. *Production costs, assembly and manufacture of Ford engines (Home Plant), 1913–26*

		Material ($) (1)	Labour ($) (2)	Overhead ($) (3)	Total ($) (4)	Material (as a % total) (5)	Labour hours (6)	Labour hours normalised (7) (*)
DEC.	1913	32.32	9.52	12.96	54.51	59	36.60	35.98
MAR.	1914	32.04	13.15	17.54	62.73	51	23.07	19.60
MAR.	1915	31.97	9.52	12.68	54.17	59	19.42	19.14
MAR.	1916	34.27	9.66	12.84	56.77	60	18.94	18.94
JUN.	1917	39.37	11.04	16.58	67.00	59	18.09	17.78
JUL.	1918	50.18	14.98	22.34	87.50	57	23.77	22.58
JUN.	1919.	42.38	14.15	16.68	73.21	58	18.61	17.98
MAR.	1920	57.58	19.42	25.65	102.65	56	25.55	23.84
MAR.	1921	58.13	12.83	18.99	89.95	65	16.88	18.28
MAR.	1922	40.18	13.02	11.38	64.58	62	16.48	17.02
MAR.	1923	43.83	9.16	6.58	59.57	74	11.17	13.77
MAR.	1924	46.17	10.44	8.10	64.71	71	12.73	15.06
OCT.	1925	22.44	17.57	19.57	59.58	38	21.42	13.56
MAR.	1926	22.05	15.54	19.49	57.08	39	18.95	12.31

Notes: (*) see table 3.4 for an explanation of how labour hours were normalised.
Sources: Ford Archive, Acc. 125, *Model T Cost Books.*

indicates that between 1913 and 1914, the labour time required fell by 45 percent, and that by 1926, the labour time required had fallen to one-third of its 1913 level. Again, after a dramatic improvement in productivity in 1914, there seemed to be a lag until the early twenties when labour productivity resumed its upward trend.

Manufacturing methods, Ford Motor Company 1906–30

Manufacturing did not play an important role in Ford's activities until 1906 when they began manufacturing engine components at the Ford Manufacturing Company. Prior to 1906, Dodge had supplied Ford with fully assembled engines and transmissions. Even in 1906, most of the 125 Ford Manufacturing employees were assemblers. Components requiring extensive machining, such as the block and crankshaft, were purchased from outside suppliers. The machines used in these early years were universal or general purpose machines that were capable of a wide range of tasks. They were fitted with jigs and fixtures to speed up production, to improve the accuracy of machining, and to make possible the use of less skilled labour in both manufacturing and assembly departments. They were single fixture machines which meant that the machine would be idle while the fixture was reloaded and that labour would have to work more than one machine in order to avoid being idle when one machine was sequencing.[74]

This presented a number of problems for management. It increased the demand for skilled workers capable of operating more than one type of machine. It also made it necessary for these workers to move about the plant, from machine to machine, making it difficult to control their whereabouts and the amount of on the job leisure they enjoyed. One contemporary author wrote: 'Where the men travel from job to job time is lost and it is impossible for the department heads to keep in accurate touch with the location of the men and at the same time to check the progress of the work.'[75] In 1907, Ford Manufacturing was absorbed by the Ford Motor Company and moved to the main Piquette Street factory. Output was increased by installing more general purpose machines fitted with what were known as duplicate fixtures.[76]

Comprehensive measures of changes in average skill levels prior to 1910 are not available.[77] It is generally assumed that skilled labour was needed to work general purpose machines. It seems quite clear that it was a skilled job to prepare a machine for new jigs and fixtures and that there were distinct advantages to employing skilled workers where they were called upon to operate different types of machines. It was also the case that on some machines special skills were needed because the machines were not sufficiently sophisticated to produce interchangeable parts without constant adjustment. Efficient production depended upon the machinist's skills which Gartman described as, 'a series of a thousand little 'knacks', jealously guarded and transmitted from generation to generation. Workers learned intuitively to 'feel' if the tool was getting dull, if the tool speed was too fast, if the casting was of poor quality'.[78] There is some question, though, as to whether skilled labour was still needed once general purpose machines were dedicated to repeating a single task and hence eliminating the need to change jigs and fixtures. Contemporary reports suggest that at an output of about 6000 vehicles, a level of output reached by Ford in 1907, many general purpose machines could be continuously employed on a single task.[79]

Initially, the machine departments at Ford Manufacturing were organised functionally into drilling, grinding and milling departments. Parts had to be moved to different departments for subsequent operations. With the move to Piquette in 1907, a similar organisation was maintained except for machine tasks on engine blocks which were reorganised sequentially and which will be examined in detail later. Klann described machine organisation at Ford in 1908 or 1909 as follows. 'Screw machines were in one department. Another department was drill presses and another department was punch presses. The second operations were someplace else again. We took parts from one machine to the other in boxes. The traffic problem was bad I'll tell you.'[80]

As long as line shafts and belts were used to power machines it was difficult to mix machines with different power requirements.[81] The move to individual electric motors in the prewar period resolved this bottleneck. An equally important barrier to machine reorganisation was the problem of machine supervision. For many years, the accepted wisdom was that a foreman could not competently supervise an assorted collection of machines. It was believed to be more efficient to have foremen with specialised expertise oversee specialised machine departments. As machine work became more specialised and work studies more prevalent it became less important to have the expert on the shop floor. Increasingly the expertise was centralised in planning and work study departments which removed this barrier to the reorganisation of manufacturing departments.

Indicative of the changing responsibilities of foremen was the centralisation of control over plant expansion and machine ordering. In the early years, it was the foremen who decided which machines and how many were needed for a new level of output. A. M. Wibel, who sometime after 1912 was placed in charge of buying machine tools, recalled:

It was up to the foreman to know how he bettered it (production efficiency), and it was up to the superintendent, who had charge of that foreman, to understand this approach, and it was up to him to use that at some general executive meeting that they might have.[82]

Sometime shortly after the launch of the Model T, Bornholdt, a tool designer, removed this responsibility from the foremen by creating a new department which catalogued all existing machines and took control of plant expansion and machine purchases.[83]

When the new Highland Park plant was opened in 1910, the principle of sequential machine organisation became almost universal. Milling and lathe departments gave way to block, connecting rod, and cylinder head departments. At about the same time, general purpose machines gave way to special and single purpose machines.[84] The terms special and single purpose machines are often used interchangeably, which is unfortunate because there were two new types of machines appearing in motor vehicle plants around 1910. The special purpose machines were clearly the glamour machines of the period. They were expensive, made to order, capable of doing many tasks at once, embodied advances in machine design, were usually worked by unskilled operators, and needed relatively large outputs to justify their cost. Minor design changes often made special purpose machines very expensive scrap.

A second type of new machine being adopted was the single purpose machine which was little more than a universal without the many options and extra sets of gears that made such machines highly versatile. Compared with special purpose machines, the single purpose machines were cheaper, were economical at a fairly low level of output, and could be adapted to design changes by simply ordering and installing a new set of gears. Of critical importance though was that since single purpose machines were dedicated to a single task they did not need frequent tool changes and hence most of them could be worked by unskilled labour.

Contemporary descriptions of plant make it clear that many of the new machines introduced after 1910 were single and not special purpose machines. R. Pierpont, the works manager of the Olds Motor Works, argued in favour of simplified standard machines setup to do only one task but which could be re-tooled by installing a new set of gears.[85] Ford also made use of single purpose machines. Wibel, Ford's machine buyer described negotiations with machine suppliers as follows:

We didn't believe in buying a couple of bushels of change gears for changing the speed of a lathe that we only wanted one speed. Why buy eight different gear changes on that machine? So we had all those left off and got credit for it. We had the machine come into us as that particular operation needed it only.[86]

A. J. Baker, from the production department at Willys-Overland, captured the critical change occurring in machine design in 1910. On the new single purpose machines, 'the feeds and speeds cannot be changed at the will of the operator – but can be changed at the will of the executive by the transportation of gears.'[87] Even some multi-task machines were in fact single purpose machines linked together. This was the case with the Bullard mult-au-matic which linked five separate single purpose machines with a circular fixture table.[88]

The introduction of special and single purpose machines meant the end of most vestiges of craft production in motor vehicle factories. As the tasks allocated to each machine became more specialised, the need for versatile skilled labour declined. This paved the way for a major influx of unskilled machine operators, with the skilled workers being limited to designing tools, repairing machines and supervising the unskilled. Meyer suggested that in 1910, 40 percent of the workforce was unskilled, while by 1913, 51 percent of all Ford employees were classified as unskilled operators and 15 percent as unskilled labourers.[89]

Management had a special interest in controlling effort norms in manufacturing departments because they tended to be more capital intensive than assembly departments. The engine block department, one of the most capital intensive of the manufacturing departments, provides a useful case study. Engine cylinder blocks were difficult to transport and required extensive machining. Prior to 1910, while still at the Piquette Street plant, a block department was created and the machines were linked together with gravity slides. Rockelman described the department as follows:

The drilling machines were multiple drills for the eight holes which were drilled in the face of the cylinder at one time. The block was passed by hand from one station to another. We put up short conveyors to push it along to the next operation. It was not automatic. It had to be hand conveyed. When the man finished the milling operation, he would take the block, put it on the slide, and shove it over to the next station. They would pick it up and put it in the drills and then would push it on. . . . They were beginning to set up progressive flow.[90]

H. L. Arnold provides a description of cylinder block machining in 1913. Hand slides and gravity conveyors, somewhat more sophisticated than those found in 1910, continued to be used to move blocks between machines. There had been a significant increase in the use of multi-jig and multi-fixture machines. On the plano–miller, four to eight fixtures were attached to a moving table. Once the first block was loaded, the sequencing cycle could be started. As the first block sequenced, the rest of the table was loaded, by which time blocks would begin to emerge from the other end of the machine where they could be unloaded. Workers on such machines were fully employed loading and unloading blocks, a job requiring physical stamina but little skill.[91] The impact on transportation needs of sequential organisation and multi-fixture machines and multi-task machines was impressive. Prior to these changes, the block had to travel 4000 feet in its journey, while after the changes, this was reduced to 334 feet.[92]

In 1918, four years after the final assembly line had been mechanised, the *Automobile Engineer* reported on further advances in the Ford cylinder block department. The need to load and unload fixtures in manufacturing operations limited the automatic nature of work progress which characterised the assembly departments. By 1918, fixtures were designed so that they could be used on a range of machines. The fixtures were fixed to small trucks which moved along a track in front of the machines. A special pin would index the truck in front of each machine.[93] Not only did this reduce the time needed to load and unload blocks it moved manufacturing departments a step closer to reproducing the automatic, mechanically paced flow employed in assembly. Another advance in multi-fixture/multi-jig machinery appeared in 1919 when fixtures were placed on revolving tables. The completed component returned to the same position it was loaded from, making it unnecessary for the operator to move from the loading/unloading station.[94]

In manufacturing departments, the same principles of work organisation found in assembly departments were adopted. However, unlike the assembly departments where the predominance of flexible human hand-labour made machine pacing relatively easy, the special needs of manufacturing departments limited the extent of machine pacing. Gravity slides, fixtures loaded on trucks, multi-fixture machines, plano-tables, circular tables and ingenious designs made it possible to link individual workers, or a small group of workers to a mechanical pace setter. But problems appeared when they attempted to link machines requiring different time cycles, or different fixtures to a mechanical pace setter. Full mechanisation of work flows in manufacturing departments was beyond technical capabilities until after World War II when advances in hydraulic clamping devices and sensing equipment made 'automation' a reality.

The institutional context of mass production at Fords

Between 1903 and 1913, production techniques were significantly changed at the Ford plants. However, the dramatic changes which took place in 1913 and 1914 had little impact on the skill content of work nor did they require large investments in new capital. Despite this, the transition to flow production doubled labour productivity in less than one year. Even Ford publicity people marvelled at the achievement. They wrote:

When the Ford shops were turning out a thousand cars a day at the lowest production costs ever attained up to that time, Ford engineers discovered a new principle of cost reduction. Costs fell two-thirds in a single period of six months, with the same machines, the same small tools, the same men – seemingly nothing done to decrease labor costs.[95]

The obvious question which needs to be answered is how did Fordism improve labour productivity so dramatically. The question is made even more puzzling by the indications that as early as 1911, three years before Ford moved to adopt flow production, the company had satisfied the preconditions for the transition to the new technology. By that date, Ford had standardised product design with the introduction of the Model T in 1908, simplified most tasks through increases in the division of labour, reached the level of output needed for simple assembly lines, and may even have seen the system in operation at local vehicle plants.

The traditional focus on shifts in factor prices to explain the timing of the adoption of new production techniques appears particularly inappropriate in this case. The Fordist system appears to have used less of nearly all inputs. There is little question about its impact on the demand for labour. We have argued that the technology was surprisingly simple and that there are good reasons to believe that it also reduced the demand for capital.

In order to understand why the new technology had such a dramatic effect on productivity and why it was adopted in 1913, it is necessary to look beyond relative factor prices to changes in production institutions and their impact on the effort bargain. The shift to flow techniques was accompanied by major changes in authority patterns within the factory. We will argue that, by 1913, the growth of output levels, the increase in the capital–labour ratio, and new tactics adopted by labour, had reduced the effectiveness of the existing production institutions used by the buyers of labour time to monitor and enforce the effort bargain. It was an effort crisis rather than a change in factor prices, which set in motion the search for a new production system.

The period preceding the transition to Fordism was a period of phenomenal output growth. In the five preceding years, output had grown from around 6000 units per annum to almost 190 000 units at the home plant. In each of the years 1911, 1912 and 1913, output at the Home Plant more than doubled. Ford found it increasingly difficult to meet output targets with the existing technology. The growth in output levels strained the capacity of the components delivery system. Klann recalled: 'The traffic problem was bad, I'll tell you. I think everyone there was thinking about getting progressive systems through the shops, all the way through.'[96] The shift to Fordism eased this transportation problem and paved the way for continued output expansion. Duggan has argued that a similar motive was behind the changes in technology implemented by the Cincinnati carriage and wagon industry. He concluded that: 'Managers seemed to seek more productive techniques primarily to raise output rather than to save labour.'[97]

While the problems associated with output growth and the need to ease transportation demands were obviously important in the decision to adopt flow techniques, they tell only part, and perhaps a small part, of the story. Not only was Ford becoming a mass producer, he was becoming a mass employer. Ford's concentration on assembly in the early period allowed him to keep his workforce surprisingly small. It was not until 1909 that employment levels first exceeded 1000, reaching 5000 in 1912 and 14 000 on the eve of the transition to flow techniques. In contrast, EMF/Studebaker employed 9000 in local plants as early as 1911. In 1910, General Motors had 10 000 employees while Packard employed 4640.[98] As the Ford workforce expanded, the institutional framework for monitoring and enforcing the effort bargain had to be revised.

The growth of employment levels had forced Ford, on more than one occasion, to significantly change the institutions employed for coordinating factory operations and for monitoring and enforcing the effort bargain. As long as the Ford workforce remained small, a paternalistic labour strategy was employed, one which encouraged high levels of effort by stressing the common interests of employer and employee. Nevins gave the following description of the factory in the early years:

Though busy chiefly in the experimental room, he (Ford) frequently moved about the factory, jesting, telling stories in off moments, and playing practical pranks on the hands, but scrutinizing every operation. Everybody used to call him Hank or Henry... and he used to know everybody by name.[99]

Given the need to employ skilled workers in the early years, Ford had few alternatives but to treat his workers as his equals and to solicit effort within a cooperative institutional context. As Gartman has argued, as long as parts required individual fitting, work tasks could not be standardised making it virtually impossible for the foremen to enforce levels and leaving the workers with significant discretion over effort norms. Another feature of this period was the use of central stores from which components and tools had to be drawn for each job. These trips to the stores created opportunities for on the job leisure. Gartman wrote: 'The foreman could not possibly specify exactly what the worker should do or how long it should take him. ... The work day was filled with pores whose size could be determined by the workers themselves.'[100]

The first stage of the transition in authority relations took place at Fords as a result of the growth of the workforce which depersonalised relations between Ford and his workers and undermined the ideological basis of paternalism. Reports during 1906 indicated that the shop was poorly supervised and that malingering, poor quality work, and cheating of the time keeper were widespread.[101] Ford was forced to increase the authority of his foremen, and delegate to them the task of enforcing effort norms. They controlled the hiring and the firing of labour, the rate of pay earned by workers in their charge and the allocation of jobs within their departments.[102] Their authority was further enhanced by a new wage system implemented in 1908.

Ford had never advocated piecework, largely because it gave labour too much say over how much work to do in a day. It was impossible to coordinate a smooth flow of work through the plant if the operator of one machine worked at a 10-percent bonus rate while the next operator worked at 20 percent.[103] Instead of piecework, Ford adopted profit sharing bonus payments for workers who were nominally on day wages. The payments were initially based on seniority, but they were later changed to reflect more directly the individual worker's productivity. In either case, getting the bonus would very much depend on getting on with the foremen. These extra payments were not automatic and were distributed at the discretion of Ford and his foremen, with obvious implications for the latter's ability to control labour. A clear indication of the role of the bonus payments can be gleaned from the fact that they were suspended in 1913 when the first lines were introduced. They were deemed no longer necessary as a new system had been devised for enforcing effort norms, or so it was believed at the time.[104]

While the growth in employment levels made a new authority structure necessary, it was the spread of the American system and improvements in machine techniques that made it possible. The American system reduced managerial dependence on the knowledge monopolised by skilled workers, thus providing new avenues for managerial control of effort norms. When Wollering set up Ford Manufacturing at Piquette in 1907, not only did he find the need to undertake crude forms of time study, but he also found that the production process was sufficiently standardised to allow such analysis. He recalled:

I had studies made on the various manufacturing operations.... We would get a man whom we had confidence in and who knew what he was doing as to whether it was a lathe or a screw machine or a grinder. He knew the fundamentals of it and he would take a stop-watch and operate the machine himself to get a fair idea what could be done.[105]

The foremen were supplied with these studies and it became their responsibility to make sure that this level of output was achieved. In the foundry, a similar pattern of centralisation of control over effort norms was reported. In 1908, the foundry workers resisted attempts to raise productivity. Klann recalled that in order to resolve the conflict: 'We had to go out and make them to prove our point. We worked hard to do it and we did it. Of course, after we did it the other boys had to do it. This is essentially what I was doing back in 1908. I was setting work standards.'[106] The systems for setting work standards were still relatively crude. There were no scientific charts or abstract paper calculations. Setting standards depended on finding a 'sympathetic' worker, be it a production worker or a low level manager.

On the eve of the transition to flow techniques, the employment relationship was subjected to a second overhaul, which further strengthened managerial control of effort norms. Just as the growth in employment levels had necessitated a shift from paternalism to control through foremen, so continued growth required a shift from foremen's control. As long as the foremen were encouraged to treat their departments as personal empires, there was a tendency for some of them to resort to harsh, arbitrary and cruel tactics to get the work out. A 1913 Ford survey listed the unintelligent handling of the men by foremen and supervisors as a major cause of labour dissatisfaction.[107] Nevins concluded: 'Many foreman were arbitrary, prejudiced and brutal.'[108] Labour responded by voting with its feet. Annual labour turnover rose to nearly 400 percent in 1913, while daily absenteeism was 10 percent. In the words of J.R.Commons: 'They (labour) are conducting a continuous, unorganized strike.'[109]

This labour crisis necessitated a massive programme to replace workers who were either absent or who had quit. These new workers were being brought into an increasingly capital intensive factory. Table 3.8 and 3.9 provide crude estimates of the capital–labour ratio. Recognising that this figure will be sensitive

Table 3.8. *Capital–labour ratio 1906–13,*
Ford Motor Company

	Ratio of capital to labour ($)
1906	700
1909	1732
1910	1909
1911	3360
1912	2975
1913	2438

Source: Tables 3.1 and 3.5.

Table 3.9. *Capital–labour ratio 1899–1919,*
US motor vehicle industry

	Ratio of capital to labour ($)
1899	2574
1904	2007
1909	2624
1914	3945
1919	6225

Source: Ford Archive, Acc. 96, Box 10, *US Census and*
Department of Commerce Year Book.

to the economic cycle and depreciation practices, it seems reasonable to conclude that the amount of capital employed per worker doubled or tripled during the years when foremen were responsible for enforcing effort norms.

Despite the deskilling which accompanied this new investment in machinery, there was still a significant delay before a new worker reached peak productivity. Gartman's data indicates that even in 1915 over one-half of the workforce needed more than a month to learn a new job while 41 percent needed two months or more.[110] With turnover rates approaching 400 percent, much of the new machinery was being operated by untrained and inefficient workers. Ford was finding that untrained workers were poor substitutes for unskilled workers within a factory organised to function as a single gigantic machine.

In response to this labour crisis, the powers of the foremen were checked in 1913, but certainly not eliminated. Responsibility for hiring and firing was centralised under the control of a new employment office organised by J.R.Lee. Foremen retained the right to dismiss workers from their own departments, but labour had the right to appeal any sacking to the employment office where the foremen would have to justify their actions. The decision as to whether the worker was released by the company, or simply transferred to another department, rested with the Employment Office. Dismissals fell 50 percent within months of these reforms. Foremen also lost control of whom they employed and their ability to allocate jobs as personal favours. Gone were the days when foremen went to the front gates and brought in new workers. Now foremen had to apply to the machine shop heads who then passed their requests on to the employment office.[111] The existing, somewhat anarchistic, wage system which gave the foremen immense power to determine a worker's wage was replaced by a less cumbersome system of eight job grades administered by a central office. Instead of promotion at the discretion of the foremen, promotion was increasingly tied to length of service on the job and the achievement of specific standards of efficiency. These reforms limited the foremen's ability to use the threat of dismissal or pay reductions to enforce effort norms.[112]

These changes in authority patterns and in the institutions for enforcing the effort bargain took place only a few months prior to the introduction of the assembly line. Our limited and less than perfect productivity data suggests that while productivity growth was slowing during 1911 and 1912, it was virtually nil in 1913. This suggests that the reduction in the foremen's power, while necessary to reduce labour turnover, created new problems. It was the moving assembly line which resolved these problems by introducing a new mechanism for controlling effort norms.

The reminiscences leave little doubt that management was conscious of the potential of the line as a means of control. Wibel recalled:

If the idea is good for one thing, it takes a lot of people that want to be paced. . . . You take the slant that we are trying to make you do things with a mechanical pace setter; that is my own version of this thing. I never thought that would take too kindly with the average working man. He didn't like to be put on a tread mill, you know, that was the idea.[113]

Professor Muther, quoted by Gartman, makes a similar point:

The operator in a production line has less control over his working speed than the job-shop employee. . . . The worker's pace is precisely determined when the speed of the line is established and the operations assigned. He is required to work at the same rate continuously. . . . The fact that the pace of work is more directly under management's control in line production is an important one. The power which management is thus given to set the speed of the line is not to be taken lightly.[114]

Another observation of moving assembly lines tells a similar story:

The movements of the men become practically automatic and . . . output is regulated by the speed at which the traveling chains are operated. Speed up the electric motors a notch and-presto! Ford production has increased another hundred cars per day without the necessity of hiring a single workman.[115]

In manufacturing departments, the shift to sequential machine organisation gave management similar power to control effort norms. Once the speed of the flow through a bank of machines was set, any bottlenecks due to slow workers would quickly appear as an accumulation of unfinished work at that particular work station. Arnold gave the following description of the impact of flow techniques in the flywheel department:

[Before reorganisation] the straw boss could never nail, with certainty, the man who was shirking, because of the many workpiles and general confusion due to shop floor transportation. As soon as the roll-ways were placed the truckers were called off, the floor was cleared, and all the straw boss had to do to locate the shirk or operation tools in fault, was to glance along the line and see where the role-way was filled up. As more than once before said in these stories, mechanical transit of work in progress evens up the job, and forces everybody to adopt the pace of the fastest worker in the gang.[116]

Oscar Bornholdt, Ford's machine specialist, recounted how with sequential machine organisation:

The first machine sets the pace and the operators of other machines must keep their machines at a similar rate so that the stock will not run short or accumulate. ... [The machines] are placed to draw from one machine doing the operation. This gives the effect of the whole operation being done on one machine.[117]

Flow production replaced the interaction between foremen and worker, an interaction which had become increasingly fractious, with a mechanical pace setter. The foremen were no longer required to push labour directly, the line now performed this job. Even Ford admitted: 'We regulated the speed of men by the speed of the conveyor.'[118] For labour, the opportunities for enjoying on the job leisure were significantly diminished by the new pacing devices.

These changes in the institutional framework, which accompanied the shift to flow production techniques, marked the beginning of a fundamental shift in authority within the workplace which has persisted up to the present. Labour very quickly lost the limited say it had over shop floor decisions and the pace of work. The authority to make these decisions was transferred to a new managerial class and to mechanical pace setters. Even when labour developed a new set of institutions of its own in the 1930s, it was restricted to bargaining over wages and other benefits. Its main success in curbing managerial authority was through the enforcement of seniority clauses.[119] Commenting on the failure of labour to regain significant control over effort norms after 1945, Lichtenstein noted that:

By the end of World War II, auto company executives largely accepted the UAW as a permanent part of their entire employee relations picture, but they were equally determined that 'managers must manage'. ... In the 1946 contract negotiations the new Ford management team readily agreed to match the best contract the UAW could secure from strikebound GM, but insisted upon a 'company security' clause codifying management prerogatives in elaborate detail, including the virtually unlimited right to set initial production standards.[120]

In his detailed study of job control, Herding also saw management as the

Table 3.10. *Ford Motor Company return to labour, 1903–32*

	Average productive wage ($) per hour (1)	Average non-productive wage ($) per hour (2)	Minimum rate ($) per hour (3)	Unskilled rate ($) per hour (4)	Hours worked per day (5)
1903	—	—	0.15	0.15	10
1905	—	—	0.15	0.15	10
1907	—	—	0.15	0.15	10
1908	0.1929	0.2711	0.175	0.15	10
1909	0.2243	0.2024	0.175	0.21	10
1910	0.2509	0.2597	0.175	0.28	10
1911	0.2190	0.2328	0.175	—	10
1912	0.2500	0.2731	0.23	—	9
1913	0.2608	0.2808	0.26	0.3016	9
1914	0.5725	0.6161	0.29	0.5574	8
1915	0.4923	0.5456	0.34	0.5217	8
1916	0.5123	0.5523	0.43	—	8
1917	0.6170	0.6403	0.50	0.60	8
1918	0.6329	0.6868	0.50	0.702	8
1919	0.7628	0.7889	0.60	0.75	8
1920	—	—	0.75	—	—
1922	0.7971	0.8563	—	—	8
1923	0.8216	0.8706	—	—	8
1929	—	—	0.875	—	8
1931	—	—	0.75	—	8
1932	—	—	0.50	—	8

Sources: Columns (1) and (2), Ford Archive, Acc. 96, Box 8; Column (3), Ford Archive, Acc. 572, Box 32; Column (4), A. Nevins, *Ford; The Times, The Man, The Company* (New York, 1954), p. 525 and Ford Archive, Acc. 96, *Dodge Estate*; Column (5), Ford Archive, Acc. 572, Box 32.

dominant power in setting effort norms after 1930. He concluded that despite a certain amount of bravado in UAW statements, their ability to control effort norms at Ford was limited. In the 1950s union influence was limited to bargaining over the amount of time labour spent on the line or in front of a machine, leaving management a relatively free hand in determining the amount of effort extracted per unit of time worked.[121]

The final component of the Fordist strategy was the adoption of the minimum Five Dollar Day wage standard in January of 1914. Table 3.10 tracks the course of daily wages at Ford from 1903 to 1932. Ford did not have a history of liberal wage rewards, paying the local going rate prior to 1914. The new wage was far from universally applied as there were service and behaviour conditions attached to receiving the new norm. It was not until 1918 that the average wage paid to Ford production workers actually reached the Five Dollar plateau. But the increase in wages was real enough. Those who received the minimum enjoyed more than a doubling of real wages for a shorter day and, from Ford's perspective, the new wage norm, even after adjusting for those who did not qualify, nearly doubled daily wage costs.

The new wage policy was motivated by a complex set of factors. It is likely that the idea of using high wages to reinforce managerial control of labour was first suggested to Ford by P.Perry the British manager of the Ford Manchester plant.[122] The recent labour unrest at EMF/Studebaker, the resistance of Ford workers to machine pacing, and Ford's growing profit pool certainly played a role in the decision to raise wages in early 1914.[123] But at the core of the new payment standard was a shrewd strategy to insure the success of the new Fordist technology and the transfer of authority to management of control over labour effort norms. Ford's own statements suggest that hard economic calculations, not charity, were behind the decision to raise wages. Testifying before the Federal Commission on Industrial Relations in January of 1915, Ford termed the Five Dollar Day 'a business proposition', while to a reporter he declared: 'I give nothing for which I do not receive compensation.'[124] The compensation in this case was a willingness to accept the new regime of managerial control over labour effort norms.

Increased surveillance from supervisors, clerks, counters and inspectors insured that output targets were reached. Arnold and Faurote wrote that every Ford worker 'is perfectly aware that he is under constant observation, and that he will be admonished if he falls below the fast pace of the department'.[125] Brody argued that, 'in the name of efficiency, they [workers] were being reduced to a cog in the great wheel of productive enterprise'.[126] But the most unique feature of Fordism was its use of new production techniques to perform the monitoring and control tasks which had previously been performed by production institutions. A contemporary observer summed up the effect of the new production techniques as follows:

Equipment obviously set the pace in the Ford Shops. That is why Ford needs no highly refined method of wage payment to furnish an incentive for output. They [labour] must very nearly do a standard day's production whether they wish to or not. ... The average Ford employee, like Barkus, is usually quite willing.[127]

It is reasonable to conclude that Ford workers disliked the new pace of work, disliked authoritarian supervision, disliked being set to a mechanical pace setter, and disliked company intrusions into their private lives. However they made a choice, albeit from a limited set of possibilities given the realities of the Detroit employment relationship, and they chose to accept managerially set effort norms and, at least in 1914, good wages.[128] They chose not to invest in their own institutions for controlling the effort bargain, nor did they sabotage managerial efforts to raise effort norms, knowing the likely managerial response to such strategies. Detroit workers showed a willingness to accept what many then viewed and many still view as intolerable and undemocratic working conditions. The impressive productivity gains of 1913 and 1914 were, to a large extent, the product of labour's willingness to limit its say over effort norms and to accept the new, managerially controlled mechanisms for monitoring and enforcing effort norms.

The new institutions succeeded because Detroit workers let them succeed. To explain why this was so would take us beyond the realm of this book and into the history of culture, politics and ideology.[129] When offered it, American workers accepted the new standard of life made possible by the Five Dollar Day. Perhaps it is in this last area that the real secrets of the success of Ford and the American system are to be found. As Rodgers has so poignantly argued, the work ethic in the United States underwent a major overhaul after the Civil War. The new technology which stripped most workers of their democratic rights within the production process was inconsistent with the ideology of American individualism. Rodgers wrote that: 'In making work easier, mechanization had made work far less easy to endure: in becoming man's indispensable servant, the machine had become a capricious master.'[130] In the United States, work became a means to an end, a means to improving material standards of living outside of working hours and a means to more leisure. The days when work itself would provide intrinsic satisfaction disappeared with the American system. The impact of the Fordist system has nowhere been captured more clearly than in the words of the wife of a Ford worker, quoted by Russell: 'The chain system you have is a slave driver!... That $5.00 a day is a blessing – but oh they earn it.'[131]

4

The effort bargain and British technical change

We will begin our study of British technical change and its links with the effort bargain by looking at trends during Britain's early industrialisation. As late as the end of the nineteenth century, the British work place, especially in industries such as engineering, continued to resemble the preindustrial work place in the sense that the owners of capital had been unable, despite numerous attempts, to create an institutional framework which would allow them to exert dominant control over effort levels. This was reflected in the slow development of a British managerial class in the years preceding World War I. British capital's inability to exert its authority over shop floor workers, was the basis of their critique of Scientific Management and other American systems for monitoring and enforcing effort levels.

The first industrial revolution and the birth of the factory system

Changes in the production process between 1750 and 1850 resulted in the centralisation of production in factories but left intact patterns of work and the effort bargain found in the prefactory period. It is now recognised that the new machine systems associated with the Industrial Revolution were adopted by only a few industries such as cotton spinning and, later on, weaving.[1] In a detailed study of the Industrial Revolution in three British towns, Foster argued:

[The Industrial Revolution] did not involve any basic change in the social system. In terms of the larger process of industrialization, it was essentially a revolution in scale, the expansion of an existing, capitalist economy to an altogether new size.... Despite the critical cost-cutting advances made in certain sectors, the bulk of industrial technology would remain primitive-scarcely mechanized at all – for a long time to come.[2]

The Industrial Revolution, and the centralisation of production in factories did change patterns of work in one important respect, namely the shift to regular working hours and new forms of 'time discipline'. Thompson has shown how prefactory work was task oriented and time patterns of work highly irregular. Holidays, short days, irregular work weeks and periods of intensive effort appear to have been the norm. With the centralisation of production under a single roof, it became important to break these irregular work patterns and instill a new discipline of regular working hours.[3] The enforcement of time discipline alone did not ensure high levels of productivity, as it was also necessary to instill a new sense of effort discipline. The limited evidence available for the period prior to 1850 suggests employers had more success enforcing time discipline than enforcing effort discipline.

According to Hobsbawm, the effort bargain and effort norms changed slowly, with effort levels remaining relatively rigid and based on existing social norms and enforced by informal collective action.[4] Attempts to enforce these effort norms or to change them were mainly of the 'stick' variety, with dismissal, fines, annual bonds or persecution under the Master and Servant Act being commonly used techniques. Where possible, women and children were employed as they were seen to be more susceptible to such strategies and could be paid lower wages.[5] For the majority of factory workers, the effort bargain continued to reflect the custom and practice of the preindustrial period. Employers appear to have accepted that effort levels could not easily be changed from the social norm, that unskilled labour should be paid a subsistence wage and that skilled labour should earn about double that wage. Given the assumed constraint on altering effort levels, employers viewed their task to be the enforcement of this relatively low effort norm and the purchasing of labour at the lowest possible price. Suggestions, by Owen and other factory reformers, that improved working conditions might significantly improve productivity were dismissed by the majority of employers. The adoption of a low wage/low effort managerial strategy is consistent with our model, which predicts that as long as capital–labour ratios remain low the buyers of labour time may see control of the ratio of income to effort as more attractive than the control of effort itself, particularly if the latter requires costly investment in institutions for monitoring and enforcing the effort bargain.

The inability of British employers to enforce new effort norms explains in part why a new managerial class, responsible for factory coordination and control, emerged slowly during the nineteenth century. Pollard, in his study of the Industrial Revolution and the origin of British management, was hard pressed to identify either a managerial class or managerial control within the shops. The managers of the day seemed preoccupied with 'external problems', the provision of roads, housing, financing, marketing and technical design, rather than the 'internal' problem of control over effort levels. The problem was not that employers had no desire to raise effort norms, but that the strategies available were limited and effort levels were viewed as being relatively fixed. Hobsbawm noted that: 'Handbooks for industrialists and managers, though devoting much attention to the economic utilisation of raw materials, neglected the problem of labour management almost completely.'[6] In many cases, the functions of control and coordination were delegated to a class of worker/managers through the internal contract system. These worker/managers were responsible for finding and disciplining labour, and in some cases for coordinating aspects of the production process.[7]

The internal contract system reflected preindustrial work habits. Pollard argued that: 'this solution... was not a method of creating factory discipline but of evading it. The discipline was to be the older form of that of the supervisor of a small face-to-face group, maintained by someone who usually worked himself or was in direct daily contact with the workers.'[8] As the capital–labour ratio rose toward the end of the century, employers sought greater control of the shop floor. Urwick, an important British management analyst, noted the changes taking place toward the end of the century:

With the advent of the modern industrial group in large factories in urban areas, the whole process of control underwent a fundamental revolution. It was now the owner or manager of a factory i.e., the employer... who had to secure or extract from his employees a level of obedience and/or cooperation which would enable him to exercise control.[9]

As employers strove for more control, the contradictions of the internal contract system became apparent. In those industries where internal contracting was employed, the owners of capital found they had at best only limited control over piecemasters or gang bosses. The cases of internal contractors driving their workers are well documented. However, it is also recognised that internal contractors, owing at least some allegiance to their fellow craft workers, were courted, organised, and to some extent controlled, by the emerging trade unions. In the building trades, the employers were concerned that union control of foremen implied union control of effort levels. One nineteenth-century building master argued that labour wanted, 'compulsion on foremen to be unionists-foremen whom they will control, and who shall not dare to do justice to the employer, nor urge the mechanic to do more work than he likes.'[10] The battle for the loyalty of worker/managers continued well into the 1920s when the Ship Building Employers' Federation noted with some alarm that many foremen were members of craft unions, and that unions were signing up foremen in Foremen's Branches.[11] In engineering, the employers tried to wean foremen from the workers by funding the Foremen's Mutual Benefit Society, in which membership was conditional upon not belonging to any other trade union.[12]

The effort bargain in the engineering trades

In engineering, it was not until the 1830s that mechanisation began to change patterns of work. Prior to 1830 the industry was organised around male workers with all-round skills such as the millwrights. Millwrights were able to use their skill to retain a significant degree of control over effort levels in a fashion similar to preindustrial artisans. However, by the 1840s, new machine systems were sufficiently widespread to allow the millwright's job to be divided between the somewhat less skilled fitter and turner and the much less skilled machine operator.[13] This change challenged labour's influence over effort levels, but did not eliminate it. Through informal and formal collective action, the relatively skilled fitter and turners were able to retain a significant degree of influence over the pace of work.

In order to protect their interests, the skilled engineering workers formed the Amalgamated Society of Engineers (ASE) during the 1850s. In 1852, the employers confronted the ASE and challenged the rights of workers to control shop floor activity. On paper, the employers won a decisive victory, but there is general consensus that the new skill-displacing production techniques being developed in the United States were not adopted. Instead, British employers exploited their international monopoly in manufactured goods which allowed them to earn respectable profits while maintaining the status quo in the factories.[14] The need to fight all of the same managerial rights battles in the 1890s, and again during World War I, supports the thesis that employers were either unable or unwilling to check the skilled workers' influence over shop floor decisons.[15]

During the 1880s and 1890s, the struggle over the effort bargain began to change dramatically. Britain lost its monopoly control of world trade in manufactured goods. Between 1870 and 1914 her share of total world industrial output fell from 31.8 percent to 14.0 percent and British output fell behind that of both the United States and Germany.[16] As competition stiffened, British employers quickened the rate at which they adopted new mechanised techniques which, in turn, made it possible to use less skilled workers more widely. Engineering industries played a central role in this transition with cycles and munitions adopting new systems of mechanised production during the 1890s while, almost from its birth, the motor vehicle industry organised the work process around the new machine systems and the less skilled machine operative.[17]

These changes in production techniques strained the existing institutional framework and the accommodation reached between labour and capital after 1852. Employers, increasingly cognizant of their deteriorating competitive position, showed a renewed interest and aggressiveness in cost saving through lower wages, labour saving methods of production, and higher effort norms.[18] Within managerial circles, the call for managerial rights was heard with renewed vigor. But labour, having established rights to set effort levels during the period of unmechanised factory production and having learned how to enforce these rights through informal and formal institutions, resisted what it viewed as managerial encroachments. The ensuing crisis in labour relations, whose severity can be measured by the mushrooming of articles appearing in the British press on the 'labour problem', moved the British economy onto a new learning path which produced a set of economic and social institutions markedly different from those found in the United States.[19]

The crisis in labour relations reached its first peak in the mid-1890s as the employers challenged the influence of the skilled engineers on the shop floor. In 1896, the employers, under the direction of Col. H. Dyer, set up the Engineering Employers Federation to win a new agreement from the engineers. In 1897, the ASE was locked-out, ostensibly over the question of hours. The main issue was actually working conditions under the new technology.[20] G. Barnes, General Secretary of the ASE, advocated trading off labour control of effort norms for higher wages. He argued that the ASE was not challenging the employers' right to install new machines, or to man them with non-ASE workers. He asked only that the introduction of these new machines and these new workers should not result in the creation of a new class of low paid workers.

Col. Dyer did not interpret ASE demands as an attempt to protect the existing effort bargain. He wrote:

The [employers] knew that these claims only masked the real attack; the council of the ASE sought either to obtain entire control of the workshops of England, or else to carry out the propaganda of the socialist party, i.e. to destroy capitalism.[21]

In engaging the ASE in this dispute, Dyer's objective was to Americanise British industrial institutions by winning, for the employers, more control over the shop floor and effort levels. Using Carnegie's Homestead struggle as a model, Dyer sought for the employers: 'The freedom to manage their own affairs which proved so beneficial to the American manufacturers as to enable them to compete... in what was formerly an English monopoly.'[22]

The stragegy of craft unions such as the ASE on new technology and the manning of machines has often been interpreted as a form of craft chauvinism, as an attempt to protect the privileges of the skilled at the expense of the unskilled. The policy of Barnes and the ASE executive, which was to give the employer the right to hire any worker as long as the rate paid was the ASE rate, seems to be more in line with Reid's reinterpretation of craft union strategies. Reid suggested that the objective of the craft workers was not to prevent the unskilled from being promoted to the skilled level of benefits, but, rather, to prevent the skilled worker from being dragged down to the working standards imposed on the less skilled.[23]

The EEF refused to make any concessions. The hours question was rejected out of hand, and a new procedure system was installed to settle disputes and to reduce work stoppages. Most important for our purposes, the compromise proposed by Barnes on the machine question was rejected. The EEF continued to demand that the wage rate be set according to the skill necessary to do the job. The EEF policy effectively meant that the new technology would result in the introduction of a large class of low paid workers. Effort levels would rise and the ratio of wages to effort would fall. It should come as little surprise that a large proportion of British engineering workers showed little enthusiasm for the new technology under these conditions.

It might be argued that the skilled engineers' original strategy, which was to resist wage cuts but not the new machines, made it unprofitable to adopt the new methods. Such a thesis is surely questionable given that the skilled British workers were demanding far less than American workers using similar production technology. In 1890, a skilled fitter in Birmingham was paid 34 (old shillings) per week, rising to 40 by 1914. The unskilled rate, the rate which the EEF proposed paying on the new technology, was 27 per week in 1913. The average wage paid to a production worker in Detroit in the vehicle industry was over 55 in 1913 and, after Ford introduced the Five Dollar Day, it exceeded 100 per week.[24] The question which some British workers asked themselves and to which we will return in a future chapter, was that if American management could make these techniques pay higher wages, why couldn't British management do the same.

The defeat of the engineers in 1898 satisfied the EEF that they had contained a pernicious challenge to their authority and to capitalism. However, the impact of the settlement on patterns of work appears to have been limited. Hinton concluded that:

On paper this (the Terms of Settlement) represented almost unqualified defeat for one of the strongest sections of the labour aristocracy. In practice, however, the employers, here as in other industries, had failed to smash trade unionism. ASE membership fell little and recovered quickly. Until the outbreak of the First World War craft control in the workshops proved surprisingly resilient.[25]

The resilience of labour's influence on the shop floor and of British trade unions can partially be explained by the emerging state policy regarding labour and collective organisation. Trade unionism had taken hold in Britain during the 1860s and 1870s when Britain's monopoly control of world markets made it easier to accommodate the demands of the minority of workers who were unionised. During the 30 years preceding World War I, when British trade union density increased from about 4 to 25 percent of the workforce, and British manufacturers lost their monopoly control of world markets, the state moved to strengthen rather than weaken British trade unionism. The 1907 Trade Disputes Act and the release of trade unions from financial liability for damages caused by the actions of their members have been seen as labour victories generated by labour's influence on the outcome of the 1906 parliamentary elections.[26] British state labour policy was shaped by the Liberals who had one eye on the polls and the other on the need to respond to the rising social tensions within late nineteenth-century British society. They came to see the need for state intervention to head off class warfare, and in the process they gave indirect and possibly unintentional support to the trade union movement and forced employers to deal with this reality.[27]

Recent research, particularly by Price and Gore, suggests that the British State and to some extent British employers had hoped that the recognition of trade unions and the formalisation of industrial relations practices would serve to discipline an increasingly non-cooperative workforce. Price argued:

As equal members fully participating within collective agreements, the acceptance of unionism was conditional upon its adoption of a partial responsibility for the preservation of work discipline.... For unionism could now perform its meliorative work only within the structures of industrial relations and only with an observance of the discipline demanded by those structures.[28]

What is notable though, is the failure of this strategy of labour control in Britain. Between 1900 to 1920 workers, and in some cases union officials, grew increasingly reluctant to accept the new forms of discipline implicit in union recognition.[29] Price concluded:

In spite of the sophisticated procedures and institutions they operated, the unions and the system of industrial relations was evidently failing to do the job that they were set up to accomplish. They were incapable, it seemed, of resolving the fundamental conflicts that they had been devised to resolve; they could not contain the struggle for control over work; they did not ensure the observance of 'reasonable' and 'rational' procedures; and they could not maintain, therefore that industrial discipline so needed by British capitalism from the 1890s.[30]

While Gore concluded:

The workers' revolt between 1910 and 1914 signaled a serious crisis for British capitalism, precisely because it represented the rejection and failure of the recently constructed framework of conciliation and control. The trade unions were unable to act as a stabilizing agency, no longer a solution, they were part of the problem.[31]

The 1898 Terms of Settlement did little to solidify a new effort bargain in British engineering. If anything, it exacerbated the problem by increasing the element of distrust between capital and labour. Between 1898 and 1914, many engineering employers tried to both lower wages and increase effort norms. It appears that they succeeded in neither. We can only speculate as to whether a concession on the wage issue in 1898 would have altered the course of British industrial history.[32] However, we can examine, in a somewhat more concrete fashion, how the failure to reach a compromise in 1898 influenced the evolution of management and technology in British engineering and, in particular, the motor vehicle industry.

The effort crisis: restrictionism and incentive payment systems

The 1880s and the 1890s can be viewed as a period of serious institutional disequilibrium in Britain, brought on by shifts in world trade patterns, the expansion of firm size, and the gradual mechanisation of production.[33] The owners of capital showed a renewed interest in controlling the effort bargain, but they were unable to convince the labour movement, which had developed its own set of institutions, that a new bargain was desirable. Davidson has recently argued that this conflict during the 1880s led to a significant shift in class relations within Britain. The social peace of the 1860s and 1870s gave way to a new interpretation of a society fractured along class lines. The New Unionism of the 1880s had weaned many workers from the class collaborationist policies of the craft unions, replacing it with a reinterpretation of labours' problems in class conflict terms. Labour had accepted the need for a broader attack on 'the structure of social and industrial power'.[34] S. Meacham has also argued that the decades prior to World War I witnessed a heightening of class tensions. He wrote:

The twenty or thirty years before the First World War in England witnessed increasing class divisions. Enmity grew between employers and workmen. No longer did clever, ambitious artisans rise into the ranks of the entrepreneurial middle class. . . . Nor could workers any longer persuade themselves of an identity of interests between capital and labor . . . . The result was a heightened sense of class consciousness . . . . All classes now felt threatened and went on the defensive.[35]

As late as 1883, the British press was complimenting British trade unionists on their cooperative attitude. The *Times* argued:

Trade unionists have little or none of the wild fancies and subversive schemes and idle rhetoric which were too commonly the stock-in-trade with their French and German fellows. There is no trace now of a deep-rooted antagonism to the capitalist class as such.[36]

However, by the end of the decade, the situation had changed dramatically and the *Times* was forced to conclude that: 'the aim of the New Unionism is nothing less than the wholesale appropriation of the property of the employers'.[37] The *Quarterly Review* argued that: 'the present condition of Capital and Labour approaches that of Civil War. . . . Two nations are in our midst: the social fabric is divided against itself.'[38]

The ensuing 'labour crisis' took a number of forms including resistance to new technology and the promotion of radical new forms of social organisation along syndicalist and cooperative lines.[39] Engineering workers tried to use the existing procedure arrangements and the 1898 Terms of Settlement to resist the new technology or to resist working with or helping the unskilled workers manning many of the new machines. They met with limited success.[40] The most successful labour strategy appears to have been labour control of effort norms. In industries such as the motor vehicle industry, resistance to the new technology was virtually absent, but there was significant resistance to managerial attempts to shift the effort bargain. For labour, restrictionism or ca'canny, the lowering of effort levels through the exploitation of incomplete labour contracts, achieved a new sense of relevance.[41]

The buyers of labour time responded to labour restrictionism by adopting new forms of the labour contract based on innovative systems of payment by results. Among industrial countries, the British interest in payments by results was not unique. Other countries also used payments systems to control the effort bargain. The lack of detailed studies of payment by results in other countries prevents us from drawing any conclusions regarding the links between payment by results and technology in these countries. We can say that in the British context, payment by results came to be seen as the solution to *all* of capital's problems and, in the process, capital's interest in new forms of supervision and new forms of machine pacing were reduced. This can be contrasted with the United States and most of Europe where Ford-style direct control was popular.[42] The central role of payment by results in British managerial strategies allowed a continuation of nineteenth-century-style social relations within the factory. As had been the case during the Industrial Revolution, employers held firm control of the ratio of wages to effort, but were forced to compromise with (or in extreme cases concede to) labour on the setting of effort levels. This pattern of authority appears to have existed as late as the post World War II period in Britain. Hugh Scanlon, a prominent British trade union leader in the 1960s, pointed out that: 'With piecework you have the man on the shop floor determining how much effort he will give for a given amount of money.'[43]

Piecework had begun to spread before 1890, but its rate of adoption accelerated as the labour crisis intensified. In the entire engineering industry, 6 percent of fitters and turners and 11 percent of machinists were paid by the piece in 1886. By 1906 the respective figures were 33 and 47 percent.[44] A similar pattern can be found in the Midlands where in 1861 14 percent of the workers were paid by the piece. By 1891, this had at least doubled, with 25 percent of those in the East Midlands, and 44 percent in the West Midlands paid by the piece. In Coventry, the home of a number of early British vehicle makers, piecework was unknown in 1861, yet by 1913 84 percent of all fitters and turners were on some form of piecework. New payment systems such as the Premium Bonus system also spread. In 1906, 4.6 percent of all engineering workers were on Premium Bonus. By 1913, this had risen to 9.2 percent and by 1914 to 11.8 percent. By 1913, 48 percent of all Coventry fitters and turners were paid on the Premium Bonus system.[45]

The move to new payment systems such as the Premium Bonus reflects the increased role of the cash nexus in controlling the effort bargain.[46] Cruder systems of straight payment by results, where the worker received a set price per piece produced, were no longer sufficient. The difficulty of setting prices accurately made it impossible to determine whether high bonus earnings were the result of increased effort or whether they were due to poorly timed jobs. With straight piecework, there was a further problem in that as labour improved its productivity through experience wages rose but labour costs per unit of output stayed constant. For both these reasons indiscriminate price cuts were often made when bonus earnings reached a certain level, particularly with employers who continued to believe that the best wage rate was the lowest wage rate possible.

It was not long before workers, both organised and unorganised, learned to play the game. They learned to resist the temptation to increase wages in the short-run by increasing effort levels and in effect creating new permanently higher effort norms. Premium bonus systems, particularly as adopted by British managers, were intended to eliminate the need to cut prices and hence to give labour new confidence that it could raise effort without the fear of piece-rate reductions. Built into the systems were safeguards against poorly set piece prices, limits on wage inflation due to learning, and automatic reductions in unit labour costs as labour productivity increased. The end result of such bonus systems, as a number of labour representatives pointed out, was to legitimate piece-rate cutting in a new form.

Employer interest in Premium Bonus systems necessitated a separate memorandum to govern them. The 1898 Terms of Settlement had given management the right to employ any payment system, but its vagueness regarding the conditions governing payment systems appears to have made it unenforceable. The 1902 Carlisle Memorandum allowed management to introduce any Premium Bonus system they desired, and in return they agreed to guarantee the day rates of all workers, and to maintain prices once they were established. The guaranteeing of day rates was a critical concession, as it limited management's ability to use payment systems to increase effort levels.[47] If labour felt that the existing piece prices required too much effort to earn a bonus they could choose straight day wages and an effort level over which they had some control. The introduction of 'established prices' marks an attempt to enforce mutuality in setting piece prices. This would have made the ratio of effort to income subject to bargaining. Evidence suggests that employers resisted sharing control over the setting of the income effort ratio and that mutuality in setting prices was rarely practiced.[48]

Barnes was criticised for accepting the deal offered in the Carlisle Memorandum. His reply is indicative of his conciliatory stance and his faith in trading off increased productivity for increased wages. He wrote:

In regards to the employers getting an undue advantage because of the workman not getting the whole of the time saved from the basis time is fallacious. The essence of the system is in the cheapening of production, and therefore a lessened price for the product, with consequent increased demand.... We believe that there will be an all round advantage in men being given *increased wages for increased effort*.[49]

The ASE rank and file had little sympathy for the new payment systems. They resisted them where possible, and ultimately rejected the agreement governing bonus systems the first time they were allowed to vote on it, 11 years after it was signed.[50]

Other union executives showed less enthusiasm for the Premium Bonus than had the ASE executive. A TUC report in 1909 strongly condemned Premium Bonus systems.[51] The Federation of Engineering and Shipbuilding Trades, which excluded the ASE, rejected Bonus systems arguing that, 'Your committee are of the opinion that the system has absolutely nothing to recommend it, it is an adaptation of the most pernicious and degrading condition of employment in modern history.'[52] In 1905, the Federation complained that the employers were relying on cheap labour and speed up through Premium Bonus systems rather than new machinery to get costs down.[53]

Evidence regarding the adoption of payment by results at the Daimler Motor Company provides one example of how the new managers were using payment systems as a substitute for direct control over labour. Straight piecework was employed in a number of shops beginning in 1897, but was significantly modified in 1898 by giving the charge hands 10 percent of the bonus earned by workers in their shops. It is obvious that simple monetary inducements were not producing the desired effort levels and hence charge hands were given an incentive to act directly to raise effort norms. There may even have been a shift back to day work between 1898 and 1903. However, the continuing unsatisfactory nature of effort levels led to major changes in 1903 under the new works manager P. Martin. Straight piecework was extended to all of the shops in what was viewed as a general movement away from driving supervision, and toward induction through the cash nexus. Martin and the Daimler Board had considered adopting the Premium Bonus system but delayed its implementation until a new costing system was installed in 1904.[54]

It was proposed by management that the Halsey system be adopted with a 50–50 split between labour and management of all times saved.[55] After an objection from the workers, the plan was modified, increasing labour's share. The executive of the United Kingdom Society of Coachmakers (UKS), the main union involved, objected to both the original and the improved proposals. Based on its earlier experience with piecework, it argued that Daimler had no intention of maintaining the system as it was, and that once output levels reached their maximum, prices would be cut. The men were anxious to give the improved version a try and it was arranged to have a three month trial period. After this period, the men voted overwhelmingly to return to day work. Daimler did not force the issue, indicating that bonuses would continue to be paid to non-society workers, and calculated for members of the UKS. These accumulated bonuses would be paid if the workers changed their minds. The firm also informed the workers that they were returning to the 50–50 split. The temptation of receiving bonus earnings, even if only in the short-run, was too great for the Daimler workers. The UKS executive was forced to agree to the Premium Bonus system, but only after a strong rebuke concerning the short-sightedness of the Daimler workers.[56]

The adoption of the Premium Bonus system at Daimler was part of a comprehensive change in production techniques and production institutions. Between 1896 and 1903, the firm had installed a great deal of new machinery, which was carefully organised. The persistence of low output levels led Martin to reject direct control of effort levels through 'driving supervision', a system where agents of capital enforced effort levels. Instead, Martin moved to a system of voluntary cooperation from labour generated through the cash nexus. Martin entitled his new strategy 'induction'.[57]

It is difficult to quantify the success or failure of incentive payment systems in enforcing a new effort bargain. In the debate regarding British economic failure between 1870 and 1920, there is a general consensus that British growth rates and improvements in productivity slowed sometime after 1870 relative to earlier British performances and relative to growth rates in other industrial countries. Between 1873 and 1913, per annum growth in total factor productivity in Britain was 0.4 percent, in the United States it was 1.2 percent, and in Germany it was 0.9 percent.[58] Growth of labour productivity in Britain showed a marked decline after 1874 when it stood at 2.2 percent per annum, falling steadily thereafter to 0.1 percent per annum in the decade preceding World War I.[59]

In the opinion of a large number of contemporary observers, and academics who have studied the period, there was a link between productivity growth slowdowns and the labour crisis. According to Davidson:

However optimistic the findings of modern economic historians may prove to be, the fact remains that a significant spectrum of contemporary middle and upper-class opinion perceived the late-Victorian economy as undergoing a crisis and identified it with the 'Labour Problem', particularly with the deterioration in industrial relations.[60]

Phelps Brown, in his study of British productivity between 1890 and 1913, also linked declining over-all productivity with the deterioration in labour relations. He suggested that the slow down in productivity growth was: 'due to the changed attitude of the worker, which to many contemporary observers was unmistakable.... There was a withholding of cooperation formerly given, an increased resistance to management, a resentment and denial of its authority.'[61]

The defeat of direct managerial control: 1914–18

We have argued that there was an effort crisis in late Victorian Britain, and that British employers tried unsuccessfully to enforce a new effort bargain through incentive payment systems. Buyers of labour time were attempting to control effort norms through indirect methods, primarily through their control of the ratio of wages to effort. There was less evidence of the direct control techniques being pioneered in America including new modes of supervision, detailed shop floor cost accounting and machine pacing. Events during World War I, made the likelihood of a shift to direct control and an American managerial strategy even more remote. The employers, through the EEF, did make one last attempt to break labour's influence over shop floor decisions and to increase direct managerial control, but they were unsuccessful. The state imposed wartime compromise between labour and capital retained, some might say increased, labour's influence over effort levels.[62]

The massive demand for labour was not foreseen in the first few months of the war. Within this context, early requests by Vickers to relax established labour customs were not sympathetically received by the Secretary of State. However, within months, the twin demands for arms and armies pressed home the need for increased productivity.[63] Between November of 1914 and January of 1915, the EEF and the ASE tried to negotiate the relaxation of prewar customs. The employers proposed that the unions should refrain from contesting any changes in the area of manning of machines, hand work, demarcation, non-union labour, female labour, and overtime. After the war there would be a return to prewar conditions, but this was a pledge which apparently neither side realistically expected to be fulfilled. The EEF proposals, which did not make any provision for consultation between management and labour on these issues, would have dramatically increased managerial control in the shops and could very well have paved the way for an American style managerial system. The unions showed little enthusiasm for the EEF proposals. They suggested that rather than relaxing working customs, the amount of private work should be reduced and the released labour transferred to arms production. Various government departments showed some sympathy for this idea, but it was strongly resisted by Sir Allan Smith representing the employers.[64]

The Shell Conference held on 21, December 1914, warned of imminent shortages of ammunition and made it imperative that some agreement be reached on increasing output. At this point, the government was drawn in as arbitrator between the EEF and the unions. On 29 December, Sir H. Llewellyn proposed that dilution (the employment of unskilled labour on jobs normally the preserve of skilled workers) be accepted by the unions in return for a 10 percent wage increase. This proposal, which looked strikingly like the Barnes proposal in 1898, was unacceptable to the employers. The idea of profit sharing was also proposed, but again dropped after objections by employers. Instead, attempts were made to resume the stalled talks between the employers and the unions.[65]

The resumed negotiations between the EEF and the unions failed, forcing the government to impose its own solution. This solution had a number of major differences from the agreement which the EEF had been seeking. The government proposals made it necessary for management and labour to agree on any changes, with the government as the final arbitrator. The other important feature of the proposals was the guarantees built into the system regarding the type of changes allowed and the restoration of changes. The Shell and Fuses agreement, signed just before the Treasury Agreement, stipulated that any changes made should not permanently alter the work so as to make it suitable for unskilled or female labour. The government proceeded very cautiously in asking the unions to change their customs. The Treasury Agreement did not require dilution of labour or relaxation of prewar customs. It simply suggested that this would be a good idea, and asked the unions to consider any such requests from the employers favourably.[66]

These early attempts by the government to alter the effort bargain by relaxing prewar customs failed. The government was forced to pass new legislation in 1915. The Munitions of War Act embodied many of the proposals of the previous agreements, extended the administrative machinery, provided sanctions for non-compliance, and introduced the limitations of profit laws. All restrictive practices were to be suspended during the war. In cases where it could not be mutually agreed whether a practice was restrictive an independent arbitrator would decide. But even at this stage, employers in general showed little real enthusiasm for changing prewar customs. The need to agree with labour on proposed changes, the effectiveness of shop stewards in areas such as the Clyde in protecting labour's interests, and the likelihood of restoration after the war, made the effort to get changes through appear greater than the reward. Equally important, employers were keeping an eye to the postwar economy. They were unwilling to dilute labour if it simply meant that they lost their skilled workers to other firms, perhaps permanently. Only when labour shortages became extremely serious in 1917 and 1918, and the army set its sights on munitions workers as recruits, was dilution pressed forward by government legislation such as the aborted Dilution Bill of 1917, and the Embargo Scheme of 1918 which set minimum levels of unskilled labour on munitions contracts.[67]

The shop steward's challenge; 1917–19

The war legislation had a direct effect on the effort bargain in that it forced management to share control with labour and encouraged the development of institutions such as shop steward committees. Shop steward movements in areas such as Glasgow and Sheffield remained the domain of skilled workers.[68] However, in Coventry and its motor vehicle plants, unskilled workers played an important role in the movement from an early date. In 1910, four craft unions, the Amalgamated Society of Engineers, the United Machine Workers (UMW), the Toolmakers (TM), and the Steam Engine Makers (SEM), formed a joint committee to coordinate union policy. In 1911, the Workers Union (WU), which represented semi- and unskilled workers, applied for membership on his committee. It was allowed to join in January of 1912, with the support of the ASE, but the relationship between the Workers Union and the committee was uneasy at best. They were suspended, at the request of the SEM and UMW, from the newly named Coventry Engineering Joint Committee (CEJC) before the year was out. In 1913, the Workers Union fought, with little support from the skilled unions, a successful strike, winning both recognition from the Coventry District Engineering Employers Federation, and a minimum wage rate of 6d per hour. In that year, their Coventry membership stood at 2166 making them the third largest union after the ASE with 2670 members and the Amalgamated Society of Toolmakers with 2634 members.[69]

The Coventry branches of the ASE had indicated a tentative interest in industrial unions. In November of 1913, the possibility of a National Union of

Mechanics, an industrial union which would organise all workers in the Iron Trades, was discussed at an ASE District Committee meeting. In 1913, the ASE withdrew from the Coventry Engineering Joint Committee, in part because it wanted to form a closer connection with the WU which the CEJC refused to readmit. A proposed formal connection between the Coventry ASE and WU was vetoed by the national executive of the ASE, but there is evidence that, at least during 1913 and 1914, there was informal cooperation. It is likely that this move was motivated by the growth of the WU in Coventry, and the adoption of machine methods by the city's motor vehicle and cycle firms which had narrowed the skill gap. The relationship between the two soured during 1914, partly as a result of the differential treatment of skilled and unskilled workers in regard to war service, and partly as a result of the WU signing up what the ASE considered to be skilled workers.[70]

The links between the skilled and unskilled were not completely shattered by their serious differences. Toward the end of 1916, there was a crisis over dilution and the introduction of low paid workers at Coventry Ordnance Works (COW), one of the largest employers of diluted labour in Coventry. When Morris, the head of the WU, withdrew three of his members in an act of symbolic defiance, he was prosecuted under the Munitions Act for disrupting production. The skilled workers, obviously feeling that the effort bargain imposed on the unskilled would affect them since many skilled workers were doing essentially unskilled tasks, supported Morris and the WU. Ryder, the local ASE Organising District Delegate, testified for him in court. Of equal, if not greater interest were the aggregate meetings called during the crisis at which the skilled workers had their say. At the first of these meetings it was decided that if Morris was convicted, the skilled workers would immediately down tools. At a second meeting, the union officials were instructed to seek legal advice on a proposal to bring employers before the courts on charges of violating the Munitions Act. In January of 1917, Morris was found guilty and sentenced to three months hard labour. His appeal was rejected, but the sentence was reduced to a five pound fine.[71]

The local ASE leaders found themselves in a delicate position. They were officially committed to a work stoppage, but could not expect the support of the national executive. At an aggregate meeting attended by over 1,000 ASE members, it was decided that it would be futile to proceed with the strike. The meeting did pass a number of resolutions indicative of the level of feelings on the issue. They criticised the judge's decision and decided:

To exert the utmost vigilance in reporting the numerous cases of employers evading their responsibilities under the Munitions orders.... The employing classes are allowed to evade the provisions embodied in the Acts of Parliament to safeguard the workers who have loyally foregone their hard won rights for the Benefit of the country.[72]

The meeting also proposed that all union officials sitting on government bodies should be withdrawn. The Morris incident foreshadowed further cooperation between skilled and unskilled workers in their struggle for a new institutional framework to regulate the effort bargain.

The Coventry ASE's policy toward unskilled labour and toward industrial unions remained confused and, in the end, self-defeating. But perhaps it was because there was some movement in the relationship between the skilled and the unskilled in Coventry that the employers took such a hostile attitude toward 'all grades movement' which proposed to formalise labour's influence on the shop floor through shop stewards representing all workers regardless of skill or union affiliation.[73] The ASE had employed shop stewards since at least 1899 when they were appointed at Daimler. In 1907 attempts were made to elect shop stewards at Humber and Coventry Ordnance Works, but the experiment was abandoned as the union could not prevent the victimisation of these stewards. By the end of 1915, the ASE was organising regular meetings of all their stewards in the various Coventry shops. In 1916, the CEJC, with ASE approval, began to investigate the setting up of 'all-grades' works committees of shop stewards. These stewards were not to be elected but, rather, appointed by the local union officials.[74]

The Coventry ASE also encouraged the formalisation of labour's influence over shop floor decisions through joint works committees of shop stewards and management officials. In October of 1915, the unions met with the managers of the controlled establishments to discuss this issue. The managers' proposals to create joint boards with equal numbers of labour and management representatives was rejected by the ASE. Their objection was that the managers were proposing only an advisory role for the new body while the ASE wanted it to have an executive function. The ASE pursued its demand through the Local Labour Advisory Board, which recommended to the National Advisory Committee in March of 1916, that such a board with executive powers might be useful.[75]

The course and speed of events were altered by the rise of an unofficial shop stewards movement in 1916. The local ASE's initial response to this challenge to their authority was to appoint more stewards. In January of 1917, five more stewards were appointed at the Coventry Ordnance Works. In March, the ASE and two other local unions set up a joint committee at COW in an attempt to check the influence of the unofficial movement. Stewards, who were being appointed by the ASE, were instructed to try to get representation on the unofficial committees.[76]

In April of 1917 the unofficial shop stewards brought out the workers at Hotchkiss in an attempt to get official recognition of their committees. The Ministry of Munitions intervened and forced the Coventry District Engineering Employers Federation (CDEEA) and the Coventry Engineering Joint Committee (CEJC) to accept an elected shop steward committee. Neither body showed any real enthusiasm for elected stewards. The Coventry employers were critical of the government's proposals and they informed the EEF that: 'We view with great concern the recognition of shop committees of this nature, as they are generally controlled by extreme men whose aim it is to secure election on shop committees.'[77] Unions, such as the ASE, had consistently resisted the election of shop stewards, preferring to keep their appointment under official control.[78]

In forming its policy, the government followed the more moderate advice it was getting from the Minister of Labour and from some union officials. The Minister of Labour argued that the shop stewards' movement was an industrial protest, not a political protest. He argued that it was based on the frustrations of workers regarding their standard of living. It was recommended that if the workers' demands for better living conditions were partially met, there would be no danger in allowing shop stewards to be elected.[79] Other advisors to the cabinet suggested that the rise of the shop stewards was part of a wider challenge to British society following the Russian model.[80] The different interpretations of the implications of recognising workers committees is indicative of the danger different groups saw in them. The state did not see a challenge to its authority in these committees. On the other hand, the employers, who would have to deal with these committees, and share managerial authority over effort levels with them, saw them as a threat.

During 1917, the CEJC changed its policies and worked out proposals to govern the election and operation of shop stewards. It was proposed that stewards be elected by all of the workers in a department, regardless of their union affiliation. The stewards would be controlled by the CEJC, not by the individual unions. After a major strike at White and Poppe, late in 1917, these proposals were submitted to national negotiations. The Coventry District Engineering Employers Association remained a strong opponent of works committees and would accept them only if their power to interfere with management was seriously restricted. It suggested that:

The shop stewards shall not interfere with the proper exercise of authority by foremen and chargehands. Works committees would be consulted on any changes in general working conditons, (but it was), to be understood that the introduction of an improved method of manufacture is not in itself to be regarded as a change in general working· conditions.[81]

The employers also wanted the right to approve of all shop stewards elected.

By the end of 1917, a National Agreement was reached regarding shop stewards which satisfied neither the national ASE, nor the local employers nor the local unions. Stewards were to be elected, but they were to represent a single union only. The novel idea of having department-wide elections was rejected. It was only with the revision of the agreement in 1919, when a system was set up similar to the original CEJC proposals, that the ASE and the CEJC became parties to the agreement.[82] By this time, unemployment had begun to rise and with it the power of the stewards collapsed. Employers, who continued to be less than enthusiastic about shop steward committees, used the downturn to rid themselves of the most vocal stewards.[83]

The wartime events had made clear the fragility of management's control of the shops, politicised many of the workers' demands and, at least in Coventry, increased the degree of common interests between skilled and unskilled workers. Management came to accept that in British factories its ability to dictate effort levels was limited, even under wartime conditions. It was within this context that British employers began the debate over the alternative strategies available for postwar reconstruction.

The search for a reconstruction strategy

As early as 1916, the EEF began formulating a postwar industrial strategy arguing that the changes made during the war could not be reversed, and that labour should be compensated for accepting these changes through shorter hours.[84] Draft proposals were circulated amongst the local employers associations concerning a shorter working week, overtime, payment by results, wage rates and shop stewards. The draft proposals favoured a reduction in wages, with some recognition of shop stewards.[85] In their comments on the proposals, the local associations were almost unanimous in their call for lower wages and the freedom to employ the payment system of their choice. Opinion on shop stewards was divided, with the new engineering centres being the most negative. The Birmingham Association replied that: 'Shop committees as known in this district are regarded as intolerable institutions.'[86] Birmingham argued that the employers should organise to take complete control of the workshops. They felt that this would be a much more effective means of reducing costs than concessions such as a reduction in hours worked, or an increase of a few pence in wages, designed to win labour's cooperation. This process culminated in a draft proposal on Postwar Industrial Problems, issued in November of 1917. Shorter hours were to be granted as a concession for lower wages, the acceptance by labour of payment by results and a renewed pledge regarding managerial freedoms. The problems of setting effort levels and the right to introduce new methods of production were treated implicitly in this last demand.[87]

Much more can be learned about the direction of thinking at the EEF from reaction to two important documents on labour relations. The first was the Whitley Committee Report and the other was the report by the Labour Committee of the Federation of British Industries.

In response to the labour tension of 1916, the government created the Whitley Committee under the direction of the Ministry of Labour. Charles argued that Whitley was perceived as an alternative to the radical restructuring of the economy along socialistic lines which was being advocated by portions of the working class. He wrote:

If there was to be a challenge to the existing system of ownership and control of industry in the post war years, as the increasing power of labour and its evident growth in self-confidence seemed to indicate, the proposals of the Whitley report seemed to be the only antidote based as these were on the solid traditon of British trade unionism, but making a considerable advance over what before the war would have been regarded as an acceptable national policy.[88]

Whitley proposed a three-tiered national bargaining system, with a National Industrial Council for each industry, District Councils and local Works Committees. Whitley proposed to gain labour's cooperation by offering them consultation and a voice on a wide range of issues. The basic philosophy was set out in the First Report: 'The object is to secure cooperation by granting to the work people a greater share in the consideration of matters affecting their industry, and this can only be achieved by keeping employers and work people in constant touch.'[89]

The essence of Whitley was not the institutional structure, which bore a number of similarities to the one being developed by the EEF, but rather the range of issues which would become subject to formal bargaining between capital and labour. Unlike the EEF procedure, which was intended to resolve labour conflicts without a work stoppage, the Whitley proposals would have granted a degree of co-management to labour through an elaborate consultative system. The following questions were specifically designated as being within the scheme's scope:

(1) better utilisation of the practical knowledge and experience of the work people;

(2) means of securing for the work people a greater share in and responsibility for the determination and observance of the conditions under which their work is carried on;

(3) settlement of the general principles governing conditions of work, including methods of fixing prices on piecework;

(4) means of ensuring to the work people the greatest possible security of earnings and employment;

(5) problems in dealing with the method and amount of pay;

(6) technical education;

(7) industrial research;

(8) provision of facilities for the full utilisation of inventions and improvements by work people;

(9) improvements of processes and machinery and organisation with special reference to cooperation in carrying out new ideas;

(10) proposed new legislation;

(11) regular means of negotiating differences between employer and employee.[90]

The degree to which the above were serious suggestions, rather than simply window dressing, is difficult to determine. The half-hearted support given to the scheme by the Ministry of Labour meant that the Whitley councils which were set up failed to embody the wide powers proposed in the initial report.[91] Rather than introducing co-management, their function was to resolve conflicts between capital and labour, along the lines of the EEF procedure. If the first report had been implemented in full, it would have altered labour's role in a modern industrial society by formalising its participation in decision making.

Sir Allan Smith, the head of the EEF, was a member of the Whitley Committee. Despite his involvement on the committee, there is little evidence that the EEF was ever really interested in the co-management proposals implicit in Whitleyism. The EEF was actively pursuing its own industrial strategy during 1918, and was trying to make it appear that capital and labour already had satisfactory lines of communication, and that there was no need for the government to impose Whitleyism on engineering.[92] The reaction of local employers' associations to the Whitley proposals was mixed. Coventry, despite its criticism of government moves to impose works committees earlier in the year, expressed a qualified but favourable opinion of the proposals. It also argued that the war had shown that the relations between 'master and men' would have to change. According to the Coventry association, the major issue between capital and labour remained the level of labour effort and labour restriction of output levels.[93] Birmingham continued to be suspicious of any move toward the liberalisation of industrial relations or the democratisation of the work place. Its reply to the EEF linked the demands of British labour with the Russian Revolution. It replied that:

The executive committee of the association have read with grave concern the published report of the Whitley Committee in which works committees were advocated and consider it extremely unfortunate that Mr. A. Smith's name should have been identified with this.[94]

A few weeks later it expanded on this issue:

Having regard to the grave peril to Industry and Society generally, from the operation of the New Organisation of Rank and File movement.... In the opinion of the Association the desired goal would be further off then ever if works committees were instituted as instanced by the recent labour trouble in the Engineering Trade, and the present situation in Russia.[95]

The differences between the Whitley proposals and the EEF procedure, implemented in 1896, are extremely pertinent if EEF policy is to be fully understood. Under the Whitley scheme, labour and management were to sit together on a works committee and were to resolve conflicts between capital and labour. They would also have had an executive role in deciding industrial policy. In this, they were similar to the joint works committees favoured by the Coventry ASE in 1915 and 1916. The proposed EEF shop steward committee was to be composed exclusively of labour representatives who could discuss any issue they liked, but whose main task was to present labour's position to management regarding shop floor grievances. There was no intention of giving these committees any decision making power regarding industrial policy. The EEF report on postwar problems made it clear that works committees were to concern themselves only with the welfare of the workers and the amenities of workshop life.[96] The EEF procedure tried to guard managerial claims over the right to manage and the right to control shop floor decisions. R. Price's analysis of the impact of formal collective bargaining in the British construction trade bears many similarities to events in British engineering. The EEF procedure reduced the bargaining power of local union officials and the workers by creating an arena for dispute settlement controlled by the EEF and the national union officials. The EEF's vision of the role of shop stewards was not as labour's voice, but rather as management's ears. The national executives of the EEF and the unions would retain control over which grievances would be acted upon.

The unions showed little enthusiasm for Whitleyism. If anything, the more vocal opinions seemed to confirm the EEF's interpretation of labour's objectives. The National Guild League, which did not officially represent any union, declared that the workers did not want the joint control offered by Whitleyism, but rather wanted complete control.[97] Charles' also suggested that the miners and the engineers were seeking more authority than the limited power sharing proposals by Whitley. He argued: '[The miners and engineers] were intent on something more than the improvement of the existing system: they had convinced themselves they wanted to replace it.'[98] The ASE had been particularly vocal and, according to Charles, had caught the public imagination and the papers' headlines with their demand for workers control.[99]

The Federation of British Industries (FBI) also devised a strategy for the postwar reorganisation of industrial society. The Federation was created in 1916 to, 'safeguard the interests of all employers within the United Kingdom'.[100] As originally constituted, the FBI would have dealt with both commercial and industrial questions, and would have included both individual firms and employers' associations as members. The EEF refused to join the new body unless it agreed to limit itself to commercial questions, and to leave labour questions to the member associations.[101]

Notwithstanding the Employers Federation's claim to jurisdiction over labour issues, the FBI created a special committee to study the Whitley Committee Report. They had serious reservations regarding the Whitley proposals and the new role of shop stewards. H. Austin, a prominent vehicle producer and a member of the committee, wanted to restrict the power of stewards should they be recognised. He argued:

Works committees should be entirely voluntary.... They should consist entirely of representatives of the employees.... Where instituted their duties should be confined to reporting to, or receiving from the management, complaints regarding breaches of any agreements which may have been made between employers and the employed.[102]

The FBI committee soon lost interest in Whitley and went on to form its own strategy for resolving Britain's industrial problems.

In November of 1917, two four-day sessions were held by the Labour Committee, and this resulted in a report titled, 'Reconstruction After the War.' In opening these talks, W.P.Ryland, the chairman, argued that the workers were not really revolutionary but were being affected by a poison for which an antidote was needed. The poison was partly capital's own making and was generated by the unsatisfactory standard of living provided for workers, and the lack of any human touch between industry and the individual.[103] According to the Labour Committee, this had caused the growth of 'Irreconcilables', and a general mistrust by labour of capital's intentions which surfaced as restrictions of effort and output. The Committee argued that the only solution to this problem was for capital to increase its contribution to the conservation of labour. A radical restructuring of society was not deemed necessary to restore labour peace. Instead, taking a page from the utopic view of American success through high wages, it was proposed that capital should increase its contribution to the conservation of labour. The Committee concluded:

Hitherto capital has not as a general rule contributed sufficiently toward what may be called the Conservation of Labour, but has rather confined itself to laying by reserve funds for the repair, renewal and replacement of plant and for the provision of dividends ... while Labour has not received corresponding consideration in terms of unemployment, sickness and old age. Your committee suggest that an increased share of the burden involved in the Conservation of Labour ought in each Industry to fall on capital.[104]

The Committee's recommendations included:

(1) Employers should match union contributions to sick benefits.
(2) Employers should provide an old age pension after 65.
(3) Employers should supplement union unemployment benefits.
(4) If the unions were to drop all resistance to new machinery, employers should pay 2/3 of a standard weeks wage for ten weeks to any displaced worker.
(5) Employers should guarantee a minimum wage to workers on short time.

The EEF rejected the basic premise that monetary incentives alone, would solve Britain's labour problem. The Federation replied:

It would rather appear that here again is the opportunity taken of laying blame upon capital. This idea permeates the whole report. Capital is doing today more for labour than ever previously, and henceforth it will do more, but there is no reason to assume that Capital has failed or will fail to appreciate its responsibilities. ... The report seems based on a misconception – that the remedy for practically all labour troubles is a monetary one. The main trend of labour opinion recently is in the opposite direction.[105]

In March of 1918, the EEF and the FBI met to discuss the FBI's report. The EEF informed the FBI that it was exceeding the agreed limits of its authority and unless it withdrew the report, the EEF would be forced to reconsider its membership in the FBI. The FBI agreed to postpone the publication of the Labour report. The question arose for a second time, later that year, when the FBI threatened to publish the report unless some progress was made toward creating a new body to represent all employers on industrial questions.[106] The EEF ultimately set up the National Confederation of Employers Organisations to serve this purpose and the FBI report was not heard of again.

The EEF reached its own policy conclusions late in 1918, when they produced an interim report on Postwar Industrial Problems.[107] The first section of the report dealt with the impossibility of restoring prewar practices and in light of this, they were prepared to reduce the working week from 54 to 48 hours. The right to introduce payment systems was to be reinforced and the unions were to remove all restrictions on output. The document's focus on restrictionism confirms the gravity of this problem. It was proposed that wages should continue to be set as they had been during the war. A central body of union and employer representatives would review wages every nine months and then impose industry-wide and nation-wide settlements. These settlements were to be binding on all employers. The report left unresolved the question of how a new effort bargain was to be reached and enforced. The problems associated with the setting of piecework prices and the allocation of jobs to different grades of labour were referred to separate committees.

The document is notable for the exclusion of the basic principles contained in the Whitley report and in the FBI proposals. Neither consultation nor liberalised wage conditions were advocated. The EEF proposals of 1918, upon which much of the postwar industrial relations strategy in engineering was based, must be seen as one of the least imaginative contributions to labour relations in the period. As will be shown in the following chapter, it did little to resolve the crisis which had been building since the 1880s. The precise rights of management and labour on the shop floor and their capacity to shift the effort bargain in their respective favour were not resolved. Management, as had been the case in the 1850s and in 1898, claimed control over the shop floor as their right, but they continued to be unable to convince labour that this should be the case. Without a working compromise, the crisis in British industrial relations deepened. It will be shown in the next chapter that many British managers viewed this struggle for shop floor authority as the main stumbling block to greater output and as the main reason for rejecting the new technologies of Fordism and Scientific Management which were being pioneered in the United States.

5

The effort crisis and British managerial strategies

During World War I, British employers placed one foot forward into the modern machine age, but were unable to completely jettison the production institutions associated with nineteenth-century craft technology. Labour was successful in defending some of its rights regarding shop floor decision making. This checked the authority of the newly emerging British managerial class. The disequilibrium between production techniques and production institutions surfaced as a struggle over the effort bargain, a struggle which pushed Britain to the edge of a social revolution in 1917. It was in this context, that British employers debated the merits of American managerial strategies, and ultimately rejected them. They opted for an alternative set of production institutions to monitor and enforce the effort bargain. We have called this alternative strategy the British System of Mass Production.

Scientific management and the crisis of control

One might have expected British employers to have enthusiastically embraced Scientific Management as it claimed to reduce tensions between capital and labour while increasing managerial control over effort levels. In the words of Rose: 'Scientific Management was also an exercise in social engineering, the primary objective of which was to remove the cleavage between management and workers and to replace it with a harmonic fellowship.'[1] There is a remarkable degree of unanimity amongst researchers that Scientific Management left Britain virtually unaffected, at least until the late 1920s.[2] Urwick was able to cite only one firm which had adopted it before World War I.[3] Among contemporary observers however, there was confusion about whether or not British management had adopted the principles of Scientific Management. Many argued that the shift to the Premium Bonus system was actually a shift to the new American management systems. Others simply saw Scientific Management as the application of common sense and some planning. One observer defined Scientific Management as anything which reduced waste, and therefore concluded that: 'In nearly every works in England, Scientific Management had already been adopted to a greater or lesser extent.'[4] British management methods were indeed changing, but the question is whether they had changed along the lines of Scientific Management, or whether a unique British managerial strategy was emerging.[5]

Littler, in his attempt to set the analysis of Scientific Management within a theoretical framework, tried to identify the unique character of Scientific Management by focusing on how managerial structures and strategies affected the effort bargain. Two factors stand out regarding Scientific Management. The first was the spread of time studies, planning, and advanced accounting methods which centralised much of the knowledge that had formerly been controlled by skilled workers and thereby increased the authority of managers. The second was a reduction in management's dependence on workers with specific skills which was achieved by fragmenting the work process and making it easier to fit any worker to any job. The new system achieved a degree of legitimacy, in the eyes of labour, through the granting of higher wages to compensate labour for its loss of shop floor authority.[6]

Within British engineering firms, prior to 1914, cost departments, planning, and labour deskilling were gaining popularity. As production units grew larger an increase in central managerial control seemed inevitable.[7] Despite the trend toward central managerial control, a closer examination of the British experience makes it clear that Britain had not proceeded as far along this road as was proposed by the advocates of Scientific Management. The continuing struggles between employers and labour over managerial rights, the very success of passive resistance between 1897 and 1919, and the postwar negotiations which will be examined below, provide proof of the incomplete nature of British managerial control.

Not only had British employers failed to centralise control over the production process in the hands of a new managerial class, they also showed a preference for adopting new production institutions which substituted direct managerial control of effort with the indirect control of the cash nexus. According to W.F. Watson, who was himself a skilled engineer during these years, British employers were, 'groping for an incentive that will successfully induce the maximum number of workers to maintain the maximum output of which they are capable'.[8] Premium Bonus systems, which played a central role in many British managerial strategies, were designed to overcome managerial weaknesses in the areas of costing and planning by imposing limitations on bonus earnings. This minimised the cost to management of inaccurate piece-rate setting and hence reduced managerial interest in improved costing and planning systems. At least part of the reason why British employers preferred to minimise the cost of inaccurate time setting rather than improve time setting itself, as proposed by the advocates of Scientific Management, was that they had little faith in the ability of any system to do the latter. Rowntree, in a postwar analysis of British management systems argued:

Some advocates of what is known as Scientific Management claim that they have discovered a method by which piece rates can be fixed with scientific accuracy. A close examination of their method does not, however, support their claim. By careful analysis of a job, and time studies of those engaged in it, a closer approximation to accuracy is gained then by the rough guess of a foreman. But many of the principal difficulties in arriving at an accurate result remain unsolved.[9]

The extent to which piece prices and effort norms could be set scientifically was the subject of an article published in 1920. In setting piecework prices with Scientific Management, a base time was set by using time and motion studies. To this base was added, first, a percentage to cover fatigue, personal care, and machine breakdowns, and a second percentage to provide an incentive to the worker. These two allowances represented between one-quarter and one-half of the total time allocated for the job. Even if it could be claimed that the base time was set scientifically, it is difficult to accept Taylor's claim that allowances for fatigue and for an incentive were free of subjective factors or relative bargaining leverage.[10]

The problems associated with scientific rate setting are captured in the following quote by W.F. Watson referring to his experiences as a worker for the Thornycroft firm:

Passive resistance and sabotage were practised at Thornycroft's.... Time limits, fixed by theoretic charts, were invariably all wrong. When excessive-as they sometimes were-we ca'cannied so as not to earn too much; if insufficient, we 'went slow' just the same, and lodged a complaint to the foreman, who sent for the rate fixer. When he arrived there ensued a wordy war between the three, then the rate-fixer timed the job with a stopwatch; but it was easy to 'swing the lead' on an inexperienced clerk by [proving] that the tool would not cut properly.... The charts disappeared from the machines – no one knew where they went.[11]

After 1918, the focus of British criticism of Scientific Management shifted from a lack of confidence in its scientific claims to a lack of confidence in how the American systems treated labour and their failure to deal with the human factor. It was argued that British workers would not accept the kind of constraints on their behaviour advocated by American practitioners.[12] It appeared to a number of British employers that Scientific Management would not succeed in Britain until labour, as a class, had been convinced that it was in its interest to accept managerial control of the production process. Borrowing heavily from the earlier British management strategies of people such as Owen and Cadbury, it was argued that there was a need to create a community of common interests within the production process and it was proposed to do this through welfarism or the human relations approach. Littler has argued that while Scientific Management employed *direct* managerial control over effort, the human relations approach followed a more *voluntaristic* strategy, a strategy he termed, 'ideological integration'.[13]

The debate over the merits of Scientific Management in the British context was continued in two important papers presented during 1919. The record of the discussion following these papers provides a rare insight into the attitudes of British employers. Many held the opinion that Scientific Management could not be applied in Britain after the war because British labour would not accept close supervision or direct managerial control. Instead, a more voluntaristic strategy was needed, one where labour would be encouraged to adopt new working habits.[14] The critics of Scientific Management pointed to its lack of attention to the human element. It was argued that:

Increased production would be obtained far more quickly by co-operation of all sections of workers in a shop and good will to give the greatest output. . . . After all the world was governed by sentiment, and a sympathetic word would get much more work from a man than standing over him with a watch or making a study of movement.[15]

Perhaps the most interesting response was from A.R. Stelling, a management consultant, who argued that a specific British form of Scientific Management was emerging, one which placed the need for better industrial relations before the need for better industrial coordination.

British Scientific Management aimed at the elimination of all waste, and it might be defined as investigation, common sense, and square dealing, both with the workers and with management. . . . The idea should be men, machinery and minutes; get the men right first, then the machinery, and after that they could go for the minutes.[16]

The British postwar attack on Scientific Management reached its peak when C.S. Myer, a Cambridge don and the director of the National Institute of Industrial Psychology, combined the prewar skepticism about the system's scientific basis with the postwar concern with the human factor. He concluded that Scientific Management's claim that there was only one best way to do a job was overly simplistic. Myer argued that workers had complex physical characteristics and psychological motivations, and that there might be many 'best' ways of doing a job. Myer was suspicious of claims that effort norms had a scientific basis, suggesting instead that optimal effort norms were very much a function of the economic agent's social position within the production process. He argued that a closer understanding of sociology would lead one to see the logic in workers restricting output as a defence against unemployment and as a means of showing group solidarity with their work mates. Myer went as far as to argue that British labour's intuitive opposition to Scientific Management actually had a sound psychological basis.[17]

Our explanation of why Scientific Management failed to gain a hold in Britain before 1930 extends, rather than replaces, the orthodox view on the subject. Urwick claimed that Scientific Management failed to take hold in Britain because of, 'the predominantly technical character of those who were responsible for management in this country'.[18] While we would not completely reject Urwick's argument, it does appear to us that there were other important factors behind the rejection of the system. There appears to have been a consensus that

Scientific Management would have had little impact on the effort bargain within the British context. Only in the late 1920s did British employers move hesitantly toward Scientific Management and even then only after Bedaux claimed to have resolved the difficulty of measuring labour effort and after British workers had been disciplined by a decade of high unemployment.[19]

High wages as a managerial strategy

Intertwined in nearly every debate about postwar managerial strategies was a debate about the advantages of raising wages as a means of increasing effort levels and reducing supervision costs. It was accepted by employers advocating higher wages that this was not an act of philanthropy but, rather, that it made good economic sense in the changed conditions of postwar Britain.[20] Charles and Currie have argued that the demand for improved living standards was at the heart of labour unrest between 1917 and 1922.[21] Garcke, a contemporary observer, made a similar point in an address to the British Electrical Federation in 1919, arguing that workers would no longer accept prewar living standards, and that it was recognised by many that wages would have to be increased. Cox argued before the Institute of Civil Engineers in 1917, that if labour's cooperation could be had by paying higher wages productivity could be improved almost without limits. He argued:

We shall get no real progress until you can demonstrate to the working class as a body that their individual and collective interest lies in more efficient production. . . . As soon as you have secured the concurrence of the workman, it will become possible to develop immensely the efficiency of our manufacturing processes, so as to obtain an increased output at less cost, while paying higher wages.[22]

Advocates of a high wage strategy argued that by granting higher wages, output could be increased by an even greater amount, thereby reducing unit costs. The experience of Ford where wages were doubled in their British and American plants in 1914 was used to support this position.[23] The debate in Britain centred on the merits of paying workers higher wages, versus paying them higher wages relative to other workers. The FBI's Labour Committee, and most writers on the high wages strategy, argued that if all workers were given higher wages, all workers would be more productive. The EEF, which approached this question with a degree of skepticism, argued that workers would be more productive only if they received relatively higher wages compared with other workers. It hypothesised that if all workers received higher wages then no improvement in productivity would be expected.[24]

The evidence we have suggests that British employers, in general, remained unenthusiastic about the advantages of paying higher wages and retained the low wage philosophy which was widespread during the nineteenth century. Turner has argued that they remained 'coercive' in their attitudes regarding the level of payment to labour, and that during the war they learned more about market

Table 5.1. *Index weekly real wages British engineering and motor vehicle industry,*
1914 = 100

	Time workers		Pieceworkers	
	Engineering	Motor vehicle industry	Engineering	Motor vehicle industry
1914	100	100	100	100
1923	95	94	97	103
1924	97	91	97	104
1925	98	91	99	104
1926	97	94	100	109
1927	104	97	105	117
1928	108	100	107	115
1929	109	107	110	118
1930	111	103	110	115
1931	112	105	109	116
1932	116	118	111	123

Source: EEF Archive, Basement, *Red File Folder.*

manipulation and control than they did about labour relations.[25] One of the
clearest indications that British employers had rejected a high wage strategy can
be found in a book published in 1926 titled *The Secret of High Wages.* In the
introduction to the book, E.T. Layton, the editor of the Economist wrote:

As to labour conditions any impartial observer must admit that the traditional wage policy
of employers in many British industries is largely to blame for the opposition to payment
by results. . . . Our recent industrial history would have been very different if more
industries had realised the economic importance of a wage system which provided big
prizes for wage earners.[26]

In the book itself, the authors described how high wages produced team effort
and greater productivity, and how they might serve as the perfect antidote for
Bolshevism, Communism and labour unrest.

   After his visit to the United States, A. Mosely, a prominent British trade
union official, argued that one of the key differences between British and
American employers was the unwillingness of the former to allow labour wages
to rise above some predetermined level. He wrote:

They [employers] say that a British workman is entitled to earn about such and such an
amount, and if, through his energy and his enterprise, he succeeds in earning larger
wages, the manufacturers begin to say, 'These men are earning too much. Good gracious
me, this sum of money is hardly fitted to their position! We must cut the price.'[27]

   Bodies such as the EEF claimed to support the principle of higher wages but
only if the workers earned them on systems of payment by results. However,
labour's lack of confidence that high earnings would be permanent, left much of

British industry in a vicious spiral of low wages and low productivity. Table 5.1 shows that real wages remained at or below their prewar level well into the twenties. Even the gains made in the early thirties had little to do with management rewarding increased effort with increased wages, but reflects rather the stickiness of nominal wages during the deflation associated with the depression.

The human factor and fatigue research

After the events of 1917 and the unrest generated by the shop stewards' challenge of British managerial authority, British employers increasingly expressed the concern that labour unrest, or, in the jargon of the period, 'the human factor', was the principal cause of Britain's deteriorating competitive position in manufacturing. One management journal went so far as to argue that the discovery by British management of the human factor had allowed them to by-pass the stage of industrial evolution where Scientific Management and efficiency experts were dominant. The Scientific Management stage could be by-passed because it had failed to appreciate the complexity of labour motivations. The human factor stage ushered in a period when the psychology and the sociology of labour were studied as a means of improving labour productivity. A contemporary report concluded: 'The needs, real or fancied, of the working man are as important in the weaving of the industrial fabric as is the quality of steel.'[28] In Rose's opinion, British developments in human factor industrial psychology have been underestimated.[29] British researchers were amongst the first to discard Taylor's vision of workers as 'greedy robots' and replaced it with a more complex model which was heavily influenced by the postwar labour crisis.

Within Britain there were two loosely related visions of what the human factor was and how it should be dealt with. Among most researchers and academics, the human factor related to the physical and psychological causes of fatigue, including lighting, heating, rest periods and monotony. However, to the employers and managers in the field, the interest in the human factor was related more to labour attitudes and the social relations between labour and capital. While the academics advocated improving working conditions, the employers showed a preference for propaganda campaigns designed to show labour that it was in its own interest to cooperate with management, i.e. to accept managerial control of production, after which the physical aspects of the work environment could be improved. The extent to which human factor problems dominated management thinking and the focus on words rather than deeds is captured in a statement made by the Bishop of Birmingham, who was also the President of the Birmingham Reconstruction League and an important figure in local industrial relations. He argued: 'The employers apparently tend to believe that the only reconstruction problem is that of smoothing the opposition amongst the workers and increasing output by brotherly love.'[30]

This interpretation of employer attitudes to the human factor is broadly consistent with Hay's analysis of their attitude to state sponsored welfare schemes. At first, employers were sympathetic to these schemes as it was felt that they might lessen the antagonism between labour and capital and hence raise effort levels. However, when it was realised how much state welfare schemes would cost they quickly removed their support. Hay concluded that employers came to view incentive payment systems as a more efficient strategy for raising effort levels than welfare schemes. Employer interest in welfare schemes was limited to their propaganda value and their potential for creating a favourable environment within which the payment systems could operate. For example, 'the practice of holding annual junkets, which were usually graced by speeches from the entrepreneurs, stressing the need for common effort, harmony of interests and shared sacrifices, was a popular and inexpensive form of company welfare, much indulged in the textile towns of the Scottish borders'.[31]

The discovery of the human factor did lead to a change in priorities in managerial thinking. Sir H. Fowler, in his presidential speech to the Institute of Automobile Engineers (IAE), stressed the need to pay attention to social relations within the work place and suggested that: 'as a rule in speaking on such subjects [productivity] it is usual to deal first with the machine and then with the man. I think this is reversing the importance of the subject, and so propose to deal first of all with the human side.'[32] But when Fowler and other speakers such as Crompton, a former president of the IAE, spoke about the human factor it is clear that they were not in the first instance referring to the need to adjust working hours, rest periods, lighting or heating within mass production factories. For this group of employers, large factories were unmanageable as they impersonalised labour relations, which had the effect of widening the ideological gulf between capital and labour which in turn reduced productivity. Fowler romanticised the past, referring to a period, 'when personal contact was possible, and it was felt that each one was a necessary and integral part of the concern'.[33] Crompton proposed that the solution to this problem was to return to the industrial world of the nineteenth century. He suggested: 'The ideal thing would be smaller towns, each town having one or two small factories, everyone living as neighbours in one district, the employers, the foremen and the men, having houses and their gardens near to one another.'[34]

In a number of cases, employers did go beyond ideological calls for industrial harmony and erected welfare type programmes which had been pioneered by early British managers such as Owen and Cadbury. This movement was particularly strong during the war, having been stimulated by the introduction of female labour into the factories. Melling has shown that when faced with a hostile labour force the gas employers chose to adopt a welfarist attitude toward labour. The objective was to contain the workers' control over what was becoming a highly integrated production process. Melling has also suggested that welfare programmes such as health care and housing were spreading rapidly in other British industries after the war.[35]

We have already noted that while much of the research on the human factor was concerned with the sources of fatigue, much of the managerial interest in these systems was with how capital–labour tensions might be reduced. In 1918 and 1919 it seemed that the Industrial Fatigue Research Board (IFRB) might conveniently join the two together. The IFRB had come to the conclusion that the main sources of fatigue in industry were not muscular exhaustion but, rather, psychological stress. Even more interesting was the argument that psychological stress might be caused by suspicion and hostility, two of the most obvious manifestations of the capital–labour conflict. By 1919, Myer had concluded that: 'The physiological factor of muscular fatigue was now fast becoming generally negligible in industry, compared with the effects of mental and nervous fatigue and of weariness, want of interest, suspicion and hostility etc.'[36]

During these debates on alternative managerial strategies, British management showed itself to be aware of the limitations of its own authority within the factories. Centralised managerial control, which Scientific Management and Fordism implied, was rejected on the grounds that British management could not achieve and British labour would not accept direct managerial control over effort. Having rejected direct control, British managers searched for a strategy which would induce labour to cooperate within a more voluntaristic context. They developed a keen interest in the human relations approach, which combined a strong ideological component calling for labour to see its self-interest in cooperating with management, with aspects of welfarism and paternalism. In the remainder of this book, we will examine how the rejection of direct control and the shift to a more voluntaristic framework was translated into an actual managerial strategy, firstly in the engineering industry generally and, secondly, in one section of the engineering industry, the motor vehicle industry.

The effort crisis and managerial strategies in engineering

The labour unrest generated by attempts to shift the effort bargain reached a peak between 1918 and 1920, with many employers expressing a concern that the labour crisis might lead to a social revolution similar to the all too recent transformation in Russia. Whether or not there was ever the likelihood of a successful workers' revolt is not in itself relevant to our thesis. We have already suggested that the workers' primary demand was for improved working conditions. Charles seems correct when he argues:

It was the deep-felt determination of the wage earners that they deserved some immediate alleviation of their lot which caused the upsurge of unrest, but it was precisely because it was not intended to be revolutionary in ends or means that it could so easily be diverted by a National Industrial Conference and a Sankey Commission.[37]

Having made this point, it is extremely important to make a distinction between what was actually taking place, and what contemporaries thought was happening. There seems little doubt that the threat of social revolution loomed larger in contemporary accounts and calculations than in the reasoned analysis of historians. Here again Charles has made an important point:

Ideologies were hardening before the 1914 war. Certain sectors of labour were becoming increasingly susceptible to the appeal to violent or revolutionary solutions.... That these views were in fact embraced by only a few is not the point. They were numerous and influential enough to confuse the issues and divert energies.[38]

Political opportunists, such as Lloyd George, inflated labour's strength to magnificent proportions bordering on revolution. What emerged, 'was a strongly expressed conviction in some quarters that the demands of labour were an English equivalent, milder and less outrageous, but basically as pernicious and destructive as the Russian Social Revolution'.[39] Even the language of the Houses of Parliament showed that the events in Britain were being interpreted as similar to events in Russia. When a successful strike at the government's Slough Transport Depot resulted in the appointment of a works committee, a member of parliament asked what was being done about the 'Soviet' now in session at the works.[40]

It was not just opportunistic or reactionary politicians who saw red in labour's demands. Numerous influential employers were also concerned. Caillard and Docker (directors of important engineering firms) both expressed concern about a shop floor revolt, with Caillard passing on alarmist reports to Lloyd George throughout the war.[41] In 1921, the chairman of the board of directors of the Birmingham Small Arms Company, which owned the Daimler Company, allocated one-third of a 15 page speech to the shareholders to the 'Illusion Behind Social Unrest'. The shareholders were told:

It is perhaps a more grievous matter that during the last thirty years political principles have been persistently inculcated into the minds of working men the world over that are quite inconsistent with economic progress, simply because they are in direct conflict with the plain facts of business. The result is that you have large classes in all countries not only utterly discontented, but convinced that the conditions of which they complain result from the greed and fraud of the wealth owning section of the community. They have been taught, and now sincerely believe, that because labour is necessary to the creation of all wealth that, therefore, all wealth is created solely by labour. Wages, therefore, seem to them only part of the product which their splendid skill and energy have brought into existence, and they consequently regard the rest of the value of their product as going wrongfully into the pockets of private individuals, when it should go either to those who do the work, or at least, to the community they compose.[42]

In order to head off the threat of unrest when the war ended, the government called a National Industrial Conference. Rhetoric or not, the employers could hardly have been encouraged by the TUC's main policy paper prepared by

G.D.H. Cole and signed by A. Henderson. It demanded the nationalisation of regulated industries, the elimination of private property in all armaments production, state control over prices, a 44-hour week and higher wages immediately. In concluding, they argued:

The fundamental causes of labour unrest are to be found rather in the growing determination of Labour to challenge the whole existing structure of capitalist industry than in any of the more special and smaller grievances which come to the surface at any particular time . . . . The second primary cause is closely linked with the first. It is that, desiring the creation of a new industrial system which shall gradually but speedily replace the old, the workers can see no indication that either the Government or the employers have realised the necessity for a fundamental change, or that they are prepared even to make a beginning of industrial re-organisation on more democratic principles.[43]

The original policy paper of the EEF, and their response to the TUC's proposal indicates that they were conscious of a potentially explosive situation. However, in their view, the cause of the problem was not economic factors but rather political factors. In a draft policy paper they argued:

A very large proportion of the unrest is due not to labour conditions but to a state of indiscipline (1) of the workpeople to their trade unions, and (2) of the workpeople generally toward the government, and (3) to the objections which were felt by a sector of the community to the present state of society . . . . It has to be kept in mind that the government has had to resort to military assistance in connection with labour unrest. That of itself assures that the trouble has gone beyond a mere question of labour conditions . . . . All the evidence available shows that that tendency is in no way connected with labour relations but it is the evidence of a world movement against established law and order.[44]

An important indication of employer concern regarding the labour crisis was the reluctant participation of the EEF in national lobby groups and propaganda clubs. Turner has attributed much of this change in policy to the leadership of Sir Allan Smith, but there were also broader factors behind the shift in policy. In 1913, when approached to join the Employers' Parliamentary Association, the EEF refused, arguing that cooperation amongst employers was not practical. The initial impetus for a national political organisation of employers came from outside the EEF from the Central Association of Employers' Organisations and from the British Manufacturing Association which led to the formation of the Federation of British Industries.[45] At first, the EEF cautiously accepted the FBI. However, as the two continued to clash over the setting of labour policy, the EEF created a new organisation, the National Confederation of Employers Organisations, a body which it controlled directly. In the postwar context, the EEF had concluded that such a body was needed to protect the wider interests of employers.[46] A memo from the EEF offices in 1918 clarifies the motives behind the formation of the new body:

Having regard to the possible effect of recent events on the continent and the possibility of maximalistic theories taking root in countries not yet definitely affected, it appears necessary that the employers as a whole should reconsider what steps they should take to ensure a satisfactory and continuous cooperation and exchange of views of all questions of general interest.[47]

As well as promoting a new national body to represent employers' interests, the EEF actively supported propaganda bodies whose objectives were to neutralise the influence of labour groups such as the Fabians. Sir Allan Smith and other representatives of the engineering industry played leading roles in creating and later supporting the National Propaganda fund. In August of 1919, the fund made its first official appeal to banking, financial and industrial interests.[48] In October of 1919, Hall, the executive director of the fund, stated its objectives:

The extremist propaganda, which it is our intention to defeat, has been at work both openly and insidiously for thirty years.... Unless a resolute and sustained effort is now made by all the responsible elements in the country, the sacrifices of the war will have been in vain and the future of the nation will be in danger.[49]

The extent of the fund's activities in trying to change labour's views is stunning. Over 4 000 000 leaflets were distributed in working class districts, 330 000 posters were exhibited, and 1000 street corner meetings were held. Some £100 000 had been subscribed by October of 1919, and expenditures totalling £265 000 were proposed for 1920. The fund claimed to have been very successful in the Coventry area reporting that: 'Reassuring reports have been received from this area which has passed through cycles of extreme revolutionary feeling.'[50]

While Smith's interest in the fund seems to have been keen, that of the member firms of the EEF was less so. The EEF's suggestion to its members that they might contribute 1/- per £100 of wages was not generally followed. By August of 1920, even the EEF's interest in the fund weakened. Smith resigned from the management committee in August of 1920, and the EEF launched an investigation into the fund's affairs. The EEF continued to advise its members to join the fund and in July of 1921, the management committee voiced its approval of the funds reorganisation under J.C. Gould and allocated £2000 to it from federation funds.[51]

Smith was also influential in promoting the Economic Study Club, which was to fulfill one of National Propaganda's main objectives, the provision of informed and acceptable opinions on issues such as nationalisation. Smith respected, but feared the efficiency of the Research Department of the Labour Party which he saw as, 'the finest piece of work which had been seen in this Country.'[52] Smith held the position that the working class had been so inundated with socialist propaganda, that they were beginning to believe it. The Economic Study Club was to supply speakers at various functions to reduce the influence of the Labour Party and other socialist propaganda groups. When the

Economic Club joined the Federation of British Propaganda Societies, Sir Allan Smith was the Club's representative.[53]

The NCEO and National Propaganda extended employer lobby groups to the national level, where they became involved in a war of words with their labour opponents. Charles has argued that this was unlikely to resolve the 'deep-rooted and complex' obstacles to harmony and industrial efficiency.[54] It would be overly cynical and incorrect to argue that the EEF purposely tried to hold down labour's standard of living, but their message of increased cooperation and effort now, and improved working conditions in the future, had little chance of success in the British context. British labour had learned from its experiences that future promises had to be highly discounted. It was within this context of labour unrest and fear of revolution that the engineering employers and the trade unions negotiated new collective agreements and searched for new methods of production after the war.

Almost before the smoke had risen from the last battlefield in Europe, the EEF and the unions began negotiating a reduction in the work week. Brownlie, leading the ASE delegation, tried to take advantage of labour's strong postwar bargaining position. He stressed that unless a sizeable concession was made on the hours question, there was the very real possibility of a revolution. He argued:

The reports that I read . . . indicate that Europe is seething with discontent, in other words on the brink of revolution. . . . If we could come to an understanding on the general principle of the reduction of hours of labour it could do much to relieve the tensions in as much as it will inspire with hope the law abiding trade unionist who observes constitutional procedures.[55]

In return for a reduction in the working week, the employers sought guarantees that changes in production techniques made during the war would be accepted by labour and that the unions would support future changes. The employers also demanded that the unions agree to work the new repetition methods of production on systems of payment by results. Brownlie accepted the demand for new technology almost without reservation: 'We have had to adapt ourselves to new conditions. . . . Many of our people will become in the near future to a great extent machine tenders, and so forth. We have got to adapt ourselves to changed conditions.'[56] However, on the question of payment by results he was less forthcoming, arguing that no special mention need be made regarding payment by results as it was implicit in the concessions on new production methods. This argument did not convince the employers. To the employers, to the workers, and probably even to Brownlie, it was clear that, in the British context, the control of the effort bargain depended largely on the indirect control of incentive payment systems. Despite the spread of deskilling production techniques, British managers lacked the authority to enforce effort norms through direct techniques such as supervision or control of the organisation of work.

Brownlie's bargaining strategy was to combine both bold statements on the desirability of the new technology with equally bold statements about the inevitability of a socialist society. Much to their discomfort, he told the employers:

I have for the past twenty odd years subscribed to a body of doctrine which I do not relinquish in the slightest degree... The difference between me and some of my friends who subscribe to the same doctrines is a difference of method.... I believe that the great changes which I anticipate in the future will be brought about by a slow gradual evolutionary process.[57]

Brownlie encouraged the employers to adopt new, capital intensive methods of production, but denied them the control over effort levels which was needed to guarantee their profitability. The employers showed little enthusiasm for Brownlie's new society, and their demands in the ensuing negotiations indicated that they would defend their position with determination. The final agreement included a 47-hour working week, with assurances that the unions would try to reduce the restricting of output by labour. The question of machinery and other working conditions was to be submitted to further conferences. The most contentious issue, payment by results, was not directly referred to in the agreement.

Within less than a year, before negotiations on the other issues could seriously begin, a further reduction in the work week to 44-hours was requested. While the resulting conference did not grant shorter hours, it does provide a useful insight into what was taking place in British engineering during the early part of 1919. Smith began the conference by complaining that the unions had not fulfilled their promises regarding the elimination of restrictions of output. He argued:

It was a condition of granting the 47 hour week that the unions would take all possible steps to ensure the greatest possible output.... Output today is, as far as we can measure it, much less than in prewar times. I am making comparisons under conditions that are exactly similar to prewar conditions.[58]

This type of labour control was not limited to engineering. Evidence suggests it was also common in British mines. One miner boasted: 'Oh, we've got the owners so scared here they don't trouble us, and it's just our good consciences that [makes] us work at all.'[59]

Brownlie advocated a policy similar to that suggested by Mann and Barnes in the prewar period. He argued that higher wages and shorter hours were desirable and that they could only be had by increasing labour output. At the same time, he warned that increased output did not necessarily mean increased effort which was the overwhelming complaint of systems of payment by results. He gave his support to new machine systems and even suggested that British engineering should follow the American example. Systems such as Scientific Management and Fordism would have to be amended to protect the health of the workers, but they should not be rejected outright. He argued: 'The individual or the organisation that stands in the way of utilising the improvements of the machine tool, or the improvements brought into being by the application of science to industry, is standing in its own light.'[60] The request for the 44-hour week was rejected.

The 1922 engineering lock-out and the right to manage

The negotiations between the EEF and the unions over new technology and working conditions did not begin in earnest until 1920.[61] The employers were in no hurry to press forward with the negotiations as long as labour held a strong hand. Instead they tried to contain labour demands by conceding the shorter week, while remaining active on the political front through the NCEO and through National Propaganda. By 1920, labour's position had been undermined by the postwar collapse of the economy. It took over three years of negotiations and a major lockout to produce this new deal. The verbatim reports of these negotiations are extensive, and no attempt will be made to give a detailed description. We will focus on how the negotiations and the final deal influenced the evolution of British production institutions.

The first conference on working conditions took place in May of 1919. The EEF met both the craft and the non-craft unions in joint session. The issues were the grading of workers, the manning of machines, shop stewards, works committees and payment by results. Labour was still bargaining from a postwar position of strength. They took the offensive demanding higher wages. There was also an indication that they would accept American production methods if it led to American level standards of living.

Union officials had accepted the need to increase output if wages were to rise. The simple redistribution of existing income did not play a significant role in these negotiations. The recognition that the path to improved living standards was through improved efficiency had spread widely in Britain prior to World War I. G.R. Searle has claimed that 'Efficiency' was the dominant slogan of the period. A journalist wrote in the *Spectator* in 1902: 'At the present time, and perhaps it is the most notable social fact of this age, there is a universal outcry for efficiency in all the departments of society, in all aspects of life. We hear the outcry on all hands . . . Give us Efficiency or we die.'[62] The war experience had reinforced this view.

If both sides agreed that increased output was necessary, they differed significantly on how this might best be achieved. The employers argued that low productivity was due to trade union restrictions while the unions blamed management for being inept. Mullins, from the ASE, argued that British workers were just as good as American workers, and given the same opportunities would be just as productive. Laying the blame for low productivity at the feet of management he argued:

The workmen have nothing to do with the methods of working; methods of working are laid down for him by the employer, and in America I think there is a larger broad-minded spirit about.... I suggest it is not a question of the adaptability of British workmen but a question of system and management that we have nothing to do with.[63]

The employers replied that there was nothing wrong with high wages but they had to be earned, and that was why the acceptance of payment by results, along the lines agreed to in the 1917 Munitions of War Act, was essential. However, nearly all observers agreed that the experiences of British workers on payment by results had been that they led to more effort with marginal increases in wages. The promise of higher wages was simply insufficient to win labour's cooperation. British management remained convinced that in the British context, it would be foolish to pay higher wages before labour showed a willingness to increase effort. This first set of negotiations broke down in February of 1920 when the ASE refused to recommend payment by results to its members.[64]

When the negotiations resumed in September, the unions found themselves in a weakened position as the postwar recession gripped the engineering industry. The workers' revolution, which Brownlie had earlier suggested was imminent, was indefinitely postponed. A new agenda for negotiations was drawn up, which divided the issues into three main sections; the manning of machines, payment by results, and working conditions such as overtime, holidays and shift premiums. The question of working conditions was the least contentious and was discussed first. In September of 1920, a package covering night shift and overtime premiums was accepted by both sides. But even in accepting this package, Brownlie foreshadowed that trouble was on the horizon by continuing to prescribe a socialist solution to Britain's industrial ills. He declared:

Without minimising or weakening in any way my devotion to the ideal which has animated me right throughout my political activities, I agree with you that it is best for industry... to settle down at the earliest possible moment and make the best of existing conditions, while striving in other channels to bring about the great historical change which society is destined to undergo.[65]

By constantly reminding the employers that the existing organisation of society was doomed, Brownlie reinforced the employers' own insecurity regarding who controlled the shop floor and provoked what must be seen as a rational response, from the employer's perspective. The palisades had to be strengthened while there was still a chance, and a strategy was needed which would minimise the cost of future labour management conflicts.

The main negotiating committee placed the questions of double day shift premiums, three shift systems and holidays in the hands of a subcommittee. It then proceeded to tackle the two main questions, the manning of machines and systems of payment by results. Brownlie began these negotiations with a strongly worded statement calling for new technology and higher productivity. He argued:

The machine is important to industry, and while we have no desire to place any obstacles in the way of the development of the machine tool, because I trust that we have learned by experience, as you have learnt by experience. I hope the results of our deliberation will be that we shall arrive at an agreement whereby we shall approach the question in a manner which will be advantageous to both parties, and that the wages paid to the machine operator will not be in any way a menace to the wages paid to the men engaged in the higher branches of the trade.[66]

It is one of the ironies of these negotiations that it was often the unions that called the loudest for American production systems, while it was the employers who expressed the greatest reservations. Some unions, including the National Union of Vehicle Builders, had gone so far as to suggest that the employers should adopt a Ford style production system. They argued that under such a system it would be possible to have both higher wages and lower per unit production costs. Smith, replying for the EEF, had little faith in such a system. He argued: 'Do you think for one moment your men would submit themselves to the principle of Henry Ford.' To which Compton of the NUVB using their experiences at Ford's Manchester factory replied: 'They do it. ... Our people seem quite well satisfied. It is true for a period they did not take to it, but today they are quite satisfied with their employment.'[67]

Worker demands for improved technology were sufficiently widespread for A. Gleason, an American journalist, to suggest that labour had recognised management's resistance to modernise and that in its eyes this diminished the legitimacy of managerial requests for labour cooperation. Labour criticism of inept managerial strategies and backward technology were particularly widespread in British mines, and iron and steel works. If management was unable or unwilling to undertake steps to improve the efficiency of the shops and raise living standards, then the logical solution was for labour to take matters into its own hands, an idea which fuelled British miners demands for nationalisation.[68]

To regulate working conditions under the new production techniques, the Amalgamated Engineering Union (AEU), a new union created through the merger of the ASE and a number of other unions, proposed an Engineering Charter. It advocated a formal training programme for all machine operators so that they would have a minimum level of skill and versatility. Trainees would begin at a rate well below the skilled rate and after two years of training they would automatically receive the skilled rate. After their training period, these machine operators would be able to set up, inspect and operate a number of machines. Equally important, they would have the skill to execute any task which these machines were capable of performing. Brownlie argued that such a charter was needed to protect workers from the undesirable effects of the new production techniques.[69]

Exactly who would have benefited the most from this charter is difficult to calculate. Without a doubt, the position of the skilled worker would have been protected. But, as well as protecting the skilled worker, the charter would have upgraded the new class of unskilled workers, and would have prevented a low wage unskilled labour ghetto from forming. Tom Mann, now representing the AEU, recognised that with the new production techniques most workers would be doing the unskilled work of a machine minder. According to Mann, the Engineering Charter implied that:

All boys shall be educated and shall be taught a trade, and shall become qualified. . . . If they are qualified to do the work --- qualified to do the highly skilled work --- the fact that you do not require that particular form of skill is not to be a sufficient reason why a man should be punished who is not exhibiting the skill, not because he does not possess it, but because he is not called upon to use it.[70]

The AEU proposals were not enthusiastically received by the employers, who rejected the idea that a single adult wage rate could be paid on a large group of machines. It argued that on every machine, different jobs were performed, and that these jobs required different levels of skill. The unions would have to accept the employers' right to pay workers according to the skill required. The EEF added further that the unions had not made any mention of payment systems. It claimed:

It is idle for us to suggest to you that these machines should be paid on time. . . . [Unless the AEU was willing to accept] that we ought to pay according to the ability which is required. . . . [and] you are prepared to give us the production which is required for the industry by the personal inducement of payment by results, then I am afraid there is absolutely no hope for these proposals going through.[71]

Negotiations continued during the next 12 months, but were hampered by disputes in other sections of the economy and by the deepening recession in the engineering industry. As the economic situation deteriorated, the EEF took a harder line. Its pamphlet, *The Present Position of the Engineering and Allied Industry*, criticised labour's restriction of output and called for wage cuts. It was argued that British engineering was hard hit by the high value of the pound, the collapse of world and domestic markets, the credit squeeze, inopportune strikes in the coal and foundry sectors, and labour productivity below prewar levels.[72]

The TUC replied to the EEF pamphlet and, foreshadowing Keynesian arguments, insisted that it was bad economics to cut wages because this would reduce the domestic market. The TUC called on the government to remove trade barriers with Russia, Germany and other European countries, and to remove tariffs on imported raw materials. The most interesting aspect of the reply was the continuing attack on British management methods and the call for the adoption of American methods. It was argued:

The British engineering industry is, with few exceptions, badly organised from one end to the other. Therefore compared with many American establishments, and even with the best in this country, the great majority of British engineering workshops are badly laid out, often badly lighted, inadequately equipped, and, many of them, wastefully managed.[73]

By the end of 1921, with no sign of a compromise from either side, the negotiations reached a crisis. In November of 1921, the EEF challenged the AEU regarding its intentions, claiming that the workers were restricting effort and output, and trying to take over the management of the factories. According to Smith, the employers:

Are asking ourselves now, Mr. Brownlie, whether the works are to be carried on by your District Committees in session in the firm's premises, or whether the management is still to have some say in the direction of the factory under ordinary work. ... The recent discussion strikes at the whole system of industry as carried on today.[74]

The talks temporarily collapsed, but were resumed a week later after an informal meeting between Brownlie and Smith. Brownlie continued to deny that the unions were currently challenging managerial rights. When Smith pressed him to clarify what he meant by currently challenging, Brownlie replied: 'We hope that at some day or other there will be no employers or workpeople, but that they will all be members of the corporate commonwealth.'[75] A managerial rights agreement was eventually reached, one in which Brownlie conceded to most of the employers' demands. Smith, taking a lesson from Brownlie on rhetoric, proclaimed the agreement was necessary to protect the rights of private property. He suggested:

At the moment we are at the head because we own the factories and this work is ours. You may be in the future at the head, and then we shall have to cow to it, but until that alteration takes place we are going to manage the factories, so I do not think I need say any more, because I have said that perhaps ad nauseum.[76]

The key concessions on paper included a strongly worded clause accepting management's right to manage, including complete control over the working of overtime and the introduction of new methods of production. New methods would be worked while disputes over them were working their way through the grievance procedure. The concessions on overtime and the working of new methods, even if under dispute, represented major victories for the employers. The overtime question was a particularly thorny one as the workers felt overtime could not be justified when unemployment was high, while the concession to work new methods while under dispute significantly eased the introduction of new methods as everyone realised that once a new machine was on the shop floor and working, a procedure decision was unlikely to cause its removal.

The AEU membership voted to reject the proposed agreement, by a large margin. Further talks broke down, and on 11 March, 1922 the AEU members were locked out by the employers.[77] The EEF was able to split the union ranks and worked out an agreement with the other engineering unions. Once this agreement was signed the AEU was isolated and on 13 June they accepted a new contract. The only real change in the new agreement was that the Federation agreed to a rather meaningless clause that its members would give as much advance warning as possible before a new method of production was adopted. This agreement did not resolve the ongoing crisis over the effort bargain, as it did little to resolve the manning of machines problem or the question of payment by results. A one-month interval was granted before Federation members would begin using their new right to manage clauses to change working conditions in these two areas. The month was supposed to allow the two sides to come to a more specific agreement in these areas. Given that the two sides had been unable to come to an agreement during three years of negotiations, it should come as little surprise that no agreement was reached in the one-month grace period.

Negotiations over payment by results did not even begin until August of 1922 when the employers proposed that they should have the right to adopt any payment system of their choice and that the AEU executive should recommend this to their members. Prices were to be set initially by the employers and were to be subject to the approval of the workers directly involved. The AEU proposed two changes. First, given the membership's well-known hostility to payment by results, the executive refused to make any recommendation to the membership, which significantly reduced the chances of the agreement being ratified. Second, and a sign that bonus earnings had become incorporated as part of normal wages, the union asked the employers to guarantee not only the day rate of the workers but also a minimum bonus level on all new jobs and new prices. Such a proposal would have made it more difficult for management to use payment systems to increase effort levels. The proposal would have greatly reduced the penalty incurred by labour if it chose to work at a pace lower than the one management preferred.

These new negotiations failed to produce a national agreement forcing the employers to rely on their right to manage clauses and local agreements to govern payment by results. In the motor vehicle industry, the Humber agreement, negotiated in Coventry in 1919, was of critical importance. After the war, the local AEU had offered the local employers two choices, retaining payment by results with a much higher recognised bonus rate or putting all work on a day rate basis with a minimum wage of 3/- per hour. Recognised bonus rates were not guaranteed, rather they acted as a guide to labour and management as to when a job's price was or was not set properly. The employers rejected the proposed move to day work on the grounds that British workers would neither supply the necessary effort voluntarily, nor submit to the kind of direct supervision which would force them to work at a given pace. In the end, the employers and the AEU agreed to continue working on payment by results, but with the important modification that recognised bonus levels would increase from the national norm of $33\frac{1}{3}$ percent to 50 percent.[78]

Throughout the interwar period, the EEF continued to see payment by results as an indispensable managerial strategy. In 1928, a circular letter was sent out to all firms, extolling the virtues of payment by results and, in particular, its ability to improve the relations between capital and labour and its ability to produce a 'contented workshop'.[79] During the 1920s, there was a steady shift from fixed day rates to payment by results in British engineering. In 1914, 30.7 percent of engineering workers were paid by the piece, rising to 40.8 percent in 1918 and 48.7 in 1927.[80]

In the British case, payment systems were seen as far more than a mechanism for fine tuning the level of labour effort. They were used as an alternative to direct supervision and as a way of granting labour some say over shop floor conditions while at the same time retaining economic control in the hands of employers. Howe, chairman of the Higher Productivity Council, emphasised this latter point in a letter to the EEF. He wrote: 'The whole point is that workmen now say that they want a share of the control of business and this scheme gives them the share that they want.'[81] If labour was to have some say over effort levels, employers retained control over the ratio of income to effort. Despite the demands for mutuality in setting prices and the provision for this in numerous local agreements, the reality was that labour had little, if any, say over piece rates prior to World War II. A report to the EEF Management Board in the early 1930s concluded: 'The facts already referred to seems to prove that mutuality or no, the vast majority of prices are accepted as fixed by management, without recourse to the procedure.' The report went on to conclude that employers could not honestly claim that mutuality was followed in setting piece-rates.[82]

Negotiations over the manning of machines made even less progress than the payment question. The machine committee did not meet until July of 1923. Even then, it was the National Federation of General Workers which proposed a meeting between themselves, the AEU and the EEF.[83] The AEU refused a joint meeting, but did agree to a meeting between itself and the EEF. The AEU proposals, similar to those made in 1919 when it called for an Engineers Charter, remained of little interest to the employers and led to the rapid end of talks. Attempts to resolve the machine question were not resumed until 1929.[84]

The 1922 lockout was the key event in shaping interwar industrial relations in the engineering and motor vehicle industries. In response to a perceived threat to management's already limited control of British workshops, an agreement was imposed on labour which minimised the formal participation of the workers in decision making. Shop stewards and works committees were tolerated but given minor responsibilities. The lockout confirmed that postwar labour relations in engineering would follow the pattern set in the prewar period. Antagonism between capital and labour was accepted as a given and was to be channelled into forms which did not damage the return to capital. Employers remained reluctant to adopt new production institutions which would have given management direct control of effort norms. Instead they relied on institutions of self-regulation which left shop floor workers with a significant say over effort levels. Studies done during the 1930s confirm that despite the virtual collapse of formal labour organisation, labour 'assertiveness' within the factories remained strong, giving labour wide latitude to slow down work and enforce demarcation boundaries.[85] This is in marked contrast to the basic thrust of the managerial revolution in the United States which was transferring control over effort levels to a new class of managers. In the end, the EEF strategy doomed British engineering to a low wage/low effort equilibrium as neither the buyers nor the sellers of labour time were willing to trust the other player in the game. British engineering was caught in what game theorists have long recognised as the Prisoner's Dilemma.

The immediate postwar years which had promised to yield many changes failed to drastically alter the institutional context of British factories. The labour crisis had been contained, but it had not been resolved and the need for a working compromise between capital and labour continued to be a pressing problem for British employers despite the weakening of the unions and the rise of unemployment. The General Strike of 1926 symbolised the underlying tension between capital and labour in Britain, and sparked a new search for a compromise. The Mond–Turner talks brought together leading industrialists and leading representatives of labour in an effort to find a way in which capital and labour could cooperate. The owners of capital, and particularly the representatives from the engineering sections, remained sceptical of the usefulness of any changes. According to Garside: 'Some of the keenest opposition came from the EEF... which saw the talks as a dangerous prelude to a trade union take over of industry.'[86] The Liberals in their report titled *Britain's Industrial Future* also dealt with labour relations. Their report clearly indicated that the environment of mistrust between labour and management remained a pressing problem.[87] No major change in direction emerged from these initiatives.

The late-nineteenth-century transition from craft production techniques to mechanised production techniques destabilised the fragile nineteenth-century equilibrium between production techniques and production institutions. In turn, this led to the collapse of the nineteenth-century accommodation between the buyers and sellers of labour time and made a new deal necessary. Influenced by wartime labour demands for control over shop floor decisions, British employers abandoned the direct control route of the Americans. Instead, control was to be achieved indirectly through incentive payment systems and self-regulation. The rejection of American style direct control of effort norms and the reliance on self-regulation by labour of effort norms is the hallmark of what we have called the British System at Mass Production.

The inability of British employers to transfer shop floor authority from labour to a new managerial class in the early 1920s had two long-run effects on British technology. It made investment in new capital equipment less attractive as employers had only partial control over how fast the machines would be operated. It also retarded the evolution of a British managerial class with the skills needed to monitor and enforce the effort bargain and the skills needed to coordinate shop floor activity. British management did not fail, it never developed.

In the next section, we will look at how the struggle over the effort bargain and the still birth of the British managerial class influenced technical change in the British motor vehicle industry.

Production techniques in the British motor vehicle industry, 1896–1914

The methods of production employed in the British motor vehicle industry evolved during one of the most tumultuous periods of British economic history. As described in the previous two chapters, the late nineteenth-century transition from craft production to the mechanised techniques pioneered by the Americans resulted in a serious labour crisis. We have described this crisis as a period of disequilibrium between British production techniques and British production institutions. During this disequilibrium, the normal competition between the buyers and sellers of labour time was exacerbated.

For the buyers of labour time, the new American production techniques increased the importance of monitoring and enforcing effort norms and increased the need for effective coordination of shop floor activity. It also created new opportunities for reducing employer dependence on skilled craft workers who, through their monopoly control of production knowledge, had played an influential role in monitoring, enforcing and coordinating tasks during much of the nineteenth century.

For the sellers of labour time, the new production techniques threatened established methods for setting the effort bargain. As Hobsbawm has argued, for much of the nineteenth century: 'The small-arms fire with which the artisans fought the big guns of the employers derived its effectiveness from the ramparts of skill which protected it as well as from the solidarity of the marksman.'[1] In the short-run, the change in production techniques forced skilled workers to seek an alternative strategy for defending their interests. They were able to use their experience with collective organisations to shift to a new strategy based, not on a monopoly control of knowledge but, rather, on a monopoly control of employment rights enforced by trade unions. Through restricting access to certain classes of jobs, they attempted to preserve the patterns of authority on the shop floor that they had come to see as normal during the earlier period.

The continued erosion of production skills via new machine techniques made the existing arrangement highly unstable. It was not long before the labour institutions themselves began to crumble. The sectionalised craft unionism of the nineteenth century proved ill-suited to the challenges of a production process dependent upon less skilled labour. The earlier craft enforced concept of a fair day's work gave way to a recognition that restrictions of output or ca'canny were potent new labour weapons. The nineteenth-century accommodation between skilled labour and the capitalist system broke down and skilled labour began to see the economic system itself as one of the causes of its plight.

As Hobsbawm has pointed out, it was at this point, during the last decades of the nineteenth century, that portions of the British working class veered toward a radical critique of capitalism and began to demand industrial democracy and socialism to protect their rights.[2] British labour's success in raising to a political level what was originally an economic crisis was one of the critical differences between the British and the American experience. American skilled workers and the American Federation of Labour did not offer a strong political challenge to the new institutional arrangement in the United States. At the political level, British labour proved a formidable foe for employers and the owners of capital.[3] Capital was no longer simply trying to install a new institutional framework for monitoring and enforcing the effort bargain; it was forced to fight to preserve the capitalist nature of the British economy.

One should not lose sight of the fact that imbedded in what was becoming a political crisis was a struggle for control over the effort bargain. Hobsbawm has argued that:

For most tradesmen the shift to anti-capitalism began simply as an extension of their trade experience. It meant doing what they had always done: defending their rights, their wages, and their now threatened conditions, stopping management from telling the lads how to do their job, and relying on the democracy of the workplace rank-and-file.... Only now they had to fight management all the time, because management was permanently threatening to reduce them to 'labourers', and now had the technical means of doing so.[4]

The centre of this institutional crisis was clearly the North of England and the established industries such as heavy engineering, textiles, coal mining, and transportation. Our task in the following chapters is to examine how this crisis influenced the course of technical change in the British motor vehicle industry, a new industry with limited links to the established industries, and located mainly in the Midlands and South of England. In this chapter, it will be shown how the British motor vehicle industry quickly left behind the production techniques of the European craft system and shifted to the mechanised production techniques of the American system. In the following chapters we will examine how British employers and British workers responded to the economic and political crisis brought on by the new demands of mass production and the challenge of Fordism and the American system. British capitalists soon found that while the machines themselves could be bought in the United States, and the optimal system for organising them could be observed during pilgrimages to Detroit, it was difficult to import American institutions, nor was it possible to erase British experiences. Throughout, we will argue that British employers, while holding the upper hand, were never successful in eliminating the authority patterns found in nineteenth-century Britain.

Model policy and scale of production prior to 1914

It is often asserted that prior to 1914 British firms were small-scale producers of luxury products and therefore they employed the production techniques and institutions of the European craft system. There is little doubt that the leading American firms produced more vehicles, that their product was less refined, and that it sold to a broader based market. However, this does not warrant the conclusion that the British market began with barons and baronesses and worked up. As Clutton and Stanford warned, it is easy to obtain an imbalanced view of what British firms were producing because the output of their luxury producers was so outstanding that it overshadowed the majority of British production which was destined for what they called the utility market.[5]

Table 6.1 summaries data on the models offered by leading British producers in various price categories prior to 1914. The luxury models, valued at over £700, represented a small number of the models being offered while inexpensive models were widely produced. This was particularly true before 1907. *The Motor Trader*, an important trade journal, was so concerned about the proliferation of low cost vehicles that in a lead editorial it declared:

Cheap and nasty is a trite style of summing up the de-merits of basing one's expenditure on quantity rather than quality.... In the motor trade it is somewhat remarkable to what extent this craze for cheapness exists. It permeates it thoroughly, and this is a circumstance the more remarkable when it is found that some of the more conspicuous offenders against the cannon of business prudence are important and flourishing firms.[6]

Table 6.1. *Models offered by leading firms by price range, 1904–14 (percentage of total in brackets)*

Price range	Number of models 1904	Number of models 1908	Number of models 1914
Less than £200	30 (16.8)	10 (4.4)	57 (21.9)
£200–£350	40 (22.4)	47 (20.7)	
£350–£700	82 (46.1)	110 (48.4)	182 (70.0)
Greater than £700	26 (14.6)	60 (26.4)	21 (8.1)

Note: In 1907, Ford models sold for $2,800 in the United States. Prior to October of 1910, the Model T sold for around $1000 before its price began to decline. When the Model T was introduced in Britain just before 1914, it sold for between £135 and £180. (See Richardson, *British Motor Industry*, p. 67; Nevins, *Ford*, p. 646.)
Source: Vehicle lists published in the *Autocar* before each Olympia Show.

Table 6.2. *Average price of models offered by major British vehicle manufacturers, 1906–14 (£)*

	1906	1908	1910	1912	1914
Argyll	404	375	306	401	376
Arrol-Johnston	416	560	325	342	267
Austin	488	625	478	455	395
Belsize	502	510	353	278	223
Calthorpe	246	313	318	297	283
Daimler	625	593	545	519	582
Dennis	438	530	531	420	388
Humber	335	293	227	272	256
Rolls-Royce	700	985	985	985	985
Rover	191	129	220	214	251
Singer	238	318	338	398	356
Standard	478	522	419	435	287
Sunbeam	368	550	428	456	465
Swift	258	318	279	204	221
Vauxhall	275	375	434	520	501
Vulcan	310	351	381	281	318
Wolseley	237	—	553	564	529
AVERAGE	383	459	419	414	393

Notes: The above data is for the model range offered by each firm. It has not been corrected for the relative importance of each model in a firm's total sales since this data is not available. Since most firms sold more of their small cars than large cars, the above table overestimates the average price of cars actually sold by these firms.
Source: W.C. Bersey, *The Motor Car Red Book* (London, nd.)

The experience of the Yorkshire Motor Car Company may have been typical of these early low cost low volume producers. It was reported by J.E. Tuke, a director, that by September of 1900, they were producing one light car every three weeks with 30 workers; they made the entire vehicle and planned to expand output to one per week in the face of strong demand; and their vehicles sold for £200. By 1901, for reasons unknown, the firm was in the hands of the receiver.[7]

Between 1906 and 1912 there was a trend away from small vehicles and toward the luxury models, a trend worth expanding upon, for it lies at the heart of much of the criticism directed at the industry. Table 6.2 shows the average price of the model range offered by various firms. It is important not to confuse the average price of a firm's model range with the average price of a model. The first tracks the change in average price caused by the introduction of new models and the abandoning of old lines. The second tracks the price of the same model during successive years. These two indexes moved in opposite directions between 1906 and 1908. The average price of existing models fell from £456 to £409 between 1906 and 1908. But as Table 6.2 shows, a number of firms increased the average price of their model range over the same period. The average price of models taken off of the market in 1908 was £429 while the average price of new models introduced in 1908 was £520. This trend resulted in a number of important British firms almost completely altering the nature of their product line and the section of the market to which they catered. Prior to 1906, Sunbeam, Vauxhall, Singer and Vulcan had been almost exclusively small car producers. After 1906 they all focused on large cars with only Sunbeam making the transition successfully. The American experience was quite the opposite. In 1907 the average price of American made cars was $2137 falling to $1545 in 1910. According to *Iron Age*, a contemporary American journal, this was the result of new cheap models being put on the market.[8]

It is unlikely that the decison by British firms to produce larger cars was the product of short-sightedness brought on by the engineer's penchant for quality or the distortions generated by a class society. The decision to produce larger cars can be seen as an entrepreneurial response to perceived short-run profit opportunities. Daimler is a case in point. As early as 1900, they had thoughts of producing a vehicle for less than £200. The decision in 1904 to abandon the small-car line rested with their assessment of potential profitability. They argued that large cars offered more profit per vehicle than small cars, a position which can be criticised as showing short-sightedness in that many more small cars could be sold than large cars. But they also argued that there were already too many firms producing small cars in Britain and that, no matter how large the market, there was too much competition.[9]

Standard's decision to produce larger cars was dictated by C. Friswel, who was their sole distributor. Friswell argued against aggressively promoting the firm's smaller models, which he felt would reduce sales of the more profitable larger cars. If small cars had to be produced they should be reserved for a 'certain class' of customer, presumably ones unable to afford larger models. Friswell seemed to be particularly concerned that the better-off customer, if given an option, would also buy the less expensive models. The company's decision to concentrate on the production of small cars in 1913 led to Friswell's departure.[10]

Perhaps the most relevant reason explaining the changing strategy of British producers was the radically different experiences of the two leading firms. Daimler, which concentrated on the upper end of the market was showing signs of significant success by 1907, while in the same year Argyll, which in 1905 had built a new plant to produce thousands of light cars, was on the brink of bankruptcy.

The switch to larger models between 1906 and 1912 shows a remarkable degree of flexibility and responsiveness, perhaps even over-responsiveness, to market signals on the part of British producers. By 1908 the number of small cars offered had fallen in absolute terms by two-thirds, while in percentage terms they represented only 4.4 percent of the market, down from 16.8 percent in 1904. Therefore, it should come as no surprise that by 1912, when the market signals began to point toward the profitability of catering to the lower end of the market, a number of British firms quickly moved in this direction. The Model T, priced

Table 6.3. *Output levels of ten leading American and British producers, 1913*

American	Output	British	Output
Ford	202 667	Wolseley	3000
Willys-Overland	37 442	Humber	2500
Studebaker	31 994	Sunbeam	1700
Buick	26 666	Rover	1600
Cadillac	17 284	Austin	1500
Maxwell	17 000	Singer	1350
Hupmobile	12 543	Arrol–Johnston	1150
Reo	7 647	Belsize	1000
Oakland	7 030	Daimler	1000
Hudson	6 401	Star	1000

Sources: U.S. data from J.P. Bardou *et. al.*, *The Automobile Revolution* (Chapel Hill, 1982), p. 74. UK, data from S.B. Saul, 'The motor industry in Britain to 1914' (*Business History*, 5, 1962), p. 25.

at £135, first sold in Britain in large numbers in 1911. In 1912, the Singer 10 was introduced at £195 and the Standard 9.5 at £175. In 1913, Morris followed with the Morris Oxford at £165[11] The switch to light cars was evident at the 1913 Olympia Motor Show where it was reported: 'Although the high priced car was much in evidence, the keynote of the show was undoubtedly the catering for the man of moderate means.'[12] By 1914, Morris, Standard, Singer, Hillman and Wolseley had major investments in smaller cars and over one-fifth of the models offered were priced at less than £200.[13] The notable exception to this trend was Austin who failed to cater to the light car market until after World War I.

Despite this activity in the low-priced portion of the market, British firms had much shorter production runs than the French and the Americans. The French were the early pace setters. By 1901, Darracq was producing 1200 of their 6/12 model while by 1905 De Dion was producing 6000 engines annually, 3000 of which were fitted to their own chassis. British levels of output lagged well behind. In 1905 only Argyll, Humber and Wolseley approached an output of 1000 per year, Daimler, Napier and Rover produced around 500, and ten to fifteen other firms produced between 100 and 200 per year.[14] By 1913, when the Americans replaced the French as the leading producers, the contrast in levels of output is even more dramatic as can be seen in Table 6.3.

Contemporary critics suggested that these low levels of output indicated a failure by the industry to expand as rapidly as the market warranted. Weir argued in 1903 that British producers were overly conservative in comparison with continental producers in setting output levels, and as late as 1912 the *Times* wrote: 'The fact is that there is no firm at present which has been sufficiently enterprising to lay down a large enough plant to make small cars in sufficient numbers to make their production really cheap.'[15] These criticisms are

Table 6.4. *Production and sale of vehicles by country, 1907*

	Domestic Production	Domestic Demand
United States	54 000	52 000
Great Britain	21 500	29 500
France	25 500	11 500
Germany	6 500	7 000
Italy	4 000	3 500
Others	4 000	11 500

Source: Motor Trader, 7 October 1908.

supported by the evidence found in Table 6.4 that Britain was the only major vehicle producer unable to satisfy domestic demand in 1907.

The strategy adopted by British motor vehicle firms was not so much backward as it was highly risk-averse and conservative. Whether this represents a failure, as suggested by Saul, very much depends upon one's attitude toward risk.[16] British firms were conservative in their rate of output expansion and they were conservative in that they resisted exploring new markets, preferring instead to follow, perhaps to a fault, the market signals generated by a few leading firms or firms in other countries. It is beyond this book to fully explain the conservatism displayed by British motor vehicle firms: however, one clear factor was the experience of the cycle trade, a trade with which many early vehicle firms had links.

In the 1890s, the cycle industry expanded rapidly and installed new production methods to service a mass market. By 1900 the industry was in disarray.[17] There was excess capacity and many firms found themselves over capitalised. On more than one occasion, contemporary critics warned the young motor vehicle industry of the mistakes of the cycle trade. The *Autocar* was somewhat charitable when their prediction came true with the collapse of Argyll. The company had been capitalised at £500 000 and had set out to produce standardised models in large numbers. They wrote: 'All concerned have our sincerest sympathy, for if they erred they erred magnificently. The lesson is a cruel one, and we hope it will not be lost upon the home industry.'[18] Argyll's error was not overexpansion itself but, rather, expansion on the eve of a major downturn in trade. It is now recognised that the motor vehicle industry is more vulnerable than most industries to wide cyclical shifts in demand.[19] Argyll, with its large fixed investment in special tools which carried a heavy debt load and which quickly became obsolete, was the victim of such a cyclical downturn in 1907.

While the above figures confirm the relative smallness of British output levels and their failure to grow as fast as the domestic market, they mask an important difference between British and American production methods which is critically

Table 6.5. *Employment levels, 1905–13*

	1905	1906	1908	1910	1911	1913/14
British Firms						
Argyll	1200	2000	—	—	—	—
Napier	—	1000	—	—	—	—
Daimler	—	2000	—	4500	—	5000
Austin	270	—	—	1500	—	2300
Belsize	—	—	—	1000	—	—
Humber	—	—	5000	—	—	2500–3000
Wolseley	—	—	—	3000	—	5500
Sunbeam	—	—	—	—	1200	2500–3000
Rover	—	—	—	—	1500	—
American firms						
Ford (Detroit)	—	700	450	2773	3976	14366
Franklin	—	—	800	750	—	700
Packard	—	—	—	—	—	6600

Sources: *Royal Commission on Motor Cars*, 1906, cmd. 3081, pp. 153–4; *Motor Trader*, 4 July and 15 August 1906, 18 March 1908, and 5 August 1911; St.John Nixon, *Daimler 1896–1946* (London, 1946), p. 112; Daimler, *Board Minutes*, March 1910; S.B. Saul, 'The motor industry in Britain to 1914' (*Business History*, 5, 1962), p. 25; 'Reprint from Institute of Mechanical Engineers, 1910' (*Veteran Car*, 15, March–April 1985), p. 581; R. Church, *Herbert Austin* (London, 1979), p. 149; J.P. Bardou *et. al.*, *The Automobile Revolution* (Chapel Hill, 1982), p. 67; A. Nevins, *Ford; The Times, The Man, The Company* (New York, 1954), p. 648; *Automobile Engineer*, 10 September 1914, p. 265; I. Lloyd, *Rolls-Royce, The Growth of a Firm* (London, 1978), p. 6; Pollitt Notebook, University of London, P2/2/5/9, Rover.

important to our study. Even though they failed to become mass producers prior to 1914, they became mass employers, as shown in Table 6.5.

The high levels of employment were partly the product of the British tendency to manufacture the entire vehicle rather than to act as assemblers of bought-out components. Many of the American firms such as Flanders and Ford, who had large output levels, also purchased a large percentage of components from outside suppliers. Ninety-five percent of the production costs of the first Fords were composed of components purchased from outside suppliers. At Argyll, less than half of their production costs represented bought-out components. Daimler, Austin, Rover, Wolseley and many other firms prided themselves on being able to make the majority of vehicle components in their own shops under their own quality control.[20] The extensive use of in-house production limited the need for vehicle producers to standardise components between firms, allowing each firm to claim that it had the most up-to-date design. Other factors making for large workforces included the greater attention to detailed machining for efficient performance on the British small-bore high-compression engine, and the seasonal nature of production.

The large employment levels presented British employers with problems which are normally associated with firms with much larger outputs. In many ways the pressures to change production technology were reversed in Britain and the United States. In the United States, expanding output levels required new and faster production techniques which, in turn, made possible and desirable new production institutions. In Britain, the initial pressure came from the institutional side to cope with the monitoring and enforcing of effort norms and the coordination of a more complex production process.

Production techniques in the British motor vehicle industry

The renewed interest in the history of the motor industry, has provided few details on how vehicles were actually produced in the pre-1914 period. Saul's 1962 article remains one of the most important pieces of research on this period. He argued that despite bright spots, the general performance of the industry was disappointing especially in reference to methods of production.[21] Church also argued that the industry failed to display, 'engineering skills and progressive workshop practices.'[22] Richardson concluded that motor firms:

Had probably never found it necessary to bother very much about human relations within its factories, which were comparatively small. . . . Small firms were by no means the only ones in engineering which were slow to realise that the efficient organisation of production was an important subject in its own right.[23]

Laux, in summing up the European experience argued that: 'The shift from skilled labor using artisan methods to mass production employing semiskilled or unskilled labor was slow in Europe.'[24]

We have already shown that British shops were not small. We will also argue that the slowness of the shift to American production techniques has been exaggerated. Musson has argued that a number of nineteenth-century firms experimented with interchangeable volume production.[25] While there is little doubt that the Americans had made much more progress in shifting to the American system, Musson's work should alert us to the possibility that the system may have taken root in Britain earlier than commonly believed. In the Midlands, for example, small arms manufacturers such as Birmingham Small Arms (BSA) were at the forefront of the British shift to the American system.[26] Another example was the Midland Railway shop where interchangeable production was standard practice by 1898, although they had not taken advantage of the change in production techniques to divide up assembly work into smaller units. The firm produced 200 wagons per week, each wagon being assembled in its entirety by one worker aided by one boy in two days.[27] This was very much the pattern of technical change in the motor industry where, despite changes in production techniques, British manufacturers had difficulty forcing through changes in the organisation of work.

One industry where the American system was widespread prior to 1914 was the British cycle industry. Harrison argued that even though the majority of innovations in production techniques were made in the United States, they were quickly adopted in Britain and that British methods were comparable to American methods.[28] A number of British motor vehicle firms, including Belsize, Dennis, Humber, Rover, Riley, Star, Singer, Sunbeam, Swift, Daimler and Rudge had close links with the cycle industry. The experiences and innovations of the cycle industry provide an important backdrop to pre-1914 changes in the motor vehicle industry.

The limited information we have suggests that in 1880 the cycle trade still employed the European craft system and capital had limited control over effort norms. Chargehands, who often worked alongside the workers, coordinated and controlled the production process. When J. Newton began at Rudge in 1879, he was one of only four office staff. There was no drawing office or even a draughtsman. Cycles were built to rules of thumb, and many of the necessary drawings were produced by the skilled workers.[29] W.H. Nelson, who was the assistant works manager at Rudge in 1908, recalled that in 1886 it was still all hand work and that the foreman was responsible for design, pattern making and ordering his material.

Around 1893, major changes in production techniques and institutions were initiated at Rudge. Centralised drawing and costing departments were introduced. These new departments would play a major role in the transfer of authority from shop floor supervisors and workers to departments under the control of a new managerial class. The shop floor supervisors responded to this encroachment of their authority by resigning en masse. But the production process had been sufficiently simplified that the firm was able to continue production and meet its obligations to a forthcoming cycle trade show without restoring authority to the shop floor.[30] In 1902, a Chemical and Physical Research Laboratory was created. In part this was a response to the growing sophistication in testing the quality of raw materials, but it also represented an increase in managerial control of production knowledge and a reduced dependence on the skills of shop floor workers. By 1905 the demand for shop floor skills had been eroded to the point that the new plant extension could be stocked mainly with milling machines and automatics tended by unskilled labour. The assembly of cycles, a much less complex product than a motor car, was divided up between a number of workers, again reducing skill demands.[31]

The trend at Rudge toward automatic machinery and unskilled labour was not an isolated event in the industry. The journals reported a particularly strong demand from the cycle trade for automatic machinery during 1896 and 1897.[32] The outbreak of labour unrest also points to this period as one of extensive changes in machine techniques. In 1898, the Nottingham cycle makers struck because the boys working the new machines were producing up to twice as much as the skilled workers, who worked on the same machines, felt was a fair output.[33]

A lengthy description of the Northfleet Engineering Works, located near

London, indicates that the American system of interchangeable production with less skilled machine operators was well entrenched and that a start had been made toward the sequential organisation of machinery. By 1899, the firm employed mainly milling machines and automatics. It was common practice for workers to operate two or three machines. There was a shift away from the functional layout of machinery to sequential layout: 'The milling machines are so arranged that the consecutive operation corresponds with the order in which they are laid down, so that the work passes straight down the line from one machine to the other, and the cycle of operations is completed upon the last machine.'[34] Rover, which continued to depend on skilled labour also moved toward a system of flow production. It was reported that: 'The keynote of the system employed is the way the work travels forward through the machining, polishing, plating, etc., departments to the final examination of the completed machine.'[35] It was the experience of the British cycle makers, rather than British heavy engineering, which provided the initial stock of knowledge upon which the British motor vehicle industry developed. It was an experience far removed from the craftsmanship of Britain's older industries, and one which moved the motor industry to the steps of mass production, or to what contemporaries labelled 'repetition production'.

Much of what we have been able to discover about pre-1914 production methods and managerial strategies comes from the relatively extensive prewar records of the Daimler Motor Company. In 1896, Daimler was the first British firm to begin commercial production. By 1905 it had established a reputation as a quality producer of luxury cars. Lack of detailed accounts of the history of other early firms forces us to generalise from the Daimler experience. While such an approach has obvious limitations, we will draw on available information on other firms to suggest that the Daimler experience was not atypical.

The history of Daimler in Britain can be traced back to a meeting between F.R. Simms and Gottlieb Daimler, the German engineer. This meeting led to Simms' purchase of the British rights to the Daimler patents in 1890 and the subsequent formation of the Daimler Motor Syndicate in 1893. This company was purchased by H.J. Lawson as part of his grand scheme to monopolise the British motor vehicle industry via the British Motor Syndicate which was to acquire all of the patents pertaining to vehicle production. The Daimler Motor Company's prospectus was issued on December 15, 1896. It easily raised the desired capital, and appointed J.S. Critchley as its works manager and F.R. Simms as their consulting engineer. Critchley had received his engineering training at a tramway works, where he developed some expertise in organising machinery.

In April of 1896, Critchley, Simms and a few directors went to the continent to acquaint themselves with continental systems of production.[36] This trip was an important one for it set the basic organisational philosophy of the Daimler Company. The Deutzer factory impressed Critchley about which he wrote:

The main object in the arrangement of these works. . . is that the raw material coming in the main entrance, after passing over the scales, are deposited or distributed right and left, and pass through the works by means of light railway, and the two overhead cranes step by step in such a manner as to avoid all possibility of a repetition of transport to and fro. . . . The final object of the plan is that the engine, etc. finally come out through the entrances by way of the testing and painting shops finished and packed ready for shipment. By this system great economy and regularity throughout is arrived at.[37]

Critchley's plans for a purpose built factory consisting of six narrow parallel sheds, carefully designed to speed the flow of work between departments, to provide good lighting, and to minimise noise levels, was rejected by the board.[38] Against his advice, the board purchased the Coventry Cotton Mills. Critchley's criticisms of this site provide insights into the type of factory he planned to set up. He argued that major alterations would be necessary especially 'with regard to the handling of the motor and parts from one department to the other, and it is especially in this direction that an economical and saving manufacture may or may not be established'.[39] It is obvious that Critchley intended to improve the flow of components between functionally organised machine departments. He had yet to see the advantages of the sequential organisation of the machines themselves.

Critchley made a number of key changes at the Cotton Mills site. Two second-hand Crossley gas engines supplied power to the factory through a series of overhead shafts. While the system used was slightly more flexible than the traditional shaft and bevel gear system, it still lacked the flexibility of individual electric motors which was necessary to make sequential organisation practical. The width of the heavy machine shop was extended so that the heavy components of the engines were completely machined in one shop, thereby limiting necessary transportation activity.[40] The first batch of machines installed included self-acting lathes and automatic gear cutting plant. Lathes represented by far the largest portion of early plant. Only a few milling and grinding machines were purchased. This is relatively important since millers and grinders were the work horses at firms producing interchangeable components. Lathes tended to require more skill to set-up and operate and were less likely to provide the accuracy needed for interchangeable production.[41]

The first description of the Daimler factory as a going concern was produced in September of 1897. This report confirms that Critchley had erected a physical plant embodying the original production philosophy.

The factory is extremely well arranged, and as far as possible all operations are consecutive, that is, the raw material goes in at one end and comes out at the other manufactured into motor cars. . . . There are some eight separate shops altogether, all equipped with the newest, the latest and most expensive machinery, mostly, as regards lathes, of American make. When we say that some £20,000 has been spent in plant alone it will be seen that the Daimler Company has laid itself out to do a big business.[42]

At the time of this visit, 250 workers were employed and 50 cars were being produced in the shops.

Another description of the works was printed in 1899. By this time a number of specialised automatic machines had been installed. Machines continued to be imported from America including two Jones and Lamson flat turret lathes and a new special capstan lathe fitted with automatic feed and self trip to turret. A number of boring machines were in use, some fitted with two headstocks to allow two components to be worked at the same time, an indication of the increasingly automatic nature of machine operations. At least one of these boring machines was continuously employed on gear cases. In another area of the plant at least one person was employed on more than one machine, a practice which was strongly resisted in other factories, and again indicates the shift toward automatic machine sequencing. For the first time, milling machines made their appearance. It was claimed that these advances allowed cylinders and combustion chambers to be made interchangeable. The report stressed that Daimler were manufacturing strictly along repetition lines, a practice which was aided by the firm's standardisation of engine design. All engines were based on a two cylinder unit offered in three sizes. Larger engines were constructed by joining more than one of these standard units together.[43]

Indicative of the rapid changes made in the machine shops, boys were hired as turners' helpers in early 1899. At one point there were 129 men and 45 boys on machine work, while in the turning department 30 of the 52 operators were boys. Boys were paid 4d per hour and shared in piecework bonuses up to a maximum of time and one-quarter. The piece prices on jobs where they assisted were reduced by about 20 percent. Skilled labour cautiously accepted the arrangement, partly because it stood to gain once the boys had reached their time and one-quarter earnings limit. The extent to which boys were used was beyond standard practices eventually creating a concern amongst the skilled workers that it might reduce the demand for their own labour. The district organiser of the Amalgamated Society of Engineers (ASE) was called in and, after discussions, management agreed to reduce the percentage of boys in the workforce. This seems to have satisfied the skilled workers, although they did take the further precaution of appointing a shop steward to watch the situation in the future.[44]

Information available on other early vehicle producers indicates that they were also moving away from the European craft system. In 1901, Lanchester employed the lessons of the cycle makers and adopted interchangeability between body, chassis and engine components. The policy of standardisation did not succeed, in part because Lanchester's was forced to delay the introduction of improvements in product design which occurred with great rapidity in these early years.[45] By 1905, British firms were having more success in shifting to the American system. At Belsize, the assembly of a vehicle was divided between 20 separate gangs. They employed American and British tools with a large automatic bay for repetition production.[46] In 1902, the Humber vehicle factory was still small, employing only 150 hands and was closely tied to the cycle works. But reports indicated that the cycle section's experience with modern machinery and repetition work had been fully absorbed by the motor vehicle section. An article commenting on the Nottingham factory of 1903 suggested:

Advantage has been taken of the long experience which Humber have had in the employment of labour saving tools for the production of bicycle parts, and it would be difficult to find a better regulated machine tool shop, or one with a greater output for its size. The machines are all worked at their maximum capacity, high speed steel being employed throughout . . . limit gauges and micrometer working are universal.[47]

The division of labour in the Humber assembly halls was still limited. Two 12-hp and one 20-hp model were produced each week. A gang of four workers and a foreman were responsible for assembling each engine. Task duration was relatively long with each gang completing just two units per week.

One of the most important of the early vehicle producers was the Hozier Engineering Company located in Scotland. They produced five vehicles per week in 1902 and 15 by 1904, a level of output which many considered extraordinary at the time. Their production process was heavily dependent upon the use of jigs and fixtures to provide standardised components. Their success in achieving standardised production was tested in 1903 by an independent agency. A vehicle was chosen at random from the assembly area and without any adjustments it was driven 100 miles. This was seen as a test of the accuracy of machine techniques, because normally a vehicle would have to be torn apart a number of times to regrind camshafts, crankshafts and other critical components before it would function without shaking itself apart. At Daimler, it was still necessary to subject the engines to careful tests, and once installed in the chassis they were run in for five hundred miles before being delivered.[48] The Argyll test being successful, the sponsor concluded:

This result is attained by the system of manufacture from standard jigs and (with strictly defined limits of accuracy) to standard gauges, so that the mechanism and workmanship of each car is exactly the same as that of every other car of the same power. . . . The personal element is by this system of manufacturing entirely eliminated.[49]

There is very little evidence on the skill profile of the workforce prior to 1905. Actions by Midland employers suggests that at least a start had been made in shifting to less skilled workers. Engineering employers in the Midlands, where many vehicle producers were located, were not very active in the late nineteenth-century struggles between organised labour and organised employers. The Coventry employers did not form an employer's association until 1907 and only affiliated with the national Employer's Federation in 1910. The Birmingham Employer's Association had a longer history, but its membership during the upheaval of 1897 was relatively small. The *Engineer* attributed this low level of employer activity to their ability to introduce new machine techniques and less skilled labour with little opposition. It wrote:

The fact is that the engineering shops in the district . . . are much less dependent upon skilled labour than some time ago. The production of engineering work by machinery has been brought to such perfection in some of the largest works in the Birmingham district, by the introduction of machinery, . . . The labour on the work of manufacturing becomes little more than itself mechanical.[50]

Despite the introduction of automatic machinery, jigs and fixtures, and the inroads of less skilled workers in some production departments, it is likely that a large proportion of the workforce in the motor vehicle industry remained skilled prior to 1905. However, the continued use of skilled labour was no longer based on its ability to produce from blue prints on universal machines without the aid of jigs and fixtures. The continued use of skilled labour was a product of three factors. First, machine techniques had not yet progressed to the point where interchangeable production could be guaranteed without the intervention of skilled workers. This was particularly true of shops which depended on ordinary centre lathes which could rarely be operated by the less skilled.[51] Second, inaccuracies in product design and the design of jigs and fixtures meant that hand fitting was necessary in some areas. Third, short production runs meant frequent changes of jigs and fixtures, which mitigated against the use of unskilled labour on production operations.

In the larger shops, many of these barriers to the spread of the less skilled were removed by 1914. Laux estimated that, at output levels of a few hundred or a few thousand, many processes in motor vehicle plants could be made suitable for less skilled labour.[52] With longer production runs, the pace of technical change accelerated. Milling machines and grinding machines appeared in larger numbers, which meant reduced demands for skilled labour to operate machines. In turn, the greater degree of interchangeability of components reduced the demand for skilled fitters to assemble cars. At Deasy in 1910, lathes still accounted for 75 percent of machine work in the plant, but there was a continual shift of work to the growing grinding department.[53] By 1911 at the Rover plant, grinders from five different companies were used and special grinders were employed in machining crankshafts and cylinders.[54] At the Institute of Automobile Engineers, interest in grinding technology led to a paper being presented on the topic in 1911.[55]

The trend toward new machine techniques and the use of less skilled labour was evident at Daimler where weekly output reached 25 in 1906 and 45 by 1909. The plant extension of 1906 included gear cutting machinery which was simple enough that it could be operated by boy labour. The hand grinding of valves, which took a skilled worker seven and one-half hours, was mechanised and now took just over one hour. By 1909, the *Motor Car Journal* described the works as one using, 'great labour saving automatic processes'.[56] Other reports indicated that in the assembly halls the work had been extensively divided and that, 'each section, year in and year out, always handling that particular part of the engine or the car'.[57] The existing gangs found that either the range of tasks they were responsible for was reduced or that the gang's work was sectionalised and allocated to individual workers. Around the same time the milling department was expanded and the existing machines were fitted with better jigs and fixtures. These allowed more unskilled labour to be used in machine departments. The milling department employed 80 hands in 1909, and almost all of them were unskilled machine operators or boys. Only three workers in the department received the recognised ASE rate for skilled labour.[58]

By 1908, the improvements in machine techniques, particularly the expansion of the milling department and the extensive use of jigs and fixtures, had made it possible for Daimler to do away with much of the hand fitting and skilled labour in the assembly departments. This was especially true in the engine department, where hand labour was all but eliminated, while in the chassis department the spread of interchangeability was less complete. It was noted in a contemporary report that:

It is a curious fact that although the firm under discussion wasted many pounds in hand fitting parts, yet the engine erecting was carried out on a totally different system. ... There was exceedingly little which was hand fitted on any of the engines ... any part, which during that operation was found to be of a size other than that necessary, had to be returned to the machine shop and replaced with one which would fit. ... Very few of the engine gangs possessed a file or other instrument which could be used for fitting in the ordinary sense of the word.[59]

The likely explanation of this anomaly was the need for precision if the engine was to operate efficiently, a need less keenly felt in other areas such as chassis and body production. Between 1908 and 1912, Daimler eliminated 50 percent of the hand fitting in the chassis shop and it was suggested that much of the remaining hand fitting was simply the product of poor jig and product design. One contemporary observer expected 1913 to witness the appearance of the first British erecting shop in which only assembly, not fitting, was performed.[60]

Between 1906 and 1914, other firms were also moving toward interchangeability and production with unskilled workers. The new Humber plant, opened in 1908, had a capacity of 150 motor cars and 5000 cycles per week. The firm claimed that all of its components were interchangeable, a position which had been attained by extensive gauging. The continued employment of benches in the assembly areas raises some doubt about the degree to which the system had been perfected.[61]

The Hozier Engineering Company had been reorganised as the Argyll Company and had undergone a rapid expansion bringing its potential output to 100 chassis per week in 1906, with plans reported which would have doubled or tripled this output. The new firm had been capitalised at the unheard of sum of

£500 000, and their initial share issue of £230 000 was oversubscribed two and one-half times. Believing that they had resolved the majority of design problems, they were ready to invest in special machines to produce their new models in large numbers. Alexander Govan, the managing director described the stages through which their production process had advanced. In 1901, parts were hand traced on marking out tables and machined by skilled labour. By 1905, with annual production reaching 1700 vehicles, nearly all work was done by less skilled workers with the aid of jigs and fixtures. In the new factory built in 1906, the jigs and fixtures were fitted directly onto the machines creating, for all intensive purposes, special purpose machines which did away with the need for skilled set-up labour. Indicative of the changes in production techniques, the time needed to machine cylinders had fallen to 45 minutes by late 1906 from an earlier figure of 30 hours. The new factory, based in part on knowledge which Govan had acquired during his visit to the United States in 1904, never realised its full capacity as the firm had to be reorganised and its production plans scaled down after a financial crisis in 1907.[62]

In 1910, the Belsize works in Manchester was referred to by one journal as an 'Anglicized embodiment of American methods and organisation'.[63] They used mainly standard machines and fitted special jigs and fixtures to them. A few special purpose machines were in use including one which bored four pairs of cylinder blocks simultaneously. Belsize had made a start toward flow production in the machining departments. The machinery was arranged so as to allow components such as cylinder blocks and cranks to be passed from machine to machine rather than be transported between departments for different operations. In 1912, after the managers had toured a number of American factories, a new works extension was opened. Semi-automatic machines and multi-fixture tools were widely used. Reports suggested that the work was sectionalised and subdivided beyond that normally found in British factories.[64]

Less complete information on other firms also suggests that a major effort was underway to shift to the American system with less skilled labour. The new Arrol Johnston factory, opened just before World War I, was modelled after the Detroit Packard factory. Pullinger, the works manager, was criticised in the trade press for wanting to get rid of all skilled labour, to which he replied that skilled labour would from now on be employed only where necessary.[65] When Loraine Dietrich bought the Ariel Motor Co. near Bournbrook, they planned to put the plant on an interchangeable principle and build only one model, the 15–20 hp.[66] The Perry Motor Company of Birmingham planned to adopt a similar strategy when they entered the market in 1913. They intended to produce one model in one standard size and they informed the press that by fixing jigs to standard machines and by severe inspection interchangeability was ensured and: 'Fitting has been reduced to a matter at most of mere assembly of finished part to finished part.'[67] At Austin, a strategy of standardisation and repetition production had been suggested as early as 1911, but product design errors and errors in the design of jigs and fixtures meant they had to use skilled fitters to hand finish components. By 1914, many of these errors had been rectified and the plant was made suitable for the large-scale employment of less skilled labour, a necessity imposed upon the firm by the shortage of skilled labour at Longbridge.[68]

The Sunbeam factory was one of the few bright spots in the industry according to Saul. The firm employed a special type of jig known as a Universal Jig which could be adjusted to work on a number of different components and which produced accurate and virtually interchangeable components. Chassis assembly was divided among a large number of small gangs. Each gang was responsible for one task, and the chassis were moved between gangs with overhead cranes, a system which must have been awkward, but which gave a rare British example of flow production prior to 1914.[69] The more common assembly systems, employed by both Wolseley and Morris, divided the work between a number of specialised gangs who moved along a row of stationary assembly stands.[70] By 1914, Wolseley had moved to sequential machine organisation in the cylinder head and crankcase departments. Assembly tasks continued to be divided into relatively small units allowing the firm 'to produce better work at a cheaper rate than would be the case if the work were more varied.'[71]

The above account focuses on the most advanced production techniques of the most advanced firms. Clearly, these new machine methods did not spread evenly to all factories, or even within factories. Some firms showed themselves particularly inept at improving their systems. At Armstrong Whitworth, vehicle production was reduced to a subsidiary activity of the main factory engaged in non-vehicle production. They used equipment that was not wanted by the main factory, and management showed little interest in this minor and, it was thought, uninteresting department. Likewise at the motor department of the Birmingham Small Arms Company, vehicle production was not treated as a main activity and showed a distinct lack of organisation and profits.[72]

The experience of Standard is closer to earlier generalisations of British production methods. Standard followed a conservative production policy keeping output below 400 as late as 1911 and producing only 750 vehicles in 1913. In 1909 vehicles were put through the works in batches of 25 and the decision to put through one batch of 100 vehicles met with severe criticism. There was great concern that either the design might prove faulty or be superseded by some improvement before the batch of 100 could be sold. The next year saw batch sizes fall back to 50 where they remained until 1913 when they again started putting vehicles through the works in batches of 100. These relatively low levels of output and small batch sizes limited the type of machinery the firm could employ. When the new works were opened in 1910 they employed high speed lathes, rejecting the use of the more advanced capstan lathes and the even more advanced automatics because their scale of output did not justify the extra cost.[73]

Even bearing in mind that few of the journals we have used would have wished to criticise firms, and that firms using the newer techniques received far more coverage in technical journals than firms using the older and therefore less newsworthy techniques of craft production, it still seems reasonable to conclude that by 1914, many British motor vehicle factories were much closer to our conception of a modern mass production factory employing the American system than they were to that of mid-nineteenth-century craft producers using the European system.[74] Such a conclusion is supported not only by the above accounts, but also by statements of contemporary observers. In 1914, a management consultant, experienced in motor vehicle methods, commented that: 'In the motor trade ... a large portion of the workers were either turret hands who do not do much more than pull certain handles, or milling machine hands who only put work in a fixture and let it go, having the speed and feed set for them and jig drillers.'[75] In a similar vein, Legros, in his presidential speech to the Institute of Automobile Engineers in 1911 claimed that: 'The tendency in the bigger factories is to diminish the amount of responsibility left to the individual worker in respect to the employment of ... shop knowledge.'[76]

If, in 1905, the majority of workers in the industry continued to be skilled workers, it seems safe to argue that by 1914, in all but the smaller shops, a significant portion of the work in engine and chassis departments was done either by unskilled machine operators and assemblers, or by skilled workers doing essentially unskilled work. In chassis and engine shops, driven by the need to work to close tolerances for efficient vehicle operation, elements of the American system were adopted. Body shops, about which we have had little to say, remained the preserve of the skilled worker well into the 1920s. *The Motor Trader* reported in 1911 that body construction, 'was one of the few branches of handicraft that so far has successfully resisted suppression by mechanical processes'.[77] These shifts in production techniques allowed and made necessary a reform of the production institutions employed to coordinate factory activity and to monitor and enforce the effort bargain. It is to these innovations that we will now turn.

The rise of management in the British motor vehicle industry, 1896–1914

As long as employers remained dependent upon skilled workers who monopolised production knowledge, their own techniques for coordinating shop floor activities and enforcing the effort bargain remained underdeveloped. This was very much the case in the early motor vehicle industry where J. Laux argued: 'Management rarely seemed to question the principle that its direct responsibility did not extend into the shops, where the parts were made and assembled. There, the foremen and older skilled workers ruled.'[1] But as the new production techniques reduced the demand for skilled labour they removed the main constraint to the development of new managerial institutions. Employers began to adopt new production institutions whose net effect was to transfer authority from labour to a new managerial class. Using information on Daimler and other firms we will argue that the transfer of authority was incomplete and that this would play a critical role in the British motor vehicle industry's response to the challenge of Fordism after 1914.

In our research, we have uncovered very few cases of labour resisting the introduction of new production techniques in the motor industry. However, attempts to alter authority relationships within the factories or to impose a new effort bargain, attempts which often coincided with the introduction of new production techniques, met with severe opposition. The Humber Beeston plant near Nottingham, provides a good example of how the new production techniques destabilised the existing effort bargain and led to serious labour unrest. We have already referred to this factory as one which benefited from the cycle trade's experience with repetition production techniques. In 1902, changes were made in the employment relationship in an attempt to boost productivity. The straight piecework system was replaced with the Premium Bonus payment system; however, the experiment failed and in 1904 Humber reverted to straight piecework. With the return to straight piecework, labour lost the guarantee that at least its day rates would be paid, regardless of individual output levels. This had been part of the compromise worked out by the EEF and the ASE at Carlisle in 1902 to regulate the use of the Premium Bonus system. The change in payment system was not popular with the workforce and set in motion four years of labour conflict culminating in the closure of the plant in 1908. At the root of the conflict was the effort bargain.[2]

The issue came to a head when prices were handed out for the new light car which Humber was putting into production. The firm had over 100 orders in hand, suggesting a level of output well above that usually found at this time. Fourteen men, working in teams of two, were involved in the assembly of the chassis. They were offered 58/- per vehicle. The employer claimed that each team could assemble at least one vehicle per week. The workers demanded between two and three weeks for each chassis. The employer concluded that: 'The inference to be drawn from the above was that the men had agreed amongst themselves not to do the work at a reasonable rate.'[3] An agreement proved impossible and, after fourteen days, the workers were dismissed.

At the local conference, at which Barnes presided for the ASE, Humber refused to alter the price on chassis assembly arguing that decent wages could be earned at the existing price. The problem, they said, was that the workers did not work hard enough. Within the ASE bargaining team there was a significant difference of opinion as to how to deal with this question. The difference of opinion reflects the changing nature of the effort bargain in the engineering industry. Barnes dismissed management's arguments as silly. He contended that it could not possibly be a question of labour not working hard enough as management 'have the authority' to enforce the intensity of work. Gardner, perhaps better steeped in the traditions of skilled workers under the European system, also thought management's arguments were silly. He felt that it could not possibly be a question of effort levels as the ASE enforced these themselves. Any worker not working hard enough would be 'fired out' by the union.[4] Barnes, if not his members, conceded the control over the effort level to management and focused on the relationship between wages and effort. For Barnes, effort could be had, but at a price. Gardner continued to advocate a strategy applicable to a production technology dependent upon skilled labour, where labour had a more direct influence over defining the level of effort that represented a fair days work.

An agreement continued to prove elusive and on 11 April 1904, the ASE called out the rest of its members from Humber. It had caught Humber in the middle of the production season, a critical time since the seasonal nature of consumer demand meant that any output lost would likely be lost permanently. Humber was unable to find sufficient labour to fill the gaps left by the ASE, indicating that interchangeability had not been completely achieved, making it difficult to produce without the services of skilled assemblers. Unless the EEF came to Humber's aid, which the firm justified on the grounds that they were a test case, they were going to give in to the union demand that day rates be guaranteed under straight piecework.[5] The requested help was not forthcoming, and Humber and the ASE reached an agreement on 13 April. Day rates were guaranteed on the following conditions:

(1)   Should any man fail to earn at piecework rates the amount of day work rate during any week, the deficit may be deducted from any excess earned by him during the following three weeks.

(2)   Should the manager discharge any man in consequence of his not having earned as much as the day work rate at the piecework price or otherwise, no complaint will be held by the other men.

(3)   It shall be the sole discretion of the Works Manager to decide what is skilled and what is unskilled labour.

(4)   The men in consideration of the above concession, agree to do their utmost to assist the firm and to turn out as much work as they have hitherto done.[6]

The agreement provides a summary of the institutional issues involved in the transfer to the American system. Clauses (1) and (2) deal with the revisions to the employment relationship. Clause (3) is indicative of the struggle going on for the control of jobs, while clause (4) leaves little doubt that effort norms were an issue in this and, we would argue, many other conflicts during the transition to the American system.

While this agreement ended the strike, it did not end the conflict over the effort bargain at Humber, a conflict which became increasingly intertwined with the spread of new production methods. In August of 1905, the company closed for a month to install new machinery. When the factory reopened, the ASE claimed that a number of their members were not taken back and that instead non-union, and likely less skilled labour was hired. Pullinger, the works manager, did not deny the charge, and in a local conference declared that union labour held up production and were less eager to work than non-union labour.[7]

By 1907, relations between Pullinger and the unions had deteriorated further. Pullinger increased his efforts to make his shop a non-union one. He went to the workforce to, 'appeal to you to cooperate with me in doing everything in your power to help us to keep this shop free from all taint of Trade Unionism'.[8] The reason for this policy was made explicit:

It was adopted because members of the ASE and the Steam Engine Makers... were always agitating... they were also dilatory in their work and did not produce such good class of work as we are producing at the present time, neither would they earn the amount that they could have earned at piecework prices.[9]

Both the ASE, and the National Union of Vehicle Builders blacked the Humber works. In 1908, the Humber Beeston factory closed down, and all vehicle production was moved to Coventry. The extent to which this was a result of the blacking by the unions and how much was due to rationalisation between the firm's Coventry and Beeston plants is unclear. What is clear though, is that the problems which plagued Humber Beeston continued in Coventry. Upon opening the new works in Coventry, Humber followed a policy of hiring only non-union foremen, introduced new rules requiring workers to operate more than one machine, allowed for the discharge of workers who were not earning at least their day rate, forced union and non-union labour to work together and gave management the right to decide what was skilled and what was unskilled work. It was reported that Pullinger continued to prefer hiring non-union labour.[10]

These rules were the major issue in an unofficial strike in 1910. The ASE district organiser suggested that unofficial strikes were common in the Coventry area. The strike succeeded in checking the authority of an unpopular foreman, provided for the recognition of a shop committee, improved night and overtime premiums, and reduced the level of disciplinary fines and made them payable to a workers' benevolent fund. A second unofficial strike was reported in 1911, which won concessions on piecework prices on new jobs.

Disputes over new methods for monitoring and enforcing the effort bargain caused strikes at other Coventry firms. In 1910, the workers at Standard objected to excessive supervision, the method of setting piece prices and the lack of a guarantee of day rates on piecework. The dispute was resolved only after the firm made concessions to labour in each of these areas. At Rover, a new system of supervision which limited bonus payments to chargehands was the cause of numerous disputes between 1909 and 1913. The conflict was resolved when chargehands were paid a 44/- minimum rate and a bonus proportional to their day rate. The production workers were put on piecework and all bonuses were paid through the office, rather than through chargehands who had a habit of taking a share of these bonus payments for themselves.[11]

A similar pattern of events can be found at the Coventry Ordnance Works (COW), a key supplier of motor vehicle components prior to 1914.[12] By 1907, they employed large numbers of unskilled workers and workers earning less than the skilled rate. Labour regularly complained that the firm was setting piece prices too tightly, making it difficult to earn bonuses at an acceptable level of effort. In an attempt to alter this situation, the local ASE allowed the election of shop stewards and began a campaign to recruit more workers into the union. In August of 1907, an overtime ban was called, but collapsed because the firm was able to maintain production levels with members of the Workers Union and with boy labour. The ineffectiveness of the overtime ban reflected the new problems created for labour by the transition to the American system. The Workers Union had expressed a desire to support the ban and wanted the Coventry Allied Trades Federation to agree to call out its own members if any Workers Union member was victimised on account of the ban. Victimisation was highly likely as the members of the Workers Union were unskilled workers and could easily be dismissed and replaced. The Federation refused to support the Workers Union in this way, and in fact instructed the members of the Workers Union to work up to 15 hours of overtime per week, undermining the skilled worker's protest.[13]

A few months later, the local ASE renewed its activities at COW and again

Table 7.1. *Coventry Ordnance Works, distribution of labour, 1908*

Category	Heavy shop	Navy shop	Small tool shop	Fuze shop	Tool room	Light machine shop
ASE	60	10	26	12	20	38
Other unions	21	3	36	1	6	8
Non-union	22	8	49	25	20	20
Youths	5	—	—	—	—	51

Notes: As well as the 56 boys listed above, the firm employed another 65 boys who were not allocated to any particular shop.
Sources: ASE(COV), *Minutes*, 4 February 1908.

attempted to recruit more workers into the union. Table 7.1 indicates the extent to which non-union labour, much of it unskilled youths, was being employed.

The local ASE continued to be critical of the practices of the firm and how it was using the new technology to alter working conditions. It was not the new production techniques themselves which the ASE criticised but rather how they were being used to alter the effort bargain. It was claimed:

The firm use jigs and fixtures extensively and claim that little skill being required they are justified in employing cheap labour.... The position is an excellent example of how modern machinery is used to lower the standard of life for men in the engineering trades.[14]

The executive of the Coventry ASE viewed the spread of the American system at COW with some alarm and responded by extending the relatively unsuccessful overtime ban to a full scale strike. But the failure to obtain the support of either the national executive of the ASE or the Coventry Allied Trades Federation, which was dominated by small craft unions, significantly weakened the effectiveness of the protest. The strike collapsed and led to the resignation of the entire local executive of the ASE. It complained bitterly of the lack of support from the national executive during the past 14 months when attempts were being made to improve conditions at COW. The rising levels of unemployment which began in late 1908 temporarily halted any further action against the firm.[15]

Late in 1909, in an attempt to increase managerial control of the effort bargain, COW introduced speed and feed men and the Premium Bonus System.[16] These attempts were resisted and, after a three-day strike in December, the speed and feed man was sacked and the firm agreed to set piece prices mutually. During the years leading up to the war, numerous strikes occurred, nearly all related to the pace of work or the level of payment. After a number of earlier setbacks, labour began to win some of these conflicts. Undoubtedly these successes were related to further organisation of the less skilled by the Workers Union. In 1913 the Workers Union achieved a major victory in winning a six pence per hour minimum wage and rights to overtime pay.[17] In 1913, the company was forced to reduce the use of boy labour, while in 1914 they were forced to sack a rate fixer, remove the power to set prices from the foremen, and undertake a general investigation of piecework prices. By May 1914 the situation was sufficiently tense that the local ASE instructed its members that in the case of a major dispute they should occupy the factory rather than simply walk off of their jobs.[18] The decision to employ a strategy of occupation reflects one of the changes adopted by labour as a result of the new technology. Under the European system, skilled labour could simply withdraw its skill and the firm was unable to operate. Under the American system, unskilled workers were relatively easy to replace necessitating a shift in tactics to occupation and picketing.[19]

Another important conflict arising from the adoption of the American system took place in Manchester at the Crossley works. Late in 1911, after a period when work had been 'specialised, sectionalised, and organised', an unofficial strike was called. The strike committee gave the following reasons for striking:

The employees of Messrs. Crossley Brothers, Openshaw, Manchester are now on strike. They are out because, only by such action can they effectively resist the treatment they have been subjected to during the past two years (when the speed-up system commenced).... The Management promised to remove the speed and feed man from direct interference with the men in the shops. This promise has been broken ... piecework prices have been repeatedly reduced, with the result that numbers of men have been displaced and the jobs given to boys.[20]

The strike lasted nine weeks, during which time the national ASE, as had been the case in Coventry at COW, withheld moral and financial support. The strike continued only because local workers were willing to provide the necessary support. The conflict was resolved by an agreement to send the issues to Central Conference. This largely defused the issue although a decision was made to create a works committee through which the workers hoped to limit the impact of what one local observer called the 'Taylorist System'.[21]

These labour conflicts all arose out of employer attempts to use changes in production techniques as an excuse for revising production institutions and shifting the effort bargain. They were responses to capital's experimentation with new payment systems, new modes of supervision and new techniques for monitoring labour effort. These experiments were designed to increase the authority of a new class of factory managers. The fullest account available on the rise of the management function at a motor vehicle firm is that of the Daimler Motor Company. The Daimler experiments were designed to resolve two related problems. The first was the need to increase control over labour in order to increase the productivity of the new capital equipment. The second was the need to improve factory coordination, particularly in the more complex manufactur-

Table 7.2 *The value of work-in-progress, 1905–14 (percentage of total capital investment)*

Year	Average thirty-four firms	Daimler	Rover	Sunbeam	Belsize	Rolls-Royce
1905	15.7	34.5	16.9	—	—	—
1906	18.8	29.4	29.4	24.0	—	—
1907	24.2	37.8	39.0	23.9	36.5	25.9
1908	23.8	41.0	39.6	32.0	47.3	31.5
1909	22.6	41.8	33.9	28.6	44.6	26.6
1910	22.6	—	34.4	35.0	42.6	31.0
1911	24.8	—	39.4	30.7	40.3	39.4
1912	25.6	—	32.7	34.4	35.5	34.6
1913	32.3	—	30.3	39.1	47.3	44.5
1914	30.9	—	36.5	35.7	47.5	45.1

Source: Company Balance Sheets.

ing establishments, so as to speed up the flow of work through the shops and reduce the investment in work-in-progress. Motor vehicles were one of the most expensive of the early mass produced commodities, and, as shown in Table 7.2, work-in-progress regularly absorbed between one-fifth and one-half of total fixed capital investment.

At Daimler, despite the glowing reports in trade journals, production was sporadic and well below the expectations of the board of directors. The board's minute books indicate a state of confusion within the works and a lack of coordination. Capacity for 1897 had been estimated at 250 vehicles, but within months this was reduced to 150 vehicles. At the same time, the board became concerned with the rising costs of production and the large amount of capital invested in work-in-progress, which exceeded investment in plant by £5000.[22] The board concluded that Critchley was not working the plant to its full capacity and they decided that they would have to intervene directly in order to insure the desired level of output. An accounting system was introduced which included weekly expenditure estimates and monthly works reports.[23] These were to be made available to the board, which intended to use them to increase its control over Critchley, and, via him, the works itself. The board retained the authority to set prices, decide on production levels and labour requirements, decide on all technical matters concerned with design, and to sanction all expenditures.

The board soon discovered how difficult it was to coordinate and control a motor vehicle factory and that they were particularly unsuited for the task. None of the active directors had any experience in vehicle production, and their knowledge of engineering methods was limited. The lack of a managing director and the fact that many board meetings took place in London rather than Coventry greatly reduced their knowledge of the day to day events which they wished to control. The board also lacked a natural leader with a major financial investment in the company. The chairman of the board often took the lead, but his ability to do so was limited by the strong personalities on the board such as the outspoken editor of *The Autocar*, J.J. Sturmey. The functioning of the board and the works which they tried to control came to depend upon a consensus of opinion within the board, a consensus which rarely existed.[24]

The first of a number of committees of investigation was set up in 1898.[25] While the directors had blamed Critchley for many of the problems and had even considered replacing him, the committee of investigation focused almost exclusively on the shortcomings of the board and largely exonerated Critchley of any blame. The Committee indicated that, thus far, every contract put through the works had resulted in a trading loss, and that it was only non-manufacturing transactions which had kept the company from bankruptcy. The Committee argued that the firm lacked a clear line of authority and that dissension within the board and board members' involvement in decision making had exacerbated the situation. The Committee proposed reducing the number of directors and hiring a managing director with a major financial investment in the firm.[26]

The Committee's report was presented to the annual general meeting in January of 1899. After an extremely stormy meeting, the board was allowed to save face and was given the support of the shareholders. Conveniently, four of the original seven board members resigned and two new directors were appointed. E.H. Bayley, a new director, was made chairman of the board and charged with the responsibility of reorganising the system of management. A closer investigation of the firm's organisation indicated that the committee of investigation had identified only one area of weakness, the impracticality of managing from the board room. Bayley would soon discover that the institutional framework for centralised managerial control simply did not exist at Daimler. There was a lack of accurate record keeping in the early period and without this data management was unable to coordinate or control factory operations. Management was forced to depend on shop floor workers to perform these functions.[27]

Even before the new board took over, important changes were taking place which began the transfer of authority from labour to management. In an attempt to systematise and control the distribution of tools, each worker was given three numbered brass tags. Tools were given out from the tool room in exchange for the brass tags. This provided an easy system for controlling the number of tools handed out and a means of maintaining a record of where the tools were. While apparently a simple change, it had important ramifications. It gave management the authority to control tool distribution and reduced its dependence on production workers knowledge of where the tools were. Labour was thereby denied one tactic it had used to control plant productivity and effort norms.

Another area which was reformed was the booking of time for workers who worked both day rate and piece-rate jobs. Each worker, or team of workers was issued two boards, one for day work and one for piecework which could be identified by their colour.[28] Only one board was allowed out of the cost office at one time and they were stored on trolleys which moved throughout the works. These boards acted as a check that labour was not booking onto day work while accumulating a stock of piecework jobs. The boards also supplied management with a steady flow of data. Each board included details on part number, batch size, workers involved, and their productivity. The collection of this data provided the information to compare the relative productivity of workers and through this control effort norms.

The relative burden of overhead costs was another area where new data collection methods were adopted. Prior to 1898, the firm had simply added a fixed percentage onto direct labour costs to cover overheads. The percentage used represented an informed guess. In 1898 large ledgers were supplied into which all overhead charges were entered. These charges were divided by the total number of labour hours to provide an exact figure for overhead costs.[29] It is easy to underestimate the importance of these changes. For the first time, management was collecting detailed data on plant operations and labour productivity. This data provided the foundation upon which a new managerial class could be erected, thereby reducing labour's authority over many aspects of shop floor operations and effort norms.

In September of 1898, in an attempt to boost productivity, the conditions of employment were changed. The workers were put on a revised piecework system and fines were levied on workers who lost time due to lateness.[30] Central to these changes was a new form of supervision. Foremen, who had been paid a fixed salary, were replaced by lead hands and chargehands who not only worked at the bench but also had a financial interest in the bonus made by the gang they supervised. They were paid a bonus equalling 10 percent of the total bonus earned by their gang.[31] The changes were resisted by the skilled workers. The Amalgamated Society of Engineers called a meeting to discuss the situation and appointed a shop committee to meet with management. It was argued that this system of supervision had already been tried at A. Herberts, the tool maker, and had not succeeded. Herbert's had decided to return to paying foremen on a fixed day rate.[32] The shop committee was unable to reach a compromise with management. No action was taken by labour as the ASE, the Steam Engine Makers, and the Toolmakers were unable to agree on a joint policy of action. The ASE decided to drop the issue when a downturn in demand threatened to force Daimler into bankruptcy.[33]

Upon assuming the chairmanship of the board, Bayley took steps both to reduce the board's direct involvement in the running of the works, and to enhance the collection of data via a new accounting system. The design of vehicles was delegated to Critchley and the newly appointed consultant, Sidney Straker. An Accounts Committee was created and given responsibility for collecting cost information and keeping a check on the state of the works and the cost of production. Overhead costs were calculated more precisely and allocated according to actual machine and building usage rather than as a single plant wide average.[34] Despite the changes, the managerial function remained underdeveloped and the new managerial class was unable to coordinate and control the production process. Productivity remained below expectations and vehicles continued to be produced at a loss.[35]

Another committee composed of the chairman of the board, the works director and Captain Longbridge, a new director, was set up early in 1901. This new committee reported that production costs continued to absorb the entire revenue from sales.[36] Longbridge was appointed to go up to Coventry and conduct a special investigation. His report, presented in July, led to an even greater centralisation of authority in the new managerial class. He emphasised the role of the draughting office as a means of controlling productivity and effort norms. This office was to be expanded and a chief draughtsman was to be appointed. More comprehensive drawings were to be supplied and the draughting office was made responsible for specifying the materials to be used and the quantity needed. Again, decisions formerly made on the shop floor were centralised under managerial control.[37]

During 1901, P. Martin was appointed works manager. When Martin took over, managerial institutions and control were still incomplete and labour showed little inclination to increase productivity on its own. Manufacturing departments failed to commmunicate either with each other or the assembly departments. Finished components were left lying around the shop while the erecting department waited for them to complete a job.[38] Under Martin, managerial institutions were formalised. A hierarchy of foremen was created giving those in the production departments a higher status. For the first time, a works supervisor was appointed to oversee the entire operation.[39] On the shop floor, Martin advocated reducing the level of direct or, as he called it, 'driving' supervision. To this end, he reduced the number of salaried foremen, leaving only nine salaried foremen in the entire shop. He increased the number of lead hands who still worked at the bench, and adopted piecework in the shops which had remained on day work.[40] The use of incentive payment systems was an integral part of Martin's strategy and one which he felt would reduce the demands on management to coordinate and control labour.[41]

The spread of ordinary piecework was only an interim policy. The board, in consultation with Martin and the sub-editor of *The Engineer*, was investigating the Premium Bonus system. Longbridge and Martin approved of the new payment system, but Martin argued that its introduction was still premature. He was concerned that the costing system in use did not allow management to set production times accurately in the entire factory.[42] By 1904, Martin's objections were overcome and the new payment system was adopted in most of the shops over the next two years. Labour resistance to the changes in the employment relationship were discussed in detail in Chapter 4. The members of the National

Union of Vehicle Builders unsuccessfully resisted the new system, while the members of the ASE accepted it on the condition that the Carlisle Memorandum of 1902 was followed.[43]

A paper presented by Martin on Works Organisation provides a rare insight into the managerial philosophy prevalent, not only at Daimler but also at a number of important firms in the vehicle industry.[44] Martin described a managerial function that went beyond the provision of entrepreneurial creativity in the areas of design and engineering. These basic tasks were to be supplemented with new responsibilities for coordinating shop floor activity and controlling the production process. Within this context, Martin stressed that the skills and creativity of the individual had to be forced into a mould which would serve management's broader administrative goals. Within the management hierarchy, the interests of the engineering department had to be made subservient to those of the sales department. In stark contrast to the accepted wisdom on British engineering practices, he wrote:

It is not my objective to disparage the fullest exercise of brilliant ingenuity and genius, yet I think we shall do better to confine ourselves, as regards the engineering department, to the strict purpose of showing profit on a manufacturing business.[45]

The collection of data on factory performance was integral to the transfer of authority to management. Martin took the process of collecting data to its logical conclusion in advocating not only the collection of historical costs, but also the analysis of production plans so as to be able to predict costs before production began. In effect, management was to completely free itself of any dependence on labour in the setting of productivity norms. Labour was to be supplied by the draughting office with precise descriptions of material needs and instructions on how the work was to be done, as well as standard labour times provided in advance by the rate setting department. Martin gave a detailed description of how the latter should operate. He suggested:

Divide the work in the factory into jobs, considering these jobs as units of work. Each of these jobs is provided with a time allowance by the rate fixing department. These allowances should not be fixed by the old method of observation, but from charts and curve tables, of data established by your actual previous results in different metals, operations etc., or from other sources.[46]

These changes went even further toward deskilling work in the sense that management, not labour, would make all decisions regarding materials employed, product design, size limits, type of machinery and class of labour. Martin stressed: 'Nothing should be left to the judgement of the workman, however simple and obvious the job looks.'[47]

However, the deskilling of labour and the enhancement of managerial control was not seen as leading to direct managerial control of effort norms along Ford lines. Martin advocated replacing the driving supervision of foremen with what he termed 'induction'. For Martin, 'induction' implied labour self-regulating the effort bargain rather than being driven by management. This self-regulation was to be achieved through the use of improved incentive payment systems such as the Premium Bonus system. According to Martin, the advantage of the Premium Bonus system was its ability to enforce effort norms without direct managerial intervention.[48] He argued that under straight piecework and day work, management was responsible for both maintaining effort norms and for coordinating shop floor activity. Under both systems, labour had an incentive to restrict output. With day work, labour did not receive any direct payment for increased effort, while with straight piecework labour feared that higher productivity would lead to price cuts. Martin supported the claim, examined in Chapter 4, that under the Premium Bonus system, labour confidence in the stability of piece prices would lead to increased output. Effort norms would be self-enforced. Perhaps even more important, labour would have an incentive to either perform itself, or ensure that management performed basic coordination tasks such as component delivery and machine maintenance which would allow labour to earn bonuses. According to Martin:

Instead of staff driving the workers for output, the workers drive the staff to supply them with material, and jobs are finished off by virtue of fresh ones pushing them out . . . . The usual driving system is absolutely reversed. The staff, and everybody connected with the company is kept on the jump all the time to keep the man supplied with material, so that he can earn more wages; and I think the greatest advantage of the bonus system is to be found in that very fact.[49]

The Daimler workers were less enthusiastic than Martin about his new institutional strategy. We have already referred to the attempts by the United Kingdom Society of Coachmakers to resist the changes in the labour contract. The new payment system did not have the expected effect on productivity and in 1908 an attempt was made to alter further the conditions of employment. Labour was informed that anyone not earning at least the day rate would be sacked. This prompted a strike which forced the firm to withdraw their threat. But once the workers had gained the initiative, they demanded even larger concessions. They claimed that rate fixers were incompetent, that prices were normally given out after a job was completed, that many jobs did not yield a bonus, and that they were forced to book times below what they had agreed was the minimum fair time. At a shop meeting, it was decided to ask management to remove the Premium Bonus system altogether. In March, the local ASE prepared for an extended strike at the firm and the Allied Trades Federation was called in to coordinate the campaign. Again, a downturn in trade forced labour to postpone any action.[50]

This was the last major attempt by labour to force the withdrawal of the Premium Bonus system prior to World War I. Labour's reluctant acceptance of the system seems to have been a function of two variables. The first was the

Table 7.3 *Employment and bonus levels, Daimler, 1910–13*

	Number employed	Average wage (£)	Bonus as a percentage of average wage
Nov. 1910	3816	1.82	13.5
Jan. 1911	4285	1.85	21.7
Apr. 1911	3868	1.79	14.7
Jul. 1911	2894	1.53	12.0
Oct. 1911	3150	1.70	13.3
Jan. 1912	3988	1.61	13.3
Apr. 1912	4330	1.96	15.6
Jul. 1912	4374	1.58	11.9
Oct. 1912	4436	1.81	14.1
Jan. 1913	3820	1.72	14.2
Apr. 1913	4165	1.39	23.8
Jun. 1913	3681	1.70	10.9

Source: Daimler, *Board Minutes*, 1910–13

continued growth of non-union labour which by 1910 represented about 55 percent of the workforce.[51] The other factor, shown in Table 7.3, was the regularity and size of bonus earnings which came to represent a significant percentage of final earnings.

Other firms were also moving in the direction of formalising managerial institutions and enhancing managerial control over the production process. Comments on Martin's paper generally supported the attempt to formalise managerial structures and to reduce the authority of both the board of directors and the shop floor workers.[52] J.S. Napier presented a paper to the IAE in 1907 describing the system used at Arrol Johnston. He claimed that his system was intended for use in a repetition factory. The workers worked without drawings, depending upon the jigs, fixtures and special tools to prevent machining errors. Detailed job cards were distributed with each job giving all of the needed information, including the labour and materials to be used. On the same cards, details of actual production times were recorded which provided management with the information needed to keep track of labour productivity and to locate potential areas of cost reductions.[53]

By 1908, Dennis had revamped its managerial structures along similar lines. All work was completely designed before any production began. Each different component had its own index number to simplify cost accounting. All job cards included information on materials, tools and the location of drawings. The system was supposedly designed to reduce the need for workers to make decisions, and to simplify the tasks of the foremen: 'The foremen is left free to look after the men and not worry about matters really outside of his province.'[54] The Premium Bonus system was used with a 50/50 split between the firm and the workers. Dennis collected cost data which was used to keep track of any deviations from average productivity. These deviations were immediately investigated and provided management with new techniques to monitor effort norms.

At Deasy, system and managerial control were also prevalent. Work was put through in batches of 10 to 20 vehicles. Before production could begin, each batch had to be sanctioned by the manager of the sales department. The drawing office was then informed and it sent drawings to the works office where requisition cards, process cards, cost cards and operator tickets were issued. Once work on the batch was begun, the Process department kept track of the rate of progress and insured that the works operated as smoothly as possible.[55]

Argyll, one of the most ambitious of the early British vehicle producers, altered managerial practices as potential output reached 2500 vehicles and employment reached 2000. Their managerial philosophy was based on nineteenth-century British welfarism and foreshadowed the interwar interest in the human factor. A contemporary observer wrote:

Their idea was to make the workman believe that he was as good as any other man, and, with the best tools, and placed in the best circumstances, he would turn out the best work ... every department is well lighted, and well ventilated, while the air of cleanliness that pervades the whole place is one of the most remarkable features of it. The directors evidently believe thoroughly in having their people work under the most advantageous and attractive conditions.[56]

The works itself was located in a palatial building, which was later criticised as being overly ornate. The entire south front facade, 425 feet long, was allocated to worker amenities including separate male and female restrooms, dining halls, recreation halls and a lecture theatre to seat 500. The latter was used for entertainment and plans were in progress to start a series of lectures for the benefit of the workers. A large amount of space was also allocated for costing, planning and ordering offices. Thirty acres of land was allocated for the construction of houses for workmen.[57]

Austin, which would soon become the largest British vehicle producer, resisted the trend toward the growth of formal managerial structures. Austin argued that a motor vehicle had to be made accurately and with high-quality materials. It was better to spend one's money on labour and material rather, 'than to spend a considerable amount on non-productive items'.[58] Austin supported the need for a costing system which could predict costs, but his statements reveal that he was suspicious of Martin's proposals to adopt work study as the method of setting labour times. Austin preferred what Martin termed 'old-fashioned direct observation'. As was the case at Daimler, Austin depended on incentive payment systems to enforce effort norms. However, at Austin's the coordinating mechanism truly was invisible. Labour was simply told that it would be on bonus, but was not told the piece price, nor even the rate of bonus earned. Austin collected information on the bonus rates which the workers were earning and adjusted prices until he felt they were making the correct rate of bonus. Even at this point, the workers were not informed of the piece price, or the bonus rate they had earned: 'The rate of bonus is not known to the men, and in any case they get more than they bargain for, provided they are at all diligent and painstaking with their work.'[59]

Having rejected the formalisation of managerial control, and not yet at a stage where flow production techniques could be used to control effort norms, Austin was forced to depend on the willingness of labour to cooperate in achieving the firm's objectives. Austin, who had long believed in the identity of interest between himself and his workforce, often preached the need for harmony. On one such occasion in 1913 at a works dinner attended by one-fifth of the workforce he argued:

We must be prepared to work harder and scheme more. We must prevent waste of materials and effort, must take advantage of every possible improvement in regard to organisation, equipment and conditions of employment, working harmoniously together inter-departmentally, and individually, all of which goes a long way toward the reduction of useless labour.[60]

For those workers not lucky enough to hear Austin's speech, or for those unconvinced by words, incentive payment systems and the threat of job loss offered concrete reasons to cooperate.

F.H. Royce, of Rolls Royce, also had reservations about formalisation of managerial institutions. Not only was Royce reported to be a poor production engineer, preferring to stop production rather than forego small improvements in product design, it was also suggested that he, 'regarded all administration as superfluous and the increasing size of what was generally, but to Royce accurately, termed the "non-productive" staff at Derby was a source of constant irritation to him'.[61] Royce's potential influence over the emerging managerial class was limited by Claude Johnson, the firm's chief executive officer, who created a special design department for Royce and located it well away from the works. Some of the firm's most productive years occurred with Johnson in charge of production at Derby and Royce ensconced in his villa in France perfecting product design.[62]

Martin and Austin were not alone in seeing incentive payment systems as an aid to enforcing effort norms and as a means of coordinating shop floor operations. In the complex manufacturing operations of the British vehicle producers, managers placed significant emphasis on getting labour to help coordinate factory operations. The veteran vehicle producer, F.W. Lanchester was quick to point out the merit of Martin's concept of 'induction'. He suggested: 'If the men urge the staff the works organization flows like a river, whereas if the staff urge the workers it is more like a pumping system in which you have pumping going on at intervals.'[63]

Recent research on the history of management strategies at Rover confirms the incomplete development of a managerial function in Britain in the early 1900s. At Rover, improvements in cost accounting were slow to materialise. Until 1908, departments were allocated an overall budget, and department supervisors given an incentive to keep costs below that budget, a system which Whipp and Clark have called 'delegated control'. Paper work, a chief mode of communication of the new factory bureaucrats, was kept to a minimum and white collar workers were noticeably absent. In reviewing the minutes of the board of directors, Whipp and Clark concluded that little attention was given to the study of work organisation: 'The economies of coordination are barely mentioned.'[64] Rather than developing managerial institutions for direct control of the production process, Rover employed a system which relied on a system of labour self-regulation, based on 'informal, ideological and cultural forms of authority.'[65]

The dependence on the less visible hand of self-regulation, where many of the tasks associated with coordinating factory affairs and enforcing effort norms were delegated to production workers, suggests that there were serious weaknesses in the British managerial function. At the Detroit Ford plants, effort norms were set by the very visible hand of the new managerial class and enforced through flow production techniques. Labour was neither asked, nor expected, to aid in shop floor coordination and the setting of productivity norms. At Daimler and probably other British vehicle firms, the division of labour and authority between labour and management was less complete. Between 1896 and 1914 a new managerial class began to emerge in Britain. But the managerial function had not evolved to the point where management could dictate effort norms to labour or where it could dispense with labour's cooperation in coordinating shop floor activity. Martin was forced to adapt his strategy to this partial transfer of authority. He used his payment systems not only as a means of encouraging labour to adopt specific effort norms, but also as an aid to factory coordination. Martin theorised that labour's desire to earn bonuses would translate into self-regulation with labour taking an interest in plant maintenance, parts delivery, and the general level of factory efficiency.[66]

In 1914, the British managerial function may simply have been in an early state of transition and all that was needed was a few more years to allow the transfer of authority to be completed. However, time was not on the side of the new British managerial class. The war, which began in 1914, altered the course of managerial evolution and, we will argue, prevented the transfer of authority from being completed. The continued dependence of British employers on British labour to monitor and enforce effort norms and to help coordinate factory operations became a long-run feature of British mass production.

The impact of new technology on the effort bargain

How successful were these changes in production techniques and production institutions in increasing productivity and generating profits? It is difficult to

Table 7.4. *Man-hours per vehicle: British
motor vehicle industry, 1902–13*

Firm	Year	Man-hours per vehicle
Wolseley	1902	5400
Thornycroft	1902	4860
Humber	1902	2700
Belsize	1903	3780
Austin	1905	5000
Daimler	1906	3780–4320
Argyll	1906	1080–1620
Crossley	1908	2268
Daimler	1909	4572
Clement Talbot	1909	1458–1782
Wolseley	1912	3240
Belsize	1912	1023
Daimler	1913	2700
Rover	1913	1620
Wolseley	1913	2862

Sources: The above data was obtained mainly from
figures provided in various contemporary journals and
from S.B. Saul, 'The motor industry in Britain to 1914'
(*Business History*, 5, 1962). See also C.R.F. Engelbach,
'Some notes on re-organising a works to increase production' (*Proceedings Institute of Automobile Engineers*, 12,
1927/28), p. 497.

accurately quantify the productivity impact of the changes we have discussed
because information on output levels, labour inputs, the capital–labour ratio, the
type of product manufactured, and the amount of the product made by each firm
is not readily available. In an attempt to compare British and American
productivity, Saul did hazard a guess, but was careful to note its impressionistic
nature. He concluded that British firms performed poorly in comparison with
American firms such as Ford. Unfortunately, Saul chose firms which our
detailed research suggests cannot be compared without major corrections to the
data. In choosing the Ford Motor Company of 1903 as a reference point, Saul
picked a firm which did little more than attach wheels and affix a name plate onto
a bought out chassis. The early Ford vehicles were, for the most part,
manufactured by Dodge. On the other hand, Argyll and Albion, like most
British firms, manufactured almost the entire vehicle. Comparisons of such
different production methods is likely to be seriously misleading.[67]

By drawing on the data found in contemporary journals, productivity
measures discussed during union and management negotiations, and from
archival records for firms such as Daimler and Rover, a better estimate is
possible. The data provided by these sources is still far from complete. For data
on American firms, we have relied on the detailed cost records kept by Ford, and
on the productivity records of Franklin which produced a more expensive car

Table 7.5. *Man-hours per vehicle: United States vehicle industry: 1906–14*

Year	Franklin	Ford
1906	—	1210
1908	1836	—
1910	1674	—
1912	1242	—
1913	—	206
1914	918	83.5

Notes: attempts to compare Ford productivity with the productivity of other firms is most problematical because Ford depended upon outside suppliers for many of his components. The estimates presented here impose British levels of bought out components on the Ford production data found in Table 3.4.
Sources: on Franklin see G. Babcock, *The Taylor System in Franklin Management* (New York, 1917), Chart 1: On Ford see Table 3.4.

than Ford. Tables 7.4 and 7.5 provide the basic data on labour productivity levels during the prewar period.

This data needs to be treated with caution as we have been unable to correct fully for two important sources of measurement error namely differences in the type of vehicle and differences in the amount of vehicle which firms produced at different times. If we had been able to correct for these errors we would almost certainly have found an improvement in British productivity relative to American productivity. This is due to the fact that British firms tended to produce more of the vehicle than did most American producers. On average, bought out components represented about 50 percent of British costs compared with between 75 and 90 percent at Ford. No direct data is available for Franklin, but based on descriptions of their production process and the types of components that they manufactured, it is likely that they used a proportion of bought out components similar to that found in British factories. The other data problem is changes in the type of vehicle produced, which influenced the amount of labour needed in production. There are strong reasons to believe, especially after 1912, that British producers moved to a cheaper type of product requiring less labour to produce. This means that our figures likely overstate the extent to which labour productivity increased.

From Tables 7.4 and 7.5, we can conclude that British producers were able to double labour productivity between 1903 and 1913. The number of man-hours required fell from a range of 3000 to 5000 hours to between 1000 to 3000 in 1913. If one accepts contemporary reports which claim that the shift to incentive payment systems increased output by between 30 and 100 percent and if one

Table 7.6. *Production costs, 1912, Rover and Ford Model T*

Vehicle	Selling price	Wages	Material	Overhead	Value added per unit of wages paid
Rover (£)	331	62/16/4	115/19/1	49/0/5	3.42
Ford (1913) ($)	550	17.39	184.72	23.13	21.04
Ford (1915) ($)	440	18.70	186.62	24.93	13.55
Ford (1917) ($)	360	37.05	203.73	55.61	4.24

Sources: for Rover see, Pollitt Notebooks (London), p2/2/5/9, *Rover*; For Ford see, Table 3.4.

adds the likely impact of closer managerial supervision as labour's monopoly of production knowledge eroded, it is entirely plausible that half of these productivity increases were the result of shifts in effort norms.[68] Relative to the two American firms, British productivity improvements compare favourably with Franklin, but are less spectacular than those at Ford. It is highly unlikely that correction of data errors would change this basic picture.

Simply looking at labour productivity levels, as was done above, produces useful comparisons of labour output in different environments, but says little about the efficiency of a managerial strategy. A managerial strategy needs to be judged, not according to the physical output per hour of labour, but rather by the physical output per unit of wages paid. For the profit maximising firm, it is the second measure, output per unit of wages, that is important. A high labour productivity strategy which is won only at the expense of very high wages may prove less profitable than a low productivity and low wage strategy.

Value added per unit of wages paid is one indicator of relative effort bargains. Data for Ford and Rover are provided in Table 7.6. By subtracting the cost of materials bought out from each firm's selling price, a simple estimate of the effort bargain is produced. The table suggests that Ford had a large advantage in the prewar period but that advantage quickly disappeared. Part of Ford's advantage can be explained by the higher level of capital investment at the Ford plant where approximately $490 per worker was invested in machinery in 1912 compared with about $350 at Rover.[69] But the rapid decline in value added per unit of wages also suggests that in the early period the price of Ford cars may have been artificially inflated by Ford's near monopoly position.

By using the productivity data in Table 7.4 and data available on wage rates we can construct an estimate of the labour cost of manufacturing motor vehicles. The labour cost per vehicle can be interpreted as a crude measure of the effort bargain. Changes in labour cost per vehicle reflect both changes in the effort bargain and changes in the effort needed to produce a vehicle. There is no way to separate out these two effects with the available data, although impressionistic data suggests that as much as half of the change in labour hours per vehicle was

Table 7.7. *The effort bargain, 1902–14 (£ of wages per vehicle)*

Firm	1902/03	1906	1912/13	1914
Daimler	—	133	90	—
Wolseley	180	—	108	—
Belsize	126	—	34	—
Rover	—	—	62	—
Franklin ($)	—	—	341	275
Ford ($)	—	—	52	49

Sources: Tables 7.4 & 7.5.

Table 7.8. *Relative yields on ordinary shares, 1905–13 (yield per annum)*

Year	British shares (1)	Non-British shares (2)	British motor vehicle shares (3)
1905	5.7	20.9	94.1
1906	1.8	5.8	48.7
1907	− 4.8	− 10.7	− 50.0
1908	− 0.6	16.4	− 28.3
1909	2.4	10.4	40.7
1910	10.6	3.2	58.4
1911	8.5	5.4	19.2
1912	2.5	2.3	32.5
1913	5.2	− 5.1	24.3

Sources: Columns (1) and (2): M. Edelstein, 'Realized rates of return on UK home and overseas portfolio investment' (*Explorations in Economic History* 13, 1976), pp. 326–7. Column (3): W. Lewchuk, 'The return to capital in the British motor vehicle industry' (*Business History*, 23, 1985), p. 15.

due to increased effort norms. Table 7.7 suggests that after taking into account the higher wage rate in the United States, the advantage of the American producers is significantly reduced.

The final measure of economic performance is the return to capital. Table 7.8 provides various measures of the yields on ordinary share capital. It is obvious that British motor vehicle firms enjoyed a relatively high rate of return on capital in all years except the depressed years of 1907 and 1908. Direct comparison with American motor vehicle firms is difficult because few were able to raise capital publicly prior to 1914. The return to capital at Fords was very high. Between 1903 and 1914 Ford earned over 82 million dollars in profits, or nearly eight million per year, of which nearly one-half was distributed as dividends. This return was the product of an initial investment of $100 000 in 1903 after which all remaining capital came from retained earnings.[70] No British firm, nor very many American firms, if any, had such a high return to invested capital.

We can conclude that British firms were profitable prior to 1914, that they enjoyed a significant rate of productivity growth, and that their performance was comparable to most British and American firms other than Ford. Saul was broadly correct in saying that British firms were less productive than Ford, however the extent of that difference is reduced once one takes into account the fact that Ford was an assembler of bought out parts and that most British firms were manufacturers. On the eve of World War I, the British motor vehicle industry had adopted many of the production techniques of the American system and had begun the transfer of authority from labour to a new managerial class. There were indications that the industry was headed along the same path followed by Ford. The experiences of the war would change this course of evolution.

Fordism and the British system of mass production, 1914–1930

World War I placed new pressures on British employers and British workers. The economic conflict between the buyers and sellers of labour time was complicated by the call of nationalism. The demand for munitions created the urgent need for a speedy resolution of the transfer of authority to the new managerial class. In this hothouse environment labour made major concessions, but we would argue that the transfer of authority remained incomplete. As was shown in Chapter 5, labour forced the state and British employers to recognise its right to a degree of shop floor democracy within the new institutional framework. Many British capitalists held the opinion that unless some concessions were made to labour, the future of British capitalism was bleak.

While employers in the British vehicle industry searched for a solution to the managerial crisis and to demands by labour for a sharing of authority on the shop floor, the Ford Motor Company in Detroit was progressing from triumph to triumph. In early 1914 the wages paid to labour in Britain and the United States were doubled. In the United States the prices of the Model T fell 26.5 percent between 1914 and 1916.[1] Fordism had become an internationally discussed and, for the most part, admired system of production.

We will begin this chapter by piecing together the fragments of information available on the transfer of Fordism to Ford's Manchester plant.[2] We will be concerned with how British labour reacted to the new technology and whether the production system was as productive in Britain as it was in the United States. We will then examine the strategies of a number of different British firms. Their varied experiences reflect the richness of institutional history. Taken together, they indicate that British employers were forced to respond to labour's demands for a share of authority on the shop floor. The direct labour control of Fordism was rejected and in its place the British system of mass production was adopted.

Fordism and the Ford Motor Company in Britain

In Chapter 3, we examined the evolution of Fordism at Ford's Detroit plants. The central elements of the new production system were the erosion of labour's control over production decisions and the direct managerial control of effort norms through close supervision and machine pacing. A similar production system was introduced at Ford's Manchester factory between 1912 and 1914. In fact, it is likely that Ford's Detroit strategy was influenced by events in Manchester during 1912 and 1913.

Neither the Ford Model A introduced in 1903, nor the Model N introduced in 1906 were very successful in the British market. The Model T, introduced in small numbers in 1909, was a success and it soon became obvious that the British market could support its own Ford factory. The new plant began operations in October of 1911, assembling knocked-down kits sent from Detroit. The first report of the new factory in 1912 indicates that 200 workers were assembling 25 '4 seater' chassis per day. As a concession to local custom and practice, labour was paid on the piecework system, but before the year was out the shops were put on day rates. It was reported that labour earned slightly more than the local average. Chassis were assembled on stationary stands, as was the practice in Detroit at the time. The frames, as they were unpacked, were placed on trestles. Gangs of four men moved along the line of seven to nine chassis doing their particular job. Once the chassis was completed, it was pushed to a second stationary line where the body was added and the final assembly was completed. In 1912, 263 workers produced 3187 vehicles. By 1914, employment had risen to 1504 and output to 8352, making Ford a large producer but a relatively small employer.[3]

Originally, the Manchester works was exclusively an assembly operation with all of the manufacturing being done in Detroit. During 1912, manufacturing operations were gradually introduced, beginning with components which were difficult to transport such as bodies, petrol tanks, radiators, and exhaust pipes. The workers hired for these new shops were informed that working conditions would be radically different from other Manchester shops: 'When a new employee was engaged, it was explained to him that he was taken on as a handyman and not as a tradesman. This enabled a man to be transferred from one job to another without conflict with the terms of employment.'[4]

A description of production methods in 1915 confirms that most tasks were unskilled, even in the body shop, one of the strongholds of the European system. It was reported:

All parts are machine cut to templates and jigs, and little indeed is left to be done by hand, except actual putting together. The processes in the department of this factory are almost automatic, little being left for hand work beyond the insertion of screws.[5]

One Ford employee recalled how the average worker could be trained to do most Ford jobs in 5 or 10 minutes.[6] Machine moulds were used in the upholstery section to eliminate hand stuffing and to simplify the sewing of seats. Metal presses were used to shape body panels making panel beaters unnecessary, and a crude system of paint spraying had eliminated the skilled brush painter. Petrol tanks were completely machine made except for tinning which remained a hand operation.[7]

Resistance to these new methods of production came mainly from the trades directly threatened: the coachmakers, the sheet metal workers and the tinsmiths. Sporadic strikes began in 1912 leading to a major confrontation in 1913 which closed the body shop for 22 weeks.[8] The officials of the United Kingdom Society of Coachmakers (UKS) argued that they were striking against a pernicious system known as the 'American system', a system which attempted to ignore trade unions.[9] Unlike earlier conflicts at COW and at Crossley, the Ford strike received the official support from the executive of the ASE and the Manchester and Salford Trades Councils. However, the support from the union officials did not translate into support at the rank and file level. Shop floor union representatives were reluctant to call out their members, and when they did the call was often ignored by the workers involved. There was widespread concern that, because Ford work required little skill, they would simply replace strikers from the ranks of the unemployed. The general reluctance of the Ford workers to support the strike prevented its spread from the body shop where it began. The chassis shop continued to produce cars during the strike with bodies imported from Detroit.

The experiences of the Joiners Union during the strike typify the inherent weakness of labour opposition to the Fordist system in Manchester. There were a number of occasions when the sheet metal workers struck, and the Joiners Union instructed its members, who did similar work, to support the strike. Many joiners refused to obey the union directive and, on one occasion, they sent a committee to the union headquarters to argue their case. The executive took a dim view of this rank and file action and forced the protesting joiners to resign from the union. Ford was quick to exploit such weaknesses in labour ranks and offered the expelled joiners regular employment as long as their behaviour was 'satisfactory'.[10]

Wages were allowed to rise during the strike and the year following the strike. Wilkins and Hill concluded that: 'By assuring strategically placed workers both job security and high wages he [Sorensen] broke the union power at Ford Manchester and ended the dispute. . . . The unionism which has always been cropping up heretofore has been absolutely broken up.'[11] It was not just the skilled worker who benefited from this wage policy. The union officials in the body plant pointed to high Ford wages as a major impediment to their attempts to reform the system.[12] In 1911, the minimum wage, which many unskilled assemblers received, was set at 5d per hour, rising to 6d in 1912. In September of 1913, the minimum was raised to 10d per hour, and in April of 1914, a 5d per hour profit sharing bonus was granted.[13] All but the last increase occurred before Ford revolutionised the wages paid to Ford workers in Detroit with the announcement of the Five Dollar Day in January of 1914.

It may very well have been P. Perry, the British manager, who first suggested

Table 8.1. *Weekly earnings Ford (UK) and other British vehicle plants (£)*

Year	Ford (UK) minimum (1)			Average British motor factory (2)	Morris Motors (3)	Austin (4)
1914	2.94			1.89		
1917	3.33			3.25		
1919	4.90			3.75	2.95	
1920	6.07			4.43		
1925	7.05	6.75	6.46	4.10		
1928	7.44	7.32	6.46	3.90	4.30	4.00
1932	5.29	4.01	3.23	3.80		

Notes: beginning in 1925, Ford introduced a three grade system of wages. No data was available to indicate how many workers were in each grade. The 1928 Morris figure is the rate paid the previous year. The 1928 Austin figure is the rate paid in 1929.
In column (2), the wage figures between 1914 and 1920 are for skilled fitters and turners on day work. Wage figures from 1925 to 1932 are for pieceworkers in EEF shops.
Sources: Wage rates for the Ford Motor Company were provided by Mr D.L.Greenbaum, Ford Motor Company; Column (2) EEF wage data; Column (3) 'Light motor car' (*Machinery*, 20 October 1927); Column (4), R.Church, *Herbert Austin* (London, 1979), p. 150.

to Ford that higher wages might resolve some of Ford's labour relations problems.[14] Perry had been critical of the wages paid in the Manchester area in 1911 and considered the going wage of $4\frac{1}{2}$ d per hour a starvation wage. However, he did little about the problem until the wave of strikes began in 1912. Perry's views on labour policies were influenced by the prewar labour crisis in Britain. When Ford visited Britain in 1912 he had long talks with Perry, who indicated that British management had come to accept British labour's demands for a say in shop floor decisions. It has been reported that:

[Ford] listened sympathetically to Perry's explanation of the differences between the idiosyncrasies of Detroit and Manchester workers, between the ultra-conservative capitalism of American industry and the growing democratic approach in England born of Lloyd George's Limehouse campaign.[15]

The coachmakers strike ended after 22 weeks. The unions were dealt a major defeat. The final settlement stipulated that Ford would not re-employ any of the strikers, and that all black-legs employed during the strike would be kept on. Ford's British plants remained virtually union free until 1944 when Bevin, as Minister of Labour, forced the firm to accept unions.[16] The ability of Ford to keep union influence at bay in his shops was the product of two factors. Ford maintained a hostile attitude toward trade unions which made life difficult for trade union sympathisers and trade union organisers.[17] The influence of trade unions was also limited by the company's willingness, until the early 1930s, to pay above the going rate for labour as shown in Table 8.1.

Actual Ford earnings were less than the minimum shown above, as workers lost time and earnings whenever there was a machine breakdown or a shortage of material. When the line stopped, it was not unusual for the workers to be put on lay-off for a couple of hours. They would congregate in the tea-houses across the road from the plant and when the problem in the plant was corrected, the foreman would know exactly where to go to get the workers to resume production.[18] Despite these interruptions, wages were still high enough to make Ford jobs desirable. One worker recounted: 'I have been in there at eight o'clock in the morning crying because I could not get my quota done. We were all fighting one another to keep a job.' Another former worker recalled that the high wages made competition between workers fierce, 'Competition for a job anywhere was keen. For a highly paid job at Ford it was cut throat.'[19]

Having resolved the transfer of authority to the new managerial class by late 1913, the firm moved to alter the production process. The first powered assembly line was installed in Manchester in September of 1914, about nine months after the first line was installed in Detroit. At first, only the chassis section was mechanised. The body line and the final assembly line remained hand powered. The chassis line was 114 feet long. The frames were loaded onto buggies and dragged along the line, taking between 50 and 90 minutes to complete the entire journey. The chassis line held about ten vehicles, while the body and finish line held about eight more. The line was designed for an hourly output of between 7 and 21 chassis. Task lengths ranged between 3 and 9 minutes, somewhat longer than the average on the Detroit lines.[20] No records of early manning levels, comparable to the Arnold and Faurote studies have been found.

As had been the case in Detroit, the Ford Manchester workers accepted tight managerial control of effort norms enforced through strict supervision and line pacing. A Ford line worker in the 1930s recalled:

Discipline was very strong ... if you didn't do your job properly and for example, keep up with the line as they used to say, you would obviously lose the job ... jobs weren't easy to come by in those days, and so most people were glad to work hard to keep their jobs.[21]

The same worker recalled that occasionally the foreman would speed up the line toward the end of the day to make up for any production shortfalls.[22] This willingness to let management control line speeds can be contrasted with similar events at Standard in the 1930s. A Standard worker recalled:

One day the foreman came along and he thought he'd ... get a little bit extra off. ... At the end of the day we found we'd done about four cars too many. So then everybody stopped until the track ... speed was put back again.[23]

Standard workers thereafter monitored the speed of the line by drawing chalk marks on the floor and keeping watch of how long it took a chassis to move between the marks.

There is no indication that labour productivity was unsatisfactory in these early years. A representative from Detroit who visited the factory indicated that

Table 8.2. *Output and productivity levels, Ford Manchester*

	Total output (1)	Employment (2)	Labour weeks per vehicle (3)
1912	3187	263	4.10
1913	7310	814	5.60
1914	8352	1504	9.00

Notes: employment figures include both sales and production staff.
In 1911, Ford employed 69 staff to administer UK sales.
Sources: Employment-*Ford Times*, June 1914; Output-L'Estrange
Fawcett, *Wheels of Fortune* (unpublished, Ford Archive, (Warley)).

Table 8.3. *Cost of Manchester touring car 1916 (£)*

	Material	Labour	Overhead	Labour (hours)
Chassis imported	61.72	—	—	—
Chassis Manchester	3.16	1.86	2.37	29.94
Body imported	4.22	—	—	—
Body Manchester	5.79	2.83	3.64	45.40
Total	74.90	4.70	6.01	75.34

Notes: to calculate labour hours, it was assumed that all workers were paid the standard hourly rate of
15d per hour.
Sources: Ford Archive (Warley), *Ford Cost Summaries*, November 1916.

the unskilled British workers were more productive than the American unskilled
workers, but that the skilled workers in Manchester were less productive than
their American counterparts. This was attributed to the smaller amount of
capital equipment the British skilled workers were given to use.[24] Tables 8.2 and
8.3 present the limited information we have on production costs and productivity levels at Manchester. They provide only a rough indication of labour
productivity as it must be remembered that the Manchester shop was mainly an
assembly shop prior to 1914 and that the amount of manufacturing activity was
slowly being increased which we suspect explains the apparent fall in labour
productivity shown in Table 8.2. Table 8.3 does suggest that the value added per
unit of wages paid in Manchester was comparable to what Ford achieved in
Detroit. Using the 1915 Model T selling price of £125, value added per unit of
wages paid was 10.65. In Detroit value added per unit of wages was 13.5 in 1914,
falling to 7.01 in 1916.[25]

By mid 1914, Ford had successfully transferred his American technology to
Britain. Labour authority over shop floor decisions had been checked and the
plant had been shifted to a high wage/high effort bargain. The Ford experiments

were keenly discussed in the journals and newspapers in America and Europe. To many workers, managers and politicians in Russia, Germany, Italy and France, Fordism was seen as the solution to their political and economic problems in the postwar period.[26] As was shown in Chapter 5, British management remained skeptical of the ability of American methods to resolve British problems. In the remainder of this chapter we will try to show how and why a different set of production institutions emerged in Britain.

World War I and British production methods

It is often argued that the war forced British firms to adopt the production techniques of the American system. This may have been true for many industries, but the effect on vehicle makers was probably less spectacular. By 1914, the larger British vehicle makers already had extensive experience with the American practices of interchangeability and production with less skilled workers. When the general engineering shops, which had been slower in accepting the new technology, began to convert during the war they turned to the vehicle firms for advice.[27] The potential for vehicle makers to benefit from their wartime experiences was also somewhat limited by the products they were asked to make. Many vehicle makers shifted to aero work which did not offer production runs much longer than those found in the larger prewar vehicle shops.[28] The firms that shifted to other types of munitions did enjoy significantly longer product runs which must have provided valuable experience. But, as Austin was to find out, the techniques employed to produce standardised shells could not easily be transferred to the production of the vastly more complex motor vehicle.

The war also presented new barriers to firms trying to invest in new production techniques. There was great uncertainty as to how long the war would last which made it risky to invest in new production technology which might be uneconomical after the war. Labour was also better organised during the war and offered strong resistance to changes which affected working conditions. Employers also faced the problem of where to get capital for the new machines and how to get permission to import them from America which continued to be the only supplier for many types of machinery. There were showcase factories, such as Austin's new shell works at Longbridge where large amounts of new machinery were employed, but most firms had to make do with the existing stock of machinery. Many simply fitted their existing general purpose machines with new and relatively inexpensive jigs and fixtures. On long runs of shells or other war material, these machines could be continuously employed on a limited range of tasks, as if they were special purpose machines.[29] As late as 1917, many munitions jobs were still being done on standard and general purpose machines set to do a single task. More, in a recent examination of changes in the skill content of work, has argued that the war resulted in a revolution in how machines were employed as distinct from the type of machine employed.[30] If there was any lesson to be learned from the war, it was that long runs allowed one to move away from complex automatic multi-task machines with long time cycles to simple machines designed for a limited range of tasks.[31]

While the war had a limited impact on the production techniques used by vehicle makers, it did stimulate the search for a new institutional framework to regulate the relations between labour and the emerging managerial class. As had been the case before the war, there continued to be calls for strengthening the new managerial class's control over the production process. Pomeroy, the manager of the Vauxhall factory, argued that the desired managerial control could be had by increasing the authority of the draughting office. However, despite the increase in managerial authority, Pomeroy was unwilling to suggest that labour be placed on day wages or that management should take direct control of enforcing effort norms. In fact, Pomeroy and many of his colleagues viewed day rate payment systems as outdated and obsolete. Incentive payments were seen as indispensable aids in enforcing effort norms and coordinating factory affairs.[32]

Other leading managers debated the merits of American management systems. A.W. Reeves, the chief draughtsman at Crossley argued:

An important factor to the author's mind, and one which appears to be entirely ignored in the wonderful systems originating on the other side of the Atlantic, and among many idealists on this side, is that of the personal or human element. Anyone with any knowledge of the independent and, it must be confessed, awkward spirit, characterising the workers of say the Northern Midlands, would hesitate before applying the extreme methods of the latest American Scientific Management, well knowing the futility of the task.[33]

T.C. Pullinger, whom we have already met as manager of the Humber works, had taken the position of managing director at Arrol Johnston. He also argued that Scientific Management and Fordism were impractical given the attitudes of British workers. Instead he suggested:

Our operatives must have instilled into them the idea that their work is an art, and that it is a high privilege to be able to operate machine tools, and produce beautifully finished interchangeable parts. ... A great deal more efficiency and interest can be obtained from employees if those in charge treat them in a kindly and sympathetic manner, taking interest in their work, pointing out to them the directions in which they can improve, and giving them a word of encouragement.[34]

C.S. Bayley had the following to say about American techniques while commenting on a paper at the Institution of Automobile Engineers:

In America, I understand, the labour available is much more amenable to systematised working. In England there is difficulty in getting a man to do exactly what he is told, because he is apt to think a great deal more for himself than do his fellows in America. Therefore, a system in this country has to be more elastic and less precise than many American systems are said to be.[35]

Perry Keene, from the Austin costing office referred to American production systems as 'herd systems'. He wrote:

In America you have to employ methods which a crowd can carry out, but the British individual will not have that. The Americans have come over here and tried to make bicycles and boots and all sorts of things in the last 50 years, but they have without exception failed because the Britisher will not have 'herd' methods. He has the individualistic tendency, and it is a British tendency that you have to allow for.[36]

The experiences of the war seem to have hardened British managerial attitudes toward Fordism and American managerial institutions. Each of the above statements viewed British workers as having different characteristics than American workers. Each argued that British workers could not be expected to accept the authoritarian and undemocratic practices of the Americans. The British worker had to be given a degree of freedom to control and influence conditions on the shop floor, reminiscent of the craft worker of the previous century. British management seems to have accepted, even in shops where the production techniques of the American system were installed, that the limit to its authority was greater than was the case in the United States.

This self-imposed limit to managerial authority was nowhere clearer than in Coventry when negotiations began for a return to private work and at Rolls-Royce which planned to mass produce their high-class product in 1919. The Coventry case is particularly interesting in that British management rejected an offer which would have forced it along the route followed by Henry Ford. The managerial strategies of Rolls-Royce and the Coventry employers foreshadowed the path of institutional development which the British motor vehicle industry would follow for the next 50 years.

The Humber agreement and the rejection of direct control in Coventry

Strengthened by their wartime experiences, the Coventry unions, and particularly the ASE, demanded major changes in the postwar negotiations. We have discussed these in some detail in previous chapters. Our interest here is solely with demands to change the payment system. A committee was created by the ASE in early 1918 to discuss postwar strategy. In March, this committee proposed that all systems of piecework and premium bonus be stopped and that there be a general return to day work. In April, the idea was presented to the National Executive. The idea was also raised at a conference of District Committees representing the Midlands area. This conference agreed that all individual piecework systems should be replaced by collective piecework systems as a prelude to a full scale return to day work. The issue came to a head in late 1918 when Humber wanted to return to prewar work. The ASE boycotted all piecework and placed its workers on day work.[37]

During negotiations with the employers, three methods of payment were proposed by the unions. Labour could continue to be paid by the piece on the basis of either old prices and a recognised bonus level of 100 percent or, alternatively, new higher prices and a lower recognised bonus level. The unions also proposed a third option of moving to day work at a rate of 3/- per hour. While the unions favoured day work, the employers thought it was the least attractive proposal.

The Coventry employers objection to day work was that they could not trust the workers to produce at the level they were promising. Their experience with the Munitions of War Act and the rise of powerful shop steward committees had convinced them that labour would not accept unilateral managerial control of effort norms or managerial control of decision making on the shop floor. To them, the proposed shift to day work involved an agreement to pay higher wages and unenforceable labour promises to work harder to earn those wages. In December of 1918, in response to union requests to shift to a fixed day rate payment system, G.H. Henson from Daimler replied: 'We might... ask what guarantee there will be on your side of no restrictions on output in the future?'[38] Again in March, the same issue came up and Henson replied: 'If we were to consider any such scheme, does it carry with it the guarantee we have asked for from your side to thoroughly urge your men to go for it all they can?'[39] Perhaps what is most revealing about these conferences is that management could not see any way to enforce the desired effort levels without the aid of incentive payment systems. At no time was the possibility raised of moving to day work at an hourly rate less than labour requested. The obvious sticking point was not the price of labour time but, rather, the price of labour effort with different payment systems.

A bargain was reached in which it was agreed to continue working piecework but with higher recognised bonus levels than before the war. The final agreement, which became known as the Humber Agreement, provided for a base rate of 45/- per week and a recognised bonus level of 50 percent. Had the Coventry employers accepted day work at this time, they would have been forced to shore up the managerial function, particularly in the areas of coordination of the production process and the monitoring and enforcing of effort levels. It is likely that they would have moved in the direction of machine pacing and direct control of effort norms along Fordist lines. Instead, management chose to control the ratio of wages to effort, leaving labour some flexibility in setting effort norms.[40] With this strategy, management could exploit the cash nexus to shift onto labour some of the responsibility for making sure that the plant ran smoothly. The Coventry employers had adopted a strategy which would later be advocated by Howe, the chairman of the Higher Productivity Council and which was referred to in Chapter 5. Both saw incentive payment systems as giving labour the control it had demanded during the war without endangering the profitability of capitalism.[41] In the short-run, as long as capital–labour ratios remained low and labour organisations were too weak to challenge managerial control of the price setting process, the strategy worked.

Rolls-Royce and management by consent

A somewhat different strategy was adopted by Rolls-Royce, which also tried to deal with the postwar managerial crisis by granting labour a degree of industrial democracy. Even before the war, management at Rolls-Royce had been keenly aware of British labour's dissatisfaction with the existing economic organisation. C.Johnson, the managing director, went as far as to suggest in 1910, that a duplicate plant should be set up in France in case the Derby works had to be closed due to strikes or socialistic legislation or war.[42] As early as 1911, concessions had been made to labour demands for a say over shop floor conditions by recognising a shop steward committee. As the war ended, management indicated its intention to resume weekly production of 135 high class vehicles along mass production lines.

Rolls-Royce had seen its employment increase four-fold during the war to around 8000. The work had been put on a repetition basis by extensive use of jigs and fixtures. The days when Rolls-Royce employed only craft workers were over and even management had to admit that the majority of workers were engaged in dull, boring and monotonous work. The postwar production process was to be simplified further and, where possible, divided into even smaller tasks suitable for even less skilled workers. Interchangeability was to be achieved by fitting new jigs and fixtures to the firm's stock of standard machines. A description of the plant in 1921 indicated that interchangeability was widely practised and that the firm had made its motto, 'Organise and Specialise'.[43]

Wormald, the works manager, continued the company's tradition of sensitivity to the problems generated by conflicts between labour and management. He argued that his plans to mass produce cars were unlikely to work without, 'a contented workforce willing to cooperate'.[44] To this end, the shop stewards were consulted and offered a role in the postwar institutional framework. A Select Committee of design and production engineers was made responsible for implementing the changes. The work process was analysed to determine the best way of doing a task and labour was given an opportunity to comment on management's proposals. Working in conjuction with the Select Committee was an Efficiency Committee composed originally of foremen but with labour representatives after 1921. This committee was made responsible for keeping a check on speeds and feeds, jigs, and tools. Ultimately it became a pricing committee.[45] Wormald's willingness to grant a degree of control to shop floor workers soon brought criticisms from shop floor supervisors. They complained:

Continually for some time past, the Shop Stewards movement, as it is now constituted at Rolls-Royce is a direct menace against discipline and management, and the whole of the Supervisors of Rolls-Royce have decided that it is impossible to carry on, unless they are allowed to supervise their jobs without this tyrannical treatment meted out by the Shop Stewards.[46]

C. Johnson wanted to extend these experiments in industrial democracy to democratic ownership of the company's capital. In 1918, he proposed that the firm should allocate 200 000 ordinary shares to the workers (one-quarter of the total issued shares). He also suggested that the workers should elect two representatives to sit on the board of directors. These radical proposals did not sit well with the other directors who thought Johnson was trying to resolve a social crisis which was really the responsibility of the state.[47] The board rejected Johnson's proposals and instead encouraged workers to buy shares on an installment plan, a strategy which was not overly successful. One of the direct results of Johnson's suggestions was the creation of a welfare fund which received a share of the firm's profits and which provided a wide range of activities.

On paper, management presented the Rolls-Royce system as a workers' utopia in which an enlightened management benefited through the increased productivity of contented workers. In reality, the system fell well short of the ideal. The company continued to employ many less skilled workers in the lower wage brackets. In 1920, the unions prevented the firm from using the introduction of new machine systems as an excuse to increase the number of low paid workers. In the same year there was a strike over the sacking of a man. Negotiations between the two sides indicated that sacking was a common form of labour discipline.[48]

The extension of industrial democracy at the firm was in many cases little more than window dressing. The basic strategy the company was to take in the postwar period was largely decided before the stewards were consulted. The shift to mass production in 1919 was accompanied by a tightening of managerial control over many aspects of the production process. Decisions regarding how long a job should take, which machine a job should be done on, and by which operator, were for the most part determined in offices separated from the work place. A cost department was employed to collect information on productivity. The control department was responsible for keeping track of material in hand, material needed and inventories of finished parts. This was all done with the aid of what was known as the Progress Board.[49] The company was looking not so much for labour participation in decision making as much as for labour consent. The fact that Rolls-Royce had even felt it necessary to respond to labour's demand for industrial democracy suggests that the wartime unrest had had an influence on managerial thinking.

Vauxhall and the movement toward direct control

Both the Coventry employers and Rolls-Royce formulated their managerial strategies at the height of labour unrest in 1918 and 1919. Vauxhall was one of the first British firms to change strategies after the collapse of the vehicle market in 1921. Vauxhall was a relatively small producer of higher grade vehicles. As late as

1925 their weekly output was only 25–30 vehicles and they employed less than 2000 workers. As was the case with many other British firms, Vauxhall's leading managers in 1914 saw the labour crisis as a critical barrier to economical production in Britain and incentive payment systems as the best way of getting labour to work at a satisfactory pace. L. H. Pomeroy, who had designed many of Vauxhall's prewar models, argued that efficient production in Britain rested on, 'above all the securing of his [labour's] implicit faith and trust in the class by whom he is employed'. This trust could not be had on the day rate system of payment: 'The payment to all men of a standard rate, irrespective of their production attainment, seems to him to be futile and obsolete.'[50] Pomeroy also advocated increasing the authority of management and reducing labour's involvement in shop floor decisions. The drawing room was to be made the nerve centre of managerial organisation from which all instructions were to be issued and all information on productivity collected.[51]

When Vauxhall returned to private work in 1919, their system of production differed little from that employed in 1914. A shop steward committee, as recognised by the Employers Federation, operated in the plant and competed with management for control of shop floor activity. Hancock complained that production costs were excessive.[52] Labour was paid on the Premium Bonus system and, according to A. J. Hancock the works manager, an excessive amount of skilled labour was employed. Vauxhall's isolation from both the London and the Midland engineering centres, and the company's concentration on more expensive vehicles, seems to have slowed the rate at which unskilled labour replaced skilled workers in the production process. As late as 1921, they continued to use fully rated skilled men on capstan lathes, milling and grinding machines. In Birmingham, semi-skilled labour was used exclusively on capstans, and 75 per cent of the work on milling and grinding machines was done by semi-skilled labour. This cannot be explained by lack of investment in new machines for they had invested heavily in advanced machine tools including a large selection of American tools such as continuous loading grinding and boring machines.[53]

The situation changed drastically when the market for motor vehicles collapsed. Vauxhall, whose least expensive car sold for £1750, was particularly hard hit. The factory was closed for six weeks to allow each of the 6000 jobs to be studied, timed and assigned to a specific and usually lower grade of labour. The incentive wage system was dropped without any consultation with labour. This signalled a change in Vauxhall's managerial strategy. It was claimed that incentive wages were no longer needed as management had taken the responsibility upon itself for determining output levels. Vauxhall withdrew from the Engineering Employers Federation, and disbanded the shop steward committee which it was argued interfered with management.[54] Hancock saw these changes as moving Vauxhall toward repetitive production on a semi-automatic basis.

The change in managerial philosophy toward direct control over labour, was not accompanied by major changes in the organisation of production on the shop floor. Machines continued to be organised along functional lines rather than in departments designed to produce a single component. Chassis were erected on the stationary principle rather than on an assembly line. The failure to shift to flow production was related to the relatively small output of the firm. It was not until 1925, that the first assembly line was installed and even then the firm was producing only 30 vehicles a week and employing 1400 workers. The chassis line was very simple, with nine assembly stations and a task cycle of one hour at each station. The firm had also installed a large amount of special purpose machinery, much of which was used for only a few hours each week. This was justified on the grounds that special purpose machines produced more accurate work than standard machines.[55] Despite these investments, the firm continued to need large amounts of skilled labour. They ran their own trade school which had both a standard apprenticeship programme of five years or more, and a shorter programme of three years to teach labour how to operate machinery.

Little is known about the success of the firm's payment system between 1921 and 1925, but reports indicate that by 1925 the firm had been forced to back off from its policy of fixed wages. But even in 1925, the managers took great care to point out that the firm did not employ piecework. It was claimed that a bonus was paid to each worker based on the worker's quality and quantity performance. The payment system was called an 'efficiency system', with the bonus reflecting the worker's 'whole value' to the firm. Managerial control of effort norms seems to have been relatively tight. All operations were given a real time in which the job was to be done, not a mystical time which included an element of slack to allow labour to earn a bonus. At Vauxhall, labour was not offered the choice of a slower work pace and lower pay. Labour was expected to produce at the task times set by management and: 'Experience shows that in the majority of instances the work is actually done in this time. Where this is not the case, an explanation is required and an investigation made to determine the cause of the discrepancy.'[56]

General Motors had begun assembling Chevrolets in London in 1924, but felt they needed a 'British' base to expand from in the face of growing British nationalism. After an unsuccessful attempt to take over Austin, GM purchased Vauxhall late in 1925.[57] Almost immediately they set out to rearrange the production process and strengthen managerial authority on the shop floor. Even though the Vauxhall managers had advocated the transfer of authority from labour to a new managerial class, statements by Hancock reveal what little progress had been made. Not only did GM raise output from 36 to 130 per week; they also, according to Hancock, took the guesswork out of planning. Hancock was impressed by the degree of preplanning practised by American managers. While in Detroit in 1926, he was exposed to various American methods including the building of a scale model of each factory which was used to plan the lay-out of the machinery, and the production of a 'brochure' which allowed management to predict, before production began, the capacity of a given plant.[58]

By 1928, the machine departments and assembly areas were reorganised along flow lines. The factory was divided into 23 self-contained departments, and each department was arranged so as to produce one component every 20 minutes, giving 130 of the relatively large 20–60 hp models per week. All machines were organised on the line principle, and assembly was done on tracks.[59] Hancock came to see machine pacing as the key to controlling labour effort. He argued that all machines should be organised in lines, and that whenever possible, mechanised tracks should be used to act as 'quantity per hour gauges'.

A change was made to the 'efficiency payment system'. Before the GM takeover, the bonus was based on the individual worker's value to the firm. Under the new flow organisation this was changed to a group bonus system, reflecting the reduced degree of freedom of individual workers. Relative to other British plants, bonus earnings were not high. They rarely exceeded 25 percent and were well below both the EEF rate and the Humber rate.[60]

Despite the GM takeover, Vauxhall retained its British character, in part as a response to GM's perception that the British buying public might resist doing business with an American firm. The board of directors remained entirely British until the 1950s.[61] The most important appointment was C. Bartlett who was made managing director in 1930, a position he held until 1953. According to Holden, Bartlett practised a form of enlightened paternalism in an attempt to create a loyal and contented workforce. Relatively high wages were paid through the group bonus system. A profit sharing scheme was begun in 1935. In 1941, the Management Advisory Committee was established to take up employee grievances. In a number of instances, Bartlett even moved to check the instability of employment generated by the seasonal nature of demand by shifting workers to non-production jobs when output was reduced. Under these conditions, labour was expected to practise a form of 'self-discipline'. Former production employees recalled that workers helped each other out when they got behind in the machine departments, that they disciplined workers who didn't pull their weight within the group, that they made sure group members showed up on time, and that they discouraged members of the group from taking excessively long breaks in the toilet etc.[62] One Vauxhall worker suggested that Bartlett's strategy was to create an environment where 'everybody should cooperate with one another'.

The Vauxhall system was clearly a step closer to Fordism than the strategy of either the Coventry employers or Rolls-Royce. Management had taken greater responsibility upon itself for setting effort norms which allowed the use of a payment system with a relatively low rate of bonus earnings. After the General Motors takeover, there was a reluctance to adopt the American system of direct control without modification. The firm employed a blend of American direct managerial control with a strong element of paternalism. By the 1950s this era was over and a new American managerial broom swept through the works. Most of the elements of paternalism were abandoned, the plant was put on Measured Day Work, and management took a greater role in controlling the operations of the firm.[63] We will return to this transition in the next chapter.

Morris Motors: mass production and early experiments with automation

The history of technical change at the Morris Motors Company is one of the most intriguing of any British firm.[64] Morris did not produce his first car until April of 1913 when he marketed the Morris Oxford at £165. From the start, he intended to mount a British challenge to the Ford invasion of British markets. Like Ford, Morris began as an assembler and it was only after the war that he expanded into manufacturing. Morris was keenly aware of American practices, having visited America in 1914 and having placed an order for engines with the Continental Manufacturing Company.[65] Morris's plans were interrupted by the war and it was not until 1919 that he was able to begin producing the Morris Oxford and Morris Cowley in volume. Even then output growth was cautious. He produced around 2000 vehicles in 1920, 7000 in 1922 and 20 000 in 1923.[66]

Little is known about the early techniques used in Oxford. Before the war, a few hundred workers assembled chassis on the stationary principle. This practice continued for a short period after the war. By the end of 1919 a simple assembly line was installed. It was hand powered and would remain so until 1934.[67] The division of labour was less extensive than at Ford in Detroit. In 1925 task cycles were still 2.6 minutes. The main line was divided into 18 operations, the rear-axle sub-assembly line had 12 operations and the steering assembly had six. As early as 1914, Ford had already divided the main assembly line into 45 different tasks in Detroit.[68]

As output expanded, Morris found it increasingly difficult to buy the volume of components he required from independent firms and so began purchasing his component suppliers. In May of 1923, Morris acquired the Coventry plant of Hotchkiss et Cie. Hotchkiss was originally a French firm which moved from St Denis to Coventry when it appeared that their French plant was going to be overrun by the Germans.[69] During the war, Hotchkiss had been a major producer of munitions. It was also the centre of labour unrest in Coventry during the shop stewards revolt in 1917 and 1918. The plant was managed by H. E. Taylor. Taylor seems to have had a clearer picture than most British managers of the changes in production techniques and production institutions resulting from the transition to the American system. Taylor argued that, with the American system, there were three parties rather than two engaged in the production process. He labelled them capital, administration, and applied labour. He argued that the success of the Americans was not a benevolent spirit of cooperation between labour and capital, which seemed to be the sole objective of many

British managerial strategies. Rather, he attributed American success to the efficiency of administration which allowed labour and capital to enjoy improved standards of living. It was in this administrative area, which we have called the managerial function, that Taylor saw the greatest British weakness.[70]

Taylor supplied a detailed account of how the Hotchkiss works was converted to vehicle production after the war. The 'difficult' workers were isolated on the remaining munitions contracts. The rest of the workforce was put on the new vehicle contracts. At first output was low, 50 engines per week, and managerial control was limited. An incentive payment system was used because, in Taylor's words: 'Some incentive to effort was necessary as the system was not sufficiently advanced to enforce the production required.'[71] Labour was allowed to earn up to 50 percent bonus on a fixed base rate. According to Taylor, the firm also began to actively educate the workforce, or, in his words, engage in 'propaganda', about future plans for expansion and increases in wages. Within a short time, output was raised to 100 per week, machinery was fully jigged and tooled and labour was put on a straight piecework system. By 1922 output was over 200 per week and elements of flow production had been installed. Most of the machine departments were organised sequentially. Components still travelled to a central stores from each department rather than directly to assembly areas which was the practice in more advanced organisations. The engine and the gear boxes were assembled on simple hand powered tracks. Hand fitting had not been completely eliminated as each assembler was still supplied with a vice. Each engine took 188 labour hours to manufacture and assemble. At Ford, where bought out components represented 60 percent of the cost of manufacturing engines, about 20 hours were needed in the early 1920s.[72]

The firm's Coventry plant, which had been at the eye of the wartime labour storm, was remarkably free of labour conflict during the period when the production process was radically transformed and output increased to 2000 per week.[73] Taylor suggested that their ability to avoid labour disputes was based on their policy of allowing wages to increase when new methods were installed. Taylor advocated paying high wages in order to avoid labour unrest and went as far as to link rising wages with social stability. He argued; 'So long as conditions are good and improving, the mass of the people will remain quiescent: should the general trend be stable or backward the mass will ultimately revolt.'[74] Taylor also saw incentive payment systems as necessary only under less advanced applications of the American system. Under advanced forms, where machine pacing was employed, Taylor suggested that fixed day rates were a more attractive payment system.[75]

With the Morris takeover F.G. Woollard was made manager of the plant which was renamed Morris Motors Engine Branch. Woollard was undoubtedly one of the pioneers of continuous production, and began experimenting with 'automation' years before other firms. He had been exposed to the principles of flow production as an apprentice with the London and South Western Railway at Eastleigh. Around 1904, the firm experimented with a simple flow system to assemble coaches. The level of output was low, initially four per week and later six. The coaches moved through a series of assembly stations advancing forward once every seven and one-third hours. From this experience, Woollard became convinced that flow systems could be applied with great benefit even at relatively low levels of output. In 1925, he lectured to the members of the Institute of Automobile Engineers that: 'The processes described hereafter are not aimed at attacking enormous quantities, but are an endeavour to secure continuous flow, so that a relatively small factory may meet the greatest overseas plants on fairly level terms.'[76]

When Woollard took over the plant, output was less than 300 per week. By installing a few machines to balance production and by putting on a second shift, output was raised to 600 in a few weeks. In July they began installing new plant costing £300 000 which increased output to 1200.[77] By a number of accounts, including the chief production engineer from Ford's Detroit plant, the organisation of the Morris engine plant was decades ahead of standard motor vehicle technology and foreshadowed the post-1945 discovery of 'automation'.[78] Woollard introduced two novel machine systems. On the cylinder block line, the Morris Hand Transfer Machine was created. This was simply the normal machines employed in machining cylinder blocks linked together by a series of conveyors. Labour moved the blocks by hand between machines and loaded the blocks by hand into the different fixtures.[79] The 53 work stations were staffed by 22 machine operators and seven inspectors and stock chasers. The machines were all on a four- or eight-minute cycle. The block took 224 minutes to move through the bank of machines and took 116 minutes of labour time. Work was carefully organised on the Hand Transfer Line. Each job was preplanned and then subjected to Time and Motion study to insure maximum productivity.[80]

The experiments with hand transfer were followed by experiments in automated transfer and clamping. Both the flywheel and the gearbox departments were automated in this way. Components were hydraulically moved between machines, hydraulically clamped into the fixtures, and then sequenced by a single control bar, in effect creating one large automatic machine. These early automated systems were not successful and they had to be reorganised on the hand transfer principle. It has been suggested that Morris did not have the volume of output to justify automatic transfer machines, but Woollard himself attributed their failure to weaknesses in hydraulic techniques.[81] Automation would not become a reality until after World War II when it was installed at Ford's new Cleveland engine plant.[82] Between 1923 and 1925, the labour time needed to manufacture and assemble an engine was reduced from 188 hours to 86 hours.[83]

Two factors seem to explain why these experiments were attempted at Morris. The first reason was the lack of space for expansion at the Coventry site, coupled with the demand for engines which had increased from 100 to 2000 per week in less than five years. The second factor was that both Woollard and Taylor approached the problem of monitoring and enforcing the effort bargain differently than many other British managers. They both argued that machine pacing was the ultimate solution to the human factor problem. Regarding the advantages of machine pacing, Taylor wrote:

By this arrangement all planning is carried out by technical men, the machine units being equipped, assembled, and maintained by skilled artisans, while the actual production is automatic. Such a system eliminates the human factor to a large extent and reduces repetition production to its proper level of an automatic mechanical operation.[84]

Woollard saw great advantages in machine pacing, not only for employers but also for labour. For employers: 'The virtue of the flow line layout resides in the fact that it helps us to take control of the time we are buying.'[85] While for labour:

Mechanical movements of the work piece are possibly even more of moral than of physical value, notwithstanding the fact that it is the physical help they give that makes the moral value possible. The mechanical movement is a metronome which beats out time for the whole work.... It is beneficial in redressing injustices to the over-worked by urging those who do less than their share.[86]

Taylor and Woollard agreed that regular increases in wages were necessary for high output. Woollard argued that the payment of high wages was not an altruistic act, but based 'upon the hard facts of business efficiency'.[87] He was also suspicious of welfare services in lieu of wages. He argued that: 'The factory is a means of enabling them [labour] to earn a decent living and they are better citizens if they control their own activities outside the factory.'[88] Woollard and Taylor differed over whether wages should be paid by the piece or on day rates. Woollard strongly favoured piecework, while Taylor had a preference for day work. Woollard remained skeptical of the ability of management to coordinate the production process or enforce effort norms without the aid of incentive payment systems. Morris factories remained on individual or, in a few cases, group piecework until after World War II. One suspects that incentive payment systems were particularly effective as control mechanisms in Oxford where much of the work force was recently recruited from rural districts.[89] This in turn helps to explain why, despite introducing a hand powered chassis assembly line in 1919, and the expansion of output from 2000 in 1920 to over 60 000 in the late twenties, the line was not mechanised until 1934.[90] The unmechanised line gave labour that much more freedom in setting the pace of work relative to the relentless mechanised line.

Austin and piecework as a managerial strategy

While our attention at Morris is drawn to their experiments with production techniques, at Austin it is the production institutions that are the most interesting. During the war, Austin had expanded rapidly and had installed large amounts of new machinery. When the war ended, they were overextended, with inappropriate plant, and producing a large car which was not well received in the market. They were forced to the brink of bankruptcy and were saved only through a reorganisation imposed by the receiver. Austin's control over the company's day to day production was restricted. C.R.F. Engelbach was appointed as the new works director, and E.L. Payton was brought in to restore financial control.[91] The shock of this financial crisis undoubtedly slowed the rate of technical change. In 1920, Austin was still assembling chassis on 120 stationary stands.[92] In other departments, crude flow techniques appeared immediately after the war. There was a shift to sequential machine organisation in the machine shops, but this must have been limited by the continued use of shafts and belts to provide power to the machines. A simple line system was used in the assembly of the rear and front axles which were mounted on mobile stands and pushed by hand past a row of specialised assemblers. Austin continued the practice of having all components sent to and drawn from a central store.[93]

It was not until Austin's visit to Detroit in 1922 that production techniques and product design began to change radically. Austin's visit had convinced him that it was unsound to simply cheapen the existing 12 HP and 20 HP models to compete with Ford and that the light car he proposed in 1921 and designed at his own expense in 1922 was the key to the company's future survival.[94] Austin was also impressed by the 'energetic' way in which the men worked in the Ford factories. He identified two factors behind Ford's ability to extract maximum effort from his workers. The first was, 'the diversity of the Races employed there ... diversity which gives to manufacturers a very large advantage in his effort to organise for rapid and economic production'. The second was the atmosphere of push and shove in the plant created by the use of flow techniques. He reported: 'The secret for obtaining the atmosphere can be explained in a few words – no excess material between operations. Each operation is being pushed forward by the one behind and drawn forward by the one in front.'[95] Austin did not see the large output of the American producers as a major advantage. He had been informed that the advantages of flow production could be had at an output level as low as 15 000 per annum and were mostly exhausted by the time output reached 50 000, constraints well within his reach.

Production techniques were transformed under the direction of C.R.F. Engelbach who had worked during the war at the Coventry Ordnance Works.[96] In an attempt to reproduce the hustle and bustle of the Ford factories, work was organised to flow from machine to machine, from machine line to machine line, and from machine line to assembly areas. The role of the central stores was reduced and sub-stores between operations were kept to a minimum or eliminated altogether. At the same time, stationary assembly methods were replaced by assembly lines in the major assembly areas. In 1924 these lines were hand powered, and it was not until 1928, 15 years after the Ford experiments, that mechanised lines were adopted. But even in 1928 the gear box line and the final chassis line were only in the process of being mechanised and it is unclear precisely when they were mechanised. Engelbach reported that the reorganisation of the plant reduced labour inputs by about one-third, somewhat less than the one-half commonly reported for the same changes at Fords.[97]

Between 1920 and 1928, there were also significant changes in the company's production institutions. There was a general enhancement and formalisation of the managerial function, something Austin had been suspicious of prior to the war.[98] By 1928, an efficiency department was created which was responsible for the overall planning of production, the investigation of ideas brought forward to increase output, and the setting of times needed to produce vehicles. From this data, the rate fixing department was able to set production times and classify the type of labour to be used on each task. Disputes between labour and the rate fixer were resolved through demonstration. An elaborate costing office was created and the task of collecting data was eased through the use of mechanical card readers which electronically recorded data. The cost department provided daily reports of overall productivity and changes in inventories, as well as daily reports on every worker's output. Armed with this data, management claimed that it was able to identify the causes of low productivity, be they design faults, tool mistakes or low labour effort. It was also claimed that the system was able to predict in advance the cost of production, although statements by Engelbach during the 1936 strike, that with a new model some time was needed to arrive at a final costing, casts doubt on this claim.[99]

Despite the shift toward flow production, and the increase in managerial authority, Austin did not adopt Ford style direct control of labour, or as Perry-Keene described the Ford system, 'herd methods'. Austin continued to depend on labour regulating itself which gave the workforce an element of control over working conditions and effort levels. In this sense the production institutions employed by Austin differed significantly from those employed by Ford. At Austin's the final transfer of authority from labour to management remained incomplete and rigid machine pacing of labour effort norms was less prevalent. Austin continued to believe that one of the keys to Ford's success was the level of effort supplied by labour. He summed up the lessons learned during his Detroit visit as follows: 'I saw the famous Ford shops ... the point that interested me and made me marvel most was the way in which everybody in the establishment seemed to be trying to be doing their best.'[100] Austin and his top managers believed that such a level of effort required a new attitude on the part of labour, one that could only be created by employing incentive payment systems. They believed that Austin's success would rest not on installing new machine methods or attempting to enforce labour effort norms through direct control but, rather, in attaining a cooperative labour spirit. Austin was sceptical of innovations such as the Morris transfer lines which he felt were inelastic and not well suited to existing needs.[101] He could not see the advantages of machine pacing which Woollard and Taylor stressed.

Perry Keene, the head of the costing department, was one of the most vocal of the Austin managers in advancing the thesis that labour 'spirit' was the key to higher productivity in Britain. In a letter to the *Times*, following the General Strike, he wrote: 'Confidence is directly the root of the whole matter.... The defensive attitude of labour has been brought about in many cases through unprincipled action on the part of management.'[102] Speaking about the problems facing Austin he argued: 'The obvious difficulty at the moment is lack of confidence as between employer and employed.' The way to resolve this lack of confidence was not to pay high wages on the fixed day wage system but, rather, to expand the use of incentive payment systems. Perry Keene suggested that with:

such a basis, many economic problems become common to both employers and employed, and interests commonly flow in one direction.... The reason why the system of control became really efficient was that they inculcated into the whole staff a maximum idea of personal responsibility to the firm itself whereby they and the firm were likely to prosper.[103]

Engelbach, who as works director might have been expected to see new machine techniques as the key to improved productivity, also stressed the need for good organisation, not up-to-date machine methods. He argued: 'Good organisation and an indifferent plant achieve better results than a good plant and indifferent organisation.'[104]

For Austin, an incentive payment system, known as Bonus on Time was specifically designed to create this atmosphere of self-regulation. Each job was assigned a time. Labour was paid the number of time credits earned per week times their base rate. All workers were on individual piecework and received 100 percent of any time saved through increased effort. Management stressed that no attempt would be made to cut prices if bonus levels increased. The rapid rise in bonus earnings to over 100 percent, which was twice the Humber rate and three times the rate recognised in the union agreements with the EEF, confirms that in general, higher bonuses were allowed before prices were cut. Management actively encouraged higher bonus earnings by giving special recognition to workers who earned particularly high bonuses over an extended period and by giving them further merit bonuses.[105] There is no evidence that after such recognition the time allowance was rolled back. Perry Keene claimed that it was better to let a worker reap the gains from a loosely set piece-rate time than to correct the mistake and jeopardise labour's willingness to go for high bonuses.[106] In order to emphasise the link between effort and earnings, bonuses were paid to the workers in the first pay envelope following the work week.[107]

The decision to recognise and encourage higher bonus earnings was a conscious one made in 1922, and coincided with the collapse of trade unions in the industry after the 1922 lock-out. Prior to this shift in strategy, the average bonus level was around 21 percent. Apparently under Perry Keene's instructions, the firm stopped cutting prices when bonus earnings reached some

Table 8.4. *Productivity effect of new production techniques and changes in labour effort, Austin Motor Company*

	Actual employee weeks per vehicle	Average bonus (% of base rate)	Estimated employee weeks, holding model line and production techniques constant
1922	55	21	55
1923	24	100	33.3
1924	20	112	31.37
1925	17	124	29.7
1926	12	136	28.2
1927	10	147	26.9

Notes: in order to calculate increase in labour productivity while holding the product line and the production techniques constant, we used 1922 as a base observation. In 1922, labour must have been allowed 66.55 labour weeks in order to earn 21 percent bonus with an actual production time of 55 hours. By using this base observation, we could isolate the productivity effect of increased effort using the following formula:

$$(66.55 - X)/X = \text{bonus earned}$$

X = estimated labour time holding model line and production techniques constant

This analysis assumes that high bonus earnings reflect increased labour effort. Prior to 1924, the lack of union organisation and the slow pace of change in production techniques makes it highly plausible that bonus earnings reflect mainly increased effort. After 1924, our confidence in this assumption is reduced. Labour remained unorganised, but there were extensive changes in production techniques. It is likely that the the post 1924 estimate of 44.7 percent overestimates the contribution of increased effort norms. Labour disputes during the period suggest that Austin may have been lowering labour base rates rather than changing piece rate times after 1924.

Sources: Actual productivity data from C.R.F. Engelbach, 'Some notes on re-organising a works to increase production' (*Proceedings Institute of Automobile Engineers*, 12, 1927/28), p. 510. Bonus levels from A. Perry Keene, 'Production a dream come true' (*Journal of the Institute of Production Engineers*, 7, 1928), p. 30. Perry Keene only provides bonus observations for shortly before and shortly after the change in policy in 1922 and 1927. We have assumed that the post policy change observation held in 1923 and that bonus rates increased at a constant rate between 1923 and 1927.

predetermined maximum. At first, labour was highly suspicious, but bonuses began to edge up reaching 100 percent within a few months and reaching a plant wide average of 147 percent by 1927.[108]

While it is difficult to disentangle the productivity effects of the shift to smaller cars in 1923, the gradual move to flow production and the increase in effort norms which accompanied the recognition of new bonus standards, the data we do have suggests that increased effort norms accounted for a large part of the improvement in productivity. The data found in Table 8.4 suggests that 67.7 percent of the increase in productivity between 1922 and 1924 can be explained by the increased labour effort needed to earn the higher bonus earnings. After 1924, a period of extensive technical change, increased effort levels accounted for 44.7 percent of the increase in labour productivity. These estimates offer tangible evidence that the Austin managers' assessment of the potential return from winning labour's cooperation versus installing new production methods may have been correct.

Managerial assessments of the Bonus on Time payment system differed. To some Austin officials its main contribution was to reduce the need to monitor and enforce effort norms. Perry Keene argued: 'The remuneration he [the worker] is able to obtain through savings is sufficient incentive to the worker to make large output effective with the minimum of supervision.'[109] It is not difficult to find statements by former workers that incentive payment systems provided a positive stimulus to effort norms. One such worker gave this vivid description of how bonus was earned:

Well you had time, so much time for doing a job, and if you were on ordinary time, you'd get £2 and then you'd have to go quicker and quicker to get more. So the track'd perhaps start at time and a quarter ... and then it would go up to time and a half, £3 a week. Time and three-quarters. Speed it up as you get used to it ... double time. And when it got to double time they'd stop. No more, no faster. And what we used to do, we'd have a real good go, we'd pick the bodies up and jump the pegs. Four men'd pick a body up ... and jump the pegs and we'd make it up to double time and a half, which was about £5 a week, and this is a lot of money in them days.[110]

Other Austin officials argued that the payment system acted as a check that management was in fact effectively coordinating factory operations. They argued: 'On piecework it is of vital importance to the man for the next job to be in sight and he acts as a whip to the shop management to be fed with work.'[111] In a very revealing statement they argued:

Every group system lacks stimulation to the individual, and the speed of the group is usually that of the slowest man. Group prices are cheap and easy to administer, but cover up Works inefficiency, hence their popularity. In fact, they are economically dangerous unless a Works is extremely well managed.[112]

What is of interest in this statement is the link between the need for individual incentives and the degree to which managerial institutions were developed. This statement could as easily have been made about day work systems which went even further than group bonus systems in breaking the link between individual effort and individual rewards. For these Austin officials, the Bonus on Time system was seen as a substitute for elements of the managerial function itself. The following statement suggests that it was particularly in the area of planning how the work was to be done, shop floor organisation, machine maintenance, and enforcement of effort norms that the Bonus on Time system was seen as a substitute for management:

The effect on the worker is to bring out all his sense of competitiveness, raise his standard of concentration, and make him take a greater interest in his work. If tactfully applied, ... a man will demand quick and clear instructions from his foreman, develop short cuts in his work and, to save delay from breakdown, will guard the welfare of his machine in no uncertain manner.[113]

The Austin managers saw their strategy as an alternative to the direct control system employed by Ford and as the only viable strategy given the characteristics of British workers and the level of development of the British managerial function. Quoting from an Austin study of their payment system, it was argued:

There are still a few employers who object to piecework on principle. Their stand-point is that an efficient management ought to be able to get the same results at an agreed rate of wage without having to pay more money to encourage the men to work harder.... Some form of extra wage must be paid to a man if he is expected to work harder. The only alternative is to pay a high wage similar to the Ford system, and insist upon task achievement.... The daily task system at fixed wages may perhaps, be workable in American, or even Continental factories, but the necessary...driving works policy, would not be acceptable either to English Labour or Management. Intelligent workmen, who rightly or wrongly consider themselves able to criticise a Works system, will not submit themselves to the injustice of a task which puts all the inefficiency of a Works upon their shoulders.[114]

We have already mentioned that the shift to high bonus earnings coincided with the collapse of the formal trade unions in 1922. Many observers, including the EEF, recognised that Austin's ability to exploit the payment system to control labour was closely related to labour's lack of an organised voice. The firm's ability to force workers into lower base rate grades made high bonus earnings a necessity if labour was to protect its standard of living. The EEF had concluded that: 'The more powerful the Union becomes, the more they will be able to break down the present system because they will be in a position to force the Company to follow the generally observed district rates.'[115]

Austin had little sympathy for trade unions or works committees, which he saw as interfering with the identity of interests between himself and his workers. The Austin works committee, recognised under an agreement between the unions and the EEF, was not allowed to function freely. By 1928, Perry Keene claimed that: 'We definitely set out to manage as managers and the result is that we have no representation anywhere from the workers' side. No shop stewards, or shop committees, or anyone wanting to interfere with management.'[116] As long as work at Austin's was seasonal, management had little trouble in keeping labour unorganised. D. Etheridge, who would later become the plant shop steward convener, recalled that in the 1920s regular work was only available part of the year. He wrote: 'Now this would give the opportunity for employers to see that you didn't create a stable situation where trade unionists could organise and build up.... If the people didn't fit the bill during the period they were at work they just didn't send for 'em back you see.'[117]

Prior to the late 1930s, labour attempts to resist aspects of the payment system were largely unsuccessful.[118] A major conflict over the grading of workers was temporarily avoided in 1928. The District Organiser for the AEU complained that Austin was notifying the workers, 'that their engagement must terminate but they can continue if they agree to a reduction in rates'.[119] Labour tensions flared up again in early 1929 over attempts to revise piece rate times. By the late 1920s, average bonus rates ranged between 100 and 150 percent. Management argued that this was excessive and that in part, it reflected the large investment in new production techniques in the late 1920s which had not been fully reflected in lower time allowances. In what may have been the first attempt to cut piece prices since 1922, management moved to retime all jobs so as to yield a 75 percent bonus.[120] Labour argued that the high bonus levels were compensation for reductions in base rates which they had suffered over the last five years.

Trade union officials at the plant believed that they were too weak to challenge the proposed changes in working conditions. During January and February of 1929, an attempt was made to settle the dispute through the procedure recognised by the EEF and the unions. The union officials proposed to accept an agreement with Austin which conceded most of the points. Their strategy was to embark on an organising drive to prepare for future confrontations. This proved unsatisfactory to the workers who took matters into their own hands and staged a stay-in strike beginning 25 March 1929. The strike by the largely non-unionised workers brought production to a halt. The strike foreshadowed postwar events in that the strikers were reluctant to let the official unions bargain for them. In the end, the strikers were defeated by a lack of solidarity in their ranks. Under the threat of dismissal, the strikers returned to work and handed over the negotiations to the union officials.

For the union officials, the action by the unorganised workers provided an unexpected windfall. Not only were they able to attract new members into the unions, they were able to wring concessions from Austin. Concessions were made on the grading issue and management agreed that piece rate times would from now on be set mutually. The shop stewards system, which had been suppressed during the 1920s, was to be revived, and for the first time in nearly a decade an organised labour voice was instituted.[121] Even though these concessions were rolled back in the early 1930s as unemployment rose, they set the basis for a future challenge to management's ability to exploit the cash nexus to control labour and to coordinate shop floor activity.[122]

The real rise of a new labour presence on the shop floor would not become apparent until after World War II when a period of prolonged full employment strengthened labour's position. But even in the late 1930s there were signs that production institutions had evolved and that labour had laid the basis for a postwar challenge to managerial authority. The problem of reclassifying workers at lower base rates was again debated during 1936. Again, a spontaneous strike spread amongst the unskilled and the unorganised workers which closed down the plant, and again recourse to official procedure yielded few tangible gains.[123] In 1938, a major conflict over the payment system erupted in the Aero Works. This time labour was better organised and the shop stewards system had grown in presence. Austin was forced to reinstate sacked workers and to remove the rate fixer and time study engineer from the shop floor. Concessions were made to prevent the strike from spreading to the vehicle factories.[124]

We would argue that Austin had adapted the Fordist system he observed in Detroit in 1922 to British conditions. The managerial function was enhanced and elements of flow production installed. However, Austin remained suspicious of direct control over labour. Mechanised assembly lines appeared only after a lag, and Austin was critical of the machine pacing experiments of Morris. Austin officials emphasised that in the British context it was not practical for management to regiment shop floor activity. British workers needed to be given some flexibility in deciding how the work was to be done and at what pace. The undemocratic methods of direct control were viewed as impractical. In the next section, it will be shown how other British managers had rejected the managerial strategy of direct control as practised by Ford.

Associated Equipment Company and Rover: the rejection of day work

The experiences of Rover and the Associated Equipment Company lend support to the thesis that British management became dependent on incentive payment systems to supplement shortcomings in the British managerial function. The Associated Equipment Company (AEC) was the first British vehicle producer to install a mechanised assembly line. The firm was incorporated in 1912. Its main business was to supply buses to the London General Omnibus Company, the London Electric Railway Company and the Metropolitan District Railway Company. Buses were sold to other firms through an exclusive agency arrangement with the Daimler Company. During the war, the firm manufactured trucks for the Ministry of Munitions and after the war assembled a few motor cars on a contract basis for the Maxwell Company.[125]

AEC was generously financed by the companies to which it supplied buses. The initial share issue of £500 000 was almost entirely supplied by the Underground Electric Company. They supplied a further £100 000 in preferred shares in 1916 while the London General Omnibus Company took £500 000 of the preferred shares in the same year. AEC paid relatively high dividends on these investments. Between 1913 and 1920, dividends ranged between 24 and 34 percent per annum. After a 5-year suspension of dividends between 1921 and 1925, payments ranged between 5 and 10 percent until 1934, when AEC became a public company.[126] AEC's average output between 1914 and 1927 was 1000 chassis. During the war years, this was increased to between 2000 and 3000 chassis.

Although some accounts suggest that AEC adopted its first assembly line in 1915, we have been unable to find any evidence to support this thesis. The first line was more likely installed in May or June of 1917 and was the culmination of a series of events which increased American influence at the company. During 1916 the business manager and the secretary toured the United States. In the same year, S.A. Wallace was appointed as the works manager. Wallace was well trained in the principles of the American system having formerly been employed by General Electric in New York. Within six months of Wallace's appointment, a large shipment of new American machines were installed. [127] This was followed in early 1917 by the chassis line in the form of a mechanised moving platform, 265 feet long, designed to hold ten chassis, and costing £3500. [128]

It is unclear precisely why the line was adopted. Output was not increased dramatically until the end of 1918 when weekly output was doubled to 100. [129] It was suggested in a number of accounts that AEC faced the special problem of moving heavy chassis through the plant, suggesting that this first line was related more to the problem of factory conveyance than either factory coordination or labour control. This need for conveyance aids may have been increased by the company's dramatic shift to female labour during the war. By late 1918 almost half the labour on the chassis line, two-thirds of the machine operators in the gear cutting department, and virtually the entire automatic department was composed of women. [130]

Despite the introduction of American techniques and the dilution of labour, the workers were able to protect a number of customs including the refusal to work more than one machine. These kept earnings high and reduced the work load. Our limited data suggests that the new methods employed after 1917 may have reduced the labour time needed to produce a chassis from about 4000 hours in 1915 to 3000 hours in 1926. [131] Union organisation remained relatively strong and by 1925, well before trade unionism revived in other motor vehicle plants, there was talk of setting up a shop steward committee which became a reality in 1926. [132]

After the war, the firm suffered from the abundant supply of surplus army trucks and buses. It was not until 1926, when the firm moved its operations from Walthamstow to Southall, that further changes were made to production techniques and production institutions. The events surrounding the transfer of operations to Southall provides a critical insight into British managerial thinking in the interwar period. As had been the case in 1917, the company had a number of contacts with American producers during the period preceding the move. In 1922, AEC had entered into an agreement with General Motors to exchange patents, to respect each others market territory and to engage in mutual assistance in the organisation of works. There is no record of the impact of this agreement, although AEC seemed reluctant to share patents and in 1926 ended the agreement. [133] G. Rushton, who was made manager of the new works, was influenced by American practices during a visit to the United States shortly before taking up a position with AEC. A spokesman for the EEF felt that Rushton, after his visit to the United States was suffering from a rare British management disease, 'Forditis'. [134]

Rushton had not suddenly come to his American views in 1926. He had been instrumental in setting up a large repair depot for the London General Omnibus Company after the war. This depot overhauled buses on a mass production basis. Each day 15 buses were disassembled, overhauled and reassembled on a series of moving lines employing 2200 workers. The task was simplified by the company's standardisation on three types of AEC chassis, the extensive use of jigs, and the installation of some special purpose machines. Much of the work was done by semi-skilled labour. Unlike most other British engineering shops, labour was paid on a time, not piece, basis and it was reported that the moving lines enforced effort norms with little encouragement from supervisors.[135]

The Southall factory is of great interest as it incorporated the two critical components of Fordism, flow production techniques and fixed high day wages. Component assembly lines, of which there were twelve, fed into the main 'L' shaped chassis assembly line. The works was designed to produce 80 to 100 chassis per week, and output may have reached a maximum of 110 per week.[136] The most radical change, and the most contentious in the opinion of the Engineering Employers Federation, was the shift to day work and high fixed wages. The London Engineering Employers Association argued that:

> The essential difference between his Southall scheme, and schemes in operation at Walthamstow and at other federation firms was a payment in *anticipation* (of output), whereas the scheme approved by the Association were payments made *after the results* had been assured.[137]

The workers were placed into three grades. Toolmakers and a few erectors were paid 2/-, the majority of erectors and some of the machinists were paid 1/9, and the rest were paid 1/6 per hour. Management had calculated these rates based on output levels and bonus earnings at the old plant. The workers were also paid a Group Bonus which amounted to around 5 percent of earnings. If output at the new plant was above or below what they expected, the managers reserved the right to change wages immediately although the record indicates this was unnecessary.[138]

From the perspective of Rushton, the new production process and the new wage payment system were a success. Average labour cost after three weeks was reduced from £39 to £27 per chassis. By the middle of 1927, the total cost of a chassis had fallen from £267 to £168. The firm paid out an extra bonus of one-half weeks wage per worker after the first six months. During the same period, profits rose from £65 000 to £118 000.[139] By 1930, the number of hours needed to produce a chassis had fallen from around 3000 during the last days at Walthamstow to just under 2000.[140]

The London District Employers Association was concerned about the experiments at AEC, particularly the shift to high fixed day rates. It was suggested that this would inflate local wages and might weaken the effectiveness of incentive wage systems in enforcing effort norms. The local association, which included firms such as Dennis and Fairly Aviation, threatened to expel AEC from the association. P. Martin, from Daimler, was in favour of taking a hard line with Rushton arguing that he was playing 'ducks and drakes' with the rules of the EEF. Representatives of the Employers Federation intervened to try to resolve the problem.[141]

In July of 1927, J.C.A. Ward interviewed Rushton on behalf of the Federation. He informed Rushton that the problem with the participating bonus scheme was that it was being operated on day work principles. Ward informed Rushton that: 'The Federation objected to the participating bonus because the Company paid over the district rate without any check that the workpeople earned their money.' Rushton replied that the firm did not need a check on the workers because that was management's task: 'The workman earned the participating bonus, otherwise the workman would not be in the works.'[142] In discussing alternatives, Rushton also revealed that one of the objectives of his payment system was to cap wages at a level below those paid by Ford. Fore-shadowing post-1945 events, Rushton argued that under piecework it might become difficult to control the upward drift of wages when new production techniques were adopted. He argued that: 'He was unwilling to adopt any system which would bind him to pay a percentage of any profit to the men; if such a percentage were adopted he might have to raise the wage indefinitely and up to a point equal to the 'Ford wage.'[143]

Ward was no more successful than the London Employers in getting Rushton to change his payment system. He appealed to Rushton on the grounds that it was not fair to the other members of the EEF. He argued:

If his (AEC) Company was allowed to pay on this system, other members must also be allowed; that Mr. Rushton's advantage in getting, as he said he did, good men and good work by paying a high fixed wage, was dependent entirely on the fact that this high fixed wage was above that ordinarily paid in the district. . . . and that this advantage of Mr. Rushton's would not exist if all members of the Federation were allowed to pay as much as they thought they could afford, the district rate would no longer exist and Mr. Rushton's advantage through paying above the district rate would disappear. . . . [The] participating bonus as practised by the Company was altogether inconsistent with the existence of the Federation.[144]

The Federation and the London Employers learned to live with the AEC system, although there was no enthusiasm to adopt it at other engineering shops.

In 1930, a similar situation developed at the Rover Company when the management was criticised by the Federation for being sympathetic to Fordist ideas. Rover had been slow to react to the challenge of both Austin and Morris and had lost ground during the 1920s. But 1929 was a particularly good year as output reached 7255 and employment reached 2460.[145] On the strength of these successes, Rover decided to increase output even further, and as part of this strategy, S. Wilks, the managing director, proposed reorganising work practices on the Bedaux system. The Bedaux system had a reputation amongst workers as leading to speedup with few tangible benefits. For the EEF, it presented new problems in that it involved an external agency setting effort norms. The Federation warned interested firms that:

The Bedaux system is different from the usual run of payment by results systems in that the 'B' is not fixed by mutual agreement between the employer and the workman concerned. In fact neither the employer nor the workman has any say in the fixing of the 'B'.[146]

Wilks was attracted to the Bedaux system by its claim that it could measure work loads scientifically. He tried to sell it to labour by arguing that it would lead to higher productivity and higher wages. Labour remained suspicious that its main effect would be to turn the effort bargain in management's favour. Wilks tried to impose the system on the less organised women workers in August of 1930. The women resisted the system and began organising themselves with the aid of the Coventry branch of the Workers Union. The women workers refused to work the system and were sacked. The rest of the shop stopped work and a picket line was placed around the works. Soon after, the male workers of the NUVB joined the women on strike.[147]

As the conflict escalated, the national officials of the EEF, the NUVB and the TGWU became involved. Wilks grew increasingly frustrated with the progress of the talks and appealed directly to E. Bevin, the General Secretary of the TGWU. A deal was struck in which the Rover workers would accept the Bedaux system in return for guarantees of higher wage norms. Rover agreed to pay female workers a minimum of £2 15s per week, about a third higher than the going rate in Coventry.[148] As Tolliday has argued, this agreement, reached with minimal consultation with the Rover workers reflected Bevin's willingness to trade off higher wages for intensification of effort.[149] Wilks' proposals to grant higher wages in return for greater managerial control of effort norms was not well received by the Employers Federation. The Secretary of the Coventry Association spoke to Wilks: 'He warned the company as to such a step being retrograde in the opinion of the Association and had mentioned the harmful effect which the giving of enhanced day rates would have on the industry of the district.'[150] Cole from the Federation was more to the point in questioning the practicality of shifting to a high wage high effort bargain. He argued that:

Captain Wilks, to my mind is suffering from some rather ill-digested views with regard to Capital and Labour. He is a great admirer of Mr. Ford and American methods. His idea is that everybody should receive a high day rate and then be compelled to work as hard as possible and if they do not then they are to be fired out.[151]

The CDEEA demanded that the firm revise the agreement and in particular lower the guaranteed rate paid to women workers. The issue was diffused when the firm reversed its decision to expand output. The pressure to increase productivity and strengthen the managerial function eased. The Bedaux system was dropped and the shop remained on ordinary piecework.[152] Relations between the firm and the Coventry Employers remained cool though, and the firm did not attend any Employers meetings for five years.

Fordism and the British motor vehicle industry

We have been concerned in this chapter with the impact of Fordism on the British motor vehicle industry between 1914 and 1930. By 1917, two important British plants had adopted a variation of Fordism, Ford's Manchester works, and the Associated Equipment Company. Managers of other British factories were critical of both of these experiments. In their view, managerial strategies which attempted to gain direct control of effort norms were not compatible with existing British social forces. In particular, they argued that British labour would not tolerate a managerial strategy which stripped them of any control over shop floor decisions. However, managerial suspicions of Fordism were not shaped entirely by labour demands for shop floor democracy. British managers were also aware of weaknesses in the British managerial function and the potential for getting labour to perform many of the tasks of shop floor coordination needed for efficient production. We have argued that a British System of Mass Production was developed in which the managerial function was less developed than in the American case and British workers retained a degree of control over how they worked which American workers had lost by 1914. British capital had adopted an institutional framework within which, to a large extent labour regulated itself.

During the interwar period, the British System of Mass Production worked well for British employers. The weakness of trade unions and the persistence of high unemployment made it difficult for labour to exploit self-regulation. This can be seen as a period of temporary equilibrium between British buyers and sellers of labour time, and between British production institutions and production techniques. However, quite invisible to contemporary participants in the industry, a gradual process of institutional evolution was underway. Under the British system, labour and management had different experiences and learned different lessons than was the case with firms employing the American system. British labour learned new ways of exploiting the institutions of self-regulation, while management became increasingly dependent on labour for many of the basic coordination tasks.

In the 1950s, this temporary equilibrium was shattered. During an extended period of full employment, labour was able to exploit the weaknesses of the British managerial function to shift the effort bargain in their favour. At the same time capital–labour ratios began a rapid rise as the result of the spread of 'automation'. This put new pressure on British management to increase labour effort norms. At this point, British capital proposed abandoning the institutional framework of the British System of Mass Production and began a process of what might be seen as Americanisation. An attempt was made to check labour's control of shop floor decisions and increase managerial authority. Incentive payment systems fell out of favour and Measured Day Work spread throughout the industry. In the final chapter of this book we will examine this transition and show how it led to the industry's ultimate collapse in the 1970s.

9

The collapse of the British system of mass production, 1930–1984

By the 1930s, a distinct alternative to the Fordist system of direct control of effort norms was in use in many British motor vehicle factories. This system of production, which we have called the British System of Mass Production, should not be confused with nineteenth-century production systems which were organised around the skilled artisan. The majority of British motor vehicle workers in the 1930s could not be classified as skilled workers. In fact, the production techniques used were surprisingly similar to those found in many American factories. New types of machinery and the emergence of volume production drastically reduced the skill required from individual workers. The most striking contrast between the American and the British system was the limited extent to which British management had been able to exert direct control over labour effort norms and the limited extent to which management had claimed responsibility for organising the work place. Labour retained a significant say over the setting of effort norms and the organisation of work, while management controlled the process by which piece-rate prices were set allowing them to control the ratio of wages to effort.

The British system of mass production, with its production techniques based on modern factory practices but its production institutions based on earlier craft technology, provided the basis for nearly three decades of unprecedented economic success. Between 1930 and 1955, output increased nearly fourfold, British firms became dominant players in the export market, and the return to capital was consistently high. Between 1929 and 1938, Austin's average return on net tangible assets was 17 percent, while at Morris the average return was 13.2 percent. After the war, the return to capital was even higher. Between 1947 and 1951, Austin earned 31.2 percent and Morris 25.5 percent per annum on net tangible assets. There is even some evidence that British firms were narrowing the productivity gap that the Americans enjoyed, although on the whole British labour productivity remained significantly lower than that found in the United States. In 1935 American labour productivity was 3.1 times that of British labour, while in 1955 the American advantage had been cut to 2.5 times as many vehicles per worker.[1]

Table 9.1. *Value of net assets, Austin, Morris, and Ford (UK)* £'000

	1929	1938	1947	1956
Austin	3028	5138		
			27 690	62 609
Morris	3316	12 555		
Ford	2717	11 464	24 366	65 369
Ratio Austin plus	2.33	1.54	1.14	0.96
Morris to Ford				

Source: G. Maxcy & A. Silberston, *The Motor Industry* (London, 1959), pp. 163, 178.

A closer look at this period of prosperity reveals a number of troublesome trends. The two largest British firms, Austin and Morris were not only profitable but also willing to distribute a high percentage of earnings as dividends. In the interwar years, Austin distributed over 65 percent of earnings to shareholders. Morris, who earned £55 million between 1927 and 1951 retained only 26 percent of these earnings in the firm.[2] Rover followed a similar pattern of overly generous dividend payments in the 1950s. Management's decision to satisfy investors' short-run desire for dividends was based on the fear that dissatisfied investors could replace the existing managers by mounting a takeover bid for the company.[3] The effect of this industry-wide preference for satisfying the short-run demands of investors rather than the long-run demands of sustained growth, can be seen in Table 9.1 which compares the rate of asset growth of Ford and the two leading British firms. Ford (UK) began the period as the smallest of the three firms, but ended the period larger than the other two combined. Austin and Morris tried to ward off the effect of their reluctance to invest in new plant through a series of 'defensive' mergers. In 1952 Austin and Morris merged to form the British Motor Corporation (BMC), while in 1968 BMC merged with Leyland to form the British Leyland Motor Corporation.

Another area of concern was the trend in the capital–labour ratio. Although the data is incomplete and somewhat unreliable, it does suggest that the capital–labour ratio, which had increased rapidly between 1900 and 1919, stopped increasing in the interwar period. Between 1924 and 1937 the capital–labour ratio actually fell 0.7 percent per annum in manufacturing as a whole. This was the only period between 1856 and 1973 that such a drop was recorded.[4] Table 9.2 indicates that the capital–labour ratio in the motor vehicle industry increased by about 50 percent between 1900 and 1919 but thereafter showed little upward movement until after World War II.

Table 9.2 includes both British firms and British based American firms such as Ford. Data on Austin, presented in Table 9.3, suggests that the reversal in the rate of growth of the capital–labour ratio may have been even more dramatic in the British sections of the industry. This is especially interesting as it supports

Table 9.2. *Capital–labour ratio*
British motor vehicle industry
(calculated at 1929 prices, 1929 = 100)

1900	65.5
1909	58.5
1919	93.6
1929	100.0
1937	95.0
1948	108.9

Source: G. Maxcy and A. Silberston, *The Motor Industry* (London, 1959). Original data from D. Creamer, 'Capital and Output Trends in Manufacturing Industries, 1880–1948', (*NBER*, Occasional Paper 41), 1954.

Table 9.3. *Capital–labour ratio Austin Motor Company (per worker employed)*

	Net tangible assets (current £)	Net tangible assets (1925–29£)	Fixed assets (1925–29£)
1907	143.8	256.8	199.3
1912	127.1	219.1	127.2
1922	404.5	381.6	220.2
1926	434.6	426.1	176.5
1929	298.8	308.0	160.2
1933	298.4	363.9	210.5
1936	259.6	298.4	168.9
1939	269.1	295.7	193.4

Source: R. Church, *Herbert Austin* (London, 1979), pp. 22, 143, 149, 213.

our thesis that British management's lack of control over effort norms discouraged investment in new capital equipment.

The slow rate of asset growth and the decapitalisation of the leading British producers surfaced in their inability to hold their market share shown in Table 9.4.

By the 1960s it was becoming obvious that something had gone terribly wrong in this once successful industry. A government study in the mid-1960s concluded that the two remaining independent British firms, British Motor Holdings and Leyland, were too small to be competitive on the international market. Turner, in his study of labour relations found an industry beset by serious problems.[5] By the early 1970s the government was forced to bail out both Chrysler and British Leyland who together controlled the majority of the companies which we examined in previous chapters. British companies were

Table 9.4. *Share of total production of cars, 1929–55*

	1929	1938	1946	1950	1955	1965	1975
Austin	25	21					
			43.4	39.4	38.9	37	36
Morris	35	23					
Ford	4	18	14.4	19.2	27.0	29	26

Sources: G. Maxcy and A. Silberston, *The Motor Industry* (London, 1959), p. 117; R. Church and M. Miller, 'The big three: competition, management and marketing in the British motor industry, 1922–1939', in B. Supple (ed.), *Essay in British Business History* (Oxford, 1977), p. 180; S.J. Prais, *Productivity and Industrial Structure* (Cambridge, 1981), p. 154.

Table 9.5. *Labour productivity British and American motor vehicle industry (annual output per employed)*

	1935	1950	1955	1960	1965
UK	2.86	3.6	4.5	5.4	5.8
US	8.76	10.4	11.2	12.4	14.8
Ratio	3.06	2.88	2.49	2.29	2.55

Sources: 1935, L. Rostas, *Comparative Productivity in British and American Industry* (Cambridge, 1948), p. 171; 1950–55, G. Maxcy and A. Silberston, *The Motor Industry* (London, 1959), p. 211; 1960–65, C. Pratten and A. Silberston, 'International comparisons of labour productivity in the automobile industry' (*Oxford Bulletin of Economics and Statistics*, **29**, 1967), p. 378.

facing new competition from a rebuilt continental industry and from the newly established Japanese producers. The inability of British firms to adapt to these changed conditions provides the focus of this final chapter.

The formalisation of shop floor labour institutions, 1930–55

It is not difficult to find claims that the rise of shop stewards and labour restrictions on output are at the heart of Britain's economic decline since 1945.[6] The difficulty with this simple thesis is that, relative to other industrial powers, British labour productivity has lagged since the last decades of the nineteenth century, particularly in industries such as motor vehicles. As shown in Table 9.5, American labour productivity has consistently been two to three times higher than British productivity. If anything, the rise of shop steward organisations in the 1950s seems to coincide with an improvement in relative productivity.

Part of this difference in labour productivity reflects the inability of British firms to exploit economies of scale and the lower level of capital investment. However, it is difficult to reject the thesis that part of the productivity difference reflects differences in labour effort norms. In his study, Rostas noted that in a number of cases identical plant was worked much more intensively in the United States than in Britain. He concluded that the lower level of productivity in these cases was caused by organisational factors and by the willingness and ability of labour to work.[7] Phelps Brown had relied on a similar argument to explain the slow rate of productivity growth in pre-1914 Britain.[8] What has changed since 1945 is not labour effort norms but, rather, the ability of British firms to turn low effort into profits. It is within this context that the formalisation of British shop floor labour organisations needs to be examined.

In previous chapters we have argued that between 1890 and 1920 British employers were unable to complete the transfer of authority from labour to a new managerial class. However, loose managerial control of shop floor activity did not work to labour's advantage in the interwar period. Trade unions and shop steward organisations were seriously weakened during the economic downturn which followed the war. High levels of unemployment, compounded by the seasonal pattern of production, left labour with little bargaining leverage. Clauses in labour contracts, which recognised mutuality in setting piece rate prices, were ignored.[9] Despite the lack of direct control over effort norms, management remained in firm control of the ratio of wages to effort and via this, the effort bargain.

The Austin strike of 1929 foreshadowed post-1945 trends in the industry. The strike over management demands to change the payment system and reduce wages was coordinated by local shop stewards. Local and national trade union officials played a minor role. At one point it looked as if the shop stewards might regain some of the authority that they had lost in the 1920s and challenge management's control of the ratio of wages to effort. However, the rise in unemployment in the early 1930s allowed Austin management to roll back the gains the stewards made in 1929.[10]

The arms build-up leading to World War II and the war itself provided a favourable environment for the resurgence of formal shop floor labour organisations. The Essential Works Order passed in 1941 restricted the right of management to fire workers and hence offered shop floor labour representatives some protection from victimisation. The formation of Joint Production Committees after 1942 provided shop stewards with new avenues for exerting their authority. Both trade union officials and employers were reluctant to formally recognise the participation of labour representatives in Joint Committees. Union officials feared a loss of control over trade union members, while management feared they might become a powerful bargaining opponent. The EEF tried to check the authority of the shop stewards by stipulating that the Joint Committees would not deal with questions of wages or working conditions which would continue to be dealt with through the existing procedure agreement controlled by local and national trade union officials.[11]

At Austin's Longbridge plant, labour elected its representatives to the Joint Committee in June of 1942. The rules of the Austin Committee restricted discussions to questions with a direct bearing on productivity. The Joint Committee was to exchange views, 'on matters relating to the improvement of production, to increase efficiency for this purpose and to make recommendations there on'.[12] The labour participants rejected the advisory role proposed for the Joint Committee by management and instead saw it as an opportunity to improve working conditions. One labour representative reported: 'The meeting closed with a feeling on our side that at least we had got a framework on which we could hammer out our production problems, and it was up to us to get the utmost out of it.'[13] In this new environment, shop floor labour organisations thrived. By the end of the war the Longbridge shop stewards were meeting regularly, had erected their own meeting hall which was referred to as the 'hut', and had begun issuing reports of activities and strikes.[14] The shop stewards had forced a reluctant management to bargain with them over working conditions.

The revival of shop stewards and the threat they posed to management needs to be interpreted in the context of interwar production institutions and management's failure to gain direct control of labour effort norms and the coordination of shop floor activity. Despite the defeat of formal shop floor labour institutions after World War I, management did not step in to complete the transfer of authority from labour to a new managerial class. Management was satisfied with preventing labour from exploiting its authority to turn the effort bargain in its favour. This was done by keeping British workers unorganised at the shop floor level. Lyddon is quite correct to point to the links between shop steward movements in World War I and World War II.[15] But the link is not the constitutional one of agreements between the unions and employers which he argues shaped the institutional shape of organised labour. He is closer to the truth when he points to labour's continuous struggle for 'job control'. In the unique British context, labour has always had a large degree of job control. What was lacking were formal labour institutions to exploit that control.

The potential shop stewards had to convert labour's control of shop floor activity into control of the effort bargain helps to explain why British management reserved its sharpest criticism for shop floor labour organisations. As was the case after World War I, the post-World War II era witnessed attacks by management on the right of formal shop floor labour organisations to exist. Even though there was no economic collapse comparable to the one which followed World War I, supply problems and unbalanced demand created opportunities for victimising shop stewards. There were 44 reported strikes over redundancy in the industry between 1947 and 1953. Over one-third of these strikes, and over one-half of the working time lost involved charges of unfair selection of shop stewards for redundancy. On more than one occasion between 1945 and 1955 firms such as Austin and Morris released and refused to rehire key shop stewards. In their report to the Royal Commission on Trade Union and Employers Organisations, the Austin shop stewards reported that it was not until the mid-1950s that shop steward fear of victimisation subsided.[16]

There was also an attempt by the employers to dismantle the Joint Production Committees created during the war. Initial negotiations between the EEF and the unions made little progress until January of 1947 when the Labour government voiced an interest in consultative mechanisms. This was backed up by more direct intervention in April when the Minister of Labour convinced the TUC and the British Employers Confederation to recommend formalisation of shop floor consultative machinery. The EEF reluctantly agreed to the continuation of Production Committees, but stressed that they were strictly voluntary and that negotiation over wages and working conditions would continue to be done through procedure and official union channels.[17]

In renegotiating postwar labour rights, management seemed less concerned with extending its authority on the shop floor and rather more concerned with reestablishing its unilateral control of the ratio of wages to effort. This was most obvious in Coventry, during 1945 and 1946, when management attempted to set piece prices without consulting the shop stewards, as had become the practice during the war. This put significant downward pressure on hourly earnings which fell by over 25 percent during 1945.[18] The workforce at Daimler and at Humber responded by reducing effort norms and demanding that labour be placed on day work. At Humber, three stewards were sacked for their aggressive negotiating stance. In protest, labour reduced output even further, which led management to declare 1500 workers redundant. This led to an all out strike at Humber, and the call for a general strike of all Coventry workers to begin March 13, 1946. Local and national union officials were unwilling to support such radical action and on the day of the strike only 10 percent of the workforce left their jobs. The Humber strike and the general strike collapsed shortly thereafter. Local union officials and the shop stewards reached an agreement with Humber. The main feature of the agreement was the recognition of a 60 percent bonus rate as the new norm for workers on incentive payment systems.[19]

The Humber agreement of 1946 looked very much like the Humber agreement of 1919. Incentive payment systems remained an integral component of the British managerial strategy and the role of the shop steward remained ambiguous. Despite Salmon's claim that mutuality was recognised in the 1946 Humber agreement, it is difficult to support this conclusion in the light of events in the industry over the next decade. We have already indicated that victimisation of shop stewards remained a problem until at least the mid-1950s. Lyddon is probably closer to the truth in arguing that shop stewards were tolerated and that where firms found it desirable to rid themselves of these organisations they were invariably successful. Such a conclusion is supported by Tolliday's work which leaves little doubt that trade unions and shop floor organisations remained weak until the late 1950s[20]

In the years immediately after World War II, management succeeded in checking the authority of shop steward organisations and thereby preserved managerial control of the ratio of wages to effort. However, given the absence of a serious economic collapse and a political climate which was more sympathetic to labour's right to organise, management was unable to completely suppress shop steward organisations. This was critical, for the new production techniques employed after the war increased the need for an organising agent to ensure continuous production. Management needed to run its increasingly expensive plant continuously to ensure a satisfactory return on investment. Labour, which very much depended on high bonus earnings to maintain their standard of living, also had an interest in continuous production. We will argue that both labour and management turned to the shop stewards to provide the needed coordination.[21] British management had failed to exert dominant control of the shop floor in the 1920s, had failed to develop new institutions for controlling labour and coordinating shop floor activity, and were therefore unprepared to assume these tasks in the early 1950s. But the cost of employing the shop stewards as organising agents was high. The cost was not loss of control of effort norms as popular interpretations would have us believe but, rather, the loss of managerial control of the ratio of wages to effort which had been used for nearly half a century to control the shop floor indirectly. In many ways, British management was hoisted on a petard of its own making.

Automation and postwar trends in production techniques

In the years following World War II, production techniques in the motor vehicle industry underwent a massive transformation. Automatic transfer mechanisms, capable of mechanically moving components from machine to machine, were perfected by American manufacturers and became standard practice in their new plants. General Motors operated a partially automated cylinder block line at their Buick plant in 1947, while in 1948 Ford began production at the new Cleveland engine plant which is reputed to have had the first fully automated cylinder block machine line.[22] The spread of automatic transfer mechanisms had as big an impact on factory life as the adoption of the first assembly lines in 1913. One observer wrote: 'The moving chain conveyor invented by Henry Ford in the early days of motor car production appear very insignificant in relation to these transfer machines.'[23]

Automatic transfer techniques had the potential to dramatically reduce overall costs. One estimate put the savings as high as 26 percent of floor space, 85 percent of direct production labour and a reduction of 30 percent in the capital–output ratio. Another study suggested that the new production techniques had the potential to reduce total labour requirements by 60 percent.[24] These were cost savings which British firms could not afford to ignore and in the late 1940s and early 1950s a number of British firms began to invest in the new technology. In the late 1940s, Morris introduced an automated system in their gear box plant. Austin began installing transfer machines in 1948 and had four large transfer lines in operation by 1952. By 1955, 120 rotary transfer machines were added to their plant. The British based plants of General Motors and Ford moved quickly to adopt the new techniques. Vauxhall had 12 transfer stations in its block line by 1948 and Ford had 24 stations by 1950. Standard, a relatively small producer in the mid 1940s, moved to automatic machinery in the late 1940s and began planning the introduction of automated systems in the early 1950s.[25]

A sure sign that automated production systems had spread to British motor vehicle plants were the conferences held in the mid-1950s to examine the new technology. The Institute of Production Engineers sponsored a major conference in June of 1955. One of its participants was F.G. Woollard who had played a role in the experiments with transfer machinery at Morris Engines in the 1920s. This conference received wide publicity and gave a generally optimistic picture of the impact of the new technology.[26]

Of more interest to our study are the two conferences held in 1955 by the shop steward organisations in the motor vehicle industry. In June of 1955, the shop stewards from the motor and ancillary industries held a conference to explore the implications of new production techniques. The conference attracted 185 shop stewards. The conference participants did not take a hostile attitude to the new technology. In fact quite the reverse seems to have been true. Les Ambrose, in summing up the discussion suggested: 'The first thing that had come from the discussion was that Trade Unions could not be opposed to automation.'[27] They were concerned, about its possible effect on workers, but they lacked a well-worked-out strategy to deal with it. The first conference failed to attract any resolutions in advance, and a last minute proposal simply pledged the shop stewards to fight for an improved standard of living, shorter hours and three weeks holiday with full pay.

At a second conference held in September of 1955 in Oxford, the shop stewards were better prepared. As had been the case in the first conference, the Austin shop stewards, and the Longbridge convener, D. Etheridge, played a central role in moulding policy.[28] The conference was attended by 320 delegates who passed a number of resolutions including a key proposal from the British Motor Corporation shop stewards. The resolution made labour concerns regarding the safety of the new techniques a priority in bargaining. It also pledged the shop stewards to bargain for higher wages, shorter hours, no redundancies, and lower vehicle prices. Perhaps more important, it signalled the basic strategy of shop stewards in negotiations over the new technology. Their strategy was a forward looking one, committed to bargaining for improvements in working conditions under the new technology. They rejected the alternative strategy of trying to preserve existing privileges by resisting new production techniques. The concern with redundancies reflected the shop stewards' recognition that the bargaining leverage of shop floor organisations was closely tied to conditions in the labour market.

It was also decided at the conference to send a delegation of shop stewards to

Table 9.6. *Capital investment per worker, Standard Motor Company, 1927–53*

	Net assets (current £)	Net assets (1925–29 £)	Fixed assets (1925–29 £)
1927	365	368	208
1932	148	178	120
1946	663	—	—
1948	721	477	349
1950	812	475	289
1952	775	384	207
1953	724	346	209

Sources: Company Balance Sheets; S. Melman, *Decision Making and Productivity* (Oxford, 1958), p. 254; Melman Papers, MRC, Mss 254/2, *Employment Data*.

London to lobby members of parliament regarding the uses of automation.[29] In November of 1955, 22 shop stewards met with members of parliament and, through D. Etheridge, the Austin convener, requested a government investigation into the potential impact of the new technology. Again the shop stewards stressed that automation must not result in massive labour redundancies and increases in unemployment. They asked that restrictions be placed on the rights of management in the area of redundancies and encouraged the state to seek new markets for the increased volume of motor vehicles made possible with the new production techniques. To this end, they threw their support behind a private member's bill which proposed creating a permanent committee to study and assess the social and economic impact of automation.[30]

The most obvious effect of the new production techniques was to increase the investment in capital per worker. Between 1937 and 1951 the annual growth in capital investment was double the growth in labour employment. Between 1951 and 1964, capital growth was almost five times greater than labour growth.[31] As shown in Table 9.6, Standard saw the level of investment per worker double during World War II.

Another indication of how automation was revolutionising investment per worker is the trend at Ford's Dagenham plant which made extensive use of the new technology. By 1960 they employed £1427 of fixed assets per worker, which represented approximately £555 in 1925–29 prices.[32] This is two to three times the investment by Austin in fixed assets in the late 1930s and double that employed by Standard who had only begun the transfer to automation in the early 1950s.

A second feature of the new technology, and almost as important as the increase in investment per worker, was the tendency of the new technology to increase the degree of task integration within the shops. Under the automated systems, localised breakdowns, labour go slows, or strikes would have serious repercussions throughout the plant. Continuous production became increasingly important to both labour and management.

The new production techniques created new problems for British managers. After nearly two decades of constant or even falling investment per worker, and a managerial strategy which gave British labour a significant say in the coordination of shop floor activity, management discovered a new need to control the production process. F. Griffiths, chief production development engineer at BMC, was one of the few British managers to appreciate the tensions between the production institutions which formed the basis of the industry's interwar prosperity, and the new production techniques employed after World War II. In the 1960s he wrote:

What is required to be automated in the motor industry.... is the relationship of our processes with each other and to the production programme.... We are losing 20 percent [of capacity].... The cause of this will be found in the fact that the right material is not at the right place at the right time, and that the motor industry is really not in proper control of its business. The piecework systems which it has to use, its lack of immediate knowledge of its relationships between supply and what is required, all mean that its output is in the hands of a large number of people.[33]

Management was being challenged to take direct responsibility for planning, maintenance and the organisation of shop floor activity. It was a challenge for which they were ill prepared.

Shop stewards as agents of coordination: the Standard Motor Company

The Standard Motor Company has been at the centre of much of the speculation regarding post-1945 developments in the British motor vehicle industry. It has fascinated researchers because it combined advanced production techniques and a management system which left many of the shop floor production decisions in the hands of labour. S. Melman, who wrote about the firm in the mid-1950s, viewed the production system employed at Standard as a challenge to the established view that modern industrial production techniques necessitated a powerful managerial class capable of making decisions without reference to shop floor workers. He wrote that: 'The management of the Standard Motor Company has successfully extended its decision-making in relation to other managements at the same time that it has formally acknowledged increasing bilateralism in decision-making within the production plants of the firm.'[34]

Recent work on the post-1945 British motor vehicle industry has stressed that the production system employed by Standard in the 1940s and 1950s was unique and was not adopted by other manufacturers. However, the uniqueness of the Standard case should not be exaggerated. The firm was unique in that labour was extremely well organised in the mid-1940s and that management, led by the maverick managing director J.P. Black, chose to recognise shop floor labour institutions and to incorporate them into their broader managerial strategy rather than resist them as was the case at other British firms.[35] But within the broader picture of the evolution of managerial strategies in the British motor vehicle industry, Standard was not unique in failing to establish direct managerial control over decision making on the shop floor.

It was not until the early 1930s that Standard joined the ranks of British mass producers.[36] In 1929, their output was about one-tenth that of the two leading British firms, Austin and Morris. In the early 1930s there was a major change in management at the firm. J.P. Black replaced R.W. Maudslay, the founder of the firm and its original managing director. Black favoured expanding output and reducing the model range. By the late 1930s, output averaged between 40 000 and 50 000 chassis per annum and Standard had taken a position as one of the 'big six' producers. Their output of private cars was comparable to Fords and about one-half of that of Morris and Austin.[37]

Standard invested heavily in new plant and machinery after 1945 in order to maintain its market share of 10 percent of private cars produced. Total investment in fixed plant nearly doubled in each of the three years following the war. Total investment in fixed assets increased from £750 831 in 1945 to £5354 241 in 1948. Over the same period, investment in fixed assets per workers increased from £134.7 to £555.2.[38] While this fourfold increase in investment per worker in less than three years, is impressive, it is changes in authority patterns on the shop floor which are most pertinent to our study.

Standard had a long history of employing paternalistic and welfarist management methods to gain the loyalty and cooperation of the workforce. In 1910, the Standard Motor Company Benevolent Fund was created to provide for workers facing hardship. During the war, a canteen was built, a recreation field and club house were provided, and a works magazine was published. They also provided child care for their workforce and subscribed to the Coventry Advisory Committee for Women's War Employment (Welfare and Recreation). Their boldest move to try and gain the workers' loyalty came in 1920 when 10 000 shares, representing about 7 percent of total share capital, were set aside for employee purchases. The scheme was unsuccessful and 16 months later only 246 shares had been taken up. During the 1920s, 10 acres of land was purchased and was made available to workers in small lots and on easy credit terms.[39]

With the arrival of Black, these various welfare programmes received a new emphasis. In 1936 the Employees Special Fund was created with the intention of providing sick benefits, death benefits and pensions for production workers, and group life insurance for the staff. The Fund was financed from employee contributions and from profits. Table 9.7 shows how company contributions rose dramatically after the war and then fell again after 1955 and were stopped in 1959.[40]

In 1941, the company announced its intention to provide pensions for all

Table 9.7. *Standard Motor Company, employee special fund*

	Dividends paid (£)	Contributions to special fund (£)	As a percentage of dividends
1936–40	398 388	45 000	11.3
1941–45	472 000	140 000	29.7
1946–55	2 631 185	1 045 000	39.7
1956–59	1 754 753	201 500	11.5

Sources: Standard Archive, MRC, *Board Minutes*, 1936–59.

workers. The plan was formally launched in 1948 when the first booklet was issued outlining benefits. The scheme was not negotiated with labour, and was not part of the collective agreement. Workers with more than 15 years of service were entitled to a pension. Male workers, who could retire at age 65, received benefits ranging from £1 a week for 15 years service to £3 5s for 30 years service. Women, who could retire at 60, received 75 percent of the corresponding male rate.[41]

The reminiscences of former Standard workers suggest that these welfare programmes created a special relationship between the workforce and management.[42] A management official emphasised Black's unique approach to labour. He recalled: 'I think it was all in his mind that he wanted to be this model employer...He loved to appear to be the big benefactor.'[43]

Despite Standard's enthusiasm for welfarist benefits, life on the shop floor could often be harsh for the workers. The company had joined the EEF in 1917 and, like most Federated firms, was unsympathetic toward shop stewards and shop steward committees. Labour had little job security, as the demand for labour was still seasonal and there were no rules regulating lay-offs or recalls. Without an organised shop floor labour organisation, management was relatively free to adjust piece-rate prices unilaterally. Labour complained of continuous piece-rate reductions and speed-up during the interwar period, as management tried to lower costs so that they could compete with Morris and Austin. It was a series of piece-rate reductions in the late 1930s which seems to have rekindled labour interest in trade unionism.[44] But it was not until the war that shop stewards were recognised by management and began to participate in shop floor bargaining. After the war, Standard was one of the few British firms which was willing to continue working with shop stewards. By 1948, Standard workers claimed to have achieved 100 percent unionisation, probably the only such motor vehicle firm in Britain.[45]

As the war came to an end, and Standard began to plan major investments in new capital equipment, they also began the search for a new set of production institutions which would insure that the capital equipment was used efficiently.[46] In late 1944, Black proposed paying labour a high fixed day rate plus a bonus based on total output. The Coventry Employers Association had reservations about this system, particularly the high level of wages being proposed. By May of 1945, perhaps because of EEF concerns, Black dropped the proposal to move to day work. In its place he proposed an incentive system with a recognised bonus rate of 100 percent and base rates much higher than before the war. The proposals, which threatened to push up wages, were unpopular with other employers and Black reluctantly withdrew from the EEF.[47]

The Standard workers saw their relative wages increase under the new agreement. In 1938, they earned 32 percent more than the average production worker in the motor vehicle industry. This increased to 42 percent by 1947.[48] Undoubtedly, the tight Coventry labour market after 1945 influenced pay policy, but there were other factors at work which help explain the rapid rise in relative wages at the company. Melman concluded that, by the early 1940s, management at Standard had come to realise that with the increase in capital–labour ratios, unit costs could no longer be kept down by squeezing wages. Instead there was a need for a new form of cooperation between labour and management which would ensure maximum utilisation of the capital equipment. This cooperation could be had only by paying higher wages and improving the working relationship between labour and management. This search for a new cooperative relationship shaped institutional innovation at Standard over the next ten years.[49]

Black remained dissatisfied with the existing wage payment system. While negotiations were being conducted with labour over revisions to the system, the board initiated a study into the possibility of adopting a profit sharing scheme.[50] In June 1947 it was proposed that, after paying labour its wages and paying capital a fair return on its investment based on the average yield on leading industrial investments, any remaining profit would be divided between labour and capital. A consultant's report made it quite clear how such a system would change the relationship between labour and the company. He wrote:

The schemes, in effect, make the existing Stockholders Participating Preference Shareholders and the employees become Ordinary Shareholders (without having a control in the Company or the necessity of investing capital).[51]

The consultant recommended a number of schemes. The scheme he preferred divided surplus profits in relation to the income of capital and labour. Capital's income was based on dividends earned and labour's income was based on wages earned. This would have resulted in labour receiving about 90 percent of surplus profits. Alternative schemes would have provided labour with as little as one-quarter of any surplus profits.

The profit sharing scheme was never put into effect. Instead, after nearly two years of negotiations with a committee of shop stewards, a new group bonus incentive payment system was adopted. Melman viewed the new scheme as being more compatible with automated production systems which required group cooperation, not individual effort maximisation. Part of management's motive in moving to the new payment system was to reduce the administrative costs involved in paying workers and reduce the variation of earnings between workers. Existing bonus rates varied from 175 to 250 percent, and over 100 base rates were used to classify workers. The company sought a system which would reduce the number of base rates, which would allow all production workers to earn the same bonus based on total output of 'complete salable units', and which could be applied to indirect labour.[52] The company obviously hoped that such a system would reduce labour unrest caused by the different workers comparing their bonus earnings with those of other workers, and labour unrest created by indirect workers who were falling behind under the existing payment system.

The company proposed establishing eight different base rates for male direct and indirect workers ranging from £7 16s to £5, and two rates for women £4 16s and £4 10s. These rates were calculated on the existing base rates and rolled in a portion of existing bonus earnings so as to reduce average bonus rates to between $82\frac{1}{2}$ and 90 percent. These proposals were to yield direct workers about the same earnings and provided indirects with a little more. The company had hoped to put all production workers in each plant into a single gang, but were forced to accept 15 gangs at the motor vehicle plant, down from 122.

The most important feature of the new payment system was the creation of large gangs and the formal recognition of the role of shop stewards in coordinating shop floor activity. The creation of large gangs meant that management ceased to control individual workers in the plant and instead turned its attention to the operation of entire gangs. Melman observed that, 'management does not attempt to keep track of, and exercise detailed control over, individual workers'.[53] Within this context, the role of the foreman was reduced to surveillance over things rather than detailed control over labour. The reduced role of the foreman allowed the company to employ only one foreman for every 200 workers, about one-quarter the number found in another British motor vehicle plant. In the United States, Ford was employing one foreman for every 18 production workers at the new Cleveland engine plant and one foreman for every 31 workers at the Detroit plant.[54]

While the responsibilities and the number of foremen were reduced the responsibilities of the shop stewards were enhanced. The stewards were no longer involved in the negotiation of individual piece-rates. Instead they acquired new responsibilities for negotiating total manning levels which had a direct bearing on the group bonus earnings and in ensuring continuous production which again influenced the group bonus. The managerial report on the new payment system argued that: 'The Shop Stewards throughout the factory, become fully conscious that nothing must stop the final track in the interest of all the workers' earnings over the whole factory.'[55] Melman argued that the shop stewards: '... acted to regularize the pace of production and thereby attain a sustained level of worker earnings. The workers in the various gangs have regarded the stewards as responsible for assuring a smooth flow of work and thereby wages.'[56] Shop stewards were also made responsible for the movement of workers between jobs and for evening out work loads. By the early 1950s, there appears to have been a managerial culture in place which stressed the minimising of managerial and supervisory work.[57]

The production institutions which were developed at Standard in the late 1940s and early 1950s can be viewed as the logical extension of the British system of mass production to the new production techniques of automation. The Standard managers chose to use the shop stewards system, which had been established during the war, to coordinate shop floor activity for management. In the opinion of Black, and other Standard managers, the shop stewards were better placed than anyone else to ensure the continuity of effort needed to achieve high productivity within an integrated production process. In the short-run this strategy worked. Standard continued to enjoy a relatively high return on invested capital, and labour saw its relative wage advantage increase from 42 percent above the average in the motor vehicle industry in 1947, to 78 percent higher in 1950, after which it began to decline but still stood 62 percent above the average in 1955.[58]

In January of 1954, Black retired as managing director. This signalled a change in managerial attitudes toward the new authority of shop stewards. Melman noted the growing anti-union element within the Standard management.[59] In January of 1955, there was a move to restrict the freedom of shop stewards. J.L. Jones, district secretary of the Confederation of Shipbuilding and Engineering Unions, complained that management was trying to increase restrictions on trade union activity within the works, including terminating the right of shop stewards to hold weekly meetings on Company premises, forcing shop stewards to seek written permission to hold gang meetings, and requiring stewards to disclose to management the business to be discussed at these meetings.[60] After a short strike, management announced it planned to renegotiate the agreement with the unions, '. . . so as to establish beyond any doubt that the management have the right to manage their own establishment'.[61]

The new restriction on shop steward rights coincided with a new investment programme in which automated techniques played a central role. Standard's position in the market was complicated by the fact that while the return to capital during the early 1950s was quite respectable, averaging nearly 25 percent between 1950 and 1955, profit margins per vehicle sold were relatively low. In 1953, Standard earned £29 12s 5d per vehicle before depreciation, while Ford earned £77 11s 8d, Vauxhall earned £107 16s 7d, and BMC earned £53. In the economic downturn of 1955 and 1956, Standard was seriously affected and saw its return to capital fall to 5 percent, a post-1945 low and only one-quarter to one-third that of its nearest competitor.[62]

In July of 1955 a meeting was held between management and labour officials to discuss working conditions under the new technology. A new hard line was taken by management which reflected an increased desire to control effort norms in order to increase the efficiency of the new capital equipment. Demands were made that managerial recommendations regarding the number of machines per operator should be acted upon as soon as the operators were trained, and that bargaining over bonus times would continue but that management would take the initiative in setting times which were to be worked during any negotiations with the shop stewards. Effort norms were at the heart of managerial concerns. They informed the labour representatives that they required a fair day's work from everyone in the plant, something which they felt they were not getting.[63]

In April 1956 an important strike took place at Standard over the question of redundancies. British labour had been waging a campaign to restrict managerial rights to make labour redundant. The installation of the new production techniques at the Standard tractor works coincided with a downturn in the demand for motor vehicles. Standard felt unable to absorb the surplus labour and announced plans to make a large number of workers redundant. This led to a strike which, despite achieving national prominence, resulted in a major set-back for the shop steward organisation and the novel set of production institutions employed by the company. By August, nearly 40 percent of the workforce had been made redundant, and in the process the leadership of the shop stewards movement was decimated.[64] The shop stewards were unable to defend their organisation as they had been unable to agree to a seniority clause with the company in earlier contracts. They refused, despite a managerial offer, to be a party to the selection of those who were to be made redundant. They preferred to continue their support for the broader British labour challenge to management's right to make workers redundant.

In his incomplete examination of the strike, Melman explained the attack on the shop stewards as a result of a shift in their objectives. Initially, the objective of the shop stewards was to extend worker decision making, but by the mid-1950s he claimed they were influenced by political agitators who were more interested in competing for managerial control of the firm. The strike provided an opportunity for the new anti-union management group to rid themselves of the troublesome shop floor labour organisations.[65] This analysis fails to explain why a new anti-union managerial philosophy emerged in the first place. It could have been a coincidence of timing and the change in personnel in the mid-1950s, or it could have been a response to increases in labour demands. We would argue that it reflects changes in production techniques. Standard had gone further than most other British firms in sharing authority with labour and in automating the production process. Standard was also one of the first to realise that as capital–labour ratios rose, labour could use its control of shop floor decisions to enhance its bargaining leverage. It was this realisation which led management to challenge the shop stewards in the mid-1950s and which led to the decline of the experiments in bilateral decision making. By early 1957, Standard had returned to the fold of the Employers Federation.[66]

Shortly after these upheavals, Standard lost its autonomy and its ability to follow an independent managerial strategy. The company had been searching for a partner for some time. In 1957 a proposed merger with Rootes was called off. By 1959 they had divested themselves of the tractor works which was sold to Massey-Harris-Ferguson Ltd, and in 1961 they became the first major acquisition by Leyland and set the stage for the eventual emergence of a single British mass producer in the 1970s.[67] In the process, Standard's problems were overshadowed by those of the vehicle industry as a whole.

New production techniques and the British system of mass production

Standard was the only major British motor vehicle firm to embark on a radical restructuring of production institutions in the late 1940s. Most other firms tried to return to the institutional framework which had worked in the interwar years. Individual incentive payment systems with relatively high bonus rates remained in vogue. Management tried to restore its unilateral control of the ratio of wages to effort by challenging the authority of the trade unions, and in particular the shop stewards. Turner was one of the first to note an emerging disequilibrium between the new techniques of automation and coordination through incentive payment systems. He argued that: 'Some of the piece-work plants, in particular, may well have allowed their payment system – and the insistences of the production process itself – to assume an unduly large part of the supervisory function.'[68]

In the immediate postwar years, management had little incentive to push for changes in shop floor authority patterns which might lead to strikes by labour. The destruction of most continental factories combined with the strong demand which followed the war created a seller's market. Maxcy suggested this was a period when, 'competition took the form of a production race rather than a battle for sales'.[69] Exports absorbed as much as 80 percent of total output and for a number of years Britain was the largest exporter of motor vehicles.[70] By the mid-1950s competition in output markets began to increase and British firms were forced to seek changes which would increase productivity and reduce costs.

One of the most serious problems British management faced was the failure of incentive payment systems to control wage growth or guarantee continuous production. Labour was enjoying a decisive improvement in its bargaining power. After years of resisting incentive payment systems, labour became their most vocal defenders. The Austin shop stewards argued:

Under the existing Piecework system we have a large measure of control over how much wages we will earn, the amount of work to be performed for these wages, and the opportunity to re-negotiate piecework prices if the material, or means of production change, or by mutual agreement. This means that from time to time our members have had to enter into struggle with management to alter prices, without this determination to fight, improvements would not have come about. Of course its not always that we have had the level of control that we have now.[71]

Table 9.8. *Reported strikes in the*
motor vehicle industry, 1921–64

	Number of strikes	Striker-days (000s)
1921–30	27	84.1
1931–39	37	225.7
1940–44	121	281.6
1945–49	78	302.5
1950–54	59	683.5
1955–59	197	820.6
1960–64	401	1366.9

Source: H.A. Turner, G. Clack & G. Roberts, *Labour Relations in the Motor Industry* (London, 1967), p. 232.

Between 1953 and 1969, shop floor bargaining over piece-rates accounted for 72 percent of all wage growth in Coventry motor vehicle plants, the remaining 28 percent was the product of national wage bargains.[72] Workers at plants paid on incentive systems quickly caught up to and surpassed workers paid by the hour at plants such as Ford. By 1968, a British worker on incentive payment systems averaged 74d an hour compared with $56\frac{1}{2}$d paid at Ford's Dagenham plant.[73]

For the first time in the industry's history, labour stoppages became a major problem. Table 9.8, which records reported strikes involving more than 100 lost labour days, reveals the rise in strike incidence.

These officially recorded strikes are simply the tip of the iceberg. The highly fragmented wage bargaining structure associated with incentive payment systems led to numerous small strikes, which were usually not officially recorded. At a single BMC plant in Cowley, there were 253 local stoppages in 1964 and 297 in 1965. At the BMC Longbridge plant there were 935 internal disputes between 1966 and 1971. The impact of these largely unreported strikes is difficult to measure. Turner estimated that in the mid-1960s, unreported strikes at BMC plants may have accounted for one-half of lost output, while at other firms they were much less important.[74] It is clear the British workers found short strikes involving only a few workers increasingly effective as the production system became more integrated and as capital–labour ratios rose.

After almost half a century of promoting incentive payment systems as the key to sound managerial practices, management began to question their efficiency. In an early study, W. Brown argued incentive payment systems presented managerial problems in setting prices and introducing new production methods. He questioned whether in fact incentive systems increased effort and was critical of management's tendency to abdicate its responsibilities for decision making under payment by result.[75] Flanders, in his analysis of the growing managerial critique of payment by results, argued that the problem was not that the systems were in 'decay', as was commonly suggested, but that they were no longer fulfilling managerial objectives. They were no longer an effective means of controlling labour or coordinating shop floor activity. As he pointed out, payment by results systems were operating with unprecedented efficiency from the perspective of labour.[76]

The first British motor vehicle firm to abandon incentive payment systems was General Motor's British subsidiary Vauxhall in 1956. Vauxhall had experimented with fixed day rate systems in the early 1920s before the GM takeover. But within a few years they returned to a group incentive system with relatively low bonus rates. Average bonus earnings were less than 25 percent prior to 1939, while after the war they began to edge up to just under 60 percent, but still well below the norm in other British plants.[77]

Vauxhall management gave two main reasons for switching from payment by results to fixed day rates. Management found that the longer incentive payment systems were in use, the more adept labour became in exploiting the system to its advantage. Managers complained that there was a tendency for bonus rates to rise without any corresponding improvement in productivity, and that the system was 'getting out of hand'. They also argued that new production techniques, installed at a cost of £34 million in 1956 and 1957, required more stringent managerial control over labour effort and shop floor activity.[78] R. Pearson, Vauxhall's managing director, stressed that the new techniques required continuous effort and balanced output, while payments by results produced uneven effort and unbalanced output. Pearson argued:

Today it is quite clear that planned production entails controlled production, and that unpredictables must as far as possible be eliminated. Output incentives must be replaced by an environment conducive to the performance of set tasks; by an inducement to meet precisely both quantity requirements and quality specifications. Put shortly and bluntly, management today is committed to preproduction planning and cannot delegate its responsibilities for coordinated output to any system other than that controlled by management.[79]

Pearson stressed the productivity effects of moving to fixed day wages and managerial control of the production process. The evidence suggests that throughout the 1960s, Vauxhall productivity was about the same as BMC which remained on incentive payment systems.[80] The real advantage of the new payment system appears to have been its ability to control wage increases. By the late 1960s, Vauxhall workers were amongst the worst paid motor vehicle workers, earning less than two-thirds the rate paid to pieceworkers at Longbridge.[81] The new payment system had ambiguous effects on productivity, but clearly shifted the wage effort bargain in management's favour.

The second group of British plants to abandon incentive payment systems were also under American control. In 1964, Chrysler acquired a major interest in the Rootes Car Company, which itself was formed through the earlier merger of a number of pioneering British firms including Humber, Hillman, Sunbeam, Singer and Vulcan.[82] As was the case at Vauxhall, management proposals to reform production institutions coincided with a major capital investment programme. In 1967 the firm began installing some £60 million in new British production facilities.

Two years of negotiations over a new payment system for the main Coventry plant had made little progress by mid-1968. The company threatened to move unilaterally and force labour to accept Measured Day Work (MDW). The workforce voted to resist any such move, and only a last minute compromise avoided a strike. Young and Hood viewed the compromise as critical in that it preserved an element of labour control over the effort bargain which had emerged under incentive payment systems. In return for unilateral control of track speeds, management agreed to share authority over decisions on staffing levels with any disputes being settled through arbitration. In 1970 labour's hand was strengthened further with the acquisition of veto rights over staffing proposals.[83] Through its control of track speeds, management was able to exert more control over the productivity of capital equipment. The cost of this concession was granting labour significant, some would say excessive, control over the ratio of wages to effort. By 1969, Chrysler (UK) workers, compared with other European producers, were by far the best paid, earning 30 to 60 percent more for identical tasks.[84] The MDW systems as applied at Chrysler was the exact antithesis to interwar incentive systems which gave labour control of effort norms and the productivity of capital, while management controlled the ratio of wages to effort. Under MDW at Chrysler, management controlled the productivity of capital but labour controlled the ratio of wages to effort.

Production institutions changed dramatically with the shift in payment system. The number of foremen employed increased from one for every 140 production workers under piecework to one for every 25 production workers under day work. The positions of lead hands and chargehands were eliminated and their responsibilities for coordinating shop floor activity and overseeing labour were transferred to the foremen. The stature of the industrial engineering department was increased as it became responsible for measuring standard work loads while a new department was created to oversee industrial relations. In this new arrangement, foremen complained that they lacked the authority to perform their tasks and that they were constantly undermined by the Industrial Relations Department's propensity to take a soft line in order to 'preserve peace at all costs'.[85]

Chrysler (UK) was the first major British motor vehicle firm to collapse in the 1970s. Many reasons have been advanced for their collapse, including their failure to rationalise and integrate their European plants, and the tensions created by employing American managers in key European positions. There is little doubt that poor labour relations played a role in the company's decline; some have even argued that it was central to their problems. The company averaged 500 disputes per annum in the early 1970s and even though between two-thirds and three-quarters of these disputes lasted less than four hours, they had a serious effect on productivity.[86]

It is of some interest that Chrysler management, having failed to regain control of the production process through MDW, decided in 1975 to renew the rights of labour to participate in company decision making. In May of 1975, a prominent Chrysler (UK) manager declared that, 'for two years we have realised that with a changing world greater participation... in the decision making process and in the operation of our company [by] the trade unions was something we ought to bring about'.[87] Detroit had directed its British managers to develop a new managerial style which was more sensitive to labour interests and which included better communication with labour and labour participation in decision making.[88]

Labour was cool to the idea of formalising its involvement in decision making and rejected the initial proposals. In August of 1975, new proposals were made in the form of an Employee Participation Programme. The reforms included; shop floor based Employee Representation Committees which would meet weekly with management to review the operation of the plant; the appointment of employee representatives to committees dealing with production levels, staffing, recruitment and quality; and the appointment of employee representatives to the board of directors.[89] Negotiations over these proposals were not completed as the company soon faced a major financial crisis.

In negotiating a rescue package with the government, the question of industrial democracy resurfaced. Chrysler agreed to overhaul its labour relations and draw labour representatives into policy making meetings. The first tangible manifestation of this new approach was the proposal for saving the company which was a joint management labour document. In late 1977 it was proposed that management's long-run economic strategy should be negotiated with labour representatives and should appear as part of the formal labour contract. This was resisted by trade union officials who feared being tied down to unforeseen implications of the plan. It was shop floor officials who showed the greatest enthusiasm for participation and for becoming formally involved in day-to-day decision making.[90] These experiments in industrial democracy were barely off the ground when they were undermined by Chrysler's decision in 1978 to sell its European operations to Peugeot.

The plants which became the nucleus of British Leyland were among the last to switch to fixed day rate payment systems. During the late 1960s, BMC management grew increasingly critical of incentive payment systems. It was argued that they led to instability of earnings and to inequality of earnings which caused numerous labour disputes. They created the need for extended bargaining over prices whenever there was a change in product design or production technique. Labour's strategy of working at a slower day rate pace and accepting lower day rate wages until times were agreed, was proving to be increasingly effective as capital investments increased during the 1960s.[91]

The move to fixed wage payment systems first appeared within BMC at those plants which were relatively new or which were built outside of the traditional vehicle building centres. In 1963, the BMC Bathgate plant moved to MDW. Labour was able to protect its interests in the effort bargain through an agreement to set work standards mutually. An investigation of the plant in the mid-1960s did not bode well for future experiments with the new payment system. H.T. Rudd, the plant director, complained that the plant was constantly losing money and that a major part of the problem was low levels of productivity. He complained that output in the Bathgate machine shop was only about 60 percent of what one would expect in a shop on incentive payment systems. He felt the plant could easily be reorganised to increase output, but that any such move would probably precipitate a 'general strike'.[92]

Management approached reforming pay systems at the older plants in Coventry, Birmingham and Oxford with much more caution. In August of 1967 they began a series of meetings with national union officials on job evaluation, work study and new payment systems. At the first meeting, management presented a carefully worded statement of intent. They wanted to reform payment systems to reflect the content of jobs and performance of the employee, indicating a managerial belief that wages were no longer representative of effort. Management was initially willing to follow historical custom and allow labour some control over effort norms. In an otherwise vaguely worded document, they clearly specified, 'acceptance of the fact that individual employees should have some influence on their own effort'.[93]

While union officials were willing to discuss new payment systems at the national level, the shop stewards and the rank and file were suspicious of management's intentions. It was not until January of 1972 that the Joint Shop Stewards Committee at the Longbridge plant dropped their refusal to discuss MDW with management.[94] A publication by an Oxford group warned BMC workers of the perils of MDW. It was seen as a system for controlling the growth of labour wages, weakening shop floor labour institutions and loosening labour control of effort norms.[95] Another publication in the early 1970s warned employees that management intended to use MDW to wrest back control over production and pay. However, the agreement at Chrysler was pointed to as an example of how the 'sting' could be taken out of pay reform. Quoting the secretary of the Chrysler Joint Shop Stewards' Committee:

The whole secret of MDW lies in one clause, namely the Company have the prerogative of saying what the track speed will be, but the unions mutually agree as to the labour load required to run at these speeds. It is this clause which takes the sting out of MDW. Without it we would be slaves to the job.[96]

Despite the shop floor workers general suspicion of managerial intentions in reforming payment systems, they were not without their own criticisms of payment by results. The rapid growth of bonus earnings relative to base rates in the postwar period increased the instability of earnings. Even more serious, the new production techniques reduced the control individual workers had over their own bonus earnings and made them increasingly dependent upon the quality of shop floor coordination and the willingness of workers in other departments and plants to work continuously. The evidence suggests that management was too weak to provide the needed coordination and control and that the task was beyond the abilities of unorganised workers. In many cases it was the shop stewards who filled this institutional gap.

The rise of shop stewards as central figures in maintaining continuous production can be detected immediately after the war, despite managerial attempts to limit their authority. On at least two occasions in 1946, labour called on the shop stewards to settle sectional labour disputes which were reducing the flow of work through the plants and thereby reduced bonus earnings.[97] As the degree of integration in the plants increased, the pressure on the shop stewards to mediate disputes also increased. In December of 1962, the shop stewards at Longbridge complained about stoppages by workers in the paint shop which were threatening to restrict plant output and bonus earnings.[98] The role of shop stewards as mediators was forcefully put forward in the submission of the Austin shop stewards to the Royal Commission on Trade Unions in 1966. Challenging the accepted wisdom that shop stewards were strike happy, they argued:

The Motor Industry has been conspicuous because of the large numbers being affected and laid off because of the actions of a few ... and the general opinion has been created that this is something that the Shop Stewards welcome. Nothing could be further from the truth and any Shop Steward in a responsible position and having to act in the general interest could easily explain why. If at the Austin for instance, thousands are laid off because of the actions of a few men, then these thousands and their representatives want to know why and whether it is justified action. There is, in an organised factory a strong sense of shop loyalty and solidarity, but it is not given without reason and the leadership in the factory gets the criticism if workers are called upon to suffer unnecessary hardship. There is also the principle that any advances should be made on behalf of the whole factory and not that any section should be well out in front because of any action they might take without having any consideration for its effect on others.[99]

The shop stewards were also called upon to provide needed coordination between production departments in the face of managerial incompetence. Reports by the convener at the Longbridge plant and the minutes of the Austin Joint Shop Stewards meetings reveal a growing sense of frustration amongst production workers regarding management's inability to keep the plant operating. In 1954, in the midst of the automation controversy, the Austin shop stewards were chastising management for failing to invest in up-to-date material handling methods in the press shop. The shop stewards became involved when low output from the press shop created shortages and loss of earnings in the rest of the plant. The shop stewards decided to take greater control over the situation by scheduling regular meetings between the stewards in the press shop and the stewards in the body shop in order to coordinate material flows.[100]

In 1967, Etheridge argued that waiting time, breakdowns and other managerial inefficiencies caused more man hours to be lost than labour stoppages.[101] In his annual report in January of 1968 he argued:

We are convinced that the real short time working is not due to the disputes, but to the lack of coordination of the management with its suppliers and that most of the disputes have been caused by this or other of management's inefficiencies.[102]

Such a conclusion is given some support in a study by Scamp of lost time at the Pressed Steel Fisher plant in Cowley in 1966. Scamp suggested that of all lost time, 19.66 percent was the result of waiting time, 14.61 percent was the result of lay-offs, 4.79 percent was caused by strikes and 13.24 percent was the result of unauthorised labour absences.[103]

Indicative of the growing involvement of the Longbridge shop stewards in filling a coordination gap, was an investigation into low output levels in the transmission case section of the East Works. At a conference held in the shops in January of 1967, labour and management criticised each other for practices which reduced productivity. One of the shop stewards criticised 'the shop floor supervision for failing in their duty'. Another steward complained: 'We are not getting the piecework conditions that we are entitled to. Get fitters and electricians on the jobs quicker and we will have a happy section and be able to earn money.' Management complained that many of the machine breakdowns were caused by labour taking short cuts in an attempt to earn bonus, or failing to do other tasks such as cleaning up the swarf or failing to oil the machines, tasks which would reduce the time available for making bonus.[104]

The committee appointed to investigate conditions in this department included the general superintendent of the East Works, the senior shop steward and the senior rate fixer. The committee concluded that the major cause of lost time and output was machine breakdowns which were particularly damaging in this department because it was organised on a line principle. Its recommendations are quite remarkable in that one would have expected such decisions to have been the responsibility of management, rather than the product of a labour inspired investigation into lost time and earnings. It recommended assigning a fitter and an electrician to the department to speed the process of rectifying breakdowns, the scheduling of downtime for preventive maintenance, improving the layout of the plant to ease maintenance operations, an increase in the number of supervisors, improvements in inspection and greater attention to stocking necessary tools.[105]

By the early 1970s, labour frustrations with production stoppages caused by aging equipment, internal and external disputes, and managerial incompetence led many workers to question the desirability of incentive payment systems. In December of 1971, the Rota Dip department in the West Works at Longbridge asked for permission to negotiate a fixed day rate system. Members complained that it was impossible to work continuously and earn high wages because of continuous congestion in other departments. They were averaging only 13/- an hour, almost 5/- below the average male piecework wage, and well below the £1 being proposed by British Leyland on the new flat rate system.[106]

Reform of payment systems was a corporate policy of British Leyland, but was carried out by local management on a plant by plant basis. One of the first plants to work Measured Day Work, and one which played an important role in the negotiations at the main Longbridge plant and probably other BMC plants, was the newly built Cofton Hackett engine plant. The plant was highly automated, and management argued that incentive systems were inappropriate since the work pace was mechanically determined. Labour was sympathetic to changing the payment system in an attempt to reduce the instability of earnings, but it wanted guarantees regarding employment, mutuality in setting effort norms, and a bonus on track output. But, perhaps most significant, was the demand for a built-in wage growth mechanism to compensate labour for the loss of the learning effect which tended to push up piecework bonus earnings over time.[107] The learning effect was an important mechanism by which labour raised earnings to keep pace with inflation.

Negotiations over the new wage system were lengthy. In 1968 an interim agreement was reached fixing hourly wages of production workers at 13/- per hour, which included a fixed 25 percent incentive bonus. The interim agreement indicated the intention to base future bonuses on performance. The clauses on mutuality in setting effort standards were relatively weak. Work study and skill analysis techniques were to be used and management gave assurances that they would discuss these with labour, but there was no guarantee that the work load would be mutually agreed.[108] It was not until 1970 that a final agreement was reached, and even then there was extreme controversy amongst the stewards about the degree to which mutuality in setting effort standards had been achieved.[109]

Negotiations over a new payment system at the BMC plants in Cowley began in 1968.[110] Management proposed graduated payment systems rather than flat rate systems. The Stepped Incentive Payment system, as it was known, gave management the authority to choose output levels while labour was offered a choice of six different manning levels for each level of output. For given levels of output, the fixed hourly wage would fall as manning levels increased. As was the case at Chrysler, the new payment system gave management greater control over the level of output and the productivity of capital equipment. Managerial control of the ratio of wages to effort was also enchanced by the proposal to have manning standards set by industrial engineers using recognised work study methods. Labour retained the right to influence effort norms and per capita earnings.

At the old Morris and Pressed Steel Fisher plants in Cowley the negotiations were quite lengthy due to labour's refusal to accept the company proposals. The two sides met at Central Conference in York, the last stage of the procedure process, in January 1971 where they registered a failure to agree. Management threatened to act unilaterally and impose a new payment system. The system suggested was not the Stepped Incentive System but, rather, a single flat rate for standard performance. Whether this was management's intention all along is not known. The workforce continued to resist any reforms. It reported for work, but worked at the pace associated with the lower pay of a grade II indirect worker, a common practice while piece prices were being negotiated. Management was forced back to the bargaining table and in February of 1971 an agreement was reached which provided for a single fixed rate of £40 and mutuality in setting effort standards.[111]

The way in which mutuality in setting effort standards evolved is of critical importance, for it lies at the heart of control over the effort bargain. Management envisioned a system where industrial engineers would establish standards which could then be discussed with the shop stewards. However, given the 'scientific' nature of this process, it was assumed that there would be little room for bargaining on the shop floor. The shop stewards claimed that, in practice, the proposals of the industrial engineers had little impact in setting standards. Instead the shop stewards formulated their own estimates of what was fair and used these as the basis for negotiations. Ford suggested that rather than checking the authority of shop stewards the new payment system actually enhanced their role as it legitimated their authority to bargain over a range of new issues including staffing levels and working conditions.[112]

Ford's evidence on the productivity effect of the new payment system needs to be treated with some caution as the company was negotiating the extension of the system to other areas of the plant at the time of this study. Nonetheless, the evidence suggests that effort norms fell as much as 20 percent. This drop reflects both the success of the shop stewards in negotiating high manning levels, and the weaknesses in shop floor supervision. The supervisors felt that their job had been made more difficult under the new payment system and that labour was less apt to report potential machine problems or material shortages when paid on a fixed day rate.[113]

In Birmingham, negotiations began at the plants of the former Rover Company in 1970. The shift away from incentive payment systems, which one commentator labelled the 'quiet revolution' was initiated by a labour-requested clause in the 1970 piecework agreement that investigations begin on ways to improve earnings security. Again, management proposed a stepped incentive system, in this case with five manning levels, and fixed rates of pay for each level of performance.[114] By early 1971, the Stepped Incentive proposals were withdrawn and replaced with a single flat rate, apparently at the insistence of labour. The fixed rate agreed to was based on an effort standard equivalent to 100 set by the British Standards Institute, which was supposed to be equivalent to the exertion required to walk four miles per hour. This new payment system came to be known as the 'Protected Earnings Plan' and was implemented in March of 1971.[115]

As was the case at Cowley, the new Rover payment system led to a reduction in the number of strikes, but led to new and serious problems regarding the enforcement of effort norms and the coordination of shop floor activity. Sutherland suggested that 'effort drift' had replaced 'wage drift' as the central problem facing management. Again, it was the supervisors who were the most vocal in criticising the new payment system claiming that it resulted in 40 hours pay for 40 hours attendance, not 40 hours work. Supervisors claimed that their jobs were more taxing and that labour had less incentive to correct production problems. In fact, supervisors argued that labour had a new positive incentive to create problems. One estimate had labour productivity falling as much as 30 percent.[116]

One shop steward suggested that part of the reason labour productivity had fallen was that labour now worked at a constant pace, and made no attempt to increase effort levels to compensate for unforeseen interruptions such as machine breakdowns or material shortages. The problem was compounded by management's inability to keep the plant running continuously. Sutherland concluded that management lacked the skills to take over the tasks of controlling labour and coordinating the production process and that there was no concerted effort to create these skills.[117] In changing payment systems, Rover also undermined the existing institutions for monitoring and enforcing the effort bargain. In a pattern similar to that found at Standard, the Rover shop stewards had played a central role as agents of coordination and control under incentive payment systems, a role they abandoned under the new fixed wage system. In comparing shop floor activity under the two payment systems, a Rover worker suggested:

If the track stopped or if there were gaps in the track, it was actually the shop stewards on the shop floor that got production out to get the bonus up. Now from the situation we went into with measured day work was, I said to my foreman ... It's all yours now.[118]

The Austin Longbridge plant was one of the last plants to begin negotiations on pay reform. The discussions were sparked by labour requests for pay during lay-offs, reflecting the growing disenchantment with the constant interruptions in work generated by strikes, machine breakdowns and poor managerial coordination. Management proposed lay-off benefits as part of a broader reform of the payment system. The Austin proposals, dated 30 November 1970, provided for a single fixed rate of pay for each grade of labour and a fixed effort norm equal to 100 on the BSI scale. There was no suggestion that labour was going to be given a choice over effort norms, as was the case in early proposals at Cowley, at Rover or at Cofton Hackett.[119]

The shop stewards were not interested in the management proposals and they

Table 9.9. *Average hourly earnings male piece workers, Longbridge (£)*

1965	0.525
1966	0.440
1967	0.469
1968	0.516
1969	0.728
1970	0.882
1971	0.925

Sources: Etheridge Papers, Mss 202/ S/J/3/2/79–160, *Animal Conveners Report*, 1967–1972. All figures except 1969 were reported as earnings per minute or hour on piecework. The 1969 figure was given as earnings per week, without any clear indication of hours worked per week. We divided the given figure by 42.5 hours to obtain an hourly rate.

withdrew their request for lay-off pay hoping this would end the discussions on reforming the payment system.[120] Management was unwilling to drop the issue and it is not difficult to see why. Until the mid-1960s, management had control of earnings in the shops, and was able to force through reductions during the downturn in 1965 and 1966. But, as Table 9.9 reveals, the shop stewards became increasingly successful in pushing up earnings in the late 1960s.

During 1971, management tried to circumvent shop steward opposition to reforming the payment system by appealing directly to small groups of workers.[121] The shop stewards at Longbridge finally dropped their refusal to discuss new payment systems in January of 1972 when they heard that a number of shops were ready to accept an agreement based on the Cofton Hackett settlement.[122] The initial proposals discussed were those made to the Kings Norton workers on the Longbridge site in December of 1971. These proposals threatened to seriously weaken labour control of effort norms. Labour was to be given an opportunity to discuss, negotiate and agree to manning schedules. What is notable about these proposals is the wording of a number of clauses which suggest that shop floor negotiations would be unnecessary as work loads were to be 'professionally' determined. Clause 30 reads:

Management undertakes to examine any disputes about schedules professionally and promptly while the Trades Unions, on their part, agree to use the above procedure only in cases of genuine and significant disagreement and not, as an automatic procedure whenever any new schedules are introduced.[123]

The shop stewards forced management to revise the mutuality clauses and provide labour with firm guarantees that its rights to bargain over effort norms would be retained. Clause 11 of the final agreement committed management to mutuality in setting manning levels. Clause 19 stipulated that current manning levels were not to be changed without full consultation with the trade unions and mutual agreement on the proposed changes. There was no suggestion in the final agreement that professional work study would take precedence over the shop stewards' proposals regarding work loads. In a new departure, the Longbridge agreement contained relaxation allowances for day workers based on the difficulty of the job, something which was unnecessary where labour's time was its own. The agreement was signed 3 November, 1972, and was implemented shortly thereafter.[124]

After 75 years of employing incentive payment systems as a means of controlling labour and coordinating shop floor activity, management throughout the motor vehicle industry had ventured into the era of direct managerial control of the production process. Within three years, British Leyland would join Chrysler in bankruptcy, and within ten years performance related payments would return to the industry.

The collapse of an industry and the belated shift to Fordism

There is little controversy regarding the impact that the shift to MDW had on labour productivity, shop floor coordination, and labour effort norms. Bill Roche, the shop steward convener at the Cowley body plant recalled, '... that the speed and the tempo and the physical effort of people changed dramatically from that of piecework to measured day work'.[125] This was partially the result of labour's ability to use mutuality clauses to negotiate lighter work loads, and partially the result of reduced labour interest in coordinating shop floor activity in order to keep plant running continuously. A union official argued:

The only thing that has happened with the introduction of MDW is that where our people used to do their own chasing ... at the present time, the management is responsible for supplying the material. Of course you do not get from individuals the same kind of approach to obtaining materials to keep the job rolling as you did previously.[126]

Another union official argued:

In the old days on piecework, because of the antiquated machinery, if anything happened to that machine, that affected their livelihood and the people who were brought up on piecework would put it right ... they would keep the machine going with a piece of string. Now, because there is no incentive there, if the machine breaks down they do not bother to use their initiative.[127]

Nor was management able to fill the coordination gap. John Barber, who had been a manager at Fords and was later brought into the British Leyland organisation recalled:

In the Measured Day Work system on the other hand, the foreman is very much a first line manager. And this probably was the biggest single thing which made the transition

Table 9.10. *Vehicles per employee, British Leyland,*
1968–83

1968	5.6	1976	5.4
1969	5.5	1977	4.0
1970	4.9	1978	4.2
1971	5.4	1979	3.9
1972	5.9	1980	3.7
1973	5.7	1981	4.2
1974	4.9	1982	4.8
1975	4.4	1983	5.5

Source: P. Willman and G. Winch, *Innovation and Management Control*
(Cambridge, 1985), p. 20.

difficult and a problem in the early days. I think that we underestimated the calibre of the experience of the BMC foreman and we underestimated the time we should have allowed for training for this major change.[128]

Table 9.10 shows how serious the decline in labour productivity was in the decade following the introduction of MDW.

The crisis brought on by the shift to MDW was the last chapter in a sequence of events which can be traced back to British management's inability to break labour's influence over the organisation of the work place in the final decades of the nineteenth cenury. Without direct control of labour effort norms, British managers lacked direct control of the productivity of capital and hence were reluctant to follow the capital intensive example of American producers in the interwar period. However, the clear superiority of the integrated and automated production techniques perfected by the Americans in the 1930s and the 1940s, forced British managers to invest in new production techniques which raised capital–labour ratios. Other than Standard, they made few changes in their production institutions as long as the postwar sellers' market continued. But when competition tightened in the late 1950s, the inconsistencies between American production techniques and British production institutions became apparent.

British managers found it was more difficult to change production institutions than it was to change machine systems. Management lacked the skills to execute the new tasks it was called upon to perform. Labour showed a great reluctance to let go of the advantages won in the 1960s, remembering all too clearly the hard times of the previous decades. This institutional crisis slowed the rate at which British firms such as BL invested in new production techniques. The crisis was compounded by some very bad model decisions.[129]

BL management was aware that the company was in trouble in the early 1970s when they first approached the government for financing. Since the mid-1920s, British motor vehicle firms have shown a willingness to use profits to satisfy short-run investor demands for dividends rather than to satisfy long-run investment requirements. There is some suspicion that post-1968 profits at BL may have been inflated by low depreciation charges. Despite this, BL distributed over 94 percent of reported after-tax profits as dividends. Retained profits were the source of only £4 million of new capital between 1967 and 1974.[130] This high payout strategy probably reflects both the scars of Edwardian social turmoil, which must have increased the perceived risk in long-run investments in Britain, and British management's inability to control effort norms which had serious implications for the productivity of capital investments.[131] When it came time to invest in new plant in the late 1960s, the company had no capital reserve, and when the banks refused to advance BL any further funds in 1974, the state was forced to intervene, paving the way for nationalisation.

As part of this funding package, Don Ryder was appointed to study the company and to bring forward a long-run policy. Ryder stressed the lack of investment in new plant as the central cause of low productivity. The Ryder plan proposed resolving the lack of investment by a massive infusion of capital. The initial estimates were for an investment of over £1 billion. The final cost was closer to £2.4 billion.[132]

Ryder noted serious problems in the coordination of shop floor activity and labour relations. The interruptions in production which had plagued British firms since the early 1960s were attributed to external labour disputes and a host of managerial weaknesses including poor maintenance, faulty scheduling, and shortages of materials and components. Ryder also recognised that there were serious problems with the existing MDW payment systems, but argued that the new payment systems had not been given a chance to prove themselves, and hence should not be altered. In the labour relations area, Ryder proposed adopting a form of industrial democracy with joint labour management committees at all levels of operations other than the Board of Management. Ryder's intention was to restore a sense of commitment by labour in the success of the enterprise, something which appeared to be lacking under the new payment systems.[133]

The failure of the Rover SDI project at Solihull seems to epitomise the problems facing BL and the industry in the 1970s.[134] Conceived by the board of BL shortly after the Leyland BMH merger in 1968, the SDI was to be the first step in the revitalisation of the British motor industry. Over £125 million in 1976 prices was invested in the project. A new model was designed to challenge BMW in the upper end of the market, and an entirely new plant was built on a green field site. The new facility opened in 1976. Within six years it was closed.

Rover had a long history of producing vehicles for the upper end of the volume market. On the shop floor, direct managerial control was weak and the detailed organisation of work was situated within the work group.[135] The new production system adopted for the SDI project was a blend of up-to-date capital intensive production techniques and old production institutions. During the transition to MDW in the early 1970s, Rover officials had admitted that prior to the 1970s, 'management had in effect ceded large areas of authority in the organisation and regulation of work on the track'.[136] The SDI did not mark a major change from this practice. Senior management officials accepted that the start-up of the SDI line depended on customary modes of labour control. Shop floor workers influenced the recruitment of labour, provided training for 'green labour', dealt with many of the problems associated with imperfect product and task design, and were largely responsible for the fine tuning needed to reach management's target of 3000 vehicles per week.[137]

Rover management seemed unable to deal with the contradictions in its plans for reorganising the production process. On the one hand management proposed shifting to measured day work and significantly increasing capital–labour ratios, while on the other hand shop floor workers were to retain control of many decisions about day-to-day operations. As Whipp and Clark have shown, the SDI project failed in part because Rover management was unable to erect new centralised managerial institutions to fill the void created in the shift away from incentive payment systems. The industrial engineering staff, whose responsibility in setting effort norms was enhanced under fixed payment systems, remained weak, isolated and constantly under attack from shop floor organisations defending custom and practice.[138] The combination of weak managerial control of the production process and fixed payment systems created serious problems. A shop steward at the SDI plant recalled that management tried to increase output by simply putting more labour on the lines. However, in the absence of planning this led to large numbers of people doing nothing. A steward recalled:

The management wasn't doing the job properly. They wasn't, because if they had've done, then they could have stopped this. And people were walking about doing nothing. ... But who do you blame? If the management are there to say, you've got to do it and they're doing the job properly, then they've got to do it, ain't they. But if you're allowed to get away with it, it's human nature, they will. ... The overmanning was ridiculous. The trade unions didn't want it. We used to go to meetings with management and tell them we didn't want this amount of labour. But they insisted because they were after quantity.[139]

By 1978, the SDI project was in such serious difficulty that a new managerial group, 'the Liverpool Gang', was brought in to try to establish managerial control of the project. One of its priorities was to reform shop floor institutions, foreshadowing changes at the main BL plants.[140]

The SDI project represented only a small share of BL's total output. It quickly became apparent that there were serious problems in the Ryder proposals for the volume portion of BL's product line, produced at the old Austin and Morris plants.[141] The company was not even close to reaching the target levels of output proposed in the plan. Perhaps even more serious, Ryder's proposals did little to address the real problems within the company, the

Table 9.11. *Fixed assets per worker in the
motor vehicle industry, 1974 (£)*

Ford (US)	5602
Volvo	4662
General Motors (US)	4346
Volkswagen	3632
Ford (UK)	2657
Renault	2396
Chrysler (UK)	1456
Vauxhall	1356
British Leyland	920

Source: Expenditure Committee, *Fourteenth Report*
(HMSO, London, 1975), Table 14, no. 89.

mismatch between production techniques and production institutions. Interruptions in the production process continued to plague the company and labour
productivity continued to decline. By mid-1977, the Ryder plan was abandoned
and a new strategy was put forward. The new strategy was implemented by M.
Edwardes. It included a drastically pared down company and one in which
production institutions were reorganised to give management greater control
over effort norms. The Edwardes' reforms are not only the final chapter of our
analysis but also the final chapter in the transfer of authority from labour to
management which had begun almost a century earlier.[142]

With the appointment of M. Edwardes, in 1978, a radical new strategy was
adopted for reversing BL's fortunes. Between 1978 and 1983, output fell 26
percent and employment 46 percent.[143] Even more significant, Edwardes
reformed shop floor production institutions and succeeded in gaining greater
managerial control over effort norms. The 'right to manage' was asserted and
practices of mutuality were abolished. In his book on his tenure at BL, Edwardes
was quite candid regarding the deficiencies of British managerial practices and
his objective of restoring management's 'right to manage'.[144]

The reassertion of the right to manage coincided with a shift to a more capital
intensive production process. Despite early interest in automation in the late
1950s, most of the expansion of output in the postwar period in the British
section of the industry was achieved through hiring more labour rather than
investing in new capital intensive plant. As shown in Table 9.11, by 1974, BL
was at the bottom of the league tables in terms of investment per worker.

As early as 1968, the company was receiving advice to invest heavily in new
capital equipment. By 1976, some two years before Edwardes' appointment as
chairman of BL, the decision was made to base BL's recovery on investment in
capital intensive methods of production.[145] In the late 1970s, this policy began
to make an appreciable impact on capital investment per worker. Between 1977
and 1979 investment per worker doubled. As Edwardes began to trim the

number of workers in the early 1980s, the capital–labour ratio increased a further 50 percent.[146] This tripling of capital investment per worker in just over five years increased managerial interest in controlling shop floor activity and, we would argue, played a central role in Edwardes's reforms of production institutions.

The reorganisation of the production process at Longbridge to produce the Metro has been extensively examined and reflects not only the fundamental shift in managerial strategy between Ryder and Edwardes, but also between Edwardes and the British system of mass production. In keeping with the long history of how changes were made in the industry and the recommendations of Ryder, the reform of production practices at Longbridge began as a joint labour–management participative exercise. Willman and Winch argued that there was never much substance to formal labour participation and that under Edwardes the experiments in industrial democracy were abandoned and there was a shift toward unilateral managerial control. They concluded that: 'The Metro line was operated from 1980 on the basis of unilaterally imposed arrangements.'[147]

Aided by the political climate created by the victory of Thatcher's Conservatives and the growing slack in labour markets, Edwardes used the threat of closure to push through extensive reforms of production institutions. One of the targets for reform was the formal shop floor labour organisations which had grown in stature during the 1950s and 1960s. The rights of shop stewards were challenged, culminating in the dismissal of D. Robinson, the Longbridge shop steward convener, in November of 1979. By 1982, the authority of the Longbridge shop stewards had been seriously eroded. The number of active stewards fell by 50 percent, and many of the facilities which the company provided for full time stewards were withdrawn.[148]

The rules regulating working conditions were revised and unilaterally imposed by management in the 'Blue Newspaper' in April of 1980. Chell argued, '(the proposals), were clearly designed to restore to management a degree of control over the production process which had not been enjoyed by them for many years'.[149] The reforms ended the practice of mutuality in setting effort norms and removed the protection of status quo clauses which allowed labour to work under existing conditions while new work standards were being negotiated. Willman and Winch argued that the new rules shifted authority over the setting of effort norms to management and isolated the industrial engineering department from bargaining pressures. Effort norms were to be set scientifically using established industrial engineering techniques.[150]

The assertion of direct managerial control of effort norms by Edwardes in the early 1980s marks the culmination of a major shift in British managerial strategies which began to surface in the mid-1960s during the negotiations over MDW. Under the pressures of rising capital–labour ratios and the growing integration of tasks within the work place, the British system of mass production and indirect control of labour was replaced by a new system of production reminiscent of the technology first employed by Henry Ford in Detroit in the early 1900s. The Edwardes reforms gained for management something they had been unable to win during the Second Industrial Revolution, direct managerial control of effort norms.

While the methods employed by BL at the new Longbridge Metro plant in the early 1980s mark a clear shift toward an American style production system, it was not a carbon copy of Fordism as practised in Detroit in the early 1900s.[151] In 1913, Ford exchanged relatively high rates of pay for managerial control of effort norms. The Edwardes system imposed higher effort norms during a period when relative wages in the industry were falling.[152] Edwardes was unwilling to offer British labour a high effort high wage deal given the precarious financial state of BL, nor is BL likely to improve relative labour remuneration in the near future given the new competition from low-cost Asian manufacturers.

It is not clear that British management has been able to overcome the lack of skills which plagued its early attempts to impose direct control of effort norms.[153] In an attempt to make management's task easier, the Edwardes reforms included a new incentive payment system based on finished output from each plant. The bonus system was non-negotiable, provided a single bonus rate for all workers in a plant and represented about 20 percent of total earnings, well below the norms established between 1920 and 1970. The effort norms upon which the bonus is based are controlled by management and as Edwardes admitted, the shop stewards have little if any influence over it.[154]

During the 1970s and 1980s, many aspects of the production system used in the British motor vehicle industry were Americanised. Many of the nineteenth-century vestiges of democratic decision making on the shop floor were erased. In this sense the reforms represent a clear break with the labour control and shop floor coordination techniques used under the British system of mass production. But the legacy of unique British social pressures and the British system of mass production remain. Labour's voice on the shop floor has been temporarily checked. Whether it has been permanently suppressed is an open question. This question is made even more intriguing given trends toward greater labour participation in Japan and in many North American companies. The British System of Mass Production was a successful adaptation to the British institutional crisis of the late 1800s. It is far from clear that the Edwardes reforms will provide the answers to the institutional crisis that the industry entered in the 1960s.

10

Technical change and the effort bargain

The preceding chapters confirm three of the propositions put forward in our theoretical analysis. First, the effort bargain has been shown to play a central role in the process of technical change. Second, important insights into the process of technical change can be had by studying the interaction between production techniques and production institutions. Third, the workplace can be modelled in a game theoretic context where buyers and sellers of labour time have incomplete control of the effort bargain and choose strategies based on their perceptions of the other party's reaction.

The historical analysis revealed that British and American employers and British and American workers reacted in different ways to the problems associated with monitoring and enforcing the effort bargain. In the United States, production techniques and production institutions emerged which provided the buyers of labour time with direct control over effort norms. Labour offered only weak resistance to the transfer of its authority over the organisation of work and the setting of effort norms to a new managerial class. Labour's willingness to accept the new deal was increased by the strategy of American employers such as Ford who allowed earnings to rise. The ability of American employers to control and increase effort norms gave them greater control over the productivity of capital equipment and encouraged them to develop and adopt capital intensive methods of production.

In Britain, the buyers of labour time were less successful in breaking labour's influence over the organisation of work and effort norms. At the turn of the century, British labour, relative to American labour, appears to have been in a more favourable position to defend its existing control over the organisation of work and effort norms. Labour also appears to have been less willing to entrust control of the production process to management, although there were signs that in the 1920s labour was willing to trade its remaining authority over shop floor decisions for a higher standard of living. The British buyers of labour time relied on the indirect control and self-regulation provided by incentive payment systems to enforce an acceptable effort bargain. Incentive systems were also employed to help coordinate shop floor activity slowing the emergence of a

British managerial class. British employers' lack of control over effort norms raised the risk associated with investing in capital intensive production methods and likely explains the dramatic slowdown in capital investment in the booming interwar motor vehicle industry.

The collapse of the British motor vehicle industry came when firms were forced to abandon the interwar strategy of labour intensive production techniques, self-regulation of effort norms and weak managerial control of the production process. The superiority of the American perfected automated production system forced British firms to shift to more capital intensive production techniques after World War II. The attempt to merge American style production techniques with British production institutions was a disaster from the employers' point of view. Labour was able to use its influence over shop floor decisions to hold the employer's capital investment to ransom. British employers had never had firm control over effort levels, and in the post-1945 context they also lost their control of the ratio of wages to effort. The employers opted to Americanise British production institutions and break labour's authority on the shop floor. However, nearly half a century of experience with the British System of Mass Production which used incentive payment systems and self-regulation to enforce effort bargains and which depended on labour to coordinate many activities on the shop floor, left the managerial class ill-prepared for its new role and labour well equipped to defend its interest. A series of reforms, many of which culminated during Edwardes' tenure at BL, were implemented. It is still too early to pass judgement on the success of these reforms.

Returning to the model proposed in Chapter 2, we can summarise the experiences of British buyers and sellers of labour time with simple decision trees. The buyers of labour time faced two options in the early 1920s. They could adopt the American system of direct control of labour through heavy investment in managerial institutions and production techniques while paying labour on a fixed wage system. Alternatively, they could adopt the British system which depended on self-regulation through incentive payment systems to enforce the effort bargain and to help coordinate shop floor activity. Under the British system the investment in managerial institutions and production techniques was lower.

Labour, on the other hand, had little direct control over the choice of technology, but did influnce the level of effort and through this the choice of technology. Any pair of production techniques and production institutions will narrow the range of income and effort bargains available to labour, but still leave labour some flexibility if it opts to invest in effort controlling institutions. For lack of a better term, we will label the labour strategy which, given the accessible set of wage effort combinations leads labour toward higher effort norms, the cooperative strategy, and the labour strategy which results in lower effort norms, the non-cooperative strategy. The level of cooperation is a broad variable which captures investments by labour in effort controlling institutions.

It is important to note that the level of effort is a function of both the level of labour cooperation and the production system employed. The non-cooperative strategy under the American system may involve higher effort norms than non-cooperation under the British system because the buyers of labour time have different capacities for constraining labour's choices under the two technologies. At the same time, under different production systems, labour investment in effort controlling institutions will have different effects.

Most game theory models use direct measures of the payoffs provided by different strategy pairs and then determine the optimal strategies. Our analysis will be somewhat cruder. We lack the data to measure the precise payoff of different strategy pairs. The best we can do is rank different payoffs and, even then, some rather heroic assumptions need to be made. In Chapter 2 it was argued that the buyers and sellers of labour time lack full information on the payoff function and are forced to estimate payoffs based on their experiences. We also argued that there was no reason to assume that the buyers and sellers of labour time estimated identical payoff functions. It appears that differences in the estimated payoff functions of British buyers and sellers of labour time holds the key to explaining both why British employers were reluctant to adopt American production technology and why at times British sellers of labour time appeared to be the strongest supporters of Americanisation.

Lacking evidence to the contrary, it will be assumed that both buyers and sellers of labour time held the same views regarding the payoffs the buyers could expect from different strategy pairs. The combination of American technology and a cooperative workforce, operating the heavy capital investment at a high speed, provided the highest profits for employers. This was followed closely by the British system and a cooperative workforce. The British system, even with a cooperative workforce, was not quite as profitable because of the lower capital investment. The British system and a non-cooperative workforce provided the third highest payoff. Under this strategy pair, the economic penalty of operating capital equipment at a slow pace would be minimised by the relatively low investment in capital and could be partially offset by paying the large workforce lower wages on incentive payment systems. The worst payoff for buyers of labour time was the American system and a non-cooperative workforce. In this case, the penalty generated by the slow pace at which capital equipment was operated would be relatively large, while the opportunity for offsetting this penalty by paying lower wages was limited mainly by the smaller labour input, but also by the use of fixed wage systems.

Turning to labour's payoffs from the different strategy pairs, the estimates made by the buyers and sellers of labour time appear to have differed. British buyers of labour time were highly suspicious of British labour's willingness to work at the pace needed to make American systems profitable. They concluded that they could not pay high enough wages to compensate British workers for the high effort norms required. They expected that any attempt to use the Fordist system would lead to a non-cooperative strategy. In the view of buyers of labour time, both pairs of strategies associated with the British system of self-regulation were superior to the strategies associated with the American system. It was felt that the British system combined with cooperation offered labour the best payoff as it could combine self-regulated effort norms with relatively high earnings. The British system and non-cooperation provided somewhat lower payoffs as earnings would fall as effort norms fell.

Labour's estimates of its payoffs differed from the employers' estimates of labour payoffs in two important respects. Particularly after World War I, British labour aspired to the wage levels offered in Ford plants and appeared willing to accept direct managerial control in return for higher wages. The combination of American systems and cooperation was ranked the highest by labour, the exact opposite of the employer's estimate. After World War I, labour remained suspicious that the buyers of labour time would try to cut piece prices if labour increased effort norms. Therefore we would suggest that it ranked the combination British system and cooperation the lowest. Labour estimated the payoff from the remaining two strategy pairs the same as employers.

These payoff functions are reproduced in Figure 10.1.

Figure 10.1 shows that in a game where the buyers of labour time choose the technical strategy first, British employers were rational to adopt the British system of mass production. Had they opted for the American system, which held out the highest potential payoff, they would have expected to in fact end up with the worst possible payoff as they would have expected labour to choose non-cooperation. Under the British system, employers expected labour to adopt a cooperative strategy. However, labour did not behave as the employers expected. Labour encouraged British firms to Americanise and argued that it would cooperate in return for higher wages. However, once British employers opted for the British system and payment by results, British labour behaved rationally in

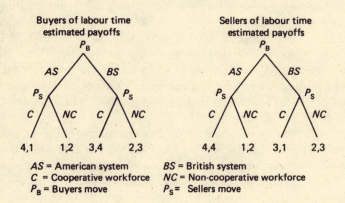

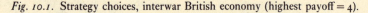

Fig. 10.1. Strategy choices, interwar British economy (highest payoff = 4).

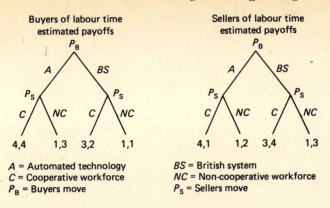

Buyers of labour time
estimated payoffs

Sellers of labour time
estimated payoffs

Fig. 10.2. Strategy choices, post-1945 Britain (highest payoff = 4).

choosing non-cooperation. This was based on its mistrust of the intentions of British employers and the strong feeling that increasing effort norms under payment by results would lead to price cuts designed to hold wages constant.

We can use the same framework of analysis to explain the post-1945 Americanisation of British production methods. In Fig. 10.2 a number of the payoffs have been changed. In particular British managers believed that automation provided an answer to their attempts to control effort norms while at the same time allowing them to raise wages enough to get labour to accept the bargain. For labour, postwar conditions enhanced it ability to control incentive payment systems which made the British system more attractive. These changes had the effect of lowering the employers' expected payoff from the British system, while for labour it raised expected payoffs under the British system. Buyers chose automated techniques, but labour resisted the new production system.

We have presented a reinterpretation of the long standing debate regarding differences in the history of technology in Britain and the United States. Our analysis has also shed light on contemporary concerns regarding the weaknesses of British management and the ability of British workers to influence shop floor activity. But perhaps of most significance, our study has suggested that an economy with rational maximising players may evolve along a path which no one prefers. Most people would agree that the British manufacturing sector is in serious trouble. However, the problem is not managerial failure or bloody minded workers. The problem is the market system and how it deals with the problems generated by incomplete labour contracts and imperfect information.

Notes

Chapter 1: Introduction

[1] The classic work in this area is H.J. Habakkuk, *American and British Technology in the Nineteenth Century* (Cambridge University Press, 1967). See also J.E. Sawyer, 'The social basis of the American system of manufacturing' (*Journal of Economic History*, 14, 1954), pp. 361–79; E.S. Ferguson, 'The American-ness of American technology' (*Technology and Culture 20*, 1979), pp. 3–24.

[2] See D. Hounshell, *From the American System to Mass Production, 1800–1932* (Baltimore, 1984).

[3] For a review of some of the literature see P. David, *Technical Choice, Innovation and Economic Growth* (Cambridge University Press, 1975). On criticisms of the market approach see W. Fellner, 'Does the market direct the relative factor saving effects of technological progress', in National Bureau of Economic Research, *The Rate and Direction of Inventive Activity* (Princeton, 1962); N. Rosenberg, *Inside the Black Box: Technology and Economics* (Cambridge University Press, 1982).

[4] On the failure of economists to examine institutions see V. Ruttan and Y. Hayami, 'Toward a theory of induced institutional innovation' (*Journal of Development Studies*, 20, 1984), p. 129.

[5] Ruttan and Hayami, 'Toward a theory', p. 205.

[6] For a recent criticism of economic theory see L. Thurow, *Dangerous Currents: The State of Economics* (New York, 1983).

[7] A. Schotter, *The Economic Theory of Social Institutions* (Cambridge University Press, 1981), p. 1.

[8] See L.E. Davis and D.C. North, *Institutional Change and American Economic Growth* (Cambridge University Press, 1971); D.C. North, *Structure and Change in Economic History* (New York, 1981); Schotter, *Economic Theory*; H. Leibenstein, *Beyond Economic Man: A New Foundation for Micro-Economics* (Cambridge Mass., 1976); O.E. Williamson, *Markets and Hierarchies* (New York, 1975); A. Chandler, *The Visible Hand: The Managerial Revolution in American Business* (Cambridge, Mass., 1977).

[9] Davis and North, *Institutional Change*, p. 7.

[10] Schotter, *Economic Theory*, p. 109.

[11] One of the earliest modern economic studies of labour and the role of management was R. Coase, 'The nature of the firm' (*Economica*, 4, 1937), pp. 387–405. More recent

work includes A. Alchian and H. Demsetz, 'Production, information costs and economic organization' (*American Economic Review*, 62, 1972), pp. 777–95. A significant amount of literature on the effort bargain now exists and has been critically reviewed by S. Bowles, 'The production process in a competitive economy: Walrasian, Neo-Hobbesian, and Marxian models' (*American Economic Review*, 75, 1985), pp. 16–36.

[12] We have borrowed heavily from the expanding literature on the labour process and the history of work. This literature is examined in more detail in chapter 2. Some of the more important works in this area include, H. Braverman, *Labor and Monopoly Capital* (New York, 1974); R. Edwards, *Contested Terrain: The Transformation of the Workplace in the Twentieth Century* (New York, 1979); M. Burawoy, *Manufacturing Consent* (Chicago, 1979); D. Clawson, *Bureaucracy and the Labor Process* (New York, 1980).

[13] M. Burawoy, *The Politics of Production* (London, 1985), p. 34.

[14] This last point is undoubtedly extremely important and, we would be the first to admit, has not been treated as thoroughly as it deserves in the following chapters. The problem is partially one of collecting good data on how workers view their longrun interests in a capitalist society. Some of the best work on this subject can be found in the most recent volume produced by Burawoy, and referred to above.

[15] For details see David, *Technical Choice*, pp. 19–94.

[16] Schotter, *Economic Theory*, p. 2.

Chapter 2: Economic models of technical change

[1] M. Abramovitz, 'Resource and output trends in the United States since 1870' (*American Economic Review*, 46, Proceedings, 1956), pp. 5–23. The modern analysis of technical change in the neoclassical tradition is predated by a number of earlier studies of which those by K. Marx, *Capital* (Moscow, 1971), and J. Schumpeter, *Capitalism Socialism and Democracy* (New York, 1942) are the most comprehensive.

[2] J.R. Hicks, *Theory of Wages* (London, 1932), p. 124.

[3] W.E.G. Salter, *Productivity and Technical Change* (Cambridge University Press, 1969), p. 43.

[4] *Ibid.*, p. 36. See also W.E.G. Salter, 'Productivity, growth and accumulation as historical processes', in E.A.G. Robinson (ed.), *Problems in Economic History* (London, 1965). For earlier, and largely ignored criticisms of Hicksian inducement mechanisms see G.F. Shove, 'Review of the theory of wages' (*Economic Journal*, 43, 1933), pp. 460–72; L.A. Morrison, 'The rate of wages and the use of machinery' (*American Economic Review*, 14, 1924), pp. 281–2; F.D. Graham, 'Relation of wage rates to the use of machinery' (*American Economic Review*, 16, 1926), pp. 434–42.

[5] Salter, *Productivity and Technical Change*, pp. 36, 128–30.

[6] C. Kennedy, 'Induced bias in innovation and the theory of distribution' (*Economic Journal*, 74, 1964), pp. 541–7. See also P. Samuelson, 'A theory of induced innovation along Kennedy–Weisacker lines' (*Review of Economics and Statistics*, 47, 1965), pp. 343–56; H.P. Binswanger, 'A microeconomic approach to induced innovation' (*Economic Journal*, 84, 1974), pp. 940–58.

[7] Except for $_n$ and $_{n-1}$, subscripts in equations represent the partial derivatives with respect to the subscripted variable.

[8] See David, *Technical Choice Innovation and Economic Growth* (Cambridge University Press, 1975), p. 47 for details.

[9] S. Ahmad, 'On the theory of induced innovation' (*Economic Journal*, 76, 1966), p. 352.

[10] *Ibid.*, p. 347.

[11] David, *Technical Choice*, p. 52.

[12] W. Nordhaus, 'Some skeptical thoughts on the theory of induced innovation' (*Quarterly Journal of Economics*, 87, 1973), pp. 208–19.

[13] David, *Technical Choice*, pp. 19–91. See also K. Arrow, 'The economic implications of learning by doing' (*Review of Economic Studies*, 29, 1962), pp. 155–73. For a discussion of the sources of learning see W. Fellner, 'Specific interpretations of learning by doing' (*Journal of Economic Theory*, 1, 1969), pp. 119–40.

[14] David, *Technical Choice*, pp. 4, 61–2.

[15] For an alternative model of technical change where the existing technology plays an important role, see H.P. Binswanger and V.W. Ruttan, *Induced Innovation* (Baltimore, 1978); Ahmad, 'Theory', p. 349 makes a similar point.

[16] F. Crouzet, *The Victorian Economy* (London, 1982), p. 383.

[17] H.J. Habakkuk, *American and British Technology in the Nineteenth Century* (Cambridge University Press, 1967).

[18] P. Temin, 'Labor scarcity and the problem of American industrial efficiency in the 1850s', in P. Temin (ed.), *New Economic History* (London, 1973), pp. 131–2.

[19] D.L. Brito and J.G. Williamson, 'Skilled labor and nineteenth century Anglo-American managerial behaviour' (*Explorations in Economic History*, 10, 1973), pp. 248–9.

[20] C.K. Harley, 'Skilled labour and the choice of technique in Edwardian industry' (*Explorations in Economic History*, 11, 1974), pp. 391–414.

[21] L.P. Cain and D.G. Patterson, 'Factor biases and technical change in manufacturing: The American System, 1850–1919' (*Journal of Economic History*, 41, 1981), p. 348.

[22] W.H. Phillips, 'Induced innovation and economic performance in late Victorian British industry' (*Journal of Economic History*, 42, 1982), p. 102.

[23] Crouzet, *Victorian Economy*, p. 395. Hounshell found that despite the fact that wages in Scotland were only one-half those in the United States, the Singer Company used exactly the same plant in its Scottish and American plants. See D. Hounshell, *From the American System to Mass Production* (Baltimore, 1984), p. 96.

[24] Some of the key works in this area include: A. Chandler, *The Visible Hand* (Cambridge Mass., 1977); L. Hannah, *The Rise of the Corporate Economy* (London, 1976); D. Nelson, *Managers and Workers: Origins of the New Factory System in the United States, 1880–1920* (Wisconsin, 1975); D. Noble, *America by Design: Science Technology, and the Rise of Corporate Capitalism* (Oxford, 1979); D. Clawson, *Bureaucracy and the Labor Process: The Transformation of U.S. Industry, 1860–1920* (New York, 1980).

[25] S. Pollard, *The Genesis of Modern Management* (London, 1965), pp. 160–208, 254–71.

[26] On changes in the nature of the managerial problem see W. Lewchuk, 'The role of the British government in the spread of Scientific Management and Fordism in the interwar years' (*Journal of Economic History*, 44, 1984), pp. 355–61. See also G. Brown, *Sabotage* (Nottingham, 1977), especially part one. For earlier treatments of the rise of labour conflict see J.R. Commons, 'American shoemakers, 1648–1895: a sketch of industrial evolution' (*Quarterly Journal of Economics*, 24, 1909), pp. 39–81;

S. Webb and B. Webb, *Industrial Democracy* (London, 1898). On the rise of trade unions and formal collective bargaining see R. Price, *Masters, Unions and Men* (Cambridge University Press, 1980).

[27] L. Hannah, 'Visible and invisible hands in Great Britain', in A.D. Chandler and H. Daems (eds.), *Managerial Hierarchies: Comparative Perspectives on the Rise of the Modern Industrial Enterprise* (Cambridge Mass., 1980), p. 42. See also C. Littler, *The Development of the Labour Process in Capitalist Societies* (London, 1982). On the contemporary British debate see L. Ulman, 'Collective bargaining and industrial efficiency', in R.E. Caves (ed.), *Britain's Economic Prospects* (London, 1968); E.H. Phelps Brown, 'Labour policies: productivity, industrial relations, cost inflation', in A. Cairncross (ed.), *Britain's Economic Prospects Reconsidered* (London, 1971).

[28] J.E. Roemer, 'Divide and conquer: microfoundations of a Marxian theory of wages' (*Bell Journal*, 10, 1979), pp. 695–705.

[29] P. Sraffa, *Production of Commodities by Means of Commodities* (Cambridge University Press, 1960); L. Pasinetti (ed.), *Essays in the Theory of Joint Production* (London, 1980); L. Pasinetti, *Lectures on the Theory of Production* (London, 1977); D.J. Harris, *Capital Accumulation and Income Distribution* (London, 1978); I. Steadman, *Marx after Sraffa* (London, 1977).

[30] The institutional assumptions made by Pasinetti are as narrow as those made by his arch opponent in economic debates, Samuelson. On Pasinetti's contention that a 'Natural Economy' exists, one where institutions are irrelevant see L. Pasinetti, *Structural Change and Economic Growth* (Cambridge University Press, 1981), pp. 153–5.

[31] F. Hahn, 'The Neo-Ricardians' (*Cambridge Journal of Economics*, 6, 1982), p. 362.

[32] *Ibid.*, p. 354.

[33] Harris, *Capital Accumulation*, pp. 120–39. See also L. Spaventa, 'Rate of profit, rate of growth and capital intensity in a simple production model' (*Oxford Economic Papers*, 22, 1970), pp. 129–47; K. Sato, 'The Neoclassical postulate and the technology frontier in capital theory' (*Quarterly Journal of Economics*, 88, 1974), pp. 353–84.

[34] For a study which suggests that this is what actually takes place in industry see E. Mansfield *et al.*, 'Social and private rates of return from industrial innovations' (*Quarterly Journal of Economics*, 91, 1977), p. 231. For studies which suggest that a critical variable in choice of technology is the lag before the new technique can be copied see Paolo-Sylos Labini, *Oligopoly and Technical Progress* (Cambridge Mass., 1962); R.R. DeBondt, 'Innovative activity and barriers to entry' (*European Economic Review*, 10, 1977), pp. 95–109.

[35] For similar attempts to modify the original Sraffian system see P. Varri, 'Prices, rate of profit and life of machines in Sraffa's fixed capital model', in Pasinetti (ed.), *Essays*; B. Schefold, 'Fixed capital as a joint product and the analysis of accumulation with different forms of technical progress', in Pasinetti (ed.), *Essays*.

[36] Harris, *Capital Accumulation*, pp. 136–7.

[37] Hahn, 'Neo-Ricardians', pp. 358–63.

[38] See R. Price, 'Rethinking Labour history: the importance of work', in J.E. Cronin and J. Schneer (eds.), *Social Conflict and the Political Order in Modern Britain* (London, 1982), pp. 204–10.

[39] For critics of the Sraffian model see A. Cutler, B. Hindess, P. Hirst and A. Hussain,

Marx's Capital and Capitalism Today (London, 1978); B. Rowthorn, 'Neo-Classicism, Neo-Ricardianism and Marxism' (*New Left Review*, **86**, 1974), pp. 63–87. For another interpretation of the possible links between technology and relative bargaining strength see D. Gordon, 'Capitalist efficiency and socialist efficiency' (*Monthly Review*, **28**, 1976), pp. 19–39.

[40] In particular see A.A. Alchian and H. Demsetz, 'Production, information costs, and economic organization' (*American Economic Review*, **62**, 1977), pp. 777-95; O.E. Williamson, *Markets and Hierarchies, Analysis and Antitrust Implications* (New York, 1975); Leibenstein, *Beyond Economic Man, A New Foundation for Microeconomics* (Cambridge Mass., 1976).

[41] W. Baldamus, *Efficiency and Effort* (London, 1961) p. 123. See also H. Behrend, 'The effort bargain' (*Industrial and Labour Relations Review*, **10**, 1957), pp. 503–15.

[42] See for instance, J.R. Commons, *Institutional Economics* (Wisconsin, 1934), where conflict is assumed to be a natural state of affairs. For a brief discussion of this point see Williamson, *Markets and Hierarchies*, p. 3.

[43] S. Bowles, 'The production process in a competitive economy; Walrasian, Neo-Hobbesian, and Marxian models' (*American Economic Review*, **75**, 1985), pp. 31–3. See also G. Clark, 'Authority and efficiency: the labor market and the managerial revolution of the late nineteenth century' (*Journal of Economic History*, **44**, 1984), pp. 1069–83.

[44] J.M. Malcolmson, 'Efficient labour organization: incentives, power and the transaction cost approach', in F.J. Stephen (ed.), *Firms, Organization and Labour* (London, 1984), p. 120.

[45] Williamson, *Markets and Hierarchies*, pp. 57–81. See also O. Williamson, 'The organization of work: a comparative institutional assessment' (*Journal of Economic Behaviour and Organization*, **1**, 1980), p. 10. For a critique of Williamson see L. Putterman, 'The organization of work: comment' (*Journal of Economic Behavior and Organization*, **2**, 1981), p. 277. See also A.L. Friedman, 'Management strategies, market conditions and the labour process', in F.J. Stephen (ed.), *Firms Organisation and Labour* (London, 1984), p. 178.

[46] Williamson, *Markets and Hierarchies*, p. 255, 21–6.

[47] Leibenstein, *Beyond Economic Man*, p. 45.

[48] *Ibid.*, p. 95; For a summary of Leibenstein's early work see M.A. Crew, *Theory of the Firm* (London, 1975) pp. 110–15.

[49] Leibenstein, *Beyond Economic Man*, pp. 99–117.

[50] Ibid., pp. 125–7. S.R.G. Jones, in, *The Economics of Conformism* (Oxford, 1984), has convincingly argued that labour's behaviour would be better interpreted as an attempt to enforce some accepted effort level. He argues that workers working above the norm would be ostracised by their mates as rate busters, while those operating below the norm would be ostracised for not pulling their fair share of the work.

[51] *Ibid.*, p. 148.

[52] Some of the more interesting work includes, J. Malcolmson, 'Unemployment and the efficiency wage hypothesis' (*Economic Journal*, **91**, 1981), pp. 848–66; J. Malcolmson, 'Work incentives, hierarchy, and internal labor markets' (*Journal of Political Economy*, **92**, 1984), pp. 486–507; J. Mirrless, 'The optimal structure of incentives and authority within an organization' (*Bell Journal*, **7**, 1976), pp. 105–31; C. Eaton and W.D. White, 'The economy of high wages: an agency problem' (*Economica*, **50**, 1983);

E.P. Lazaer, 'Agency, earnings profiles, productivity, and hours restriction' (*American Economic Review*, **71**, 1981), pp. 606-20; C. Shapiro and J.E. Stiglitz, 'Equilibrium unemployment as a worker discipline device' (*American Economic Review*, **74**, 1984), pp. 433–44.

53 For an attempt to move beyond the simple models see W.B. Macleod and J.M. Malcolmson, 'Implicit contracts, incentive compatibility, and involuntary unemployment' (Institute for Economic Research, Queen's University, *Discussion Paper*, p. 585).

54 H. Braverman, *Labor and Monopoly Capital* (New York, 1974). For other works based on Braverman's thesis see R. Edwards, *Contested Terrain; The Transformation of the Workplace in the Twentieth Century* (New York, 1979); Noble, *America by Design*; Clawson, *Bureaucracy*; Littler, *Development*.

55 Braverman, *Labor*, p. 195. For criticisms of Braverman see T. Elger, 'Valorisation and deskilling: a critique of Braverman' (*Capital and Class*, **7**, 1979), pp. 58–99; R. Coombs, 'Labour and monopoly capital' (*New Left Review*, **107**, 1978), pp. 79–96.

56 In particular see A.L. Friedman, *Industry and Labour: Class Struggle at Work and Monopoly Capitalism* (London, 1977).

57 M. Burawoy, 'Toward a marxist theory of the labour process: Braverman and beyond' (*Politics and Society*, **8**, 1978), pp. 267–312. Burawoy has expanded his analysis in *Manufacturing Consent: Changes in the Labour Process under Monopoly Capitalism* (Chicago, 1979).

58 Burawoy, 'Toward a Marxist', pp. 263–8. For an interesting attempt to link experiences and the evolution of ideology, see F. Hearn, *Domination, Legitimation and Resistance: The Incorporation of the Nineteenth Century Working Class* (USA, 1978).

59 Littler, *Development*, pp. 3–28.

60 This thesis is expanded on in D. Noble, *Forces of Automation: A Social History of Production* (New York, 1984).

61 *Ibid.*, p. 32.

62 Noble, *America by Design*, p. xxiv.

63 Burawoy, *Manufacturing Consent*, p. 30.

64 Leibenstein, *Beyond Economic Man*, p. 169; Bowles, 'Production process', pp. 27–9.

65 W. Lazonick, 'Work, effort and productivity; some theoretical implications of some historical research' (unpublished paper), p. 35.

66 For a model which uses similar assumptions see Mirrless, 'The optimal structure of incentives', pp. 105–31.

67 L' Grundberg, 'The effects of the social relations of production on productivity and workers' safety: an ignored set of relationships' (*International Journal of Health Services*, **13**, 1983), p. 627.

68 For an examination of how American workers evaluated the trade off between effort and wages see D.J. Rodgers, *The Work Ethic in Industrial America, 1850–1920* (Chicago, 1974). Rodgers suggests that American workers were encouraged to follow a high consumption style of life which in turn necessitated high wages and, by implication, high effort levels.

69 W. Lazonick, 'Work effort'.

70 *Ibid.*, p. 13.

71 With linear profit-effort Curves, changes in (W) will rotate both lines but will leave E' unaffected.

$$E' = (r(K - K'))/(P(\alpha - \alpha'))$$

Where K and K' and α and α' represent the capital stock and effort productivity coefficients of two methods of production.

[72] For an attempt to link changes in technology and relative bargaining power see T. Bruland, 'Industrial conflict as a source of technical innovation: three cases' (*Economy and Society*, **11**, 1982), pp. 91–121. For other work which suggests that there is a link between capital/labour ratios and labour relations see D. Gallie, *In Search of the New Working Class* (Cambridge University Press, 1978).

[73] F.Y. Edgeworth, *Mathematical Psychics; An Essay on the Application of Mathematics to the Moral Sciences* (New York, reprint 1967, original 1881), p. 137.

[74] R. Price, *Masters, Unions and Men* (Cambridge University Press, 1980), p. 78. On the question of restriction of output by labour see S.B. Mathewson, *Restriction of Output Among Unorganized Workers* (Carbondale, Ill)., 1969, original 1931).

[75] A. Schotter, *The Economic Theory of Social Institutions* (Cambridge University Press, 1981), p. 150.

[76] For other studies using game theory to examine economic questions see in particular, K. Lancaster, 'The dynamic inefficiency of capitalism' (*Journal of Political Economy*, **81**, 1973), pp. 1092–109; M. Hoel, 'Distribution and growth as a differential game between workers and capitalists' (*International Economic Review*, **19**, 1978), pp. 335–50; M. Osborne, 'Capitalist–Worker conflict and involuntary unemployment' (*Review of Economic Studies*, **51**, 1984), pp. 111–27; R. Hardin, *Collective Action* (Baltimore, 1982). Also of interest is R. Axelrod, *The Evolution of Cooperation* (New York, 1984).

[77] M. Shubik, 'Game theory models and methods in political economy', in K.J. Arrow and M.D. Intriligator (eds.), *Handbook of Mathematical Economics* (Amsterdam, 1981), p. 285.

[78] J. Elster, *Explaining Technical Change* (Cambridge University Press, 1983), p. 75. See also J. Elster, 'Marxism, functionalism and game theory: the case for methodological individualism' (*Theory and Society*, **11**, 1982), pp. 453–82.

[79] Elster, *Explaining Technical Change*, p. 77.

[80] See Schotter, *Economic Theory*, pp. 152–3 for a critique of abstract game theory.

[81] For a more formal treatment of the concepts used in game theory see J. Harsanyi, *Rational Behavior and Bargaining Equilibrium in Games and Social Situatons* (Cambridge University Press, 1977).

[82] J. Harsanyi, 'Games with incomplete information' (*Management Science*, **14**, 1967), 163–7.

[83] Harsanyi, *Rational Behaviour*, pp. 12, 113. Kreps and Wilson have used a similar concept which they have termed 'sequential equilibrium'. The critical characteristic of sequential equilibrium is as follows, 'Starting from every information set, the player whose turn it is to move is using a strategy that is optimal for the remainder of the game against the hypothesized future moves of its opponent... and the assessment of past moves by other players and by nature (given by the assessment over nodes in the information set)'. See D.M. Kreps and R. Wilson, 'Reputation and imperfect information' (*Journal of Economic Theory*, **27**, 1982), p. 257.

[84] Clark, 'Authority and efficiency', pp. 1069–83.

[85] Schotter, *Economic Theory*, p. 79.

Chapter 3: *The American motor vehicle industry, 1984–1930*

[1] The Ford Motor Company has been the subject of three recent studies which have helped significantly in clarifying what actually took place in Detroit between 1900 and 1930. See S. Meyer III, *The Five Dollar Day: Labor Management and Social Control in the Ford Motor Company, 1908–1921* (Albany, 1981); D.A. Hounshell, *From the American System to Mass Production, 1800–1932* (Baltimore, 1984); W. Gartman, Auto Slavery: The Development of the Labor Process in the Automobile Industry of the United States, 1897–1950 (Ph.D., 1980, University of California (San Diego)).

[2] See P. Fridenson, 'The coming of the assembly line to Europe', in W. Krohn *et al.* (eds.), *The Dynamics of Science and Technology* (Dordrecht, 1978). See also A.E. Musson, 'Joseph Whitworth and the growth of mass production engineering' (*Business History*, **17**, 1975), pp. 109–49. On British attempts to emulate the Americans see J. Foreman-Peck, 'The American challenge of the twenties: multi-nationals and the European motor industry' (*Journal of Economic History*, **42**, 1982), pp. 865–82.

[3] On the broad social impact of Fordism see the chapter titled 'Americanism and Fordism' in A. Gramsci, *Selections from the Prison Notebooks* (New York, 1971). For a more recent treatment see Hounshell, *American System*.

[4] Some of the most important works in this area include, N. Rosenberg, *The American System of Manufacture* (Edinburgh 1969); P. Uselding, 'An early chapter in the evolution of American industrial management', in L. Cain and P. Uselding (eds.), *Business Enterprise and Economic Change* (Kent State University Press, 1973); Merrit Roe Smith, *Harpers Ferry Armory and the New Technology: The Challenge of Change* (Ithaca, 1977); Hounshell, *American System*.

[5] H.B. Binsse, 'Some reasons for the excellence of American machinery' (Cassiers, **16**, 1899), p. 591.

[6] Rosenberg, *American System*, p. 14. E.S. Ferguson has advanced the thesis that American successes in adopting new machine technology were influenced less by economic forces than with cultural proclivities. He wrote. 'I am concerned in this essay with the connections between the distinctive qualities of American technology and the great central dream of democracy, in which everyone can share in the good life; with the missionary zeal with which the technological benefits of American democracy have been proclaimed to the rest of the world.' E.S. Ferguson, 'The American-ness of American technology' (*Technology and Culture*, **20**, 1979), pp. 3–4.

[7] See Merrit Roe Smith, *Harpers Ferry*, p. 22; Uselding, *Early Chapter*, p. 73.

[8] For an example of these arguments in the British motor vehicle industry see L.H. Pomeroy, 'Automobile engineering and the war' (*Proceedings of the Institute of Automobile Engineers*, **9**, 1914), p. 34.

[9] Hounshell, *American System*, pp. 4 and 25.

[10] *Ibid.*, p. 29.

[11] *Ibid.*, pp. 5–7, 116, 178. See also R.S. Woodward, 'The legend of Eli Whitney and interchangeable parts' (*Technology and Culture* **1**, 1960), pp. 235–53.

[12] Hounshell, *American System*, pp. 23, 41, 81, 204–15.

[13] J.A. Litterer, 'Systematic management: the search for order and integration' (*Business History Review*, **35**, 1961), p. 476.

[14] Noble has developed this thesis in detail in his book, *America by Design* (Oxford, 1977). See especially Chapters three and four. A leading advocate of endogenous institutional development is D. North, *Structure and Change* (New York, 1981).

[15] Gartman, Auto Slavery, p. 154.

[16] For details see D. Montgomery, *Workers' Control in America: Studies in the History of Work, Technology and Labour Struggles* (Cambridge University Press, 1979), pp. 48–90.

[17] D. Brody, *Workers in Industrial America* (New York, 1980), pp. 25–7. For an extended discussion of the history of American labour legislation see T.A. Kochan, *Collective Bargaining and Industrial Relations* (Homewood, 1980), especially pp. 55–68. See also C.L. Tomlins, *The State and the Unions; Labor Relations, Law, and the Organized Labor Movement in America* (Cambridge University Press, 1985).

[18] D. Montgomery, 'New tendencies in union struggles and strategies in Europe and the United States; 1916–1922', in J.E. Cronin and C. Sirianni eds.), *Work Community, and Power, The Experience of Labor in Europe and America; 1900–1925* (Philadelphia, 1983), p. 97.

[19] Montgomery, 'New tendencies', p. 100–1.

[20] Gramsci, *Selections*, p. 286.

[21] G. Heliker, 'Detroit labor 1890–1910' (Ford Archive, Acc. 958), pp. 2 and 24. See also Montgomery, *Workers Control*, p. 55.

[22] G. Heliker, 'Detroit labor 1900–1916' (Ford Archive, Acc. 958), p. 8; Heliker, 'Detroit labor 1890–1910', p. 35.

[23] Heliker, 'Detroit labor 1890–1910', p. 15. Heliker, 'Detroit labor 1900–1916', p. 6.

[24] J. Russell, 'The coming of the line' (*Radical America*, **12**, 1978), p. 30.

[25] A. Nevins and Frank Hill, *Ford: The Times, the Man, the Company* (New York, 1954), pp. 513–17; Russel, 'Coming of the line', p. 31.

[26] See D.M. Gordon, R. Edwards, M. Reich, *Segmented Work, Divided Workers* (Cambridge University Press, 1982), for an elaboration of the thesis that the weakness of the American working class movement can be attributed to its numerous internal divisions.

[27] Russel, 'Coming of the line', p. 31.

[28] Heliker, 'Detroit labor 1900–1916', p. 18. See also M. Dubofsky, *We Shall Be All, A History of the IWW* (New York, 1969), p. 287.

[29] Russel, 'Coming of the line', p. 42

[30] Heliker, 'Detroit labor 1890–1910', p. 69.

[31] Brody, *Workers*, p. 17.

[32] On the rise of trade unionism in the thirties see P. Friedlander, *The Emergence of a UAW Local, 1936–39* (Pittsburg, 1975); A. Meier and E. Rudwick, *Black Detroit and the rise of UAW* (Oxford, 1979); N. Lichtenstein, 'Auto worker militancy and the structure of factory life; 1937–55' (*Journal of American History*, **67**, 1980), pp. 335–56.

[33] Montgomery, *Workers Control*, p. 44.

[34] K. Sward, *The Legend of Henry Ford* (New York, 1948), p. 49.

[35] Nevins, Ford, p. 517.

[36] W. Lazonick, 'Technical change and the control of work: the development of capital–labour relations in the US mass production industries', in H.F. Gospel and

C.R. Littler (eds.), *Managerial Strategies and Industial Relations* (London 1983), p. 115.

[37] Nevins, *Ford*, p. 152.

[38] *Ibid.*, p. 186; Ford Archive, *Reminiscences*, O. Barthel, p. 25.

[39] On Olds' early activities see Sward, *Legend of Henry Ford*, pp. 6–9; Nevins, *Ford*, pp. 220–1.

[40] Nevins, *Ford*, pp. 211–13.

[41] Sward, *Legend of Henry Ford*, p. 8.

[42] Nevins, *Ford*, pp. 225–38. The difficulty that Ford had in attracting capital to his new venture reflects the riskiness of automobile production in the United States at this time. Of the 502 companies formed between 1900 and 1908 to produce cars, 273 failed shortly after they were created.

[43] Ford Archive, *Reminiscences*, Pring, p. 28.

[44] Ford Archive, *Reminiscences*, F. Rockelman, p. 9.

[45] Ford Archive, *Reminiscences*, Wandersee, p. 9.

[46] Ford Archive, *Reminiscences*, Rockelman, pp. 10–11.

[47] Sward, *Legend of Henry Ford*, p. 32.

[48] W.J. Abernathy, *The Productivity Dilemma* (Baltimore, 1978), p. 158. Task duration refers to the length of time taken to complete one full cycle of the different tasks allocated to a worker.

[49] Ford Archive, *Reminiscences*, Litogot, p. 7.

[50] H.L. Arnold, 'Ford methods' (*Engineering Magazine*, 47, August 1914), p. 673.

[51] Ford Archive, *Reminiscences*, Pring, p. 29; Ford Archive, *Reminiscences*, Dickert, p. 13; Abernathy, *Productivity*, p. 138; J.O. 'Connor, *Reminiscences*, cited in Russell, 'Coming of the line', pp. 33–4.

[52] Ford Archive, *Reminiscences*, Pring, p. 9; Arnold, 'Ford methods', p. 673. The estimate of ten percent for the chassis assembly only comes from the Model T cost books. In March of 1914, the total labour cost of manufacturing and assembling a car was $24. The cost of assembling the chassis alone was $2.20.

[53] Meyer, *Five Dollar Day*, p. 72.

[54] A.E. Musson, 'Joseph Whitworth and the growth of mass production engineering' (*Business History*, 17, 1975), pp. 109–49' See also Hounshell, *American System*, pp. 239–44.

[55] Gartman, *Auto Slavery*, pp. 120–2, 262.

[56] Ford Archive, *Reminiscences*, Pring, p. 33; C.F. Sorensen, *My Forty Years with Ford* (New York, 1956), p. 115; *Detroit Free Press*, p. 15, November 1956.

[57] Ford Archive, *Reminiscences*, Wollering, p. 24.

[58] Hounshell, *American System*, p. 221.

[59] Ford Archive, Acc. 96, Box 1. The EMF car was well known in Britain as early as 1910 and was noted for its special attention to parts standardisation. See 'American invasion' (*Motor Trader*, 12 October 1910), p. 108. See also E.K.H., 'Factory transportaton II' (*Machinery*, November 1917).

[60] Ford Archive, *Reminiscences*, Wollering, p. 43. See also F.H. Colvin, 'Continuous assembling in modern automobile shops' (*American Machinist*, 43, 1915), p. 370. One can only speculate whether there was any connection between the IWW strike at Studebaker in 1913, and their use of the assembly line.

[61] Ford Archive, *Reminiscences*, Pring, pp. 37, 48.

[62] For some of the debate regarding precisely where and when Ford moved to moving assembly see Hounshell, *American System*, pp. 244–53.

[63] Arnold, 'Ford methods', p. 673.

[64] 'The manufacturer much to be admired' (*Automobile Topics*, 45, 24 February 1917).

[65] 'Conveyor system aids big production' (*Automobile*, 35, July 1916); Ford Archive, *Reminiscences*, Liogot, p. 7; Arnold, 'Ford methods', p. 673; *Ford Times*, 8 April 1915, p. 299.

[66] Ford Archive, *Select Research Papers*, Acc. 572 Box 21; *Reminiscences*, Rough Draft, Klann (np.).

[67] Abernathy, *Productivity*, p. 138.

[68] Ford Archive, *Reminiscences*, Pring, p. 45.

[69] Ford Archive, Acc. 73, *Department Appraisals, 1919*; Ford Archive, Acc. 571, *Plant Accounts, February 1922*, Highland Park.

[70] Arnold, 'Ford methods', p. 673.

[71] *Ibid.*, p. 677.

[72] Sward, argued that by 1921 Ford had attained all the possible economies from reorganising machinery and therefore resorted to speed-up to reduce costs further. He referred to the pre-1921 period as the 'era of goodwill'. See *Legend of Henry Ford*, pp. 79, 353.

[73] Ford Archive, *Reminiscences*, Wollering, p. 9; H.L. Arnold. 'Ford methods (*Engineering Magazine*, 47, July 1914), pp. 525–32.

[74] Ford Archive, *Reminiscences*, Wollering, pp. 6–13. In general, jigs were fitted to the part being machined and guided the tools to the part. Fixtures were fixed to the machine, and once the part was loaded in the fixture it could be guided to the tools.

[75] Cited in Gartman, *Auto Slavery*, p. 149.

[76] Ford Archive, Reminiscences, Wollering, pp. 6 and 20.

[77] For a discussion of the fragmentary evidence see Meyer, *Five Dollar Day*, pp. 47–52.

[78] Gartman, Auto Slavery, p. 143.

[79] G.D. Babcock, *The Taylor System in Franklin Management* (New York, 1917), p. 125.

[80] Ford Archive, *Reminiscences*, Klann, p. 10; Ford Archive, *Reminiscences*, Wollering, pp. 22–3. Dodge may have retained this form of machine organisation as late as 1913. See 'A modern plant for automobile parts; the work of Dodge Bros.' (*Iron Age*, January 2, 1913), pp. 1–3.

[81] Ford Archive, *Reminiscences*, Dickert, p. 22.

[82] Ford Archive, *Reminiscences*, Wibel, p. 24.

[83] *ibid.*, pp. 46–7.

[84] Nevins, *Ford*, p. 382; Ford Archive, *Reminiscences*, Dickert, p. 11; Ford Archive, *Reminiscences*, Wibel, pp. 40, 58; Ford Archive, *Reminiscences*, Pioch, p. 38. See also Hounshell, *American System*, pp. 227–8.

[85] R. Pierpont, 'Automobiles and machine tools' (*Iron Age*, June 2 1910), p. 1314.

[86] Ford Archive, *Reminiscences*, Wibel, p. 58.

[87] A.J. Baker, 'The selection of machine tools' (*Journal of the Society of Automobile Engineers*, December 1922), p. 522.

[88] 'Ford Mult-Au-matic practice' (*Machinery*, 5 February 1920), pp. 579–85.

[89] Meyer, *Five Dollar Day*, pp. 48, 103.

[90] Ford Archive, *Reminiscences*, Rockelman, p. 9.

91 H.L. Arnold and F.L. Faurote, *Ford Methods and Ford Shops* (New York, 1915), p. 73. Colvin, in his description of the block department during this period, noted the ingenious design of many of the multi-task fixtures. See F.H. Colvin, 'Machining the Ford cylinders-II' (*American Machinist*, 38, 1913), p. 971.

92 Arnold and Faurote, *Ford Methods and Ford Shops*, p. 83.

93 'American practice in work handling' (*Automobile Engineer*, April 1918), p. 95.

94 'Ford Mult-Au-Matic practice' (*Machinery*, 5 February 1920), pp. 580–5. This principle may have been applied at Ford as early as 1915. See Gartman, Auto Slavery, p. 301.

95 Detroit Public Library, *Company Publications Pre-1950*, Ford Motor Company, Flyer advertising Ford Methods and Ford Shops.

96 Ford Archive, *Reminiscences*, Klann, p. 10.

97 E.P. Duggan, 'Machines, markets and labor: the carriage and wagon industry in late-nineteenth-century Cincinnati' (*Business History Review*, 51, 1977), p. 321. See also Hounshell, *American System*, pp. 223–4.

98 See Table 3.5; Ford Archive, Acc. 96, Box 1; Nevins, *Ford*, p. 523.

99 Nevins, *Ford*, p. 271.

100 Gartman, Auto Slavery, p. 133.

101 Nevins, *Ford*, p. 382.

102 Heliker, 'Detroit Labor 1900–1916', p. 25.

103 Prof. J. Younger, 'How Ford obtains low production costs' (*Machinery*, December 6 1928), p. 297.

104 See H. Braverman, *Labor and Monopoly Capital* (New York, 1974), p. 148; Heliker, 'Detroit Labor 1900–1916', pp. 27–8; Sward, *Legend of Henry Ford*, p. 48; Nevins, *Ford*, p. 531.

105 Ford Archive, *Reminiscences*, Wollering, p. 26.

106 Ford Archive, *Reminiscences*, Klann, p. 7.

107 Russell, 'Coming of the line', p. 42; Meyer, *Five Dollar Day*, p. 101.

108 Nevins, *Ford*, p. 526.

109 Quoted in Meyer, *Five Dollar Day*, p. 85.

110 Gartman, Auto Slavery, p. 359.

111 Arnold and Faurote, *Ford Methods and Ford Shops*, pp. 45–7.

112 Heliker, 'Detroit Labor 1900–1916', pp. 26 and 53. See also Russell, 'Coming of the line', p. 43; Meyer, *Five Dollar Day*, pp. 101–7.

113 Ford Archive, *Reminiscences*, Wibel, p. 18.

114 R. Muther, *Production Line Technique* (New York, 1944), p. 233, cited in Gartman, Auto Slavery, p. 188.

115 H.W. Slauson, cited in Meyer, *Five Dollar Day*, p. 64.

116 H. Arnold, 'Ford Methods and the Ford Shops' (*Engineering Magazine*, 48, December 1914), p. 349.

117 Quoted in Meyer, *Five Dollar Day*, pp. 60–1.

118 Cited in Gartman, Auto Slavery, p. 277, 283–4.

119 S. Fine in, *Sit Down: The General Motors Strike of 1936–37* (Ann Arbor, 1969), argued that the central issue in these strikes was the workers' total lack of control over the speed of the line, see pp. 55–6. See also R. Herding, *Job Control and Union Structure* (Rotterdam, 1972), pp. 17–28.

120 Lichtenstein, 'Auto worker militancy', p. 349.

[121] Herding, *Job Control*, p. 126.

[122] See discussion of Ford in Britain in Chapter 8.

[123] Braverman, *Labor*, p. 149; Russell, 'Coming of the line', pp. 42–5; Nevins, *Ford*, pp. 536–40. The few written records and popular folklore claim that the decision to pay five dollars per day was taken on a dare by Sorensen who was indicating his dissatisfaction with Ford's proposal to pay four dollars per day.

[124] See Sward, *Legend of Henry Ford*, p. 63.

[125] Cited in Sward, *Legend of Henry Ford*, p. 47.

[126] Brody, *Workers*, p. 14.

[127] H.F. Porter, 'Four big lessons from Ford's factory', (*System*, 31, June 1917), pp. 643–4, cited in Meyer, *Five Dollar Day*, p. 37.

[128] The Fordism we have described is unique to only a short period of time from 1914 to 1921. Most historical accounts recognise that in 1921 Fordism left what has been called the 'era of goodwill', and resorted to harsher and more brutal labour control mechanisms. S.S. Marquis, the religious figure who coordinated Ford Sociology in a humane, if undemocratic fashion, was replaced by H. Bennett who resorted to intimidation, spies, and fear tactics, to get the work out. Marquis recalled, 'There came to the front men whose theory was that men are more profitable to an industry when driven than led, that fear is a greater incentive to work than loyalty' (Meyer, *Five Dollar Day*, p. 198.) For the workforce the new regime of speed-up and continuous insecurity over one's tenure at Fords led to heightened stress and a common affliction known as 'Ford Stomach' (see Sward, *Legend of Henry Ford*, p. 204).

[129] For an attempt to examine these factors see M. Burawoy, *The Politics of Production* (London, 1985).

[130] D.T. Rodgers, *The Work Ethic in Industrial America, 1850–1920* (Chicago, 1974), p. 233. Rodgers has provided an excellent survey of the evolution of the work ethic in the United States.

[131] Russell, 'Coming of the line', p. 45.

Chapter 4 The effort bargain and British technical change

[1] See R. Samuel, 'Workshop of the world: steam power and hand technology in mid-Victorian Britain' (*History Workshop*, 3, 1977), pp. 6–72.

[2] J. Foster, *Class Struggle and the Industrial Revolution* (New York, 1974), p. 18–19.

[3] E.P. Thompson, 'Time, work-discipline, and industrial capitalism' (*Past and Present*, 38, 1967), pp. 71–9. For the problem or irregular work patterns in early American factories, see Merrit Roe Smith, *Harpers Ferry Armory and the New Technology, The Challenge of Change* (Ithaca, 1977).

[4] E. Hobsbawm, 'Custom, wages and work load in nineteenth century industry', in A. Briggs and J. Saville (eds.), *Essays in Labour History* (London, 1960), pp. 120–4.

[5] S. Pollard, *The Genesis of Modern Management* (London, 1965), pp. 188–90.

[6] Hobsbawm, 'Custom', p. 124.

[7] See Pollard, *Genesis*, pp. 38–47; C. Littler, *The Development of the Labour Process in Capitalist Societies* (London, 1982), pp. 65–73.

[8] Pollard, *Genesis*, p. 189.

[9] L. Urwick and E.F.L. Brech, *The Making of Scientific Management* (London, 1946), vol. II, p. 11. For other work on the rise of the new factory system see A. Chandler,

The Visible Hand (Harvard, 1977); D. Nelson, *Managers and Workers, Origins of the New Factory System in the United States* (Wisconsin, 1975); R. Edwards, *Contested Terrain* (New York, 1979).

10 *Building News* (27 May 1859), pp. 501–2, quoted in R. Price, *Masters, Unions and Men* (Cambridge University Press, 1980), p. 53.

11 EEF Archive, *U(1)24, Memo Ship Building Employers' Federation to all Secretaries*, 8 August 1920. See J. Melling, 'Non-commissioned officers: British employers and their supervisory workers, 1880–1920' (*Social History*, 5, 1980), pp. 191–210.

12 J.R. Hay, 'Employers' attitudes to social policy and the concept of social control, 1900–20', in P. Thane (ed.), *The Origins of British Social Policy* (London, 1978), p. 118.

13 See K. Burgess, *The Origins of British Industrial Relations* (London, 1975), pp. 5–12.

14 K. Burgess, *The Challenge of Labour* (London, 1980), pp. 13–15; R. Davidson, *Whitehall and the Labour Problem in Late-Victorian and Edwardian Britain* (Kent, 1985), p. 36; R.A. Church, *The Great Victorian Boom, 1850–73* (London, 1975), pp. 71–3.

15 J. Zeitlin, Craft Regulation and the Division of Labour: Engineers and Compositors in Britain, 1890–1914 (Ph.D Thesis, Warwick, 1981), pp. 99–107, 167. For an examination of the inability of employers to challenge the authority of skilled workers see E. Wigham, *The Power to Manage; A History of the Engineering Employers' Federation* (London, 1973).

16 F. Crouzet, *The Victorian Economy* (London, 1982), p. 379.

17 On early engineering technology see B. Weekes, The Amalgamated Society of Engineers, 1880–1914 (Ph.D, Warwick, 1970), pp. 9–21; Zeitlin, *Craft Regulation*, pp. 44–7, 99–107, 167.

18 Burgess, *Origins*, p. 27.

19 Davidson, *Whitehall*, p. 35. White has argued that the British transition to monopoly capitalism or managerial capitalism was simply slower than in the United States and that by 1930 the transition was complete in Britain. We will argue below that this is an over simplification and that the economic institutions emerging from the British experience during the second Industrial Revolution were distinctly different from those found in the United States, particularly in the areas of monitoring and enforcing the effort bargain. See J. White, '1910–1914 reconsidered', in J.E. Cronin and J. Schneer (eds.), *Social Conflict and the Political Order in Modern Britain* (London, 1982), p. 77.

20 For details on the 1897 lockout see J. Zeitlin, 'The labour strategies of British engineering employers, 1890–1922', in H. Gospel and C. Littler (eds.), *Managerial Strategies and Industrial Relations* (London, 1983), pp. 25–54.

21 Col. H.C.S. Dyer, 'The engineering dispute' (*Cassier's*, 1897), pp. 97–4. In this article Dyer also rejects any possibility that the new technology can be run without a reduction in wages.

22 *Times*, (7 September 1897), cited in J. Hinton, *Labour and Socialism* (Amherst, 1983), p. 67.

23 A. Reid, 'Intelligent artisans and aristocrats of labour: the essays of Thomas Wright', in J. Winter (ed.), *The Working Class in Modern British History* (Cambridge University Press, 1983).

24 British rates are based on information available in the EEF Archive, *Wage*

Movements. In the case of unskilled labour, the rate is based on the 6d minimum won by the Workers Union in Coventry. The American rates are based on earning levels cited in Chapter Three.

[25] Hinton, *Labour and Socialism*, p. 68.

[26] See White, '1910–1914 reconsidered', pp. 85–9; J. Hinton, 'The rise of a mass labour movement: growth and limits', in C.J. Wrigley (ed.), *A History of British Industrial Relations, 1875–1914* (Brighton, 1982). On union density see A. Booth, 'A reconsideration of trade union growth in the United Kingdom' (*British Journal of Industrial Relations*, 21, 1983), pp. 377–91.

[27] On the rise of state intervention into industrial relations see C.J. Wrigley, 'The government and industrial relations', in Wrigley (ed.) *British Industrial Relations*, pp. 139, 152. See also R. Davidson, 'Government administration', in Wrigley (ed.), *British Industrial Relations*.

[28] Price, *Masters*, p. 198.

[29] See T. Adams, 'The British labour movement and working-class unrest, 1918–1921' (*Society for the Study of Labour History, Bulletin no. 46, 1983*), pp. 12–3, for a useful argument that union officials may have been less willing to accept the new rules than Price suggested.

[30] Price, *Masters*, p. 257.

[31] V. Gore, 'Rank and file dissent', in Wrigley (ed.), *British Industrial Relations*, p. 66.

[32] See B. Austin and W. Francis Lloyd, *The Secret of High Wages* (London, 1926); Hobsbawm, 'Custom', pp. 128–32.

[33] On the growth of firm size see C. Shaw, 'The large manufacturing employers of 1907' (*Business History*, 25, 1983), pp. 42–60.

[34] Davidson, *Whitehall*, p. 41.

[35] S. Meacham, 'The sense of an impending clash: English working-class unrest before the First World War' (*American Historical Review*, 77, 1972), pp. 1351–2.

[36] *Times* (15 September 1883), cited in Davidson, *Whitehall*, p. 52.

[37] *Times* (6 January 1890), cited in Davidson, *Whitehall*, p. 53.

[38] 'The conflict between Capital and Labour' (*Quarterly Review*, 173, 1891), p. 253, cited in Davidson, *Whitehall*, p. 53.

[39] Within the UKS/NUVB, a section of the membership responded to the deterioration of capital labour relationships by calling for workers control in the form of cooperatives. This idea had been proposed as early as 1848 without any success. (*UKS/NUVB Journal*, August 1920, p. 32). The idea was raised at both the 1899 and the 1903 rules conferences where it was suggested that there should be a levy on members to provide the needed capital (UKS/NUVB Archive, *Revision of Rules, 1899*, and *UKS/NUVB Journal*, May 1903, p. 84). During the war, interest in worker cooperatives was renewed, and most actively pursued by the London Shop Stewards Committee (*UKS/NUVB Journal*, January 1917, 'Statement by the president of the Swindon branch', and *UKS/NUVB Journal*, April 1920, 'Statement by the Midland organiser'). In 1921, they actually took over a shop and ran it on a cooperative basis (*UKS/NUVB Journal*, June 1921). The London Shop Stewards sent a delegate to the Guild conference in October of 1921, and published a pamphlet outlining how a cooperative would work, but the collapse in trade in late 1921 stalled any further activity (UKS/NUVB Archive, *London Shop Stewards Minutes Books*, 31 January 1922).

[40] For data on the outcome of procedure decisions see Zeitlin, *Craft Regulation*, Tables 10 and 11.

[41] On the rise of restrictionism see G. Brown, *Sabotage* (Nottingham, 1977). On restrictionism and unorganised workers see S.B. Mathewson, *Restriction of Output Among Unorganized Workers* (Carbondale, 1969). On trade unions and restrictionism see F. Zweig, *Productivity and Trade Unions* (Oxford, 1951); J. Hilton *et al.*, *Are Trade Unions Obstructive?* (London, 1935); Gore, 'Rank-and-file', pp. 60–1. C.S. Myer, a British labour psychologist, argued in the twenties that it was a mistake to see restrictionism as being a product of unions. He argued that non-union workers were just as likely to react to fears concerning unemployment, and to feel it necessary to show class solidarity. Given these factors, they were just as likely to reduce output levels as unionised workers. C.S. Myer, 'Industrial efficiency from the psychological standpoint' (*Engineering and Industrial Management*, 15, May 1919), p. 427.

[42] See C.S. Maier, 'Between Taylorism and Technocracy: European ideologies and the vision of industrial productivity in the 1920s' (*Journal of Contemporary History*, 5, 1970), pp. 27–61.

[43] R. Price, 'Rethinking labour history: the importance of work', in J.E. Cronin and J. Schneer (eds.), *Social Conflict*, p. 201.

[44] M. Holbrook-Jones, *Supremacy and Subordination of Labour* (London, 1982), p. 69.

[45] Hobsbawm, 'Custom', p. 136; Zeitlin, *Craft Regulation*, p. 518; E. Wigham, *Power to Manage*, p. 73. The 1906 figure is from the 1906 Wages Census. Figures for 1913 and 1914 are from the EEF Archive, *EEF Surveys*, 30 September 1913 and 31 July 1914.

[46] Most Premium Bonus systems entailed some sharing of bonus earnings with the employers. One ingenious system was the Rowen system which had the effect of limiting bonus earnings to 100 percent of regular earnings, regardless of the level of productivity or the looseness which piece prices were set. The Rowan bonus was calculated on the following basis:

Bonus = ((Time Allowed for Job − Time Taken)/Time Allowed) *Time Taken.

On early employer attitudes to new forms of piece work see EEF Archive, P(2) 15, Section II, *W.G. Banister Lecture*, March 11, 1904.

[47] See Holbrook-Jones, *Supremacy and Subordination*, pp. 76–7, for a discussion of union policy regarding the guarantee of day rates.

[48] Details of the negotiations over the Carlisle Memorandum can be found in the EEF Archive, P(2)15, *Conference between the ASE and the EEF*, August 1902. See also *Terms of Settlement*, 1898. C. Kinsgate, president of the United Kingdom Society of Coachmakers (UKS), claimed in 1905 that prices were fixed without consultation and were often fixed only after the work was in progress. See *UKS/NUVB Journal*, August 1905.

[49] EEF Archive, P(2)15, *ASE Executive to Home Branches*, 14 October 1902.

[50] In 1907, the guarantee of day rates was extended to all piecework systems, as was a guarantee of some form of mutuality in setting prices. Weekes has pointed out that any system of mutuality which falls short of labour having an actual role in setting the price in the first instance seriously compromises labour's bargaining power. Under the majority of mutuality systems, labour was given a choice of accepting or rejecting the price which in most cases gave labour little bargaining leverage. See Weekes,

Amalgamated, p. 183. On the 1907 agreement see EEF Archive, files A(2)5, A(2)6, A(2)7, and A(2)8.

[51] *Report of TUC Committee of Enquiry on Premium Bonus Systems*, 1909. Extracts of the report are reproduced in Urwick and Brech, *Scientific Management*.

[52] EEF Archive, P(2)15, *Annual Conference of the Federation of Engineering and Shipbuilding Trades (F.E.S.T.)*, 30 August 1904.

[53] EEF Archive, P(2)15, *Barrow Meeting of F.E.S.T.*, 14 April 1905.

[54] ASE (COV), *Minutes*, 2 September 1898 to 10 October 1898 and 1 July 1903–16 September 1903. See also Daimler, *Board Minutes*, 14 August 1902 and 18 September 1902.

[55] The Halsey system was proposed by an American manager in about 1884. Under this system once the agreed normal level of output was reached, the price per additional piece was reduced. This gave labour a bonus for increased output but also reduced per unit labour costs. See Nelson, *Managers and Workers*, pp. 52–3.

[56] *UKS/NUVB Journal*, September–December 1904. The ASE accepted the new payment system as long as day rates were guaranteed. See ASE (COV), *Minutes*, 14 December 1906 to 24 January 1907.

[57] See P. Martin, 'Works Organisation' (*Proceedings of the Institute of Automobile Engineers*, 1, 1906), pp. 109–52.

[58] R.C. Floud, 'Britain 1860–1914: a survey', in R. Floud and D. McCloskey (eds.), *The Economic History of Britain since 1700* (Cambridge University Press, 1981), vol. 2, p. 22. For a review of the debate see Crouzet, *Victorian Economy*, pp. 371–422. For a recent investigation of the hazards of quantifying economic performance see S. Nicholas, 'Total factor productivity growth and the revision of post-1870 British economic history' (*Economic History Review*, 35, 1982), pp. 83–96.

[59] Crouzet, *Victorian Economy*, p. 388.

[60] Davidson, *Whitehall*, p. 63.

[61] See E.H. Phelps Brown and M. Browne, *A Century of Pay* (London, 1968), pp. 185. See also pp. 144, 175–82.

[62] Britain was not the only European country for which the war meant a shift in shop floor authority patterns. See C.J. Sirianni, 'Workers control in the era of World War I' (*Theory and Society*, 9, 1980), pp. 29–88. Britain seems unique though in terms of the longrun impact of this management crisis.

[63] EEF Archive, W(4)2, *Memo Admiralty to the EEF*, 3 August 1914, and *Memo Vickers to Sir Trevor Dawson*, 15 September 1914; *History of the Ministry of Munitions* (London, 1918–22), reproduced by Harvester Press (Sussex, 1976), vol. I, part II, p. 1.

[64] EEF Archive, W(4)3, *Special Conference, EEF, ASE, SEM, UMWA*, 10 December 1914; W(4)3, *Letter Smith to H. Lawson*, 22 December 1914; W(4)3, *Special Conference, EEF and Various Unions*, 13 January 1915; W(4)3, *Letter to J.H. Richmond*, 2 February 1915. When the government was considering legislation to enforce restoration, it was pointed out by an official at the Ministry of Reconstruction, that the government was obligated to sanction restoration. It was also suggested that any such bill could not and would not be literally implemented, but would simply give added weight to the unions' position when bargaining with management for concessions after the War. See PRO. RECO/1/800, *Statement from Ministry of Reconstruction*, October 1918.

[65] EEF Archive, W(4)3, *Letter Smith to Lawson*, 22 December 1914; *History of the Ministry of Munitions*, vol. I, part II, pp. 38, 77–8.

[66] *History of the Ministry of Munitions*, vol. I, part II, pp. 51–2, 87.

[67] *Ibid.*, vol. I, part IV, pp. 1–18; vol. I, part II, pp. 98–9; vol. IV, part IV, pp. 91–2; vol. V, part I, pp. 43–59; vol. VI, part II, pp. 61–6. For other work on the impact of the war on the production process see Hinton, *Labour and Socialism*, pp. 96–118; C. More, *Skill in the English Working Class, 1870–1914* (London, 1980).

[68] For details see J. Hinton, *The First Shop Stewards Movement* (London, 1973), p. 41; *History of the Ministry of Munitions*, vol. VI, part I, pp. 35–8. On the narrowing gap between skilled and unskilled workers see G.D.H. Cole, *Trade Unionism and Munitions* (Oxford, 1923). Hinton suggests that as the war dragged on, skilled and unskilled formed closer alliances. See Hinton, *Labour and Socialism*, p. 107.

[69] The Workers Union was a Midlands based union which began to grow rapidly in 1912. In that year, its membership increased fourfold to over 90 000. See Cole, *Trade Unionism*, pp. 24–8. On its activity in Coventry see ASE (COV), *Minutes*, 11 December 1911, 9 January, 7 and 11 November 1912. For a detailed examination of labour in Coventry see F.W. Carr, Engineering Workers and the Rise of Labour in Coventry, 1914–1939 (Ph.D, Warwick, 1979), pp. 26–7, 36.

[70] ASE (COV), *Minutes*, 17 March, 3, 11 and 18 November, 17 December 1913, 21 January, 17 April, 18 November 1914. In March of 1915, the Coventry ASE began to keep a list of skilled workers signed up by the WU. See ASE (COV), *Minutes*, March 1915. On the war service question see WU Archive, MRC, Mss. 126/WU/4/2/1, 'The manpower question' (*The Record*, February 1918).

[71] ASE (COV), *Minutes*, 12 April, 7, 18 and 25 November 1916, 1, 2 and 4 January 1917.

[72] ASE (COV), *Minutes*, 4 January 1917.

[73] The Coventry ASE's tentative but confused movement toward industrial unions and cooperation with the unskilled can be contrasted with the policy of the ASE in Oxford. In 1919 they made no move to absorb the growing semi-skilled workforce or low rated workers, and remained an unimportant union until at least the thirties. See R. Whiting, *The Working Class in the New Industrial Towns between the Wars: The Case of Oxford* (Ph.D, Oxford, 1978). During 1917, the Coventry ASE refused to let the WU join the CEJC unless it released to other unions the skilled workers it had signed up, yet one year later it was the ASE which called for reconciliation given the 'changed conditions'. See ASE (COV), *Minutes*, 18 December 1917 and 20 December 1918. That the alliance was not closer between different grades of workers can partially be explained by the differential treatment of skilled and unskilled regarding military conscription. This issue was likely more divisive in Coventry than in other engineering centres because the new technology had advanced the furthest; hence the differences between the tasks of members of the ASE and the WU were the least. This could only have made the preferential treatment of ASE members appear even more unfair.

[74] ASE (COV), *Minutes*, 15 August 1899, 26 July 1907, 10 October 1911, 5 October 1915, 7 March and 5 August 1916.

[75] ASE (COV), *Minutes*, 4 October 1915, 3 April 1916.

[76] ASE (COV), *Minutes*, 12 April 1916, 20 February, 6 and 17 March and 3 April 1917.

[77] EEF Archive, S(4)6, *Memo CDEEA to EEF*, 14 April 1917.

[78] ASE (COV), *Minutes*, 5 August 1916, 23 January 1917.

[79] PRO, CAB/24/14 GT/897, *Ministry of Labour Report to War Cabinet on the Rise of Shop Stewards.*

[80] PRO, CAB/24/24 GT/1849, *Memo Prof. E.V. Arnold*, August 1917; PRO, CAB/24/26 GT/2073, *Memo J.M. Mactavish.*

[81] EEF Archive, S(4)11, *Memo CDEEA to EEF*, 11 December 1917. See also G.D.H. Cole, *Workshop Organisation* (London, 1923) pp. 139–41.

[82] ASE (COV), *Minutes*, 13 May 1919; EEF Archive, P(5)27, *Local Conference CDEEA and CEJC*, 6 March 1919, and *Shop Stewards and Works Committee Agreement*, 20 May 1919.

[83] ASE (COV), *Minutes*, 17 June 1919 and 7 September 1920.

[84] J.A. Turner, in 'The politics of the business community in the First World War' (unpublished paper, 1980), has examined the political activities of businessmen and concluded that in general they were disorganised and ineffective. The EEF did not begin to promote joint political activities by businessmen until near the end of the war. This will be examined in some detail in the next chapter.

[85] EEF Archive, I(1)7, *Emergency Committee to Local Associations*, 19 September 1916.

[86] EEF Archive, I(1)7, *Replies from Associations.*

[87] EEF Archive, I(1)7, *Draft on Postwar Industrial Problems*, 23 November 1917.

[88] R. Charles, *The Development of Industrial Relations in Britain, 1911–39* (London, 1973), p. 85.

[89] *First Report of the Committee of the Ministry of Reconstruction on Relations Between Employers and Employed*, paragraph 14.

[90] *Ibid.*

[91] Charles, *Development*, pp. 202–7.

[92] EEF Archive, H(3)17, *Conference EEF and AEU*, 15 November 1918.

[93] EEF Archive, I(1)9, *Memo CDEEA to EEF*, 19 July 1917.

[94] EEF Archive, I(1)9, *Memo Birmingham EEA to EEF*, 9 July 1917.

[95] EEF Archive, I(1)9, *Memo Birmingham EEA to EEF*, 23 July 1917.

[96] EEF Archive, I(1)12, *Postwar Industrial Problems*, 21 January 1918.

[97] EEF Archive, I(1)10, *National Guild League to the Trade Unions*, 14 July 1917.

[98] Charles, *Development*, p. 216.

[99] *Ibid.*, p. 85.

[100] EEF Archive, *EEF Report on the NCEO and the FBI*, May 1934.

[101] EEF Archive, *Minutes Emergency Committee EEF*, 27 October 1916 and *Minutes EEF Management Committee*, 21 December 1916.

[102] FBI Archive, FBI/c/10/, vol. 21, *Special Committee*, 13 July 1917; EEF Archives, I(1)10, *Letter FBI to Whitley Committee*, 3 August 1917.

[103] FBI Archive, FBI/c/84, vol. 178, *Report Labour Committee*, 10 to 13 November 1917.

[104] FBI Archive, FBI/c/84, *Postwar Industrial Policy.*

[105] EEF Archive, I(1)12, *EEF Reply to FBI*, 21 January 1918.

[106] FBI Archive, FBI/c/81, vol. 174, *Report of Conference EEF and FBI*, 11 October 1918; vol. 178, *Report of Conference FBI and EEF*, 15 March 1918.

[107] EEF Archive, *Postwar Industrial Problems*, 29 July 1918.

Chapter 5: The effort crisis and British managerial strategies

1   M. Rose, *Industrial Behaviour* (London, 1975), p. 40. See also D. Noble, *America by Design* (Oxford, 1977), p. 271.
2   See L. Urwick and E.F.L. Brech, *The Making of Scientific Management* (London, 1946); C. Littler, *The Development of the Labour Process in Capitalist Societies* (London, 1982), pp. 99–145; G. Brown, *Sabotage* (Nottingham, 1977), pp. 148–59. For general works on Scientific Management see H.J. Aitken, *Taylorism at Watertown Arsenal* (Cambridge University Press, 1960); M.J. Nadworny, *Scientific Management and the Unions, 1900–1932: A Historical Analysis* (Cambridge University Press, 1955). For a recent reappraisal see D. Nelson, *Management and Workers, Origins of the New Factory System in the U.S., 1880–1920* (Wisconsin, 1975).
3   This firm was Hans Renold Ltd. See L. Urwick, *The Golden Book of Management* (London, 1956), p. 49.
4   A. Vines, 'Engineers' views on scientific management' (*Engineering and Industrial Management*, 1 January 1920). For other views on the spread of Scientific Management to Britain see W.F. Watson, *Machines and Men* (London, 1935), p. 90; E. Cadbury, 'Some principles of industrial organisation: the case for and against Scientific Management' (*Sociological Review*, 7, 1914), p. 104.
5   See J.A. Litterer, 'Systematic Management: the search for order and integration' (*Business History Review*, 35, 1961), pp. 461–76, for an examination of the American managerial movements which preceded Scientific Management.
6   C. Littler, 'Understanding Taylorism' (*British Journal of Sociology*, 29, 1978), pp. 185–202.
7   An excellent example of what was taking place in the larger factories were the changes being made at the Elswick factory of Sir William Armstrong and Co. By 1887, when Noble testified before a government enquiry, the firm had a comprehensive cost accounting system, employed over two hundred workers in the design office, and operated with a large proportion of unskilled labour. See *Committee of Enquiry into the Organization and Administration of the Manufacturing Department of the Army*, Morley Commission 1887, c5116, qs. 8892–9026, cited in J. Zeitlin, *Craft Regulation and the Division of Labour: Engineers and Compositors in Britain* (Ph.D., Warwick, 1981).
8   W.F. Watson, *Bedaux and Other Systems Explained* (London, 1932), p. 3, cited in Brown, *Sabotage*, p. 148.
9   S. Chapman, *Labour and Capital After the War* (London, 1918), pp. 247–8.
10   J.B. Conway, 'Standard time in connection with time study work' (*Machinery*, 1 April 1920). A good example of the subjectivity inherent in systems such as Scientific Management can be found in 'The human factor in time setting' (*Engineering and Industrial Management*, 10 April 1919), where it is suggested that times given out to workers should be adjusted according to how much actual work above the norm was expected. The assumption was that workers would always try to earn the same weekly pay, so their effort could be directly controlled by the price paid per piece. Clark Kerr in 'The effects of environment and administration on job evaluation', in Clark Kerr (ed.), *Labor Markets and Wage Determination* (Berkeley 1977), argued that all job description and job evaluation schemes, of which Taylorism is a crude form, have large elements of subjectivity even in their most objective elements. See p. 71.

[11] Watson, *Machines and Men*, p. 92.

[12] For contemporary criticisms of Scientific Management's treatment of labour see Sir R. Hadfield, 'The industrial situation after the war' (*Managing Engineer*, 1917). See also 'Applied time studies' (*Automobile Engineer*, December 1920), where the chairman of the Institute of Automobile Engineers argued that Scientific Management could not be applied in Britain because the human element was more important in Britain than in the United States.

[13] Littler, '*Understanding Taylorism*', p. 196.

[14] A copy of J. Scott Maxwell's paper to the Institute of Electrical Engineers can be found in *Machinery*, 11 December 1919 and 18 December 1919. H.W. Allington's paper before the Manchester Association of Engineers can be found in *Engineering and Industrial Management*, December 1919. A copy of the discussion following both of these papers can be found in *Engineering and Industrial Management*, January 1920.

[15] *Engineering and Industrial Management*, 1 January 1920, pp. 12–14.

[16] *Ibid.*, p. 14. Details of Stelling's own views can be found in 'Taylor's principle in modern British management' (*Engineering and Industrial Management*, 9 October 1919).

[17] Rose, *Industrial Behaviour*, pp. 84–5.

[18] Urwick and Brech, *Making of Scientific Management*, p. 89.

[19] Littler, *Development*, pp. 99–116.

[20] See the references to Sir Maurice Fitzmaurice in an article by Hadfield, 'Industrial situation'.

[21] See R. Charles, *The Development of Industrial Relations* (London, 1973); R. Currie, *Industrial Politics* (Oxford, 1979).

[22] Hadfield, 'Industrial situation', p. 189. L.A. Legros, the president of the Institute of Automobile Engineers, advocated paying higher wages and following the American example of which Ford was the leading figure. See his presidential address (*Proceedings of the Institute of Automobile Engineers*, 11, October 1916), p. 27.

[23] See S. Meyer III, *The Five Dollar Day* (Albany, 1981). Unfortunately, the Ford experience does not offer a convincing test of this thesis due to the nearly simultaneous introduction of the five dollar day and the moving assembly line.

[24] This point is made by, O. Stromborg, 'Some point in manufacturing' (*The Engineer*, 30 December 1921).

[25] J.A. Turner, 'The politics of the business community in the First World War' (unpublished paper, 1980).

[26] B. Austin, and W. Francis Lloyd, *The Secret of High Wages* (London, 1926), Introduction.

[27] A. Mosely, 'British views of American workshops' (*Cassier's*, 1903), p. 477.

[28] 'The three phases of industrial evolution' (*Engineering and Industrial Management*, 5 February 1920), p. 161.

[29] Rose, *Industrial Behaviour*, p. 65.

[30] PRO, RECO 1, 781, *Memeo Bayes to the Minister of Reconstruction*, 23 October 1918.

[31] J.R. Hay, 'Employers' attitudes to social policy and the concept of social control, 1900–1920', in P. Thane (ed.), *The Origins of British Social Policy* (London, 1978), p. 116.

[32] Sir H. Fowler, 'Some notes on productivity' (*Proceedings of the Institute of Automobile Engineers*, 15, 1920/1921), p. 8.

[33] *Ibid.*, p. 11.

[34] *Ibid.*, p. 29.

[35] J. Melling, 'Employers industrial welfare and the struggle for workplace control in British industry, 1880–1920', H. Gospel and C. Littler (eds.), *Managerial Strategies and Industrial Relations* (London, 1983), pp. 55–81. For further work on welfarism see J. Melling, 'Industrial strife and business welfare philosophy: the case of the South Metropolitan Gas Company from the 1880s to the war' (*Business History*, 21, 1979), pp. 163–79; E. Cadbury, *Experiments in Industrial Organisation* (London, 1912); T. Lawson, 'Paternalism and labour market segmentation theory', in F. Wilkinson (ed.), *Essays in the Dynamics of Labour Markets* (London, 1981); E.T. Kelly, *Welfare Work in Industry* (London, 1925); J.C. Skaggs and R.L. Ehrlich, 'Profits, paternalism, and rebellion: a case study in industrial strife' (*Business History Review*, 54, 1980), pp. 155–74.

[36] C.S. Myer, 'Industrial efficiency from the psychological standpoint' (*Cassier's*, 24 April 1919), p. 332.

[37] Charles, *Development*, pp. 231–2.

[38] *Ibid.*, p. 24.

[39] *Ibid.*, p. 230.

[40] W. Hannington, *Unemployed Struggles* (London, 1977), pp. 3–6.

[41] Turner, 'Politics', p. 34.

[42] Coventry Record Office, Acc. 594, box file 8, *Birmingham Small Arms Co. Ltd, General Meeting*, 11 April 1921, p. 9.

[43] EEF Archive, C(8)6, *Memo on the Causes of Labour Unrest*, presented by Trade Union representatives to the Joint Committee to the National Industrial Conference, 27 February 1919.

[44] EEF Archive, C(8)2, *Draft of EEF policy for the National Industrial Conference.*

[45] See Turner, 'Politics', pp. 17–24. For a study of Smith's personal involvement in politics as a member of parliament see T. Rodgers, 'Sir Allan Smith: outsider in politics 1918–1924' (unpublished paper, 1979). See also EEF Archive, *General Letter 170*, 22 April 1913. On the formation of the FBI see Turner, 'Politics', pp. 11–12.

[46] The EEF's commitment to the NCEO extended to almost complete financing during the early years, and as late as October of 1921, the EEF agreed to provide the necessary funds for the NCEO which was having trouble balancing its books. See EEF Archive, *Minutes Management Committee*, 22 February 1918.

[47] EEF Archive, I(1)12, *Memo on FBI*, January 1918.

[48] EEF Archive, *Circular Letter from Rear Admiral W.R. Hall Regarding National Propaganda.*

[49] EEF Archive, P(13)4, *Note Regarding National Propaganda*, October 1919.

[50] EEF Archive, P(13)4, *National Propaganda Bulletin no. 3*; P(13)4, *Draft Constitution, National Propaganda.*

[51] EEF Archive, P(13)4, *Minutes Executive Meeting, National Propaganda*, 5 August 1920; P(13)4, *Memo EEF to Sporberg*, 21 May 1921; *Minutes of Management Committee EEF*, 22 July 1921.

[52] EEF Archive, *Circular Letter no. 82*, 'Precis of Address by Sir A. Smith', 12 March 1924.

[53] *Ibid.*, p. 2; EEF Archive, P(13)10, *Economic Study Club.*

[54] Charles, *Development*, p. 108.

[55] EEf Archive, H(3)17, *Conference EEF, ASE, WU, and other Unions*, 15 November 1918, pp. 2–3.

[56] EEF Archive, H(3)17, *Conference EEF, ASE, WU, and other Unions*, 19 November 1918, pp. 54, 63.

[57] EEF Archive, H(3)17, *Conference EEF, ASE, and other Unions*, 19 November 1918, p. 67.

[58] EEF Archive, *Conference between EEF and the Confederation of Engineering and Shipbuilding Trades*, 24 July 1919, p. 18.

[59] W. Williams, *Full Up and Fed Up: The Workers Mind in Crowded Britain* (New York, 1921), cited in J. Cronin, *Labour and Society in Britain* (London, 1984), p. 26.

[60] EEF Archive, *Conference EEF and Confederation of Engineering and Shipbuilding Trades*, 24 July 1919, p. 29.

[61] One of the first labour groups to settle postwar working conditions was the National Union of Vehicle Builders who began negotiations in May of 1919 and reached an agreement in 1920. The most novel feature of the agreement was the recognition of a number of grades of labour. The majority of workers were classified as either fully skilled workers or semi-skilled workers. The latter received about two pence per hour less than the skilled workers. The wage differential between the two groups was surprisingly small, being less than ten per cent after war bonuses were included. The NUVB had tried to win automatic promotion to Grade I, similar to the ASE demands under the Engineers Charter, to be described in what follows, but failed. See EEF Archive, W(8)6, *Conference, EEF, NUVB, ASWM*, May 1919; W(8)7, *Conference EEF, NUVB, ASWM*, 3 December 1919; W(B)10, *Conference EEF, NUVB, ASWM*, 19 February 1920. The NUVB had expected that in times of unemployment, the 1920 agreement would protect the jobs of skilled workers by forcing firms to release Grade II workers first. In actual fact this was not done. During the interwar recession in the industry, a number of Grade I workers were made redundant and offered new jobs as Grade II workers at Grade II wages. See EEF Archive, W(8)29, *Conference EEF and NUVB*, 28 November 1922; W(8)40, *Conference EEF, NUVB and ASWM*, 22 July 1924. The inability of the vehicle builders to control the conditions under which the 1920 agreement was applied led them to call for the abolition of grades in 1924 and a shift to all workers being paid the same rate irrespective of skill. A rate of 1/9d was suggested. In return, the employers were to be given complete freedom to move workers about as they desired. This proposal was rejected by the employers. See EEF Archive, Basement EEF, *Special Conference, EEf, NUVB and ASWM*, 23 May 1924.

[62] Spectator, 16 August 1902, cited in G.R. Searle, *The Quest For National Efficiency* (Oxford, 1971), p. 1.

[63] EEF Archive, *Conference, EEF and Engineering Trade Unions*, 20 May 1919, p. 33.

[64] *Ibid.*, p. 95. See also 'Engineer's views on Scientific Management' (*Engineering and Industrial Management*, 1 January 1920), p. 12, for a critique of payment by results.

[65] EEF Archive, *Conference EEF and AEU*, 20 September 1920, p. 235.

[66] EEF Archive, *Conference EEF and AEU*, 27 October 1920, p. 496.

[67] EEF Archive, *Special Conference, EEF and NUVB*, 1 May 1925, p. 7. By the early twenties the NUVB executive had accepted that modern machine methods would be adopted in vehicle body production. In fact, they showed a keen fascination with the new technology. The report of the executive's visit to the works of the London,

Midland, and Scottish Railway Company at Derby makes this clear. 'Your representatives were impressed beyond measure as they saw the skill of the hand craftsman carried through by jig and machine in minutes, that once represented hours of skilled labour . . . . We cannot stay this progress; our policy must be to demand that the advance of the machine shall be to lighten labour, and that rapid and cheaper production shall be accompanied by a commensurate return to the wage earner.' (*UKS/NUVB Journal*, 1923).

68 See A. Gleason, *What the Workers Want* (London, 1920), p. 153, cited in Cronin, *Labour and Society*, p. 25. See also the discussion in Cronin, p. 26.

69 EEF Archive, *Conference EEF and AEU*, 27 October 1920, pp. 497–502.

70 *Ibid.*, pp. 525–7.

71 *Ibid.*, pp. 508–19.

72 EEF Archive, *General Letter 231*, 'The present economic position of the engineering and allied industries', produced by the EEF, 23 March 1921.

73 TUC Archive, *Comments on the Present Economic Position of the Engineering and Allied Industries*, Trades Union Congress, pp. 23–4.

74 EEF Archive, *Conference EEF and AEU*, 10 November 1921, p. 256.

75 EEF Archive, *Special Conference, EEF and AEU*, 17 November 1921, p. 348.

76 EEF Archive, *Special Conference, EEF and AEU*, 17 November 1921, p. 394.

77 EEF Archive, *Conference EEF and AEU*, 28 February 1922. See also E. Wigham, *Power to Manage* (London, 1973), p. 119.

78 EEF Archive, P(5)27, *Local Conferences, CDEEA and CEJC*, 6 March 1919 and 13 March 1919; *Memo EEF to UKS of Coachmakers*, 25 March 1919; M(17)6, *Fifty percent Agreement*, 26 June 1919; W(27)1, *EEF Proposals to the National Federation of General Workers*, 1923.

79 EEF Archive, P(14)44, *Circular Letter no. 41*, 24 March 1928.

80 EEF Archive, *Thirty Years of Industrial Conciliation*, p. 35.

81 EEF Archive, P(13)5, *Letter from Howe to EEF*, 29 October 1919.

82 EEF Archive, W(9)4 app. 46, part 1, *Report to the Management Board by the Special Committee Regarding Working Conditions*, 1930 or 1931, p. 8.

83 EEF Archive, M(22)1, *Letter NUGW to AEU*, 19 June 1923.

84 EEF Archive, *Special Conference EEF and AEU*, 25 July 1923. See Also *Conference EEF and NFGW*, 1 August 1923; M(22)1, *Miscellaneous Correspondence Regarding the Grading of Labour*, 1919–23 and 1929–30.

85 See J. Hilton, *et al.*, *Are Trade Unions Obstructive?* (London, 1935).

86 W.R. Garside, 'Management and men: aspects of British industrial relations in the interwar period', in B. Supple (ed.), *Essays in British Business History* (Oxford, 1977), p. 259. On Mond-Turner see G.W. McDonald and H.F. Gospel, 'The Mond-Turner talks: 1927–33: a study in industrial co-operation' (*Historical Journal*, 16, 1973), pp. 807–29; H.F. Gospel, Employers' Organizations: Their Growth and Function in the British System of Industrial Relations in the Period 1918–1939 (Ph.D, London, 1974).

87 Report of the Liberal Industrial Inquiry, Britain's *Industrial Future* (London, 1928).

Chapter 6: Production techniques in the British motor vehicle industry, 1896–1914

[1] E.J. Hobsbawm, 'Artisan or labour aristocrat?' (*Economic History Review*, 37, 1984), p. 363.

[2] Hobsbawm, 'Artisan', p. 308.

[3] On British labour politics See M. Cowling, *The Impact of Labour, 1920–24* (Cambridge University Press, 1971); K. Middlemas, *Politics in Industrial Society* (London, 1979); R. Currie, *Industrial Politics* (Oxford, 1979). A broader analysis is offered in K. Burgess, *The Challenge of Labour* (London, 1980).

[4] Hobsbawm, 'Artisan', p. 308.

[5] C. Clutton and J. Stanford, *The Vintage Motor Car* (London, 1954), p. 116.

[6] 'The quest of the cheap' (*Motor Trader*, 13 November 1907), p. 407.

[7] 'Car building in Yorkshire' (*Autocar*, 1 September 1900); K. Richardson, *The British Motor Industry, 1896–1939* (London, 1977), pp. 54–5.

[8] *Iron Age*, 27 October 1910.

[9] Coventry Record Office, Bound Newspaper Clippings, *Herald*, 16 November 1900; Simms Papers, 16/10 and 16/119/i, *Misc. Correspondence*; Daimler, *Board Minutes*, 2 February to 14 March and 17 October 1899, 11 February 1901, 11 June 1902, 29 January 1902; *Report Sixth Annual General Meeting*, Daimler Company, 27 November 1902.

[10] Standard Motor Company Archive, MRC, Mss 226/ST/1/2/1, *C. Friswell Notes*, 4 May 1909; Richardson, *British Motor Industry*, pp. 39–40.

[11] W.C. Bersey, *The Motor Car Red Book* (London, nd.); P.W.S. Andrews and E. Brunner, *The Life of Lord Nuffield* (Oxford, 1955), p. 61.

[12] 'The motor show at Olympia' (*Machinery*, 20 November 1913), p. 240.

[13] Richardson, *British Motor Industry*, p. 40; R. Church, *Herbert Austin: The British Motor Car Industry to 1941* (London, 1979), p. 39.

[14] See *Motor Trader*, 26 September 1905 and 7 March 1906; S.B. Saul, 'The motor industry in Britain to 1914' (*Business History*, 5, 1962), p. 24.

[15] W. Weir, 'Motor car manufacturing in Great Britain' (*Engineer*, 8 May 1903).

[16] Saul, 'Motor industry', p. 43.

[17] A.E. Harrison, 'The competitiveness of the British cycle industry, 1890–1914' (*Economic History Review*, 22, 1969), p. 291.

[18] 'Over expansion' (*Autocar*, 18 July 1908), p. 82. For contemporary criticisms of ambitious expansion plans at Argyll, Daimler, Humber and Rover see (*Autocar*, 11 April 1905), and *Motor Trader*, 6 January 1909, p. 47.

[19] For recent work on the vehicle industry and economic cycles see M. Miller and R.A. Church, 'Motor manufacturing', in N.K. Buxton and D. Aldcroft (eds.), *British Industry Between the Wars* (London, 1979).

[20] See Saul, 'Motor industry', pp. 34–5; *Royal Commission on Motor Cars*, 1906, cmd. 3081, p. 154. Maxcy argued that Wolseley's decision to produce in house was a function of its inability to control the quality of made out components. See G. Maxcy, 'The motor industry', in P.L. Cook and R. Cohen (eds.), *Effects of Mergers* (London, 1958), p. 361. Church has argued that the decision to manufacture raised capital demands and constrained the growth of firms in the industry. However, there is little evidence of a shortage of capital in the industry prior in 1914. On the availability of

capital in the industry see A.E. Harrison, 'Joint stock company flotation in the cycle, motor vehicle and related industries: 1882–1914' (*Business History*, **23**, 1981); W. Lewchuk, 'The return to capital in the British motor vehicle industry: 1896–1939' (*Business History*, **27**, 1985), pp. 3–25.

21 Saul, 'Motor industry', p. 40.

22 Church, *Herbert Austin*, p. 187.

23 Richardson, *British Motor Industry*, pp. 94–9.

24 J.P. Bardou, *et al.*, *The Automobile Revolution: Impact of an Industry* (Chapel Hill, 1982), p. 63.

25 A.E. Musson, 'J. Whitworth and the growth of mass production engineering' (*Business History*, **17**, 1975), p. 132.

26 J. Salmon, Organised Labour in a Market Economy (Ph.D., Warwick, 1983), p.109.

27 C.H. Jones, 'Carriage and wagon building on the Midland Railway' (*Cassier's*, **13**, May 1897/98), p. 231.

28 Harrison, 'Competitiveness of the british cycle industry', pp. 294–5. See also M. Holbrook-Jones, *Supremacy and Subordination* (London, 1982), pp. 72, 80.

29 J. Newton, 'Looking backward' (*Rudge Record*, January 1909).

30 W.H. Nelson, 'Works and working' (*Rudge Record*, December 1908).

31 *Rudge Record*, October and December 1908.

32 *Engineer*, 18 June 1897, p. 620; F. Coxon, 'Machine tool design' (*Cassier's*, November 1909), pp.19–20.

33 *Cycle Referee*, 20 January 1898.

34 'Repetition bicycle plant' (*Cycle Referee*, 16 February 1899, supplement).

35 'Firms you do business with' (*Cycle and Motor Trades Review*, 7 June 1906), p. 541.

36 See Simms Papers, 9/33, *Directors' Journey to Paris*, April 1896. They toured the Panhard and Levassor, Peugeot, and De Dion–Bouton factories in France and the Deutzer (Otto) Gas Engine and the Daimler Motorem Gesellschaft factories in Germany. There were few links between the British and German Daimler except for the initial patents and some production advice during 1896 and 1897.

37 Simms Papers, 9/30, *Remarks regarding Plans for the Daimler Motor Works.*

38 An article in 1914 commented that while more shops were being heated and lighted properly, this was still far from universal. In 1919, it was claimed that the old idea that a worker should be able to keep himself warm by working hard had been finally discredited. See 'London association of foremen' (*Managing Engineer*, May 1914); 'The heating and ventilation of workshops' (*Engineer*, 23 May 1919).

39 Simms Papers, 9/33, *Directors' Journey to Paris*, April 1896.

40 Simms Papers, 16/10, *Letter Critchley to Simms*, 8 May 1896; Simms Papers, 16/3, *Letter Critchley to Simms*, 12 May 1896.

41 Simms Papers, 16/20ii, *Machine List*, 21 May 1896, and 16/15/ii, *Machine Orders*, 24 July 1896.

42 Simms Papers, 16/33, *Letter Drake to Simms*, 7 July 1896.

43 'The English motor industry, description of the plant and practice at the Daimler Company Works' (*Cycle Referee*, 19 January 1899, supplement), pp. ii–xii. There may be some doubt as to whether the above article refers to Daimler or the Great Horseless Carriage Company which was located on the same site. St John Nixon, refers to an article in a cycle journal in 1898, titled 'A visit to the Daimler works', which incorrectly claimed to be the Daimler works (p. 53). Such an article was written, but in

1897 and not by a cycle journal. The Daimler Board of Directors gave their approval to publishing the 1899 article, and it is highly unlikely that they would have made such a fundamental mistake.

[44] ASE(COV), *Minutes*, 12 July to 26 July 1899, and 15 August 1899.

[45] Saul, 'Motor industry', p. 38.

[46] 'The Belsize works' (*Engineer*, 8 May 1903), pp. 465–72.

[47] 'The Humber works (Beeston)' (*Engineer*, 4 September 1903), p. 232.

[48] 'The English motor industry' (*Cycle Referee*, 19 January 1899, supplement), p. x.

[49] 'Direct assembly' (*Autocar*, 4 July 1903), p. 24. For information on other early factories see: On Wolseley, Church, *Herbert Austin*; 'The Wolseley works' (*Auto Journal*, 17 May 1902), p. 123; 'A walk through the Wolseley works' (*Autocar*, 8 February 1902), pp. 126, 153; On Thornycroft see 'Some motor car works' (*Engineer*, 28 November 1902), pp. 509–12. On Clement Talbot see 'A visit to the new Clement Talbot factory' (*Autocar*, 11 February 1905), pp. 1–12.

[50] 'The engineering strike' (*Engineer*, 27 August 1897), p. 207. There were few recorded disputes over machinery in the motor vehicle industry in this early period. In 1901, a strike was threatened at Motor Manufacturing over low rated men being employed on machines. The firm decided to back down on the issue rather than face a confrontation. See ASE(COV), *Minutes*, 26 April 1899 to May 1899, 9 October 1901, and 13 June 1901, 16 July 1901.

[51] 'Motor car manufacture in Great Britain' (*Engineer*, 8 May 1903), p. 481.

[52] Bardou, *et al.*, *Automobile Revolution*, p. 64.

[53] 'The Deasy works' (*Automobile Engineer*, August 1910), p. 80.

[54] Pollitt Notebooks (London), P2/2/5/9 *Rover*.

[55] J.J. Guest, 'Grinding' (*Proceedings of the Institute of Automobile Engineers*, **6**, 1911), p. 327.

[56] *Motor Car Journal*, 11 December 1909, p. 905. See also 'The Daimler Motor Car works' (*Engineer*, 4 May 1906), p. 448.

[57] *Motor Trader*, 29 May 1907; ASE(COV), *Minutes*, 5 March 1907.

[58] Indicative of the strategy followed in the Coventry vehicle shops regarding questions such as the manning of milling machines, the local workforce appears to have offered very little resistance to the adoption of milling equipment. Instead they tried to recruit the men working in the department into the ASE. See ASE(COV), *Minutes*, 24 June 1909, 30 June 1909.

[59] 'Erecting shop methods' (*Automobile Engineer*, July 1912), p. 216. See also 'Modern erecting shop methods' (*Internal Combustion Engineering*, 28 May 1913). Saul claimed that Daimler chassis continued to be erected by gangs of three or four men until the war. See Saul, 'Motor industry'. By 1907, new machines were on the market which eliminated the need to hand fit camshafts, a particularly troublesome component. See *Cassier's*, July 1907, p. 263.

[60] 'Erecting shop methods' (*Automobile Engineer*, July 1912), p. 216–17. Napier was another British quality producer which produced cars in small batches but also showed an interest in skill displacing machinery. In 1907 they employed a large number of automatics including a new system for cutting bevel gears which was claimed to be virtually automatic and capable of producing extremely accurate work. See 'A modern car in construction' (*Autocar*, 19 January 1907), p. 85.

[61] 'The new Humber works' (*Motor Trader*, 18 March 1908), p. 682.

⁶² For details on Argyll's new plant see *Motor Trader*, 28 November 1906 and 5 June 1907; 'The opening of the new Argyll factory' (*Autocar*, 30 June 1906), pp. 844–45; 'Capitalisation and over capitalisation' (*Autocar*, 1 April 1905); *Royal Commission on Motor Cars*, cmd 3081, p. 154. The Argyll experiment failed, largely as the result of the downturn in trade which began only a few months after the factory opened. Running well below capacity, and in an industry where machine improvements were made rapidly, the firm soon found itself with outdated equipment against which little in the way of depreciation had been set aside. The firm was voluntarily wound up in 1908. See *Motor Trader*, 8 July and 25 November 1908. A second important factor in the company's decline was the death of Govan during 1907. See *Motor Trader*, 5 June 1907.

⁶³ *Motor Trader*, 8 October 1913, p. 101.

⁶⁴ *Motor Trader*, 7 September 1910, p. 1036. See also *Motor Trader*, 20 December 1911 and 7 August 1912.

⁶⁵ *Motor Trader*, 4 February 1920 and *Motor Trader*, 6 August 1913, pp. 370–9, 386. Pullinger, formerly with Humber, was in charge of this new factory.

⁶⁶ *Times Engineering Supplement*, 24 July 1907, p. 238.

⁶⁷ 'The manufacture of a light car' (*Machinery*, 1913), p. 225.

⁶⁸ Church, *Herbert Austin*, pp. 29–30. See also Saul, 'Motor industry', p. 38; 'The Austin factory' (*Automobile Engineer*, 13 August 1914), pp. 244–6; *Motor Trader*, 11 December 1914, p. 462.

⁶⁹ 'Modern erecting shop methods' (*Internal Combustion Engineer*, 11 June 1913).

⁷⁰ 'A walk through the Wolseley works' (*Autocar*, 8 February 1902) p. 126; Andrews and Brunner, *Lord Nuffield*, pp. 87–8.

⁷¹ 'The Wolseley works' (*Automobile Engineer*, 10 September 1914), p. 265–8. See also 'A visit to the Wolseley Tool and Motor Company' (*Machinery*, 9 January 1913), p. 475. For information on Crossley Motors where jigs and limit gauges were universal by 1908 see *Motor Trader*, 12 May 1909, p. 290; 'A Manchester motor car works' (*Engineer*, 12 June 1908). On Thornycrofts see 'J.I. Thornycroft' (*Cassier's*, December 1914). On Rover see 'The production of a famous car' (*Automobile Engineer*, 14 May 1914), pp. 147–50; Pollitt Notebooks (London), p2/2/5/9, *Rover*. On Clement Talbot see *Motor Trader*, 24 February 1909.

⁷² On Armstrong Whitworth see R.J. Irving, 'New industries for old? Some investment decisions of Sir W.G. Armstrong, Whitworth and Co. Ltd, 1900–1914' (*Business History*, 17, 1975), pp. 150–75; Richardson, *British Motor Industry*, pp. 99–100. On Birmingham Small Arms see BSA Archive, MRC, 19/a/7/re/1, and 19/a/1/2/3, *Reports of Motor Department*; 19/a/1/2/12–14, *Reports to the BSA Board of Directors*. See also Files 19/a/1/2/18, 19a/1/2/17.

⁷³ Standard Motor Company Archive, MRC, Mss. 226/ST/1/2/1, *Friswell Notebook*, 23 November 1909, 19 April 1910; Mss 226/ST/1/1/1, *Minute Books*, 29 April 1913; Mss 226/ST/1/2/1, *Friswell Notebook*, 'Report by Budge to Friswell', 26 June 1910.

⁷⁴ H. Coffin, past president of the American Society of Automobile Engineers argued before the Institute of Automobile Engineers, in 1911, that while the British paid more attention to finish than the Americans on the vital working components of a car there was little difference between British and American techniques. See H. Coffin, 'American tendencies in motor car engineering' (*Proceedings of the Institute of Automobile Engineers*, 6, 1911), p. 25.

[75] Owen Linley, 'Manufacturing on a medium scale' (*Motor Trader*, 8 July 1914).

[76] L.A. Legros, 'Influence of detail in the development of the automobile' (*Proceedings of the Institute of Automobile Engineers*, 6, 11 October 1911).

[77] 'Some notes on the Regent Carriage Company works' (*Motor Trader*, 29 March 1911), p. 695. See also G. Eastwood, 'Wood-working tools and motor car body manufacture' (*Machinery*, 30 January 1913), p. 573; 'The New Humber Works' (*Motor Trader*, 18 March 1908), p. 684.

Chapter 7: The rise of management in the British motor vehicle industry, 1896–1914

[1] J.P. Bardou, *et al.*, *The Automobile Revolution* (Chapel Hill, 1982), p. 63.

[2] EEF Archive, P(5)8, *Letter ASE to Humber*, 1 February 1904; *Report of Meeting Humber and ASE*, January 1904.

[3] EEF Archive, P(5)8, *Report of Meeting Between Humber and ASE*, late January 1904; P(5)8, *Letter Humber to ASE*, 6 February 1904.

[4] EEF Archive, P(5)8, *Local Conference Nottingham EEA and ASE*, 17 March 1904, pp. 40–3.

[5] EEF Archive, P(5)8, *Letter Humber to EEF*, 11 April 1904.

[6] EEF Archive, P(5)8, *Agreement Humber and ASE*, 13 April 1904.

[7] EEF Archive, E(1)12, *Local Conference Nottingham EEA and ASE*, 7 November 1905.

[8] EEF Archive, E(1)14, *Humber Notice*, 23 January 1907.

[9] EEF Archive, A(2)3, *Memo from T.C. Pullinger*, 18 December 1906.

[10] EEF Archive, E(1)1, *Memo*, 7 December 1905; UKS/NUVB Archive, *UKS/NUVB Journal*, March 1905, February and May 1906, May 1907; ASE(COV), *Minutes*, 1 March 1906, 30 September, 8 and 22 October, 1 December 1908.

[11] On Standard see ASE(COV), *Minutes*, 27 September 1910 to 23 October 1910. On Rover see ASE(COV), *Minutes*, 22 March 1909, 10 May 1910, 31 January, 27 April, 17 October 1911, 24 July 1912, 17 September to 25 November 1913.

[12] COW was set up by three armaments producers, John Brown, Cammell Laird, and Fairfield Shipbuilding and Engineering Company in 1905. Originally it was to produce only ordnances for these three firms, but by 1907 was taking in motor vehicle work from a number of firms. See (*Engineer*, 31 May 1907); ASE(COV), *Minutes*, 8 April 1907; Pollitt Notebooks (London), *Letter T. Cordesn to Pollitt* (nd).

[13] ASE(COV), *Minutes*, 8 April, 26 July and 15 August 1907; Meeting Coventry Allied Trades Federation, as reported in ASE(COV), *Minutes*, 2 September and 20 September 1907.

[14] ASE(COV), *Minutes*, 21 January 1908.

[15] *ASE Monthly Reports*, May 1908 and October 1909; ASE(COV), *Minutes*, 18 April 1908, 15 April 1908.

[16] *ASE Monthly Report*, January 1910; ASE(COV), *Minutes*, 19 November and 31 December 1909.

[17] R. Hyman, *Workers Union* (Oxford, 1971), p. 61.

[18] EEF Archive, M(8)2 and M(15)19, *Correspondence and Conferences Regarding Coventry; ASE Monthly Reports*, March 1913; ASE(COV), Minutes, 13 and 21 February 1913, 25 March to 7 April 1914.

19 The most famous examples of factory occupations by unskilled labour are the labour sit-down strikes at American automobile plants which led to the recognition of the UAW during the 1930s. See S. Fine, *Sit Down: The General Motors Strike of 1936–37* (Ann Arbor, 1969).

20 EEF Archive, S(4)2, *Memorandum from Strike Committee*, 13 December 1911.

21 For more details on Crossley see 'A Manchester motor car works' (*Engineer*, 12 June 1908); *Manchester Weekly Citizen*, 16 December and 23 December 1911; *ASE Monthly Reports*, July 1906, May and July 1908, January 1912, January 1914; EEF Archive, S(4)2, *Report on Strikes and Central Conference*, 27 February 1912.

22 While the entire investment in plant at this time was £12 000, the investment in work-in-progress was £17 000.

23 Birmingham Collection, *Chairman's Report Daimler Motor Co., Extraordinary Meeting*, 4 March 1897; Daimler, *Board Minutes*, 13 May to 12 August, 9 December 1897, 20 October 1898.

24 See Nixon, *Daimler*, pp. 24–31 for details on the early board. In order to partially bridge the knowledge gap, F.R. Simms was appointed as a consulting engineer. The original share issue was taken up by 450 different individuals. The largest single holding represented less than five percent of the shares.

25 The committee was composed of shareholders including W.B. Avery the largest shareholder.

26 Nixon, *Daimler*, pp. 30–7; Simms Papers, 9/58, *Report of Committee of Investigation*, 10 December 1898.

27 Nixon, *Daimler*, p. 64. Indicative of the lack of cost accounting systems was the company's inability to give an estimate of the cost of their new 4 BHP vehicle until they were actually in production. Dealers were asked to place orders on the strength of the promise that the cost would be somewhat less than £200. See Simms papers, 16/119/i, *Letter*, 30 January 1899.

28 A similar system was in operation at the Elswick munitions plant of Sir William Armstrong Ltd. in 1887. See *Report from Commissioner and Inspector Army (Manufacturing Department)*, c 5116, 1887, testimony of Capt. Noble, 9009.

29 'Description of the plant and practice at the Daimler Company's works' (*Cycle Referee*, 19 January 1899), supplement p. xiv.

30 ASE(COV), *Minutes*, 2 September 1898.

31 Daimler, *Board Minutes*, 13 February 1899. Nixon estimated that approximately 12 foremen were removed at this time. The workforce numbered 400. This example seems to go against the progression which tends to normally be found from piece masters or chargehands to foremen paid a salary by the firm.

32 ASE(COV), *Minutes*, 2–12 September 1898.

33 ASE(COV), *Minutes*, 3–10 October 1898.

34 Daimler, *Board Minutes*, 18 April, 15 November, 28 November 1899.

35 In October of 1899, it was discovered that of the 220 vehicles sanctioned for production in March, none had been delivered despite over 100 orders on the books. No explanation for this state of affairs was recorded, but the state of the works when Martin took over in 1901 suggests that there was still a lack of managerial organisation and control over labour. See Daimler, *Board Minutes*, 17 October 1899.

36 Daimler, *Board Minutes*, 24 April 1901. Sturmey, a former Daimler director, wrote a revealing article in 1902. He argued that British firms, a polite way of referring to

Daimler, had found that costs exceeded their estimates and that they were forced to sell at a loss. 'The capitalist (was) taught that the development and bringing to a satisfactory issue of new things in motor cars is not so easy as it looks, that it is not to be had on the cheap' (Simms papers, 9/67).

37 Daimler, *Board Minutes*, 29 January and 2 July 1901. It is not clear whether Critchley was forced out of his position or simply wished to move on to his own business. He submitted his resignation during 1900 to become effective when the Brush Company, in which he had a financial interest, began production. He left Daimler either late in 1901, or early 1902. In their search for a new works manager the board approached J.D. Siddeley. He refused, and later became the works manager at Wolseley which hastened Austin's departure from the firm.

38 *Motor Trader*, 9 January 1917, p. 585; Birmingham Collection, *Report Daimler Annual General Meeting*, 26 November 1903, and *Chairman's Report, Sixth Annual General Meeting*, 27 January 1902.

39 Daimler, *Board Minutes*, 24 July and 14 August 1902. Leading foremen were appointed in the machine, erecting and carriage shops. Ordinary foremen were appointed in the repair, pattern, tool, smiths, and millwrights shops.

40 Piecework had formerly been worked only in the machine shops. The ASE gave their approval to the new system as long as day rates were guaranteed and all wages were paid through the office. See ASE(COV), *Minutes*, 1 July to 16 September 1903.

41 For a useful study of how incentive payment systems altered the employment relationship see M. Holbrook-Jones, *Supremacy and Subordination* (London, 1982), especially pp. 186–94.

42 Daimler, *Board Minutes*, 14 August and 18 September 1902.

43 After a trial period, the vehicle builders voted to return to day work. The firm continued paying bonus rates to non-society men and the United Kingdom Society of Coachmakers was forced to accept the system or lose all of its members. United Kingdom Society of Coachmakers, Quarterly Report, September and December 1904. See also ASE(COV), *Minutes*, 14 December 1906, 3 and 24 January 1907.

44 P. Martin, 'Works organisation' (*Proceedings of the Institute of Automobile Engineers*, 1, 1906–7), pp. 109–52.

45 *Ibid.*, p. 116. Chandler and Noble suggest that the conception of management as a team working toward a common objective was a precondition for them seeing themselves as a unique group within the production process, and eventually, according to Noble a separate class. See A. Chandler, *The Visible Hand* (Cambridge University Press, 1977), Part Four; D. Noble, *America by Design* (Oxford, 1979), Chapter 8.

46 Martin, 'Works organisation', p. 125.

47 *Ibid.*, p. 117.

48 *Ibid.*, p. 148.

49 *Ibid.*, p. 126.

50 ASE(COV), *Minutes*, 9 and 20 March, 13 April 1908.

51 EEF Archive, *Membership Files*, Daimler.

52 Martin, 'Works organisation', pp. 132–46.

53 J.S. Napier, 'A system of costing, book-keeping and recording suitable for a motor or other engineering factory' (*Proceedings of the Institute of Automobile Engineers*, 1,

1907). Napier had been selected by Sir W. Arrol to manage the Mo-Car works because of his organisational skills. He stayed on to become managing director when the firm changed names. He left in 1908 to join the Humber Company and in 1911 formed a consulting firm with A. Craig. J.S. Napier was a relative of the well-known founder of the Napier Company.

[54] J. Younger, 'Putting orders through the plant' (*System*, 1908), p. 598. At the time, Dennis employed between 500 and 700 workers.

[55] 'Deasy works' (*Automobile Engineers*, August 1910), p. 79–83.

[56] 'Argyll opening' (*Motor Trader*, 4 July 1906), pp. 32–3.

[57] *Motor Trader*, 16 September 1908; *Engineer*, 24 March 1905, p. 291.

[58] Martin, 'Works organisation', p. 136. Non-productive items, also referred to as indirect costs, included all charges not accounted for by labour or materials used directly in manufacturing goods. Most of the functions now associated with management such as planning, costing, supervision and inspection were included in non-productive items.

[59] *Ibid.*, p. 138.

[60] Cited in Church, *Herbert Austin*, p. 31.

[61] I. Lloyd, *Rolls-Royce, The Growth of a Firm* (London, 1978), p. 33.

[62] Charles Rolls, had long since ceased to be a factor in the firm. The same eccentricity which drew him to motor vehicles during his Cambridge undergraduate days attracted him to airplanes in 1908. This new interest cost him his life in 1910 when a plane he was flying crashed.

[63] Martin, 'Works organisation', Discussion, pp. 132–48.

[64] R. Whipp and P. Clark, *Innovation and the Automobile Industry* (New York, 1986), pp. 59–61.

[65] *Ibid.*, p. 71.

[66] The extensive use of the cash nexus at Daimler was noted by a contemporary journalist, 'Every official and every workman in the Daimler concern had a direct monetary inducement to waste neither time nor material.' See *Motor Trader*, 14 November 1906, p. 319.

[67] Saul, 'Motor industry', pp. 43–4.

[68] See EEF Archive, P(4)53, *Notes on Cooperative Production*; P(3)9, *Memo North West District EEA to EEF*, 1919; P(4)3, *EEF Survey of the Impact of Premium Bonus Systems*, 1910–14.

[69] See Rover Company balance sheets for estimates of investment in machinery. See Ford Motor Company balance sheets, Ford Archive, Acc. 96, Box 8.

[70] A. Nevins, *Ford: The Times, The Man, The Company* (New York, 1954), pp. 647–50.

Chapter 8: Fordism and the British system of mass production, 1914–1930

[1] A. Nevins and F. Hill, *Ford, The Times, The Man, The Company* (New York, 1954), p. 647.

[2] For a brief survey of the spread of the assembly line to Europe see P. Fridenson, 'The coming of the assembly line to Europe', in W. Krohn, *et al.* (eds.), *The Dynamics of Science and Technology* (Dordrecht, 1978).

[3] M. Wilkins and F. Hill, *American Business Abroad, Ford on Six Continents* (Detroit, 1964), pp. 23–47, 436. See also *Ford Times*, June 1912, July 1913 and June 1914.

⁴ Ford Archive (Warley), *Historical Notes*, 1912.

⁵ 'The English works of the Ford Motor Company' (*Automobile Engineer*, July 1915), p. 189.

⁶ BBC Interview for series, All Our Working Lives, *Royal*, Tape 141, p. 2.

⁷ 'English works of the Ford Motor Co.' (*Automobile Engineer*, July 1915), pp. 188–9, 'Body works of the Ford Motor Co.' (*Automobile Engineer*, October 1915), pp. 289–92.

⁸ Wilkins and Hill, *American Business*, p. 47.

⁹ *UKS/NUVB Monthly Report*, July 1913.

¹⁰ For the ASE policy, see *ASE Monthly Report*, November 1913. On the Joiners see Ford Archive (Warley), *Historical Notes*, 1914.

¹¹ Wilkins and Hill, *American Business*, p. 49.

¹² 'The Ford dispute' (*UKS/NUVB Monthly Report*, January 1914).

¹³ Wages rates were supplied by the Ford Motor Company, Dagenham. L'Estrange Fawcett, Wheels of Fortune (unpublished), claimed that Perry raised wages immediately after opening the Manchester plant, but this is unlikely given other accounts of the plant's wage history.

¹⁴ In the 1950s, Patrick Hennessy argued that the successful application of high wages in Manchester encouraged Ford to adopt a similar strategy in Detroit. See H. Friedman and S. Meredeen, *The Dynamics of Industrial Conflict, Lessons from Ford* (London, 1980), p. 22.

¹⁵ Fawcett, *Wheels*, pp. 23, 38.

¹⁶ By April of 1914, Sorensen was receiving reports that the trade unions in the plant had been completely broken up. See Wilkins and Hill, *American Business*, p. 49. See also *UKS/NUVB Monthly Report*, January 1914; Friedman and Meredeen, *Dynamics*, p. 56.

¹⁷ See H. Benyon, *Working for Ford* (Harmondsworth, 1973), for a summary of the early history of labour politics at Ford plants. See also Fawcett, *Wheels*, p. 26; Friedman and Meredeen, *Dynamics*, p. 53.

¹⁸ Fred Harwood, former worker, quoted in the *Manchester Evening News*, 23 June 1978 (Ford Archive, Warley).

¹⁹ *Manchester Evening News*, June 1978 (Ford Archive, Warley).

²⁰ *Special Edition of the Ford Times*, 1914. See also 'English works of the Ford Motor Co.' (*Automobile Engineer*, 1915).

²¹ BBC interviews, *Fred Harrop*, p. 3.

²² *Ibid.*, p. 7.

²³ BBC interviews, *Mr and Mrs Clark*, Tape 63, p. 7.

²⁴ *Motor Trader*, 6 March 1912. See also 'Some notes on Manchester district factories' (*Motor Trader*, 7 August 1912).

²⁵ See Table 3.6.

²⁶ For the influence of Taylorism in Russia see R. Traub, 'Lenin and Taylor: the fate of 'Scientific Management' in the (early) Soviet Union' (*Telos*, 37, 1978), pp. 82–92. For its impact in France, Germany and Italy see C.S. Maier, 'Between Taylorism and Technocracy' (*Journal of Contemporary History*, 5, 1970), pp. 27–51.

²⁷ A.A. Remington, 'Some probable effects of the war on the automobile industry' (*Proceedings Institute of Automobile Engineers*, 13, 1918), p. 7.

²⁸ During 1915, Rolls-Royce was making 15 Eagle engines per week, 5 to 6 Hawks, and

5 to 20 Falcons. By the end of 1917, the firm had delivered a total of 1480 Eagles and 756 Falcons, and plans were afoot to double that output in 1918. See I. Lloyd, *Rolls-Royce: The Years of Endeavour*, pp. 121–154.

[29] 'Special tools for making munitions of war' (*Cassier's*, July 1915); 'Machine tools for shells' (*Times Engineering Supplement*, 27 August 1915); L. Pomeroy, 'Automobile engineering and the war' (*Proceedings Institute of Automobile Engineers*, **9**, 1914/1915), p. 22.

[30] C. More, *Skill in the English Working Class, 1870–1914* (London 1980), pp. 30–4.

[31] 'Shop topics, the simple machine again' (*Machinery*, 8 November 1917).

[32] Pomeroy, 'Automobile engineering', p. 21.

[33] A. W. Reeves and C. Kimber, 'Works organisation' (*Proceedings Institute of Automobile Engineers*, **11**, 1916/1917), p. 375.

[34] T.C. Pullinger, 'Opening address' (*Proceedings Institute of Automobile Engineers*, **12**, 1917/1918), p. 432.

[35] Comments on paper by Reeves and Kimber, 'Works organisation', p. 396.

[36] A. Perry Keene, 'Prodution – a dream come true' (*Journal of the Institute of Production Engineers*, **7**, 1928), p. 31.

[37] For early debates on the merits of day work see ASE (COV), *Minute Books*, 15 January, 24 March, 9 April, 9 July 1918. Demands for a return to day work were also the issue in a short strike by carpenters and joiners at Austin in 1919. See EEF Archive P(3) 15, *Strike at Austin*, 1919. On the piecework boycott see ASE (COV), *Minute Books*, 14 and 21 January, 25 February, 25 March 1919.

[38] EEF Archive, P (5) 27, *Local Conference CEJC and CDEEA*, 18 December 1918.

[39] EEF Archive, P (5) 27, *Local Conference CDEEA and CEJC*, 6 March 1919.

[40] EEF Archive, P (5) 27, *Local Conference CDEEA and CEJC*, 6 and 13 March 1919; P (5) 27, *Memos CDEEA to EEF*, 11 February, 26 and 30 March 1919.

[41] EEF Archive, P (13) 5, *Letter from Howe to EEF*, 29 October 1919.

[42] Lloyd, *Rolls-Royce*, p. 36.

[43] See 'Rolls-Royce methods' (*Engineering Production*, 15 December 1921), pp. 565–9, 589–95; 'Quality production' (*Engineering Production*, August 1923), pp. 364–9; 'The works of Rolls-Royce' (*Automobile Engineers*, February 1927), pp. 48–51; 'An interesting works visit' (*Engineering Production*, 4 January 1923), p. 8. On postwar plans see H. Swift, 'Efficiency' (*Managing Engineer*, October 1920), pp. 111–15; A. Wormald, 'How we solved our labour and output problem' (*Works Management*, November 1919), pp. 17–19.

[44] Swift, 'Efficiency', p. 114. See also Wormald, 'How we solved', p. 10.

[45] Wormald, 'How we solved', p. 18.

[46] EEF Archive, M (15) 54, *Memo RR to Local Association and EEF*, 18 May 1920.

[47] Lloyd, *Rolls-Royce*, p. 20.

[48] During the war, there were a number of conflicts between the firm and the unions over the use of low paid women in the factory. See EEF Archive, D (8) 3, *Correspondence Derby EEA and Various Unions*; M (9) 49, *Local Conference RR and ASE*, 17 March 1920. On the incidence of dismissal see EEF Archive, M (15) 54, *Memo RR to Local Association and EEF*, 18 May 1920.

[49] See A. Wormald, 'How we keep track of 6,000 chassis parts' (*Works Management*, December 1919), p. 95; Swift, 'Efficiency', p. 111.

50 L.H. Pomeroy, 'Automobile engineering and the war' (*Proceedings Institute of Automobile Engineers*, 9, 1914), pp. 11, 21.

51 *Ibid.*, p. 22.

52 *Luton News*, 6 October 1921, in EEF Archive, *Membership Files*, Vauxhall.

53 'The works of Vauxhall Motors' (*Automobile Engineer*, June 1920), p. 233; 'Vauxhall Motors Ltd' (*Engineering Production*, 8 June 1922), p. 532; EEF Archive, D (8) 2, *Memo Birmingham EEA to EEF*, 1917, and *Memo Bedfordshire EEA to EEF*, 7 December 1917.

54 EEF Archive, *Memo Vauxhall to EEF*, 15 July 1921, and *Luton News*, 6 October 1921, in *Membership Files*, Vauxhall. See also EEF Archive, W (3) 48, *Miscellaneous Correspondence Vauxhall and Payment by Results*.

55 'The works of Vauxhall Motor Ltd' (*Automobile Engineer*, October 1925), p. 343.

56 *Ibid.*, p. 347.

57 The Austin Board agreed, in 1925, by a five to three vote to let GM invest £1 000 000 in the firm and to have the right to appoint members to the Austin board while, 'Taking great care to preserve the British character of the board'. When GM heard that there was some dissent over their investment they immediately withdrew their offer. See Austin Archive, MRC, Mss 226/AU/1/1/1, *Board Minutes*, 9 July 1925 to 14 September 1925.

58 BBC Interviews, *E.W. Hancock*, Tape 14d, pp. 1–5.

59 On the changes in production techniques see the series of articles titled, 'Motor manufacturing practice' (*Machinery*, 15 March 1928), pp. 761–74 (*Machinery*, 7 June 1928), pp. 297–300, and (*Machinery*, 19 April 1928), p. 65.

60 E.W. Hancock, 'The trend of modern production methods' (*Proceedings Institute of Production Engineers*, 7, 1928), pp. 69–83; 'The works of Vauxhall Motors' (*Automobile Engineer*, August 1930), p. 384.

61 L. Holden, 'Think of me simply as the skipper: industrial relations at Vauxhalls' (*Oral History*, 9, 1981), p. 21.

62 *Ibid.*, p. 24.

63 On the shift to MDW and the increase in managerial control see Holden, 'Think of me as skipper', pp. 21, 30.

64 There are two general works on the history of Morris. See P.W.S. Andrews and E. Brunner, *The Life of Lord Nuffield* (Oxford, 1955); R.J. Overy, *W. Morris, Viscount Nuffield* (London, 1976). See also R.C. Whiting, *The View From Cowley* (Oxford, 1983).

65 Andrews and Brunner, *Lord Nuffield*, pp. 59–74.

66 Overy, *Morris*, p. 128.

67 Andrews and Brunner, *Lord Nuffield*, pp. 87–8, 196–7; Fridenson, 'Coming of the assembly line', p. 163; 'Visit to Cowley works of Morris Motors Ltd' (*Proceedings Institute of Production Engineers*, 1924/25), p. 162.

68 'Morris production methods' (*Machinery*, 26, 7 May 1925), p. 161; H.L. Arnold and F.L. Faurote, 'Ford methods' (*Engineering Magazine*, August 1914), p. 685.

69 Andrews and Brunner, *Lord Nuffield*, p. 92.

70 H.E. Taylor, 'Principles and psychology of production' (*Machinery*, November 1928), p. 137.

71 *Ibid.*, p. 138.

72 See the series of articles titled, 'Manufacturing practice on light motor car power

units' (*Machinery*, 9 March 1922 to 7 September 1922). See also 'Production of an automobile power unit' (*Engineering Production*, 27 July 1922 and 3 August 1922). For Ford productivity levels see Table 3.7.

73 Despite numerous local labour conflicts, there is no record of labour unrest at Hotchkiss or Morris Motors during these years in the minute books of the Coventry ASE or the Coventry District Employers Association. Even though Morris Motors Ltd in Oxford did not join the EEF until 1943, Morris Engines Ltd was a member from 1923. They simply maintained a membership taken out by the original Hotchkiss company in 1917. See EEF Archive, *Membership Files*, Morris Motors and Morris Motors (Engine Branch).

74 H.E. Taylor, 'Production and psychology' (*Journal Institute of Production Engineers*, December 1929), p. 23.

75 H.E. Taylor, 'Efficiency and production' (*Automobile Engineer*, December 1927), p. 498.

76 F.G. Woollard, 'Some notes on British methods of continuous prodution' (*Proceedings Institute of Automobile Engineers*, 19, 1924), p. 420. Woollard discussed his unique views of mass production in his book, *The Principles of Flow Production* (London, 1954), p. 35–41.

77 Overy, *Morris*, p. 27.

78 Woollard Obituary, *Times*, 28 December 1957, p. 8e.

79 There are numerous descriptions of these experiments. See Woollard, 'Some notes', pp. 419–51; Woollard, *Principles of Flow Production*; 'Morris production methods' (*Machinery*, 25, 19 March 1915), pp. 773–88. There is some uncertainty regarding the contribution of H.E. Taylor. I have been unable to determine how long he stayed in Coventry before taking a position with Hotchkiss et Cie. in France. In an article in 1928, Taylor claims to have developed the new machine systems at Morris Engines and called them, Unit Continuous Systems. See Taylor, 'Principles and psychology' pp. 137–41.

80 'Morris production methods' (*Machinery*, 19 March 1925), p. 784.

81 Woollard, 'Some notes', p. 437–8; Woollard, *Principles*, p. 30.

82 For details on the rise of automatic transfer machines in the United States see W. Gartman, *Auto Slavery* (Ph.D, University of California, 1980) chapter 7 and particularly pp. 306–14.

83 'Morris production methods' (*Machinery*, 19 March 1925), p. 775.

84 Taylor, 'Principles and psychology', p. 137.

85 Woollard, *Principles*, p. 85.

86 Woollard, 'Some notes', p. 441.

87 Woollard, *Principles*, p. 180. See also Taylor, 'Production and psychology', p. 23.

88 Woollard, 'Some notes', p. 424. Accounts of factory life at Morris by A. Exell suggests that the philosophy of work as a means to an end, the end being an improvement of the quality of life outside of the factory, was carried to an extreme. Inside the factories, life was most uncomfortable, and questions of health and safety received little attention. See A. Exell, 'Morris Motors in the 1930s' (*History Workshop Journal*, nos. 6 and 7, 1978–9), pp. 52–78, 45–65.

89 See Woollard, 'Some notes', p. 424; Taylor, 'Efficient production', p. 498; W.R. Morris, 'Policies that built the Morris Motors business' (*System*, February 1924), pp. 73–6; H.A. Goddard, 'Profit sharing and the amenities of the Nuffield factories',

in F.E. Gannett and B.F. Catherwood, *Industrial and Labour Relations in Great Britain* (New York, 1939), pp. 265–9. On the rural composition of the Oxford workforce see Whiting, *View From Cowley*, pp. 5–28.

90 Andrews and Brunner, *Lord Nuffield*, p. 197. For other works on the Morris policies during this period see R. Church, 'Myths, men and motor cars: a review article' (*Journal of Transport History*, 4, September 1977), pp. 102–12; 'Developments at the works of Morris Motors Ltd' (*Automobile Engineer*, September 1926), pp. 322–8.

91 See R. Church, *Herbert Austin* (London, 1979), Chapter 4 for details. See also C.R.F. Engelbach, 'Some notes on re-organising a works to increase production' (*Proceedings Institute of Automobile Engineers*, 12, 1927–28), pp. 497–8; 'The Austin works' (*Engineer*, 5 April 1918). On the war period see PRO, Mun/4/966, *Misc. Austin Correspondence with the Ministry of Munitions*.

92 'Picture of the assembly shop, Austin Motor Company' (*Automobile Engineer*, August 1920), p. 310.

93 See the series of articles titled 'The Austin Motor Company' (*Machinery*, 6 May 1920, to 24 June 1920). See also 'Works practice of the Austin Motor Company' (*Automobile Engineer*, February 1922), p. 44; 'Making the Austin Twelve' (*Automobile Engineer*, August 1931), pp. 291–8.

94 Austin Archive, MRC, Mss 226/AU/1/1/1.ii, *Visit to USA by Chairman and E.L. Payton*, September 1922, p. 13; Austin Archive, MRC, Mss 226/AU/1/1/, *Board Minutes*, 6 April 1921 to 9 September 1921 and 13 March 1922.

95 Austin Archive, MRC, Mss 226/AU/1/1/1.ii, *Visit to USA by Chairman and E.L. Payton*, September 1922, pp. 6–7.

96 Engelbach was heavily influenced by American practices which he observed first hand during a visit to Detroit in 1927 and which he claims led him to order nearly half the new machines from American suppliers. See Austin Archive, MRC, Mss 226/AU/1/1/, *Board Minutes*, 23 February 1927 and 25 May 1927; 'The modern production engineer' (*Automobile Engineer*, October 1927), p. 376.

97 This account was drawn largely from Engelbach, 'Notes', pp. 497 – 508. See also 'Making the Austin Twelve' (*Automobile Engineer*, August 1931), pp. 291–8.

98 On the formalisation of Austin's managerial structure see 'The Austin works system' (*Automobile Engineer*, October 1927), pp. 380–4; A. Perry Keene, 'Production a dream come true' (*Journal of the Institute of Production Engineers*, 7, 1928), pp. 27–35; Engelbach, 'Notes', pp. 512–14.

99 'Stoppage at Austin works' (*Times*, 13 November 1936), p. 18e.

100 'Third Annual Meeting of the Institute of Production Engineers' (*Proceedings Institute of Production Engineers*, 1924–25), p. 7.

101 See Austin's comments in, Woollard, 'Some notes', p. 459.

102 *Times*, 'Letter to the Editor', 31 May, 1926, p. 10c.

103 Ward Papers, MRG 1, W/8/29–34/13/476, *Organisation Section*, pp. 3 – 14. The Austin Bonus system had already been discussed at an MRG 1 meeting on 2 May 1929. See Ward Papers, MRG 1, W/8/29–34/12/474.

104 Ward Papers, MRG 1, W/8/29–34/13/476, *Organisation Section*, p. 2.

105 Engelbach, 'Notes', p. 511. See also 'The Austin works system' (*Automobile Engineer*, October 1927), p. 381.

106 Perry Keene, 'Production', p. 34.

107 'Austin works system', p. 380.

108 Perry Keene, 'Production', p. 30.

109 Ward Papers, MRG 1, W/8/29–34/476, *Memo Perry Keene to MRG1*, 2 December 1930.

110 BBC Interviews, *Tom Ward*, tape 56, p. 3.

111 EEF Archive, *Austin Motor Company Ltd*, *Piecework in the Toolroom*, loose file in folder titled Payment by Results, also on microfilm W(3)129, p. 3.

112 *Ibid.*, p. 20.

113 *Ibid.*, p. 20

114 *Ibid.*, p. 26–8.

115 EEF Archive, A(1)51, G.E. Nines, *Austin Payment on Time System*. See also Coventry District Engineering Employers Association, *Minutes of Executive Meeting*, 27 July 1931. On the strike in the Austin aero-works over the system see EEF Archive, A(1)51, *Strike Austin Aero Works*, See also 'The Austin works system' (*Automobile Engineer*, October 1927), p. 301; Ward Papers, W/8/29–34/12/474, *Labour Results (Labour Control)*, Labour Section MRG 1, 2 May 1929.

116 Perry Keene, 'Production', p. 28; Church, *Herbert Austin*, pp. 31, 45. It was reported that Engelbach was highly suspicious of works councils. See 'The employer and welfare' (*Times*, 12 April 1932), p. 11c.

117 BBC Interviews, *Etheridge*, tape 55, p. 1. On the seasonal nature of work and the sacking of union activists in Oxford see BBC Interviews, *Hayden Evans*, tape 90, p. 3. Salmon argued that between 1920 and 1939 the average July August unemployment rate in the vehicle trade was 50 percent higher than the November rate. He suggested that employment for many production workers was almost casual. See J. Salmon, Organised Labour in a Market Economy (Ph.D., Warwick, 1983), p. 143–4.

118 EEF Archive, P(5)40, *Central Conference EEF and ASE*, 29 July 1919; P(3)15, *Miscellaneous Correspondence*; P(4)21, *Local Conference EEF and Various Unions*, 27 January 1920; *ASE Monthly Report*, March 1920, April 1926, June and July 1928.

119 Salmon, *Organised Labour*, p. 165.

120 EEF Archive, S(4)9, *Austin Memo*, 13 April 1929, p. 4.

121 For accounts of the strike see Salmon, *Organised Labour*, pp. 160 – 72; Church, *Herbert Austin*, pp. 151–2; EEF Archive, S(5)9, *Sit-in at Austin, Grading Strike 1929*; S(4)9, *Austin Memo*, 13 April 1929; *ASE Monthly Report*, February 1929.

122 On the erosion of these institutions during the early 1930s see Salmon, *Organised Labour*, p. 173; Church, *Herbert Austin*, p. 152.

123 Salmon, *Organised Labour*, pp. 173–4; EEF Archive, D(8)44, *Austin Working Conditions*, 1936.

124 EEF Archive, A(1)51, *Strike at Austin Aero Works*, 1938; Salmon, *Organised Labour*, pp. 191–3.

125 AEC Archive, MRC, Mss 226/AE/1/1/1, *History of Articles of Association and Board Minutes*, 23 December 1912; Mss 226/AE/1/1/2, *Board Minutes*, 6 January 1920.

126 AEC Archive, MRC, Mss 226/1/1/1–10, *Board Minutes*. Actual dividends on ordinary shares were only half of those reported above. However this would give a false picture of the real return as the firm issued one fully paid up deferred share for each ordinary share held in 1914. These shares earned the same dividend as the ordinary shares.

127 AEC Archive, MRC, Mss 226/AE/1/1/1, *Board Minutes*, 9 March 1916 and 12 October 1916; 'The AEC Truck works' (*Motor Trader*, March 1919), p. 367.

[128] AEC Archive, MRC, Mss 226/AE/1/17, *Board Minutes*, June 1917; 'Quantity production in lorry building' (*Engineer*, 4 October 1918), p. 290; 'The AEC Truck works' (*Motor Trader*, 19 March 1919), p. 408; 'Conveyor in relation to engineering works' (*Cassier's*, 10 April 1919), p. 288.

[129] AEC Archive, MRC, Mss 226/AE/1/11, *Board Minutes*, 10 April, 8 May, and 9 October 1918.

[130] 'Quantity production in lorry building' (*Engineer*, 4 October 1918), p. 290.

[131] AEC Archive, MRC, Mss 226/AE/1/11, *Board Minutes*, estimated output for 1915 was 1300. EEF Archive, *Membership File*, AEC, employed 2116 workers in 1915. For 1926 estimate see EEF Archive, *Membership File*, *AEC*, 'Interview', 22 June 1927.

[132] EEF Archive, *Membership File*, *AEC*, 'Failure to Observe Rules'; *ASE Monthly Report*, 1926.

[133] AEC Archive, MRC, Mss 226/AE/1/12–3, *Board Minutes*, 28 August 1922, 10 April 1923 and 3 June 1926.

[134] EEF Archive, *Membership File*, AEC, 'Letter W.L. Bayley to A.C. Bayley', 18 March 1927; AEC Archive, MRC, Mss 226/AE/1/13, *Board Minutes*, 1 July 1926.

[135] 'An omnibus overhauling depot' (*Engineer*, 3 February 1922), pp. 121–4.

[136] EEF Archive, *Membership File*, *AEC*, 'Interview', 21 March 1927; 'The works of Associated Daimler Company' (*Automobile Engineer*, January 1928), pp. 9–12; AEC Archive, MRC Mss 226/AE/1/13, *Board Minutes*, 6 October 1927.

[137] EEF Archive, *Membership File*, *AEC*, 'Failure to Observe Rules', p. 4.

[138] AEC Archive, MRC, Mss 226/AE/1/14, *Board Minutes*, 3 April and 19 June 1928.

[139] EEF Archive, *Membership File*, *AEC*, 'Failure to Observe Rules, Interview,' 19 July 1927.

[140] AEC Archive, MRC, Mss 226/AE/1/16, *Board Minutes*, 4 December 1930; EEF Archive, *Membership File*, *AEC*, 'Interview', 22 June 1927.

[141] EEF Archive, *Membership File*, *AEC*, 'P. Martin to the EEF', 13 June 1927. See also 'Memo A.C. Bayley to W.L. Bayley', 25 July 1927.

[142] EEF Archive, *Membership File*, *AEC*, Memo regarding interview G. Rushton and J.C.A. Ward, 19 July 1927, pp. 2–3.

[143] *Ibid.*, p. 6

[144] *Ibid.*, pp. 5–6.

[145] G. Oliver, *The Rover* (London, 1971), pp. 89–103; EEF Archive, *Statistical Files, Employment Data*, basement folders.

[146] EEF Archive, P(20)14, *Letter Sec, EEF to Lincoln, Gainsborough and Newark Employers Association*, 16 March, 1934.

[147] EEF Archive, P(20)5, *Memo Telephone Call Verley (CDEEA) to Campbell (EEF)*. See also *Local Conference 14 April 1930;* S. Tolliday, 'Militancy and organisation: women workers and trade unions in the motor trades in the 1930s' (*Oral History*, 11, 1983), p. 47.

[148] EEF Archive, P(20)5, *Proposed Solution*, 11 September 1930; CDEEA, *Minutes Executive Meeting*, 15 September 1930.

[149] Tolliday, 'Militancy and organisation', p. 47.

[150] CDEEA, *Minutes Executive Meeting*, 31 March 1930.

[151] EEF Archive, P(20)5, *Cole Memo*, 10 September 1930.

[152] Oliver, *Rover*, p. 103. See CDEEA, *Minutes Executive Meeting*, 26 January 1931, on the delay in adopting Bedaux at Coventry.

Chapter 9: The collapse of the British system of mass production 1930–1984

[1] For an overview of events during this period see G. Maxcy and A. Silberston, *The Motor Industry* (London, 1959), pp. 160, 175, 211, 222–8.

[2] R. Church, *Herbert Austin* (London, 1979), pp. 214–15; R.J. Overy, *William Morris, Viscout Nuffield* (London, 1976), p. 129.

[3] R. Whipp and P. Clark, *Innovation and the Automobile Industry* (New York, 1986), p. 69.

[4] R.C.O. Mathews, C.H. Feinstein and J.C. Odling-Smee, *British Economic Growth, 1856–1973* (Stanford, 1982), pp. 232, 240, 378–86. See also H.A. Turner *et al.*, *Labour Relations in the Motor Industry* (London, 1967), p. 80.

[5] See P. Willman and G. Winch, *Innovation and Management Control* (Cambridge University Press, 1985), p. 25; Turner, *et al.*, *Labour Relations*.

[6] See Central Policy Review Staff, *The Future of the British Car Industry* (London, 1975), for arguments regarding the role of labour restriction in the industry's post-1945 decline. For a recent debate on the strength and origin of shop stewards see J. Zeitlin, 'The emergence of shop steward organization and job control in the British car industry' (*History Workshop*, 10, 1980), pp. 119–37; D. Lyddon, 'Workplace organization in the British car industry' (*History Workshop*, 15, 1983), pp. 131–40.

[7] L. Rostas, *Comparative Productivity in British and American Industry* (Cambridge University Press, 1948), p. 64.

[8] E.H. Phelps Brown and M.H. Browne, *A Century of Pay* (London, 1968), p. 141–4, 175–85.

[9] EEF Archive, W(9)4 app. 46, part 1, *Report to the Management Board by the Special Committee Regarding Working Conditions*, 1930 or 1931, p. 8.

[10] On the lack of labour organisation in the 1930s see S. Tolliday, 'Militancy and organisation (*Oral History*, 11, 1983), pp. 42–55.

[11] See S. Tolliday, 'Government, employers and shop floor organisation in the British Motor industry, 1939–69', in S. Tolliday and J. Zeitlin (eds.), *Shop Floor Bargaining and the State* (Cambridge University Press, 1985), p. 112; J. Salmon, Organised Labour in a Market Economy (Ph.D., Warwick, 1983), pp. 219–20.

[12] Etheridge Papers, MRC, Mss 292/S/J/3/1/9, *Rules of the Austin Joint Production Consultative and Advisory Committee*, 24 June, 1942.

[13] Etheridge Papers, MRC, Mss 202/S/J/3/1/10, *The Report of the Shop Stewards Committee*, April 1944, p. 2.

[14] The first Report was published in April of 1944, which was followed by a lengthy report of the dispute at Longbridge in September of 1944. See Etheridge Papers, MRC 202/S/J/3/1/6.

[15] Lyddon, 'Workplace organization', p. 131.

[16] On victimization of shop stewards see Salmon, *Organised Labour*, pp. 336–8; Tolliday, 'Government', p. 118; Etheridge Papers, MRC, *Austin Joint Shop Stewards, Report to Royal Commission on Trade Union and Employer Organisations*, July 1966.

[17] Salmon, *Organised Labour*, pp. 281–7.

[18] K.G.J.C. Knowles and D. Robinson, 'Wage movements in Coventry' (*Bulletin of the Oxford University Institute of Economics and Statistics*, 31, 1969), p. 3.

[19] See Salmon, *Organised Labour*, pp. 292–9 for details on the Humber strike.

[20] See Lyddon, 'Workplace organization', p. 136; Tolliday, 'Government'.

[21] See Turner *et al, Labour Relations*, p. 214, regarding the role of shop stewards in maintaining continuous production. Lyddon makes a similar point in, 'Work organization', p. 137.

[22] See W.D. Gartman, Auto Slavery (Ph.D., University of California, San Diego, 1980), pp. 306–14 for a description of early automation experiments in the United States.

[23] Secretariat of the Trade Unions International of Metal and Engineering Industries, 'Today's problems in the automobile industry' (*International Bulletin of Workers in The Metal and Engineering Industries*, January 1957), p. 20.

[24] Maxcy and Silberston, *Motor Industry*, p. 59; Turner, *et al., Labour Relations*, p. 82.

[25] On Austin see Etheridge Papers, MRC, Mss 202/S/J/3/4/14, *Untitled Survey on Automation*, p. 40; Turner *et al., Labour Relations*, p. 78. On GM and Ford see *Ibid.*, p. 79. For a description of new production methods at Briggs Motor Bodies see Etheridge Papers, MRC, Mss 202/S/J/3/3/8, *Plants Developments, Mechanical Aids and Automation at Briggs Motor Bodies*, 9 May, 1956. On Standard see S. Melman, *Decision Making and Productivity* (Oxford, 1958), pp. 154–5.

[26] See F.G. Woollard, 'Machines in the service of men', in *The Automatic Factory – What Does it Mean?*, Report of the conference held at Margate, 1955 (published by the Institute of Production Engineers), cited in Maxcy and Silberston, *Motor Industry*, p. 60.

[27] Etheridge Papers, MRC, *M.A.S.S. Report*, Conference held 5 June 1955 in Birmingham, p. 7.

[28] Etheridge was a leading figure in the union movement at Austin between 1940 and 1970. For details see A. Tough's forthcoming biography.

[29] Etheridge Papers, MRC, 'All in favour say aye' (*2nd Conference of Motor Car Shop Stewards*, Oxford, 25 September, 1955), pp. 4–5.

[30] Etheridge Papers, MRC, 'All in favour', pp. 5, 19. See also Etheridge Papers, MRC, Mss 202/S/J/3/2/14, *Automation and Electronics, Bill 60*, 9 November, 1955.

[31] Mathews *et al, British Economic Growth*, p. 240.

[32] Expenditure Committee, *Fourteenth Report, The Motor Vehicle Industry* (London, 1975), p. 235.

[33] F. Griffiths, 'Automation in motors calls for much re-thinking' (*Financial Times*, 23 January, 1961), Automation and Electronics Supplement, p. 37.

[34] Melman, *Decision Making*, p. 135. See also Melman, pp. 3–10 for a discussion of how trends at Standard were distinctly different from trends at the majority of manufacturing firms which had moved toward unilateral managerial decision making. For other accounts of the Standard gang system see D. Rayton, 'Shop floor democracy in action' (*Industrial Common Ownership Movement*, pamphlet no. 1, Nottingham, 1972); R. Wright, 'The gang system in Coventry' (*Anarchy*, **2**, 1961), pp. 47–52; R. Wright, 'Erosion inside capitalism' (*Anarchy*, **8**, 1961), pp. 237–45.

[35] Melman was well aware of this unique feature of the Standard system. He noted that the majority of British managers had a perference for payment systems which emphasised the individual nature of the contract between labour and the company because they feared that collective systems would strengthen labour's voice and would allow labour to challenge managerial authority even further. See Melman, *Decision Making*, p. 35.

[36] On the company's early history see Standard Archive, MRC, Mss 226/ST/1/2/1,

Friswell Notes, 7 December 1909. See also Standard Archive, MRC, Mss 226/ST/1/1/1, *Board Minutes*, 1903–14, Mss 226/ST/1/1/3/1, 6 July 1920 and 25 July 1922; 'A modern chassis assembly plant' (*Automobile Engineer*, March 1921), p. 102.

37   Maxcy and Silberston, *Motor Industry*, p. 107; Standard Archive, MRC, Mss 226/ST/1/1/5–7, *Board Minutes*, 12 February 1930, 29 August 1933, 4 January 1935.

38   Standard Archive, MRC, Mss 226/ST/2/1/1–49, *Balance Sheets*; Melman Papers, MRC, Mss 254/2, *Draft Table of Employment Levels*.

39   On wartime programmes see Standard Archive, MRC, Mss 226/ST/1/2/1, *Friswell Notes*, 15 November 1910; Mss 226/ST/1/1/2/1, *Board Minutes*, 7 March 1916 to 12 July 1918. On the proposed share issue see Mss 226/ST/1/1/3/1, *Board Minutes*, 26 August 1920, 13 December 1921 and 24 January 1922. On the land purchase see Mss 226/ST/1/1/5, *Board Minutes*, 25 June 1923.

40   On the winding down of the fund and a discussion which suggests it was not certain that pensions and other benefits would be continued after the fund was exhausted see Standard Archive, MRC, Mss 226/ST/3, *Misc. Documents*, 'Notes on Employee Special Fund', 18 October 1962.

41   Standard Archive, MRC, Mss 226/ST/1/1/7 and 10, *Board Minutes*, 5 October 1936 and 28 October 1946; Standard Archive, MRC, Mss 226/ST/3, *Misc. Correspondence*, 'Letter to R.W. Spittal', 24 April 1952 and 'Standard Motor Company Pension Scheme'.

42   See BBC Interviews, *Cathy Smith*, tape 69, p. 17; *Freddy Troop*, tape 3, pp. 1–2.

43   BBC Interviews, *George Turnbull*, tape 84, p. 6.

44   BBC Interviews, *Mr and Mrs Clark*, tape 63, pp. 1–4. See also *Cathy Smith Interview*, p. 2.

45   Melman, *Decision Making*, p. 31.

46   See BBC Interviews, *Elwood*, tape 216, p. 8, for a discussion of how Standard had saved its machinery in 1939 which allowed the company to begin production before other firms after the war.

47   EEF Archive, W(9)5, App. 67, *Misc. Documents Regarding Standard Withdrawing from the EEF*. See especially, *Memo*, 26 June 1945; *Memo Regarding a Meeting Between Black and the CDEEA*, 22 June 1945; *Internal Notes Regarding Black*, 22 June 1945. The clearest evidence of the CDEEA displeasure with Black's day work proposals was the CDEEA request to be kept informed and Black notifying the CDEEA in September of 1944 that he intended to resign his position as vice-president of the Employers Association because he could not agree with their postwar policy. See EEF Archive, W(9)5 App 67, *Letter from Vingen to Black*, 4 September 1944. See also *Letter by Black to the Workforce*, 25 May 1945 and reproduced in Melman, *Decision Making*, pp. 221–2.

48   Melman, *Decision Making*, p. 144.

49   *Ibid.*, pp. 62–73, 110–111.

50   Standard Archive, MRC, Mss 226/ST/1/1/10, *Board Minutes*, 19 June 1947. See also Mss 226/ST/3, *Report by R.E. Herington Regarding Profit Sharing Schemes*, 18 June 1947.

51   Herington, *Report on Profit Sharing*, p. 1.

52   Standard Archive, MRC, Mss. 226, *Misc. Documents*, 'Standard Motor Company Wage Structure', pp. 1–2. See also TGWU Archive, MRC, Mss 208B/TBN 10,

Agreement Between TGWU and Standard Motor Company, 22 November 1948.

53 Melman, *Decision Making*, p. 111.

54 *Ibid.*, p. 128; Turner *et al.*, *Labour Relations*, p. 94.

55 Standard Archive, MRC, Mss 226, *Standard Wage Structure*, pp. 5–6.

56 Melman, *Decision Making*, p. 162.

57 *Ibid.*, pp. 57, 63, 114. See also Wright, 'The gang system', pp. 47–52.

58 Melman, *Decision Making*, p. 144.

59 *Ibid.*, pp. 187–99.

60 TGWU Archive, MRC, Mss. 208b/TBN 10, *Statement by J.L. Jones*, 12 January 1955.

61 Cited in Melman, *Decision Making*, p. 113.

62 See Maxcy and Silberston, *Motor Industry*, pp. 169, 175; Standard Archive, MRC, Mss 226, *Misc. Documents*, 'Statement of Corporate Profits', 10 May 1954.

63 TGWU Archive, MRC, Mss 208b/TBN 10, *Statement by Standard Official During Meeting*, 1 July 1955.

64 For details on the 1956 strike see Salmon, *Organised Labour*, pp. 551–79.

65 See Melman, *Decision Making*, pp. 179–91.

66 EEF Archive, *Membership Files, Standard Motor Car Company*. R. Wright claims that management was not fully successful in rolling back shop floor authority. When the firm was taken over by Leyland in the 1960s, Wright claims they were forced to turn to labour to keep the factory operating. See Rayton, 'Shop floor democracy', p. 23.

67 Standard Archive, MRC, Mss. 226/ST/1/1/12–13, *Board Minutes*, 21 March to 1 April 1957 and 20 July to 4 November 1959; A. Friedman, *Industry and Labour* (London, 1977), pp. 197, 218.

68 Turner *et al.*, *Labour Relations*, p. 95.

69 G. Maxcy, 'The motor industry', in P.L. Cook and R. Cohen (eds.), *Effects of Mergers* (London, 1958), p. 376.

70 P. Dunnett, *The Decline of the British Motor Industry* (London, 1980), pp. 32–6.

71 Etheridge Papers, MRC, Mss 202/S/J/3/3/64, *Statement on Measured Day Work by the Austin Works Committee* (nd.).

72 W. Brown, 'Piecework wage determination in Coventry' (*Scottish Journal of Political Economy*, 18, 1971), p. 3.

73 D.G. Rhys, 'Employment, efficiency and labour relations in the British motor industry' (*Industrial Relations Journal*, 5, 1974), p. 8.

74 On the incidence of unofficial strikes see Scamp Papers, MRC, Mss 178 TBN6, *Testimony of A.J. Scamp to the Royal Commission on Trade Unions and Employers' Associations*, 10 May 1966, p. 6; Etheridge Papers, MRC, Mss 202/S/J/3/2/79–144, *Annual Convener's Reports*, 1967 to 1972; Turner *et al.*, *Labour Relations*, pp. 52–3.

75 W. Brown, *Piecework Abandoned* (London, 1962), pp. 8–38. See also *Report of the Office of Manpower Economics, Measured Daywork* (London, 1973), p. 4.

76 A. Flanders, 'Measured daywork and collective bargaining' (*British Journal of Industrial Relations*, 11, 1973), p. 373.

77 R. Pearson, 'From group bonus to straight time pay' (*Journal of Industrial Economics*, 8, 1960), pp. 114–15.

78 Expenditure Committee, *Fourteenth Report*, paragraph 29.

79 Pearson, 'From group bonus', p. 117.

⁸⁰ Dunnett, *Decline*, p. 19; Rhys, *Employment*, p. 20; Expenditure Committee, *Four-teenth Report*, Table 14.

⁸¹ Rhys, *Employment*, p. 9.

⁸² For work on Chrysler (UK) see S. Young and N. Hood, *Chrysler* (UK), *A Corporation in Transition* (New York, 1977); S. Wilks, *Industrial Policy and the Motor Industry* (Manchester, 1984); J. Salmon, A View of Industrial Relations in the British Car Industry (M.A. Thesis, Warwick, 1975).

⁸³ See Young and Hood, Chrysler, p. 230; Salmon, View of Industrial Relations, pp. 26–32.

⁸⁴ Young and Hood, *Chrysler*, p. 231.

⁸⁵ Salmon, *View of Industrial Relations*, p. 24–8.

⁸⁶ Young and Hood, *Chrysler*, pp. 232–46.

⁸⁷ Statement by G. Hunt, cited in Young and Hood, *Chrysler*, p. 239.

⁸⁸ Wilks, *Industrial Policy*, p. 201.

⁸⁹ Young and Hood, *Chrysler*, p. 239.

⁹⁰ Wilks, *Industrial Policy*, pp. 202–3.

⁹¹ P.W. Ford, Changing the Wage Payment System at a Car Factory (M.A. Warwick, 1972), pp. 27–8; J. Sutherland, The Impact of Measured Day Work on Company Industrial Relations (M.A. Warwick, 1974), p. 30.

⁹² Scamp Papers, MRC, Mss 178 TBN1, *Notes Regarding a Meeting Between A.S. Kerr and H.T. Rudd*, 7 September 1965.

⁹³ Etheridge Papers, MRC, Mss 202/S/J/3/2/87, *Report of a Meeting Between Officials of BMC and National Officials of the Trade Unions*, 3 August 1967, p. 3. On early proposals for job evaluation see Etheridge Papers, MRC, Mss 202/S/J/3/2/93, *Job Evaluation*, late 1960s.

⁹⁴ Etheridge Papers, MRC, Mss 202/S/J/3/3/64, *Austin Special Bulletin*, 27 January 1972.

⁹⁵ Etheridge Papers, MRC, Mss 202/S/J/3/2/88, *New Deal or New Fetters*, published by the Oxford Liaison Committee for the Defence of Trade Unions, 1967.

⁹⁶ Etheridge Papers, MRC, Mss 202/S/J/3/2/104, *Measured Daywork*, published by L.R.D. Publications, February 1972, p. 8.

⁹⁷ On the AEU-Sheet Metal Workers demarcation dispute see Etheridge Papers, MRC Mss 202/S/J/1/1, *Minutes Joint Shop Stewards Committee*, 10 July 1946. On the NUVB strike in the body shop see Etheridge Papers, MRC, Mss 202/S/J/1/1, Works Committee Meeting, 14 August 1946.

⁹⁸ Etheridge Papers, MRC, Mss 202/S/J/1/9i, *Joint Shop Stewards Committee*, 31 December 1962.

⁹⁹ Etheridge Papers, MRC, *Submission by D. Etheridge and Austin Works Committee to the Royal Commission on Trade Union and Employer Organisations*, July 1966, Appendix on Restrictive Practices–Protective Practices (np).

¹⁰⁰ Etheridge Papers, MRC, Mss 202/S/J/1/3i, *Works Committee*, 27 September 1954.

¹⁰¹ Etheridge Papers, MRC, Mss 202/S/J/3/2/79, *Conveners Report*, 2 January 1967, p. 3.

¹⁰² Etheridge Papers, MRC, Mss 202/S/J/3/2/92, *Annual Conveners Report*, 1 January 1968.

¹⁰³ Scamp Papers, MRC, Mss 178 TBN 2, *Analysis of Lost Time at Pressed Steel Fisher*, Cowley, 2 April 1966 to 26 August 1966.

[104] Etheridge Papers, MRC, Mss 202/S/J/3/2/82, *Report on An Investigation into the Excessive Loss of Production Time on the Transmission Case Section*, March 1967, pp. 2–6.

[105] Etheridge Papers, MRC, Mss 202/S/J/3/2/82, *Report*, pp. 5–8.

[106] Etheridge Papers, MRC, Mss 202/S/J/3/2/159, *Letter from Bro. F. Edwardes to Works Committee*, 16 December 1971.

[107] Etheridge Papers, MRC, Mss 202/S/J/3/2/108, *Annual Meeting Austin Joint Shop Stewards Committee*, 6 January 1969.

[108] Etheridge Papers, MRC, Mss 202/S/J/9/5, *Interim Pay Arrangements, Cofton Hackett*, 9 May 1968.

[109] Etheridge Papers, MRC, Mss 202/S/J/3/2/144, *Conveners Annual Report*, 4 January 1971, p. 4; Mss 202/S/J/3/2/160, *Conveners Annual Report*, 3 January 1972, p. 6.

[110] See Ford, *Changing the Wage Payment System*.

[111] *Ibid.*, pp. 62–8.

[112] *Ibid.*, p. 83–91.

[113] *Ibid.*, pp. 72, 84, 97.

[114] See Whipp and Clark, *Innovation*, pp. 119–23.

[115] Sutherland, *Impact of Measured Day Work*, pp. 30–3.

[116] *Ibid.*, pp. 35–45.

[117] *Ibid.*, pp. 46–9.

[118] Former P6 paint rectifier, cited in Whipp and Clark, *Innovation*, p. 178.

[119] Etheridge Papers, MRC, Mss 202/S/J/3/2/141, *Proposals for a New Payment Structure at Longbridge*, 11 November 1970.

[120] Etheridge Papers, MRC, Mss 202/S/J/3/2/144, *Conveners Annual Report*, 4 January 1971, p. 5.

[121] Etheridge Papers, MRC, Mss 202/S/J/3/2/160, *Annual Conveners Report*, 3 January 1972, p. 7–8.

[122] Etheridge Papers, MRC, Mss 202/S/J/3/3/64, *Austin Special Bulletin*, 27 January 1972.

[123] Etheridge Papers, MRC, Mss 202/S/J/, *Longbridge Standard Daywork Proposals for Kings Norton No. 2*, December 1971.

[124] Etheridge Papers, MRC, Mss 202/S/J/9/7, *Longbridge Plant, Standard Daywork Agreement*, 3 November 1972.

[125] BBC Interviews, *Bill Roche*, Convener Pressed Steel, roll 95, p. 5.

[126] Expenditure Committee, *Fourteenth Report*, vol. II, p. 43.

[127] Expenditure Committee, *Fourteenth Report*, vol. II, p. 358.

[128] BBC Interviews, *John Barber*, tape 152, p. 39.

[129] On the lack of capital investment see Expenditure Committee, *Fourteenth Report*, Table 14. K. Williams, 'BMC/BLMC/BL – a misunderstood failure', in K. Williams, J. Williams and D. Thomas, *Why are the British Bad at Manufacturing?* (London, 1983), places great weight on BL concentrating on models which provided low profit margins and did not hold up well during economic cycles. Under investment and labour control question are seen to play a secondary role. While we agree with much of Williams' argument, we feel it fails to give proper weight to the long-run production problem the industry experienced.

[130] See Ryder Committee, *British Leyland: The Next Decade* (London, 1975), p. 18–19; Expenditure Committee, *Fourteenth Report*, no. 31; Wilks, *Industrial Policy*, p. 97; Williams, 'A misunderstood failure', p. 228.

131   On the Edwardian crisis and its link with high pay-out ratios see W. Lewchuk, 'The return to capital in the British motor vehicle industry, 1896–1939' (*Business History*, 27, 1985), pp. 3–25.

132   See Ryder Committee, *Next Decade*. See also Wilks, *Industrial Policy*, p. 231.

133   Ryder Committee, *Next Decade*, p. 31–8.

134   My information on the Rover SD1 project is based on the research of P. Clark and R. Whipp. I would like to thank both for providing me with copies of work in progress and for discussing their findings with me. For details on the failure of the SD1 project see Whipp and Clark, *Innovation*

135   R. Whipp, 'Management, design and industrial relations in the British automobile industry: the SD1 project' (unpublished paper), p. 15.

136   *Ibid.*, p. 26.

137   *Ibid.*, p. 28. See also Whipp and Clark, *Innovation*, pp. 182–3.

138   Whipp and Clark, *Innovation*, pp. 115–23, 148–9, 166–7.

139   BBC Interviews, *Jean Rivers*, SD1 shop steward, tape 59, pp. 3–4. For similar stories from a management official see interview with *Peter Grant*, tape 58.

140   Whipp, 'Management Design', p. 28.

141   See Wilks, *Industrial Policy*, chapter 5; Willman and Winch, *Innovation*, chapter 2.

142   The Edwardes era is analysed in great detail by both Wilks, *Industrial Policy*, and by Willman and Winch, *Innovation*. M. Edwardes, *Back from the Brink* (London, 1983), provides a popular, but nonetheless interesting account of the period.

143   Willman, *Innovation*, p. 20.

144   Edwardes, *Back from the Brink*, pp. 52, 167.

145   Willman and Winch, *Innovation*, p. 25, 63.

146   Wilks, *Industrial Policy*, p. 206.

147   Willman and Winch, *Innovation*, p. 16.

148   See Wilks, *Industrial Policy*, p. 209; Willman and Winch, *Innovation*, pp. 81–3, 159; Edwardes, *Back from the Brink*, pp. 108–25.'

149   Cited in Willman and Winch, *Innovation*, p. 124.

150   Wilks, *Industrial Policy*, p. 211.

151   For discussions of this point see W. Lewchuk, 'The motor vehicle industry', in W. Lazonick and E. Elbaum (eds.), *The Decline of the British Economy* (Oxford, 1985), pp. 135–61. See also P. Willman, 'Labour relations strategies at BL Cars', in S. Tolliday and J. Zeitlin (eds.), *Between Fordism and Flexibility: The International Automobile Industry and its Workers* (Oxford, forthcoming).

152   In 1971, motor vehicle workers earnings were 23.4 percent higher than the average British manual wage. By 1982, their advantage had fallen to 3.2 percent. See P. Willman, 'The reform of collective bargaining and strike activity in BL Cars, 1976–82' (*Industrial Relations Journal*, 15, 1984), p. 12.

153   Thoms and Donnelly attribute much of Jaguar's success in the early 1980s '. . . to an imaginative scheme of quality control monitored by shop floor workers', while a senior shop steward at the company suggested that '. . . as usual, the shop floor is leading the way.' See D. Thoms and T. Donnelly, *The Motor Car Industry in Coventry Since the 1890s* (London, 1985), pp. 211–2. For statements by senior shop stewards see 'Workers in quality street' (*New Society*, 67, 12 January 1984), p. 60.

154   Edwardes, *Back from the Brink*, p. 135. For details of the bonus system see Willman and Winch, *Innovation*, pp. 166–9.

Bibliography

(1) Archival sources

(a) The Engineering Employers Federation (EEF Archive)

The Federation holds an extensive collection of both original and microfilmed records relating to the engineering industry from 1895 to the present. The collection includes verbatim reports of works conferences, local conferences and central conferences, correspondence, and studies on managerial methods. Those records which have been microfilmed are cited by their file number. A portion of the collection was uncataloged and stored in the basement of the Federation's London office. Most of the records of the Federation are now housed at the Modern Record Centre in Coventry.

(b) Coventry District Engineering Employers Association (CDEEA)

The bulk of this collection is composed of the minutes of executive meetings of the association which run from 1915 to 1932 with a gap between 1916 and 1919.

(c) Federation of British Industries (FBI Archive)

The Federation was involved in labour relations and managerial strategies during World War I. Their papers are now held by the Modern Records Centre in Coventry.

(d) Etheridge Papers

Dick Etheridge played a major role in union activities at the Austin Longbridge plant from the 1940s to the 1970s. His papers provide a comprehensive picture of life in an automobile plant from a union perspective. These papers are housed at the Modern Records Centre.

(e) Amalgamated Union of Engineering Workers, London (ASE (London))

Formerly the Amalgamated Society of Engineers, the AUEW holding includes numerous union journals published by the union and a small holding of correspondence and conference reports.

(f) Amalgamated Union of Engineering Workers, Coventry (ASE (COV))

The Coventry office of the AUEW holds an almost complete run of the minute books of the Executive Committee. They also have a limited collection of other records.

(g) National Union of Vehicle Builders (UKS/NUVB)

The NUVB museum in Coventry holds the archive of the United Kingdom Society of Coachmakers. The archive includes union journals, minute books and other records.

(h) Ford Motor Company (US) (Ford Archive)

The records of the Ford Motor Company make up a significant portion of the collections of the Henry Ford Museum and Greenfield Village. They include factory accounts and cost books and a large selection of recorded interviews with former Ford employees.

(i) Ford Motor Company (UK) (Ford Archive Warley)

A limited amount of uncataloged material is held in Warley on Ford's operations in Europe.

(j) British Leyland Historic Vehicles Ltd.

The surviving papers of the companies which now form British Leyland have been deposited at the Modern Records Centre. Of particular use in our research were the papers of the Austin Motor Company, Standard Motor Company, and the Associated Equipment Company.

(k) Daimler Motor Company

The minute books of the Daimler board of directors have survived for the periods from 1897 to 1903 and from 1910 to 1913. The earliest books were of particular interest in light of the board's direct involvement with the running of the works. They have been referred to as Daimler Board Minutes. Housed with the minute books is a small collection of records referred to as the Birmingham Collection. These records are held privately. For more information contact the Coventry Record Office.

(l) BBC Interviews

A large number of interviews were conducted for the BBC series 'All Our Working Lives'. The collection is particularly strong regarding post-1945 events, although there are a number of interviews of interwar workers and managers and few interviews of pre-1914 motor vehicle workers. The transcripts of the interviews are currently held by the BBC in London.

(m) Coventry Record Office (CRO)

The Coventry Record Office has a major deposit of records relating to the early history of
the Daimler Company. These records include correspondence and various submissions
to the board of directors. They are cited by accession and file number. They also hold
papers relating to the early history of the Rudge Company.

(n) R. Simms and J. Pollitt Papers

Most of these papers are held by the University of London for the Veteran Car Club.
They are particularly rich in material on the early history of Daimler and Rover. Those
papers deposited with the University of London are cited according to their catalogue
numbers. A further collection of papers belonging to Pollitt remain in the hands of the
Veteran Car Club. They comprise mainly secondary sources from a range of journals and
are uncataloged.

(o) Ward Papers

The Ward papers held by the Business History Unit provide a valuable insight into the
operation of the Management Research Group One (MRG I). These records are cited by
the new catalogue system introduced by the Business History Unit.

(2) Periodical literature

Contemporary periodical literature provided an extremely rich source of information not
only on the machine methods used in the vehicle factories but on the debates over
managerial strategies. These articles have been cited in the main body of the thesis but
have been excluded from the bibliography. The majority of these journals are available
either at the British Museum, Newspaper Division, or the Science Reference Library.
The following Journals proved particularly useful:

Auto Car
The Automobile and Carriage Builders Journal (becomes *The Automobile*)
The Automobile Engineer
The Automotor and Horseless Vehicle Journal (becomes *The Automotor Journal*)
Cassiers Magazine (becomes *Engineering and Industrial Management*)
The Commercial Motor
The Cycle Referee
The Engineer
The Engineer in Charge
The Engineering Magazine
Engineering Production
Engineering Review
The Industrial Engineer
Internal Combustion Engineering
Iron Age
Iron Trade Review
Journal Society of Automobile Engineers (US)

Machinery (UK)
Machinery (US)
The Managing Engineer
Mechanical World
Monthly Review of Modern Machine Shop Practices
The Motor
The Motor Trader
Practical Engineering
Proceedings of the Institute of Automobile Engineers (becomes *Journal of the Society of Automotive Engineers*) (UK)
Proceedings of the Institute of Production Engineers (becomes *Journal of the Institute of Production Engineers*)
Stock Exchange Year Book
System
Times Engineering Supplement
Works Management

(3) Books

Abernathy, W.J., *The Productivity Dilemma* (John Hopkins Press, Baltimore, 1978).

Abernathy, W.J., K.B. Clark and A.M. Kantrow, *Industrial Renaissance, Producing a Competitive Future for America* (Basic Books, New York, 1983).

Aglietta, M., *A Theory of Capitalist Regulation; The US Experience* (New Left Books, London, 1979).

Aitken, Hugh, *Taylorism at Watertown Arsenal* (Harvard University Press, Cambridge Mass., 1960).

Aitken, Hugh, *Syntony and Spark: The Origin of Radio* (John Wiley & Sons, New York, 1976).

Allen, G.C., *The Industrial Development of Birmingham and the Black Country* (Cass, London, 1966, reprint).

Andrews, P.W.S. and E. Brunner, *The Life of Lord Nuffield* (Basil Blackwell, Oxford, 1955).

Arnold, H.L. and F.L. Faurote, *Ford Methods and Ford Shops* (*The Engineering Magazine*, New York, 1915).

Austin, Bertram and W. Francis Lloyd, *The Secret of High Wages* (T. Fisher Unwin Ltd, London, 1926).

Axelrod, R., *The Evolution of Cooperation* (Basic Books, New York, 1984).

Babbage, C., *On the Economy of Machinery and Manufactures* (Charles Knight, London, 1832).

Babcock, G.D., *The Taylor System in Franklin Management* (Engineering Magazine Company, New York, 1917).

Baldamus, W., *Efficiency and Effort* (Tavistock Publications, London, 1961).

Balfour, A. Sir, *Factors in Industrial and Commercial Efficiency* (Committee on Industry and Trade, London, 1927).

Barclay, Hartley W., *Ford Production Methods* (Harper, New York, 1936).

Bardou, J.P., J.J. Chanaron, P. Fridenson and J.M. Laux, *The Automobile Revolution: The Impact of an Industry* (Chapel Hill, 1982).

Bendix, R., *Work and Authority in Industry* (University of California Press, Berkeley, 1974).

Benyon, H., *Working for Ford* (Allen Lane, Harmondsworth, 1973).

Bersey, W.C., *The Motor Car Red Book* (London, no date).

Binswanger, H.P. and V.W. Ruttan, *Induced Innovation* (John Hopkins University Press, Baltimore, 1978).

Blank, Stephen, *Industry and Government in Britain: The Federation of British Industries in Politics 1945–65* (Saxon House, England, 1973).

Bluestone, B. and B. Harrison, *The Deindustrialization of America* (Basic Books, New York, 1982).

Brady, R.A., *The Rationalization Movement in German Industry* (University of California Press, Berkeley, 1933).

Branson, N., *Poplarism 1919–1925* (Lawrence and Wishart, London, 1979).

Braverman, H., *Labour and Monopoly Capital* (Monthly Review Press, New York, 1974).

Bremner, D.A., *The Pathology of Unrest* (Lakeman and Tucker, London, 1920).

Briggs, Asa, and John Saville, *Essays in Labour History 1918–39* (Croom Helm, London, 1977).

Brody, D., *Workers in Industrial America* (Oxford University Press, New York, 1980).

Brown, Geoff, *Sabotage* (Spokesman Books, Nottingham, 1977).

Brown, W., *Piecework Abandoned* (Heinemann, London, 1962).

Burawoy, M., *The Politics of Production* (Verso, London, 1985).

Burawoy, M., *Manufacturing Consent: Changes in the Labor Process under Monopoly Capitalism* (University of Chicago Press, Chicago, 1979).

Burgess, Keith, *The Challenge of Labour* (Croom Helm, London, 1980).

Burgess, Keith, *The Origins of British Industrial Relations* (Croom Helm, London, 1975).

Cadbury, Edward, *Experiments in Industrial Organisation* (Longman's Green and Co., London, 1912).

Central Policy Review Staff, *The Future of the British Car Industry* (HMSO, London, 1975).

Chandler, Alfred D. Jr., *The Visible Hand, The Management Revolution in American Business* (Harvard University Press, Cambridge, Mass., 1977).

Chapman, S.J., *Labour and Capital After the War* (John Murray, London, 1918).

Charles, Rodger, *The Development of Industrial Relations in Britain 1911–39: Studies in the Evolution of Collective Bargaining at National and Industry Level* (Hutchinson, London, 1973).

Child, John, *The Business Enterprise in Modern Industrial Society* (MacMillan, London, 1969).

Church, R.A., *The Great Victorian Boom 1850–73* (MacMillan, London, 1975).

Church, R.A., *Herbert Austin* (Europa Publications Ltd, London, 1979).

Clawson, D., *Bureaucracy and The Labour Process, The Transformation of US Industry, 1860–1920* (Monthly Review Press, New York, 1980).

Clegg, H.A., A, Fox and A.F. Thompson, *A History of British Trade Unions Since 1889* (OUP, Oxford, 1964).

Clinton, Alan, *The Trade Union Rank and File: Trade Councils in Britain 1900–40* (Manchester University Press, Manchester, 1977).

Clutton, C. and J. Stanford, *The Vintage Motor Car* (Batsford, London, 1954).

Cole, G.D.H., *Self Government in Industry*, 1st published 1917 (Hutchinson Educational Ltd, London, 1972).

Cole, G.D.H., *Workshop Organisation*, 1st published 1923 (Hutchinson Educational Ltd., London, 1973).

Cole, G.D.H., *The World of Labour*, 1st published 1913 (Harvester Press, Brighton, 1973).

Cole, G.D.H., *The Payment of Wages*, 1st published 1918 (George Allen & Unwin, London, 1928).

Cole, G.D.H., *A Short History of the British Working Class Movement* (George Allen and Unwin Ltd, London, 1927).

Cole, G.D.H., *Trade Unions and Munitions* (Clarendon Press, Oxford, 1, 1923).

Commons, J.R., *Institutional Economics* (MacMillan, New York, 1934).

Cowling, M., *The Impact of Labour* (Cambridge University Press, 1971).

Crew, M., *Theory of the Firm* (Longman, London, 1975).

Cronin, James E., *Industrial Conflict in Modern Britain* (Croom Helm, London, 1979).

Cronin, J., *Labour and Society in Britain* (Batsford, London, 1984).

Crouzet, F., *The Victorian Economy* (Methuen, London, 1982).

Currie, Robert, *Industrial Politics* (Clarendon Press, Oxford, 1979).

Cutler, A., B. Hindess, P. Hirst and A. Hussain, *Marx's Capital and Capitalism Today*, Volume II (Routledge & Kegan Paul, London, 1978).

Darbyshire, L.C., *The Story of Vauxhall* (Vauxhall Motors, n.d.).

David, P.A., *Technical Choice, Innovation and Economic Growth* (Cambridge University Press, 1975).

Davidson, R., *Whitehall and the Labour Problem in Late-Victorian and Edwardian Britain* (Croom Helm, London, 1985).

Davis, L.E., and D.C. North, *Institutional Change and American Economic Growth* (Cambridge University Press, 1971).

Davison, G.S., *At the Wheel* (Industrial Transport Publications Ltd, London, 1931).

Davies, S., *The Diffusion of Process Innovations* (Cambridge University Press, 1979).

Derber, Milton, *The American Idea of Industrial Democracy 1865–1965* (University of Illinois Press, Chicago, 1970).

Douglas, P., *Real Wages in the United States, 1890–1926* (A.M. Kelly, New York, 1966), reprint of 1930 original.

Dubofsky, M., *We Shall be All, A History of the IWW* (Quadrangle, New York, 1969).

Dunnett, P., *The Decline of the British Motor Industry* (Croom Helm, London, 1980).

Edgeworth, F.Y., *Mathematical Psychics: An Essay on the Application of Mathematics to the Moral Sciences* (A.M. Kelley, New York, 1967) originally published 1881.

Edwardes, M., *Back from the Brink* (Collins, London, 1983).

Edwards, Richard, *Contested Terrain: The Transformation of the Workplace in the Twentieth Century* (Basic Books, New York, 1979).

Elster, J., *Explaining Technical Change* (Cambridge University Press, 1983).

Expenditure Committee, *Fourteenth Report, The Motor Vehicle Industry* (HMSO, London, 1975).

Fine, S., *Sit Down: The General Motors Strike of 1936–37* (Ann Arbor, University of Michigan Press, 1969).

Floud, R., *The British Machine Tool Industry 1850–1914* (Cambridge University Press, 1976).

Ford, H., *My Life and Work* (W. Heinemann, London, 1922).

Foster, J., *Class Struggle and the Industrial Revolution* (Methuen, London, 1974).

Fox, Alan, *Beyond Contract: Work, Power, and Trust Relations* (Faber and Faber, London, 1974).

Freeman, C., *The Economics of Industrial Innovation* (Penguin Books, London, 1974).

Friedlander, P., *The Emergence of a UAW Local 1936–1939* (University of Pittsburg Press, Pittsburg, 1975).

Friedman, Andrew, *Industry and Labour: Class Struggle at Work and Monopoly Capitalism* (MacMillan, London, 1977).

Friedman, H. and S. Meredeen, *The Dynamics of Industrial Conflict, Lessons from Ford* (MacMillan, London, 1980).

Frost, G.H., *Munitions of War: A Record of the Work of BSA Daimler* (n.d.).

Gallie, D., *In Search of the New Working Class*, (Cambridge University Press, 1978).

Georgano, G.N., *The Complete Encyclopedia of Motor Cars, 1885 to the Present* (Ebury Press, London, 1968).

Goodrich, Carter, *The Frontier of Control*, 1st published 1920 (Pluto, London, 1975).

Gordon, D.M., R. Edwards and M. Reich, *Segmented Work, Divided Workers* (Cambridge University Press, 1982).

Gramsci, A., *Selections from the Prison Notebooks* (International Publishers, New York, 1971).

Guilleband, C.W., *The Workers Council: A German Experiment in Industrial Democracy* (Cambridge University Press, 1928).

Gutman, Herbert G., *Work Culture and Society in Industrializing America* (A.A. Knopf, N.Y., 1976).

Habakkuk, H.J., *American and British Technology in the 19th Century* (Cambridge University Press, 1967).

Haber, Samuel, *Efficiency and Uplift: Scientific Management in the Progressive Era 1890–1920* (University of Chicago Press, Chicago, 1964).

Hahn, F.H., *On the Notion of Equilibrium in Economics* (Cambridge University Press, 1973).

Hannah, Leslie, *The Rise of the Corporate Economy* (Methuen, London, 1976).

Hannah, L. and J.A. King, *Concentration in Modern Industry* (MacMillan, London, 1977).

Hannington, W., *Unemployed Struggles* (Barnes and Nobel, London, 1977).

Hardin, R., *Collective Action* (John Hopkins Press, Baltimore, 1982).

Harris, D.J., *Capital Accumulation and Income Distribution* (Routledge & Kegan Paul, London, 1978).

Harsanyi, J.C., *Rational Behaviour and Bargaining Equilibrium in Games and Social Situations* (Cambridge University Press, 1977).

Hearn, Francis, *Domination Legitimation and Resistance, The Incorporation of the 19th Century Working Class* (Greenwood Press, USA, 1978).

Heertje, A., *Economics and Technical Change* (Weidenfeld and Nicolson, London, 1973).

Herding, R., *Job Control and Union Structure* (Rotterdam University Press, Rotterdam, 1972).

Hicks, J.R., *Theory of Wages* (MacMillan, London, 1932).

Hilton, J. *et al.*, *Are Trade Unions Obstructive?* (Gollancz, London, 1935).

Hinton, James, *The First Shop Stewards Movement* (George Allen & Unwin, London, 1973).

Hinton, J., *Labour and Socialism* (University of Massachusetts Press, Amherst, 1983).

Hobsbawm, Eric J., *Industry and Empire* (Penguin, London, 1969).

Hobsbawm, Eric J., *The Age of Capital 1848–75* (Weidenfeld and Nicolson, London, 1975).

Hobsbawm, Eric J., *Labouring Men, Studies in the History of Labour* (Weidenfeld and Nicolson, London, 1968).

Hodgkinson, George, *Sent to Coventry* (Robert Maxwell and Co. Ltd, UK, 1970).

Holbrook-Jones, M., *Supremacy and Subordination of Labour* (Heinemann, London, 1982).

Holton, B, *British Syndicalism* (Pluto Press, London, 1976).

Hounshell, D., *From the American System to Mass Production, 1800–1932* (John Hopkins Press, Baltimore, 1984).

Hudson, K., *Working to Rule: Railway Workshops and Rules* (Adams and Dart, Bath, 1970).

Hunt, E.H., *British Labour History, 1815–1914* (Weidenfeld and Nicolson, London, 1981).

Hyman, Richard, *The Workers' Union* (Clarendon Press, Oxford, 1971).

Jarman, L.P. and R.I. Barraclough, *The Bullnose Morris* (MacDonald, London, 1965).

Jewkes, J., D. Sawers and R. Stillerman, *The Sources of Invention* (Norton, London, 1969 2nd eds).

Jones, S.R.G., *The Economics of Conformism* (Basil Blackwell, Oxford, 1984).

Joyce, Patrick, *Work Society and Politics: The Culture of the Factory in Later Victorian England* (Harvester Press, London, 1980).

Karslake, K. and L. Pomeroy, *From Veteran to Vintage* (Temple Press, London, 1956).

Kelly, E.T., *Welfare Work in Industry* (Pitman, London, 1925).

Kochan, T.A., *Collective Bargaining and Industrial Relations* (Richard D. Irwin, Homewood, 1980).

Labini, Paolo-Sylos, *Oligopoly and Technical Progress* (Harvard University Press, Cambridge Mass, 1962).

Lambert, Z.E. and R.J. Wyatt, *Lord Austin, The Man* (Sidgwick Jackson, London, 1968).

Landes, David S., *The Unbound Prometheus* (Cambridge University Press, 1969).

Layton, F, Jr, *The Revolt of the Engineers* (Press of Case Western Reserve University, Cleveland, 1971).

Leibenstein, H., *Beyond Economic Man: A New Foundation for Microeconomics* (Harvard University Press, Cambridge Mass., 1976).

Leverhulme, Lord, *The Six Hour Day and Other Industrial Questions* (G. Allen and Unwin, London, 1918).

Levine, A.L., *Industrial Retardation in Britain* (Weidenfeld & Nicolson, London, 1967).

Littler, C., *The Development of the Labour Process in Capitalist Societies* (Heinemann, London, 1982).

Lloyd, I., *Rolls Royce, The Growth of a Firm* (MacMillan, London, 1978).

Lloyd, I., *Rolls-Royce, The Years of Endeavour* (MacMillan, London, 1978).

Mansfield, E., *The Economics of Technical Change* (Longmans, London, 1968).

Mansfield, E., *Research and Innovation in the Modern Corporation* (MacMillan, London, 1971).

Marx, Karl, *Capital* (Progress Publishers, Moscow, 1971).

Matthews, R.C., C.H. Feinstein and J.C. Odling-Smee, *British Economic Growth, 1856–1973* (Stanford University Press, Stanford, 1982).

Mathewson, S.B., *Restriction of Output Among Unorganized Workers* (Southern Illinois Press, Carbondale, 1969), originally published 1931.

Maxcy, G. and A. Silberston, *The Motor Industry* (George Allen & Unwin, London, 1959).

Melman, S., *Decision Making and Productivity* (Blackwell, Oxford, 1958).

Merrett, A.J. and A. Sykes, *The Finance and Analysis of Capital Projects*, 2eds (Longman, London, 1973).

Meyer III, S., *The Five Dollar Day: Labour Management and Social Control in the Ford Motor Company, 1908–1921* (State University of New York Press, Albany, 1981).

Middlemas, Keith, *Politics in Industrial Society* (MacMillan, London, 1979).

Meier, A. and E. Rudwick, *Black Detroit and the Rise of the UAW* (Oxford University Press, Oxford, 1979).

Mond, Alfred, (Sir), *Industry and Politics* (MacMillan, London, 1927).

Montgomery, David, *Workers Control in America: Studies in the History of Work, Technology and Labour Struggles* (Cambridge University Press, 1979).

More, Charles, *Skill in the English Working Class 1870–1914* (Croom Helm, London, 1980).

Moss, Bernard H., *The Origins of the French Labor Movement 1830–1914: The Socialism of Skilled Workers* (University of California Press, Berkeley, 1976).

Musson, A.E., *Science, Technology and Economic Growth in the Eighteenth Century* (Methuen and Co. Ltd, London, 1972).

Nabseth, L. and G.F. Ray (editors), *The Diffusion of New Industrial Processes* (Cambridge University Press, 1974).

Nadworny, M.J., *Scientific Management and the Unions, 1900–1932; A Historical Analysis* (Harvard University Press, Cambridge, 1955).

Nelson, D., *Managers and Workers: Origins of the New Factory System in the United States, 1880–1920* (University of Wisconsin Press, Wisconsin, 1975).

Nevins, Allan and Frank Hill, *Ford: The Times, the Man, the Company* (Scribner, NY, 1954).

Nixon, St John C., *Daimler, A Record of Fifty Years of the Daimler Company* (G.T. Foulis and Co., London, 1946).

Noble, D.F., *America by Design: Science* (Oxford University Press, Oxford, 1979).

Noble, D.F., *Forces of Automation: A Social History of Production* (Knopf, New York, 1984).

Nordhaus, W., *Invention Growth and Welfare* (MIT Press, Cambridge, Mass., 1969).

North, D.C., *Structure and Change in Economic History* (Norton, New York, 1981).

Oliver. G., *The Rover* (Cassell, London, 1971).

Overy, R.J., *William Morris, Viscount Nuffield* (Europa Publications, London, 1976).

Pagnamenta P. and R. Overy, *All Our Working Lives* (British Broadcasting Corporation, London, 1984).

Pasinetti, L., *Structural Change and Economic Growth* (Cambridge University Press, 1981).

Pasinetti, Luigi (editor), *Essays on the Theory of Joint Production* (MacMillan, London, 1980).

Pasinetti, Luigi, *Lectures on the Theory of Production* (MacMillan, London, 1977).

Pavitt, Keith, *Technical Innovation and British Economic Performance* (MacMillan, London, 1980).

Pelling, Henry, *A History of British Trade Unionism* (Penguin Books, Harmondsworth, 1963).

Pemberton, Max, *The Life of Sir Henry Royce* (Selwyne and Blount, London, n.d.).

Phelps Brown, E.H., *The Growth of British Industrial Relations* (MacMillan, London, 1959).

Phelps Brown, E.H. and M.H. Browne, *A Century of Pay* (MacMillan, London, 1968).

Piore, M.J. and C.F. Sabel, *The Second Industrial Divide, Possibilities for Prosperity* (NY, 1984).

Pollard, Sidney, *The Genesis of Modern Management* (Edward Arnold Ltd, London, 1965).

Pollard, Sidney, *The Development of the British Economy 1914–67* (Edward Arnold Ltd, London, 1969).

Powell, J.E., *Payments by Results* (Longman's, Greene and Co., London, 1924).

Prais, S.J., *Productivity and Industrial Structure* (Cambridge University Press, 1981).

Pribicevic, Branko, *The Shop Stewards Movement and Workers' Control* (Basil Blackwell, Oxford, 1959).

Price, R., *Masters, Unions and Men* (Cambridge University Press, 1980).

Proud, E.D., *Welfare Work, Employers' Experiments for Improving Working Conditions in Factories* (G. Bell, London, 1916).

Reich, R.B., *The Next American Frontier* (Times Books, New York, 1983).

Report of the Liberal Industrial Inquiry: Britain's Industrial Future (E. Benn Ltd, London, 1928).

Report of the Office of Manpower Economics, Measured Daywork (HMSO, London, 1973).

Rayton, D., *Shop Floor Democracy in Action; A Personal Account of the Coventry Gang System* (Russell Press, Nottingham, 1972).

Richardson, Keith, *The British Motor Industry 1896–1939* (MacMillan, London, 1977).

Rodgers, D.T., *The Work Ethic in Industrial America, 1850–1920* (University of Chicago Press, Chicago, 1974).

Rose, M., *Industrial Behaviour* (Allen Lane, London, 1975).

Rosenberg, N., *The American System of Manufactures* (Edinburgh University Press, Edinburgh, 1969).

Rosenberg, N., *The Economics of Technical Change* (Penguin, Harmondsworth, 1971).

Rosenberg, N., *Perspectives on Technology* (Cambridge University Press, 1976).

Rosenberg, N., *Inside the Black Box: Technology and Economics* (Cambridge University Press, 1982).

Rostas, L., *Comparative Productivity in British and American Industry* (Cambridge University Press, 1948).

Rothschild, Emma, *Paradise Lost: The Decline of the Auto-Industrial Age* (Vintage Books, NY, 1973).

Rowe, J.W.F., *Wages in Practice and Theory* (Routledge and Kegan Paul, London, 1928).

Ryder Committee, *British Leyland, the Next Decade* (HMSO, London, 1975).

Salter, W.E.G., *Productivity and Technical Change* (Cambridge University Press, 1969 2nd edition).

Schloss, D.F., *Methods of Industrial Remuneration* (Williams and Norgate, no place of publication given, 1892).

Schotter, A., *The Economic Theory of Social Institutions* (Cambridge University Press, 1981).

Scott-Moncrieff, David, *Veteran and Edwardian Motor Cars* (Batsford, London, 1955).

Scott, W.H. *et al.*, *Technical Change and Industrial Relations* (Liverpool University Press, Liverpool, 1956).

Schmookler, J., *Invention and Economic Growth* (Harvard University Press, Cambridge, 1966).

Schumpter, J.A., *Capitalism Socialism and Democracy* (Harper and Bros., New York, 1942).

Searle, G.R., *The Quest for Efficiency* (Basil Blackwell, Oxford, 1971).

Slater, P. (editor), *Outlines of a Critique of Technology* (London, 1980).

Smith, Merrit Roe, *Harpers Ferry Armory and the New Technology: the Challenge of Change* (Cornell University Press, Ithaca, 1977).

Smith, Samuel G., *The Industrial Conflict* (Fleming H. Revell Co., NY, 1907).

Sorensen, C.F., *My Forty Years with Ford* (Collier, NY, 1956).

Spicer, R.S., *British Engineering Wages* (E. Arnold and Co., London, 1928).

Sraffa, P., *Production of Commodities by Means of Commodities* (Cambridge University Press, 1960).

Steadman, I., *Marx after Sraffa* (New Left Books, London, 1977).

Stoneman, Paul, *Technological Diffusion and the Computer Revolution* (Cambridge University Press, 1976).

Strassman, W.P., *Risk and Technological Innovation* (Cornell University Press, Ithaca, NY, 1959).

Sward, K., *The Legend of Henry Ford* (Rinehart, New York, 1948).

Thompson, E.P., *The Making of the English Working Class* (Pantheon, NY, 1963).

Thoms, D. and T. Donnelly, *The Motor Car Industry in Coventry Since the 1890s* (Croom Helm, London, 1985).

Thurow, L., *Dangerous Currents: The State of Economics* (Vintage NY, 1983).

Tomlins, C.L., *The State and the Unions: Labour Relations, Law and the Organized Labour Movement in America* (Cambridge University Press, 1985).

von Tunzelmann, G.N., *Steam Power and British Industrialization to 1860* (Clarendon Press, Oxford, 1978).

Turner, G., *The Leyland Papers* (Eyre and Spottiswoode, London, 1971).

Turner, H.A., G. Clack and G. Roberts, *Labour Relations in the Motor Industry* (George Allen & Unwin, London, 1967).

Unofficial Reform Committee, *The Miners Next Step* (1912).

Ure, A., *Philosophy of Manufactures*, 1st published 1835 (A.M. Kelley, NY, 1967).

Urwick, L. and E.F.L. Brech, *The Making of Scientific Management: Volume II–Management in British Industry* (Management Publication Trust, London, 1946).

Urwick, L., *The Meaning of Rationalisation* (Nisbet and Co., London, 1929).

Vorob'ev, N.N., *Game Theory Lectures for Economists and Systems Scientists* (Springer-Verlag, New York, 1977).

Walker, Charles and Robert Guest, *The Man on the Assembly Line* (Harvard University Press, Cambridge, Mass, 1952).

Watson, W.F., *Machines and Men* (G. Allen and Unwin, London, 1935).

Whipp, R. and P. Clark, *Innovation and the Automobile Industry; Product, Process and Work Organization* (St Martin's Press, NY, 1986).

Whiting, R.C., *The View From Cowley, The Impact of Industrialization upon Oxford, 1918–1939* (Clarendon Press, Oxford, 1983).

Wigham, Eric, *The Power to Manage: History of the Engineering Employers Federation* (MacMillan, London, 1973).

Wilkins, M. and F.F. Hill, *American Business Abroad, Ford on Six Continents* (Wayne State University Press, Detroit, 1964).

Wilks, S., *Industrial Policy and the Motor Industry* (Manchester University Press, Manchester, 1984).

Williams, K., J. Williams and Dennis Thomas, *Why are the British Bad at Manufacturing?* (Routledge and Kegan Paul, London, 1983).

Williamson, G., *Wheels Within Wheels* (Geoffrey Bles, London, 1966).

Williamson, O.E., *Markets and Hierarchies* (Free Press, NY, 1975).

Willman, P. and G. Winch, *Innovation and Management Control* (Cambridge University Press, 1985).

Wilson, C. and W. Reader, *Men and Machines: A History of D. Napier and Son, Engineering Ltd* (Weidenfeld and Nicolson, London, 1958).

Winter, J.M., *Socialism and the Challenge of War. Ideas and Politics in Britain 1912–18* (Routledge and Kegan Paul, London, 1974).

Woollard, F.W., *The Principles of Flow Production* (Iliffe and Sons, London, 1954).

Wyatt, R.J., *The Motor for the Million, The Austin Seven* (MacDonald, London, 1968).

Yellowitz, Irwin, *Industrialization and the American Labour Movement 1850–1900* (National University Publications, Washington, 1977).

Young, S. and N. Hood, *Chrysler (UK), A Corporation in Transition* (Praeger, NY, 1977).

Zeuthen, F., *Problems of Monopoly and Economic Warfare* (G. Routledge and Sons, London, 1930).

Zeuthen, F., *Economic Theory and Method* (Harvard University Press, Cambridge, 1957).

Zweig, F., *Productivity and Trade Unions* (Blackwell, Oxford, 1951).

(4) Articles

Abernathy, W.J. and K. Wayne, 'Limits of the learning curve' (*Harvard Business Review*, **52**, 1974).

Abramovitz, M. and Paul David, 'Reinterpreting economic growth, parables and reality' (*American Economic Review*, **58**, 1973).

Abramovitz, M., 'Resource and output trends in the United States since 1870' (*American Economic Review*, **46**, Proceedings, 1956).

Adams, T., 'The British Labour movement and working class unrest, 1918–1921' (*Society for the Study of Labour History, Bulletin no. 46*, 1983).

Ahmad, S., 'On the theory of induced invention' (*Economic Journal*, **76**, 1966).

Alchian, A. and H. Demsetz, 'Production, information costs and economic organization' (*American Economic Review*, **62**, 1972).

Aldcroft, D.H., 'Technical progress and British enterprise 1875–1914' (*Business History*, **8**, 1966).

Aldcroft, D.H., 'Factor prices and the rate of innovation in Britain 1875–1914' (*Business History*, **9**, 1967).

Allen, G.C., 'The British motor industry' (*London and Cambridge Economic Service, Bulletin no. 18*, 1926).

Ames, E. and N. Rosenberg, 'The Enfield arsenal in theory and history' (*Economic Journal*, 78, 1968).

Arrow, K., 'The economic implications of learning by doing' (*Review of Economic Studies*, 29, 1962).

Asher, E., 'Industrial efficiency and biased technical change in American and British manufacturing: the case of textiles in the nineteenth century' (*Journal of Economic History*, 32, 1972).

Atkinson, Anthony B. and Joseph E. Stiglitz, 'A new view of technological change' (*Economic Journal*, 79, 1969).

Behrend, Hilde, 'The effort bargain' (*Industrial and Labour Relations Review*, 10, 1957).

Binswanger, Hans P., 'A microeconomic approach to induced innovation' (*Economic Journal*, 84, 1974).

Blanchard, Ian, 'Labour productivity and work psychology in the English mining industry 1400–1600' (*Economic History Review*, 31, 1978).

Booth, A., 'A reconsideration of trade union growth in the United Kingdom' (*British Journal of Industrial Relations*, 21, 1983).

Bowles, S., 'The production process in a competitive economy: Walrasian, neo-Hobbesian, and Marxian models' (*American Economic Review*, 75, 1985).

Brainard, W.C., J.B. Shoven and L. Weiss, 'The financial valuation of the return to capital' (*Brookings Papers on Economic Activity*, 1980).

Brecher, Jeremy (The Work Relations Group), 'Uncovering the hidden history of the American workplace' (*Review of Radical Political Economics*, 10, 1978).

Brighton Labour Process Group, 'The capitalist labour process' (*Capital and Class*, 1, 1977).

Brito, D.L. and Jeffrey G. Williamson, 'Skilled labour and nineteenth century Anglo-American managerial behavior' (*Explorations in Economic History*, 10, 1973).

Brown, William, 'Piecework wage determination in Coventry' (*Scottish Journal of Political Economy*, 18, 1971).

Brown, William and Michael Terry, 'The changing nature of national wage agreements' (*Scottish Journal of Political Economy*, 25, 1978).

Bruland, T., 'Industrial conflict as a source of technical innovation: three cases' (*Economy and Society*, 11, 1982).

Burawoy, Michael, 'Toward a Marxist theory of the labour process: Braverman and beyond' (*Politics and Society*, 8, 1978).

Cadbury, Edward, 'Some principles of industrial organisation: the case for and against scientific management' (*The Sociological Review*, 7, 1914).

Cain, L. P. and D.G. Patterson, 'Factor biases and technical change in manufacturing: the American system, 1850–1919' (*Journal of Economic History*, 41, 1981).

Carpenter, L.P., 'Corporatism in Britain 1930–45' (*Journal of Contemporary History*, 11, 1976).

Caves, R.E. and M.E. Porter, 'From entry barriers to mobility barriers' (*Quarterly Journal of Economics*, 91, 1977).

Chandler, Alfred D. Jr, 'The development of modern management in the US and UK' in *Management Strategy and Business Development*, edited by L. Hannah (MacMillan, London, 1976).

Chapman, Stanley. D., 'The textile factory before Arkwright: a typology of factory development' (*Business History Review*, 48, 1974).

Chenery, H.B., 'Process and production functions from engineering data' in *Studies in the Structure of the American Economy*, edited by W. Leontief (Oxford University Press, NY, 1953).

Chinoy, Ely, 'Manning the machines: the assembly line worker' in, *The Human Shape of Work*, edited by Peter Berger (MacMillan, NY, 1964).

Chiodi, Guglielmo, 'Some reflections on Marx, Sraffa and the theory of distribution' (*Science and Society*, 42, 1978).

Church, R.A., 'Nineteenth century clock technology in Britain, the US and Switzerland' (*Economic History Review*, 28, 1975).

Church, R.A., 'Myths, men and motor cars: a review article' (*Journal of Transport History*, 4, 1977).

Church, R.A., 'Innovation, monopoly and the supply of vehicle components in Britain: the growth of J. Lucas Ltd' (*Business History Review*, 52, 1978).

Church, R.A. and M. Miller, 'The big three: competition, management, and marketing in the British motor industry, 1922–1939' in, *Essays in British Business History*, ed. B. Supple (Oxford University Press, Oxford, 1977).

Clark, G., 'Authority and efficiency: the labour market and the managerial revolution of the late nineteenth century' (*Journal of Economic History*, 44, 1984).

Coase, R., 'The nature of the firm' (*Economica*, 4, 1937).

Commons, J.R., 'American Shoemakers, 1648–1895: a sketch of industrial evolution' (*Quarterly Journal of Economics*, 24, 1909).

Coombs, Rod, 'Labour and monopoly capital' (*New Left Review*, 107, 1978).

Coriot, Benjamin, 'The restructuring of the assembly line: a new economy of time and capital' (*Capital and Class*, 11, 1980).

Cressy, Peter and John MacInnes, 'Voting for Ford: industrial democracy and the control of labour' (*Capital and Class*, 11, 1980).

Dasgupta and Stiglitz, 'Industrial structure and the nature of innovative activity' (*Economic Journal*, 90, 1980).

David, P., and Th. Van de Klundert, 'Biased efficiency growth and capital labour substitution in the US' (*American Economic Review*, 55, 1965).

Davidson, R., 'Government administration', in *A History of British Industrial Relations, 1875–1914*, edited by C.J. Wrigley (Harvester, Brighton, 1982).

Davidson, W.H., 'Patterns of factor saving innovation in the industrial world', (*European Economic Review*, 8, 1976).

Davis, M., 'The barren marriage of American labour and the Democratic Party' (*New Left Review*, 123, 1980).

Davis, M., 'Why the US working class is different', (*New Left Review*, 123, 1980).

Davis, M., 'The stop watch and the wooden shoe: scientific management and the IWW' (*Radical America*, 9, 1975).

DeBondt, Raymond R., 'Innovative activity and barriers to entry' (*European Economic Review*, 10, 1977).

DeGregori, Thomas, 'Technology and ceremonial behaviour' (*Journal of Economic Issues*, 11, 1977).

Dowie, J. A., '1919–20 is in need of attention' (*Economic History Review*, 28, 1975).

Drandakis, E. and E.S. Phelps, 'A model of induced invention, growth and distribution' (*Economic Journal*, 96, 1966).

Duffy, A.E.P., 'New unionism in Britain 1889–90: a reappraisal' (*Economic History Review*, 14, 1961).

Duggan, Edward P., 'Machines, markets and labour: the carriage and wagon industry in late-nineteenth-century Cincinnati' (*Business History Review*, 51, 1977).

Duval. L.F., 'The motor industry', in *Britain in Recovery*, prepared by the British Association (London, 1938).

Eaton, C. and W.D. White, 'The economy of high wages: an agency problem' (*Economica*, 50, 1983).

Edelstein, M., 'Realized rates of return on UK home and overseas portfolio investments in the age of high imperialism' (*Explorations in Economic History*, 13, 1976).

Elger, Tony, 'Valorisation and deskilling: a critique of Braverman' (*Capital and Class*, 7, 1979).

Elster, J., 'Marxism, Functionalism and game theory: the case for methodological individualism' (*Theory and Society*, 11, 1982).

Exell, A., 'Morris Motors in the 1930s' Parts I and II (*History Workshop Journal*, 6 &7, 1978/1979).

Fellner, W., 'Two propositions in the theory of induced innovation' (*Economic Journal*, 71, 1961).

Fellner, W., 'Specific interpretations of learning by doing' (*Journal of Economic Theory*, 1, 1969).

Fellner, W., 'Does the market direct the relative factor saving effects of technological progress', in *The Rate and Direction of Inventive Activity* (NBER, Princeton, 1962).

Ferguson, Eugene S., 'The American-ness of American technology' (*Technolgy and Culture*, 20, 1979).

Ferguson, E.S., 'Toward a discipline of the history of technology' (*Technology and Culture*, 15, 1974).

Flanders, A., 'Measured daywork and collective bargaining' (*British Journal of Industrial Relations*, 11, 1973), pp. 368–92.

Floud, Roderick, 'Changes in the productivity of labour in the British machine tool industry 1856–1900', in *Essays on a Mature Economy*, edited by Donald McCloskey (Methuen, London, 1971).

Floud, R., 'Britain 1860–1914: a survey', in *The Economic History of Britain Since 1700*, Volume Two, edited by R. Floud and D. McCloskey (Cambridge University Press, 1981).

Foreman Peck, J.S., 'Tariff protection and economies of scale: the British motor industry before 1939' (*Oxford Economic Papers*, 31, 1979).

Foreman Peck, J.S., 'The effect of market failure on the British motor industry before 1939' (*Explorations in Economic History*, 18, 1981).

Foreman Peck, J.S., 'The American challenge of the twenties: multinationals and the European motor industry' (*Journal of Economic History*, 42, 1982).

Fridenson, P., 'The coming of the assembly line to Europe', in *The Dynamics of Science and Technology*, ed. W. Krohn, *et al.* (D. Reidel, Dordrecht, 1978).

Friedman, A.L., 'Management strategies, market conditions and the labour process', in *Firms, Organization and Labour*, edited by F.J. Stephen (MacMillan, London, 1984).

Fries, Russel, 'British response to the American system: the case of the small arms industry after 1850' (*Technology and Culture*, 16, 1975).

Garside, W.R., 'Management and men: aspects of British industrial relations in the interwar period', in *Essays in British Business History*, edited by B. Supple (Clarendon Press, Oxford, 1977).

Gintis, Herbert, 'The nature of labor exchange and the theory of capitalist production' (*Review Radical Political Economics*, 8, 1976).

Goddard, H.A., 'Profit sharing and the amenities of the Nuffield factories', in *Industrial and Labour Relations in Great Britain*, ed. Gannett, F.E., and Catherwood, B.F. (NY, 1939).

Gordon, David M., 'Capitalist efficiency and socialist efficiency' (*Monthly Review*, 28, 1976).

Gore, V., 'Rank and file dissent', in *A History of British Industrial Relations, 1875–1914*, edited by C.J. Wrigley (Harvester, Brighton, 1982).

Graham, F.D., 'Relation of wage rates to the use of machinery' (*American Economic Review*, 16, 1926).

Groh, D, 'Intensification of work and industrial conflict in Germany 1896–1909' (*Politics and Society*, 8, 1978).

Grunberg, L., 'The effects of the social relations of production on productivity and workers' safety: an ignored set of relationships' (*International Journal of Health Services*, 13, 1983).

Hahn, F.H., 'The Neo-Ricardians' (*Cambridge Journal of Economics*, 6, 1982), pp. 353–74.

Hannah, L., 'Visible and invisible hands in Great Britain', in *Managerial Hierarchies: Comparative Perspectives on the Rise of the Modern Industrial Enterprise*, edited by A.D. Chandler Jr. and Herman Daems (Harvard University Press, Cambridge, 1980).

Hannah, L., 'Managerial innovation and the rise of the large scale company in inter-war Britain' (*Economic History Review*, 27, 1974).

Hannah, L., 'Strategy and structure in the manufacturing sector', in *Management Strategy and Business Development*, edited by L. Hannah (MacMillan, London, 1976).

Harley, C.K., 'Skilled labour and the choice of technique in Edwardian industry' (*Explorations in Economic History*, 11, 1974).

Harrison, A.E., 'The competitiveness of the British cycle industry, 1890–1914' (*Economic History Review*, 22, 1969).

Harrison, A.E., 'Joint stock company flotation in the cycle, motor vehicle and related industries: 1882–1914', (*Business History*, 23, 1981).

Harsanyi, J.C., 'Games with incomplete information' (*Management Science*, 14, 1967).

Harsanyi, J.C., 'Approaches to the bargaining problem before and after the theory of games: a critical discussion of Zeuthen's, Hicks', and Nash's theories' (*Econometrica*, 24, 1956).

Hay, J.R., 'Employers' attitudes to social policy and the concept of social control, 1900–20', in *The Origins of British Social Policy* edited by P. Thane (Rowan and Littlefield, London, 1978).

Hayes, H.G., 'Rate of wages and use of machinery' (*American Economic Review*, 13, 1923).

Heilbroner, Robert L., 'Do machines make history' (*Technology and Culture*, 8, 1967).

Hinton, J., 'Coventry communism: a study of factory politics in the second world war' (*History Workshop Journal*, 12, 1980).

Hinton, J., 'The rise of a mass labour movement: growth and limits', in *A History of British Industrial Relationships 1875–1914*, edited by C.J. Wrigley (Harvester, Brighton, 1982).

Hobsbawm, E.J., 'Custom, wages and work load in nineteenth century industry', in *Essays in Labour History*, edited by Asa Briggs and J. Saville (MacMillan, London, 1960).

Hobsbawm, E.J., 'Artisan or labour aristocrat?' (*Economic History Review*, 37, 1984).

Hoel, M., 'Distribution and growth as a differential game between workers and capitalists' (*International Economic Review*, 19, 1978).

Holden, L., 'Think of me simply as the skipper, industrial relations at Vauxhalls 1920–1950' (*Oral History*, 9, 1981).

Hughes, T.P., 'Emerging themes in the history of technology' (*Technology and Culture*, 20, 1979).

Irving, J., 'New industries for old? Some investment decisions of Sir W.G. Armstrong, Whitworth and Co. Ltd, 1900–1914' (*Business History*, 17, 1975).

Jelinek, Mariann, 'Towards systematic management; Alexander Hamilton Church' (*Business History Review*, 54, 1980).

Jorgenson, D.W. and Z. Griliches, 'The explanation of productivity changes' (*Review of Economic Studies*, 34, 1967).

Kaldor, N., 'A model of economic growth' (*Economic Journal*, 67, 1957).

Kamien, M.I. and Nancy L. Schwartz, 'Market structure and innovation: a survey' (*Journal of Economic Literature*, 13, 1975).

Kennedy, Charles, 'Induced bias in innovation and the theory of distribution' (*Economic Journal*, 74, 1964).

Kennedy, Charles and A.P. Thirlwall, 'Surveys in applied economics: technical progress' (*Economic Journal*, 82, 1972).

Kerr, C., 'The effects of environment and administration on job evaluation', in *Labour Markets and Wage Determination*, edited by C. Kerr (University of California Press, Berkeley, 1977).

Klundert, Th. van de and R.J. De Graef, 'Economic growth and induced technical progress' (*DE Economist*, 1977).

Knowles, K.G.J.C. and D. Robinson, 'Wage movements in Coventry' (*Bulletin of the Oxford University Institute of Economics and Statistics*, 31, 1969).

Kreps, D.M., and R. Wilson, 'Reputation and imperfect information' (*Journal of Economic Theory*, 27, 1982).

Lancaster, K., 'The dynamic inefficiency of capitalism' (*Journal of Political Economy*, 81, 1973).

Landes, David, 'Factor costs and demand: determinants of economic growth: a critique of Professor Habakkuk's thesis' (*Business History*, 7, 1965).

Laux, J.M., 'Rochet-Schneider and the French motor industry to 1914' (*Business History*, 8, 1966).

Lawson, T., 'Paternalism and labour market segmentation theory', in *Essays in the Dynamics of Labour Market Segmentation*, edited by F. Wilkinson (Academic Press, London, 1981).

Layton Edwin T. Jr., 'Technology as knowledge' (*Technology and Culture*, 15, 1974).

Layton, Edwin T. Jr., 'American ideology of science and engineers' (*Technology and Culture*, 17, 1976).

Layton, Edwin T. Jr., 'Millwrights and engineers, science and social roles', in *The Dynamics of Science and Technology*, edited by Krohn, Layton and Weingart (D. Reidel, Dardrecht, 1978).

Lazaer, E.P., 'Agency, earnings profiles, productivity, and hours restriction' (*American Economic Review*, **71**, 1981).

Lazonick, William, 'The subjection of labour to capital: the rise of the capitalist system' (*Review of Radical Political Economics*, **10**, 1978).

Lazonick, W., 'Technical change and the control of work: the development of capital–labour relations in the US mass production industries', in *Managerial Strategies and Industrial Relations*, edited by H.F. Gospel and C.R. Littler (Heinemann, London, 1983).

Leibenstein, H., 'Allocative efficiency and X-efficiency' (*American Economic Review*, **56**, 1966).

Lequin, Yves, 'Labour in the French economy since the Revolution' in, *Cambridge Economic History of Europe*, edited by P. Mathias and M.M. Postan (Cambridge University Press, 1978).

Lewchuk, W., 'The role of the British Government in the spread of scientific management and Fordism in the inter-war years' (*Journal of Economic History*, **44**, 1984).

Lewchuk, W., 'The motor vehicle industry', in *The decline of the British economy*, edited by W. Lazonick and E. Elbaum (Oxford University Press, Oxford, 1985).

Lewchuk, W., 'The return to capital in the British motor vehicle industry: 1896–1939 (*Business History*, **27**, 1985).

Lichtenstein, N., 'Auto worker militancy and the structure of factory life, 1937–55' (*Journal of American History*, **67**, 1980).

Litterer, Joseph A., 'Systematic management: the search for order and integration' (*Business History Review*, **35**, 1961).

Litterer, Joseph A., 'Alexander Hamilton Church and the development of modern management' (*Business History Review*, **35**, 1961).

Littler, Craig R., 'Understanding Taylorism' (*British Journal of Sociology*, **29**, 1978).

Lyddon, D., 'Workplace organization in the British car industry' (*History Workshop*, **15**, 1983).

Maier, Charles S., 'Between Taylorism and technocracy: European ideologies and the vision of industrial productivity in the 1920's' (*Journal of Contemporary History*, **5**, 1970).

Malcolmson, J.M. 'Unemployment and the efficiency wage hypothesis' (*Economic Journal*, **91**, 1981).

Malcolmson, J.M., 'Work incentives, hierarchy, and internal labor markets' (*Journal of Political Economy*, **92**, 1984).

Malcolmson, J.M., 'Efficient labour organization: incentives, power and the transaction cost approach', in *Firms Organization and Labour*, edited by F.J. Stephen (MacMillan, London, 1984).

Manegold, Karl Heinz, 'Technology Academised' in *The Dynamics of Science and Technology*, edited by Krohn, Layton and Weingart (D. Reidel, Dordrecht, 1978).

Mansfield, E., J. Rapoport, A. Romeo, S. Wagner and G. Beardsley, 'Social and private rates of return from industrial innovations (*Quarterly Journal of Economics*, **91**, 1977).

Marglin, Stephen, 'What do bosses do?', (*Review of Radical Political Economics*, **6**, 1974).

Marriner, S., 'Company financial statements as source material for business history' (*Business History*, **22**, 1980).

Maxcy G., 'The motor industry', in *Effect of Mergers*, edited by P.L. Cook and R. Cohen (George Allen and Unwin, London, 1958).

McCloskey, D.N., 'International differences in productivity? coal and steel in America and Britain before World War I' in *Essay on a Mature Economy*, edited by D. McCloskey (Methuen, London, 1971).

McCloskey, D.N., 'Did Victorian Britain fail' (*Economic History Review*, 23, 1970).

McCloskey, D.N. and L. Sandberg, 'From damnation to redemption' (*Explorations in Economic History*, 9, 1971).

McDonald, G.W. and H.F. Gospel, 'The Mond-Turner talks, 1927–33: a study in industrial co-operation' (*Historical Journal*, 16, 1973).

McKendrick, Neil, 'Josiah Wedgwood and factory discipline' (*Historical Journal*, 4, 1961).

Meacham, Standish, 'The sense of an impending clash: English working class unrest before the First World War' (*American Historical Review*, 77, 1972).

Melling, J., 'Industrial strife and business welfare philosophy: the case of the South Metropolitan Gas Company From the 1880's to the War' (*Business History*, 21, 1979).

Melling, J., 'Non-commissioned officers: British employers and their supervisory workers, 1880–1920' (*Social History*, 5, 1980).

Melling, J., 'Employers industrial welfare and the struggle for workplace control in British industry 1880–1920', in *Managerial Strategies and Industrial relations*, edited by H. Gospel and C. Littler (Heinemann, London, 1983).

Miller, M. and R.A. Church, 'Motor manufacturing', in, *British industry between the Wars*, edited by N.K. Buxton and D. Aldcroft (Scolar Press, London, 1979).

Mirrless, J., 'The optimal structure of incentives and authority within an organization' (*Bell Journal*, 7, 1976).

Monds, Jean, 'Workers' control and the historians: a new economism' (*New Left Review*, 97, 1976).

Montgomery, D., 'New tendencies in union struggles and strategies in Europe and the United States: 1916–1922', in *Work, Community, and Power; The Experience of Labor in Europe and America: 1900–1925*, edited by J.E. Cronin and C. Sirianni (Temple University Press, Philadelphia, 1983).

Morrison, L.A., 'An issue in economic theory: the rate of wages and the use of machinery' (*American Economic Review*, 14, 1924).

Multhauf, Robert P., 'The historiography of technology' (*Technology and Culture*, 15, 1974).

Musson, A.E., 'Joseph Whitworth and the growth of mass-production engineering' (*Business History*, 17, 1975).

Nelson, Richard R. and Sidney G. Winter, 'Neo-classical vs evolutionary theories of economic growth' (*Economic Journal*, 84, 1974).

Nelson, Richard R. and Sidney G. Winter, 'Toward an evolutionary theory of economic capabilities' (*American Economic Review*, 63, 1973).

Nicholas, S., 'Total factor productivity growth and the revision of post 1870 British economic history' (*Economic History Review*, 35, 1982).

Noble, David F., 'Social choice in machine design: the case of automatically controlled machine tools, and a challenge for labor' (*Politics and Society*, 8, 1978).

Nordhaus, W., 'Some skeptical thoughts on the theory of induced innovations' (*Quarterly Journal of Economics*, 87, 1973).

Osborne, M., 'Capitalist–worker conflict and involuntary unemployment' (*Review of Economic Studies*, **51**, 1984).

Palloix, Christian, 'The labour process: from Fordism to new Fordism' (*C.S.E. Pamphlet No. 1 – The Labour Process and Class Strategies*).

Palmer, Bryan, 'Class, conception and conflict: trust for efficiency' (*Review of Radical Political Economics*, **7**, 1975).

Payne, P.L., 'Industrial entrepreneurship and management in Great Britain', in *The Cambridge Economic History of Europe*, Volume VII, pt. 1, (Cambridge University Press, 1978).

Pearson, R., 'From group bonus to straight time pay' (*Journal of Industrial Economic*, **8**, 1960).

Phelps Brown, E.H., 'Labour policies: productivity, industrial relations, cost inflation', in *Britain's Economic Prospects Reconsidered*, edited by A. Cairncross (Allen and Unwin, London, 1971).

Phillips, W.H., 'Induced innovation and economic performance in late Victorian British industry' (*Journal of Economic History*, **42**, 1982).

Pollard, Sidney, 'Labour in Great Britain', in *Cambridge Economic History of Europe*, Volume VII, pt. 1 (Cambridge University Press, 1978).

Pollard, Sidney, 'Factory discipline in the Industrial Revolution' (*Economic History Review*, **16**, 1963).

Price, R., 'Rethinking labour history: the importance of work', in *Social Conflict and the Political Order in Modern Britain*, edited by J.E. Cronin and J. Schneer (Croom Helm, London, 1982).

Putterman, L., 'The organization of work: comment' (*Journal of Economic Behavior and Organization*, **2**, 1981).

Reid, A., 'Intelligent artisans and aristocrats of labour: the essays of Thomas Wright', in *The Working Class in Modern British History*, edited by J. Winter (Cambridge University Press, 1983).

Rhys, D.G., 'Employment, efficiency and labour relations in the British motor industry' (*Industrial Relations Journal*, **5**, 1974).

Robinson, J., 'The Unimportance of reswitching' (*Quarterly Journal of Economics*, **89**, 1975).

Roemer, J.E., 'Divide and conquer: microfoundations of a Marxian theory of wages' (*Bell Journal*, **10**, 1979).

Rosenberg, N., 'Another advantage of the division of labour' (*Journal of Politcal Economy*, **84**, 1976).

Rosenberg, N., 'Technological interdependence in the American economy' (*Technology and Culture*, **20**, 1979).

Rowthorn, Bob, 'Neo-classicism, neo-Ricardianism and Marxism' (*New Left Review*, **86**, 1974).

Rurup, Reinhard, 'Historians and modern technology' (*Technology and Culture*, **15**, 1974).

Russell, J., 'The coming of the line' (*Radical America*, **12**, 1978).

Ruttan, V. and Y. Hayami, 'Toward a theory of induced institutional innovation' (*Journal of Development Studies*, **20**, 1984).

Salter, W.E.G., 'Productivity growth and accumulation as historical processes', in *Problems in Economic Development*, edited by E.A.G. Robinson (MacMillan, London, 1965).

Samuel, R., 'Workshop of the world: steam power and hand technology in mid-Victorian' Britain (*History Workshop Journal*, 3, 1977).

Samuels, W.J., 'Technology vis a vis institutions' (*Journal of Economic Issues*, 11, 1977).

Samuelson, P., 'A theory of induced innovations along Kennedy–Weisacker lines' (*Review of Economics and Statistics*, 47, 1965).

Sato, Kazuo, ' The neoclassical postulate and the technology frontier in capital theory' (*Quarterly Journal of Economics*, 88, 1974).

Saul, S.B., 'The engineering industry', in *The Development of British Industry*, edited by D. Aldcroft (Allen and Unwin, London, 1968).

Saul, S.B., 'The market and the development of the mechanical engineering industry in Britain 1860–1914' (*Economic History Review*, 20, 1967).

Saul, S.B., 'The American impact on British industry 1895–1914' (*Business History*, 2, 1960).

Saul, S.B., 'The motor industry in Britain to 1914' (*Business History*, 5, 1962).

Sawyer, J.E., 'The social basis of the American system of manufacturing' (*Journal of Economic History*, 14, 1954).

Sayers, R.S., 'The springs of technical progress in Britain 1919–39' (*Economic Journal*, 60, 1950).

Schefold, B., 'Fixed capital as a joint product and the Analysis of accumulation with different forms of technical progress', in *Essays on the Theory of Joint Production*, edited by L. Pasinetti (MacMillan, London, 1980).

Shapiro, C. and J.E. Stiglitz, 'Equilibrium unemployment as a worker discipline device' (*American Economic Review*, 74, 1984).

Shaw, C., 'The large manufacturing employers of 1907' (*Business History*, 25, 1983).

Shove, G.F., 'Review of the theory of wages' (*Economic Journal*, 43, 1933).

Shubik, M., 'Game theory models and methods in political economy', in *Handbooks of Mathematical Economics*, Volume 1, eds. K.J. Arrow and M.D. Intriligator (North Holland, Amsterdam, 1981).

Sirianni, Carmen J., 'Workers control in the era of World War I' (*Theory and Society*, 9, 1980).

Skaggs, J.C. and R.L. Ehrlich, 'Profits, paternalism, and rebellion: a case study in industrial strife' (*Business History Review*, 54, 1980).

Spaventa, Luigi, 'Rate of profit, rate of growth, and capital intensity in a simple production model' (*Oxford Economic Papers*, 22, 1970).

Stark, David, 'Class struggle and the transformation of the labour process' (*Theory and Society*, 9, 1980).

Stone, Katherine, 'The origins of job structures in the steel industry' (*Review of Radical Political Economics*, 9, 1974).

Temin, Peter, 'Labour scarcity in America' (*Journal of Interdisciplinary History*, 1, 1971).

Temin, Peter, 'Labour scarcity and the problem of industrial efficiency in the 1850s' (*Journal of Economic History*, 26, 1966).

Thomas Ewart A.C., 'On technological implications of the wage–profit frontier' (*Journal of Economic Theory*, 11, 1975).

Thompson, E.P., 'Time, work-discipline and industrial capitalism' (*Past and Present*, 38, 1967).

Tolliday, S., 'Militancy and organization: women workers and trade unions in the motor trades in the 1930s' (*Oral History*, 11, 1983).

Tolliday, S., 'Government, employers and shop floor organization in the British motor industry, 1939–69', in *Shop Floor Bargaining and the State*, edited by S. Tolliday and J. Zeitlin (Cambridge University Press, 1985).

Traub, Rainer, 'Lenin and Taylor: the fate of scientific management in the (early) Soviet Union' (*Telos*, 37, 1977).

Ulman, L., 'Collective bargaining and industrial efficiency', in *Britain's Economic Prospects*, edited by R.E. Caves (Brookings Institute, Washington, 1968).

Uselding, Paul, 'Factor substitution and labour productivity growth in American manufacturing 1839–1899' (*Journal of Economic History*, 32, 1972).

Uselding, P., 'An early chapter in the evolution of American industrial management', in *Business Enterprise and Economic Change*, edited by L. Cain and P. Uselding (Kent State Univesity Press, 1973).

Uselding, Paul, 'Studies of technology in economic history', in *Research in Economic History*, edited by R. Gallman and P. Uselding (J.A.I. Press, Connecticut, 1977).

Varri, P., 'Prices, rate of profit and life of machines', in *Essays on the Theory of Joint Production*, edited by L. Pasinetti (MacMillan, London, 1980).

White, J., '1910–1914 reconsidered', in *Social conflict and the Political Order in Modern Britain*, edited by J.E. Cronin and J. Schneer (Croom Helm, London, 1982).

Wilkinson, Frank, 'Collective bargaining in the steel industry in the 1920's', in *Essays in Labour History*, edited by A. Briggs and J. Saville (Croom Helm, London, 1977).

Williamson, O.E., 'The organization of work: a comparative institutional assessment' (*Journal of Economic Behavior and Organization*, 1, 1980).

Willman, P., 'The reform of collective bargaining and strike activity in BL Cars 1976–1982' (*Industrial Relations Journal*, 15, 1984).

Willman, P., 'Labour relations strategies at BL Cars', in *Between Fordism and flexibility: the international automobile industry and its workers*, edited by S. Tolliday and J. Zeitlin, (Oxford University Press, Oxford, forthcoming).

Woodward, R.S., 'The legend of Eli Whitney and interchangeable parts' (*Technology and Culture*, 1, 1960).

Wright, R., 'Erosion inside capitalism' (*Anarchy*, 8, 1961).

Wright, R., 'The gang system in Coventry' (*Anarchy*, 2, 1961).

Wrigley, C.J., 'The government and industrial relations', in *A History of British Industrial Relations 1875–1914*, edited by C.J. Wrigley (Harvester, Brighton, 1982).

Zeitlin, J., 'The emergence of shop steward organization and job control in the British car industry' (*History Workshop*, 10, 1980).

Zeitlin, J., 'The labour strategies of British engineering employers, 1890–1922', in *Managerial Strategies and Industrial Relations*, edited by H. Gospel and C. Littler (Harvester, London, 1983).

(5) Unpublished sources

Carr, F.W., Engineering Workers and the Rise of Labour in Coventry 1914–39 (Ph.D., Warwick, 1979).

Chartres, J., Payment by Results, An Analysis of Wage System Described or Discussed in the Ministry of Munitions, 1915–1918 (Ministry of Munitions, 1919), located in PRO Mun 4, 6359.

Ciccolo, J.C. Jr., Changing Balance Sheet Relations in US Manufacturing Sector, 1926–77 (NBER Working Paper, 702).

Committee of Inquiry into the Organization and Administration of the Manufacturing Departments of the Army, 1887, Earl of Morley Chairman, C 5116 (HMSO, London).

Croucher, R., The Amalgamated Society of Engineers and Local Autonomy 1898–1914 (MA Thesis, Warwick, 1971).

Ford, P.W., Changing the Wage Payment System at a Car Factory (MA Thesis, Warwick, 1972).

Foreman-Peck, J.S., The Quality of Management in the Rover Company, 1890–1939 (unpublished paper, 1979).

Fridenson, P., Corporate Policy, Rationalization and the Labour Force: French Experiments in International Comparison 1900– 29 (unpublished paper).

Gartman. W., Auto Slavery: The Development of the Labour Process in the Automobile Industry of the United States: 1897–1950 (PhD Thesis Southern California at San Diego, 1980).

Gospel, Howard F., Employers Organizations: Their Growth and Function in the British System of Industrial Relations in the Period 1918–39 (Ph.D. Thesis, London 1974).

Holme, A., Some Aspects of the British Motor Manufacturing Industry During the Years 1919–1930 (MA Thesis, Sheffield, 1964).

Lazonick, W., Work, Effort and Productivity: Some Theoretical Implications of Some Historical Research (unpublished paper, 1984).

Macleod, W.B. and J.M. Malcolmson, Implicit Contracts, Incentive Compatibility, and Involuntary Unemployment (Institute for Economic Research, Queen's University, Discussion Paper 585).

Report of the Tariff Commission: The Engineering Industry, Volume 4 (London, 1909).

Rodgers, T., 'Sir Allan Smith: Outsider in Politics 1918–1924' (unpublished paper, 1979).

Royal Commission on Motor Cars, Minutes of Evidence, Cmd 3081 (HMSO, London, 1906).

Salmon, J., A View of Industrial Relations in the British Car Industry (MA Thesis, Warwick, 1975).

Salmon, J., Organized Labour in a Market Economy (PhD Thesis, Warwick, 1983).

Sutherland, J., The Impact of Measured Day Work on Company Industrial Relations, (MA Thesis, Warwick, 1974).

Turner, J.A. The Politics of the Business Community in the First World War (unpublished paper, 1980).

Weekes, B.C.M., The Amalgamated Society of Engineers 1880–1914 (PhD Thesis, Warwick, 1970).

Whipp, R., Management, Design and Industrial Relations in the British Automobile Industry: The SD1 Project (unpublished paper).

Whiting, R., The Working Class in the New Industry Towns Between the Wars: The Case of Oxford, (PhD Thesis, Oxford, 1979).

Zeitlin, J.H., Craft Regulation and the Division of Labour: Engineers and Compositors in Britain 1890–1941 (PhD Thesis, Warwick, 1981).

Index